Literacy Plus

Language · Lifeskills · Civics

Joan Saslow

Consultants

Lisa Agao	Robert Breitbard	Virginia A. Cabasa-Hess	Janet S. Fischer	Carol Garcia
California	*Florida*	*Illinois*	*Massachusetts*	*Illinois*
Glenda Gartman	David L. Red	Lynn Reed	Margaret B. Silver	Gordon Thomas
California	*Virginia*	*Arizona*	*Missouri*	*Virginia*

Teacher's Edition by
Sarah Lynn and Laura Brooks

Edwina Hoffman
Series Advisor

Longman

Literacy Plus A: Language, Lifeskills, Civics
Teacher's Edition

Pearson Education, 10 Bank Street, White Plains, NY 10606

Vice president of instructional design: Allen Ascher
Senior acquisitions editor: Marian Wassner
Senior development editor: Jessica Miller-Smith
Vice president, director of design and production: Rhea Banker
Executive managing editor: Linda Moser
Senior production editor: Christine Lauricella
Associate production editor: Scott Fava
Production manager: Liza Pleva
Director of manufacturing: Patrice Fraccio
Senior manufacturing buyer: Dave Dickey
Cover design: Ann France
Cover photo (coins and bills, CD-ROM): Corbis Stock Market
Text design and composition: TSI Graphics
Illustrators: John Amoss; Burmar Technical Corporation; Seitu Hayden; Len Shalansky; Tom Sperling; Steve Sullivan; Jill Wood

ISBN:0-13-099622-X
3 4 5 6 7 8 9 10—BAH—07 06 05 04

LONGMAN ON THE **WEB**

Longman.com offers online resources for teachers and students. Access our Companion Websites, our online catalog, and our local offices around the world.

Longman English Success offers online courses to give learners flexible study options. Courses cover General English, Business English, and Exam Preparation.

Visit us at **longman.com** and **englishsuccess.com**.

Introduction to the *Literacy Plus* Teacher's Edition

WHAT IS *LITERACY PLUS*?

Literacy Plus A is the first level of a two-level course that starts at absolute beginner language and literacy level. Written for adult immigrant learners, *Literacy Plus A* is for students who are preliterate in their own language and who know no English. Recognizing the reality that adults can't wait to become literate in order to work and carry on their lives, *Literacy Plus* offers instruction in survival English, basic literacy, and elemental civics concepts at the same time.

The Teacher's Edition contains this Introduction to *Literacy Plus* as well as Lesson Plans for teaching each page of the Student's Book.

SCOPE AND SEQUENCE

On pages ix and x there is a scope and sequence chart that shows at a glance the content of each of the 10 units, broken into four columns: literacy, survival language, civics concepts, and vocabulary. Reading the scope and sequence of the first and the last units presents a concise summary of *Literacy Plus A*'s starting and ending points:

Literacy. Students move in logical and sequential steps from holding a writing instrument and moving from left-to-right and top-to-bottom at the beginning of the book to completing personal information on a printed form at the end of the book.

Survival Language. Students practice communicative conversations in a variety of everyday contexts. Embedded in these essential conversational models are the lifeskills necessary for daily community, family, and workplace life. [Note that "survival language" is sometimes known as "functional language" or "social language."]

Civics Concepts. In *Literacy Plus,* the term "civics" is used to describe the fundamental concepts necessary for understanding the culture of the American community and workplace. The term "civics" is not used here to refer to citizenship education or even to what is sometimes termed "civic participation." Rather, the term "civics" in *Literacy Plus* refers to a set of concepts that introduce learners to the expected social behavior of this culture, an understanding of which is essential before students can participate fully or truly understand their rights and responsibilities as citizens. The scope and sequence chart on pages ix and x fully lists the civics concepts included in *Literacy Plus A.*

In order to navigate their daily lives with confidence in this new land, preliterate beginning ESL learners need to understand what is socially permissible and what is culturally expected of them. Before students can understand formal rights and responsibilities, they need more fundamental information, such as "It's OK to ask a stranger for directions," "Jobs are not determined by gender," or "It's OK to ask for a receipt." It is only by understanding concepts such as these that a student can be ready to understand the rights and responsibilities that are normally included in discussions of civics, civic participation, or citizenship.

Vocabulary. Students gain a full vocabulary of words and phrases urgently needed every day outside of class.

ORGANIZATION OF THE STUDENT'S BOOK

Ten units provide alternating two-page lessons centered on either Survival Language or Literacy so that students are constantly learning both. A tinted TEACHER box at the bottom of each page clearly and simply lists for the teacher the new content on that page.

Survival language pages
Where are the words?
Since students entering *Literacy Plus* are preliterate, the survival language [vocabulary and conversations] must be taught by means of pictures and sound. On each Survival Language page, you will see instructions such as "⌒ Look and listen" and "⌒ Listen again and repeat." Those directions have a headphones symbol ⌒. All survival language is presented through illustrated and recorded model conversations. Complete tapescripts of the recorded language are on each Lesson Plan page of this Teacher's Edition.

Where is the grammar?

The conversations have been purposely written so that they can be used in students' life without explicit presentation or manipulation of grammar. Nevertheless, the conversations contain the following essential beginning grammatical <u>concepts</u>, which students will master by repeating and practicing the conversations in the Student's Book: singular and plural; possessives *my, your, his, her;* subject pronouns *I, you, he, she;* and demonstrative pronouns *this, that, these, those.*

What are the teaching steps and methods?

Look and listen. Read the model conversation out loud or play the cassette. Have students listen and look at the pictures in their books. If you read the conversation yourself, attempt to distinguish between the two speakers by changing your voice or position for each role.

Check that students understand the model conversation. The Lesson Plans offer specific suggestions on how to check comprehension and convey the meaning of any new language that is introduced. Read the tapescript or play the cassette as many times as necessary for students to understand the conversation.

Listen again and repeat. Encourage students to imitate the rhythm, stress, and intonation of the conversation as closely as possible. Some methods for focusing on the intonation and rhythm include having students demonstrate the intonation with their hands or tapping out the number of syllables of each line. Specific suggestions are found in the Lesson Plans.

Pair work. Following the presentation of the new conversations and vocabulary, students have an opportunity to personalize and practice the new language. An image of two people in conversation is the students' signal to role-play the conversation, using either their own information or the picture cues to the side.

Students should be encouraged to create their conversations with minimal correction and interruption by the teacher. The pair work is an opportunity for experimentation with the conversational model, which has been included because of its practicality and value for immediate use outside of the English class. See Student's Book page 75 for an example.

Literacy pages

How to help students understand page orientation

Some students may not be accustomed to following the page top-to-bottom and left-to-right and thereby might wander over to another line as they work on an exercise. Distribute blank sheets of paper for students to place over their pages. As students complete the first line, show them how to move their sheets down to work on the next line. As students work independently, circulate around the room, helping them to adjust their sheets.

As students become more confident, encourage them to pull the sheet away and follow the line by themselves; however, some students might want this aid throughout *Literacy Plus.*

As students work through exercises, have them point to what they are working on. Pointing gives the teacher immediate feedback on students' page orientation and reinforces the left-to-right, top-to-bottom directionality of reading. It also helps keep the student focused on an activity. Literacy students often have a hard time looking away from the page and returning to the same place. A finger anchored there will help the student pick up immediately where he or she left off.

How to develop handwriting skills

Good practices established early on ensure legibility later, when students relax and write more rapidly.

Learning the strokes. Have students use large arm movements to practice the strokes used to write each letter and number. Research has indicated that using large arm movements while imitating the strokes best helps students remember the shapes and sequence of the strokes. The kinesthetic activity helps the student encode and retain the complex shapes and sequences required in handwriting.

Grip. Students should do a few simple warm-up exercises before working with a writing instrument. Have students hold up their arms, rotate their wrists, and flex their fingers to loosen up their arm, hand, and finger muscles. You may also want students to take occasional breaks from their writing practice to stretch and relax their muscles.

The pencil should be held between the thumb and first two fingers, about an inch above the point. The index finger, which controls the pressure on the pencil, should rest on top of the pencil. The pencil rests against the first (small) knuckle of the middle finger. The top of the pencil should point toward the shoulder of the writing arm. The first (small) knuckle of the index finger should be bent slightly upward as the student writes. If the knuckle is bent downward, the writer is applying too much pressure and will tire quickly.

Posture. Make sure students' posture is forward-facing and relaxed. Both arms should rest lightly on the edge of the desk. In this position the large muscle in the forearm can move easily as the student writes.

Paper position. Show students how to position the paper properly whether they are right- or left-handed. The proper paper position for a right-handed student is perpendicular to the edge of the desk. Be certain the paper is placed a little to the right of the student. The writer's hand motions are restricted by crossing over the body to write. The left-handed paper position rests at a 45-degree angle from the edge of the desk. You may want to place a strip of tape on each student's desk to establish the bottom line of the paper.

Self-evaluation. Students should evaluate their own handwriting after completing each line of free handwriting. Students can circle their best letter (or number) and draw an x below a letter (or number) that needs improvement. This process of self-evaluation gets students to pay close attention to their own work and forces them to closely study the distinctive shape of each alphabet letter.

Authentic practice pages

Near the end of each unit, a TEACHER box is titled Authentic Practice.

What are the teaching steps and methods?
Look and listen. Before class, read the tapescript to anticipate its content and language. Set the scene for the conversation. One method is to focus students' attention on the pictures. For example, point to the pictures and identify the context or specific items. Or you can point to the picture and have students identify the setting or specific items. Be mindful of what students are capable of saying; don't elicit information or language that students would not know prior to listening to the conversation.

If a student asks for the meaning of a new word, give the meaning but avoid spending a lot of time on it. Keep in mind that a major cause of lack of comprehension is the natural panic that occurs when learners hear unknown words. For this reason, it's helpful to point out to students that it's not necessary for them to understand every word to understand the selection.

Listen and respond. To help you remember all the language previously presented, note that in the Lesson Plans, every "Listen and respond" activity features a "Possible student responses" section which lists all the relevant language students have learned and are able and likely to produce. Actual student responses will vary, depending on each student's ability or ideas. Teachers can use this listing to remind students of what they have learned and to encourage the use of this language outside of class.

To encourage risk-taking and experimentation, avoid correcting students until the end of the activity and praise them for creativity and expressiveness. Have students say as much as they can.

Survival language review pages

A full-page illustration has been especially created to prompt oral review of all language taught (vocabulary and conversational survival language) in the unit as well as some review and recycling of language learned in prior units.

What are the teaching steps and methods?
Begin by allowing students time to look at the illustration. To remind students of the vocabulary, say several items and have students locate them in the picture. Then have students identify items in the picture. Finally, have students work with a partner to role-play conversations for the people in the picture.

Circulate around the room, offering help as needed. Again, to encourage the risk-taking and improvisation that are the major goals of these activities, avoid interrupting students with corrections. Instead, take notes on common student mistakes and review them as a class at the end of the activity. Encourage students to say as much as they can and to extend the suggested tasks as much as possible. A "Possible student responses" section lists language from the unit that students are likely to produce. A separate "Your students can also say" section lists all relevant language from previous units that students may recycle.

ASSESSMENT OF PROGRESS

Tests
Assessment of progress is key to demonstrating student achievement and district accountability. A complete series of performance-based achievement tests is included on the **Teacher's Resource Kit CD-ROM** in the back of this Teacher's Edition. The tests measure progress in all four skills and will build student and teacher confidence in the success of your instruction. In addition, a **Placement Test** in the back of this Teacher's Edition and on the CD-ROM ensures correct student placement within the *Literacy Plus* series.

COMPONENTS OF EACH *LITERACY PLUS* LEVEL

Student's Book
The illustrated textbook contains alternating literacy and survival language lessons.

Cassettes

This essential recording ensures mastery of vocabulary and conversation models; provides intensive pronunciation and intonation practice, making students' new language understandable; and builds students' listening comprehension of spoken English.

Teacher's Edition

Includes wraparound Lesson Plans for each page of the Student's Book. Special features include at-a-glance tapescripts of all recorded material on the Student's Book page; step-by-step instructions for presenting each lesson; numerous additional activities, challenge activities, civics enrichment ideas; a placement test; and a Teacher's Resource Kit CD-ROM.

Teacher's Resource Kit CD-ROM

Contains a downloadable and reproducible Placement Test, Performance-Based Achievement Tests, and Extra Practice Worksheets. All items can be printed out and photocopied for teacher and student use.

Placement test. A short and simple test quickly determines whether students are literate in English or their native language and places them appropriately in *Literacy Plus*.

Performance-based achievement tests. All tests can be printed out from the Teacher's Resource Kit CD-ROM at the back of this Teacher's Edition. They are organized by unit. Each unit contains the following tests:

> **Test 1.** Reviews literacy concepts introduced in the unit. Can be administered to the class as a whole.

> **Test 2.** Assesses students' receptive comprehension of new vocabulary and survival language in the unit. Can be administered to the class as a whole.

> **Listening-speaking tests.** Designed to assess each student's speaking and aural comprehension. Because the tests must be administered one-on-one, they are considered optional, but they are highly recommended if you want to determine if your students have acquired all the survival language in the unit.

Extra Practice Worksheets. The worksheets provide students the opportunity to practice the literacy concepts they learned in class. The worksheets are designed for independent work. All worksheets can be printed out from the CD-ROM.

The worksheets are designed to be predictable and easy to understand so that students can complete them without instruction or assistance. Many of the worksheets can be assigned for homework. Occasionally, the Lesson Plans will recommend a worksheet for in-class practice. In these instances, the work in progress is more relevant than the end product. For example, it is best to do the letter and number tracing worksheets in class so the teacher can monitor students' stroke sequences and handwriting practices (posture, paper position, and grip).

When students have completed a worksheet, they can hand it in to you for correction. Students should keep a folder of all of their completed and corrected worksheets. Occasionally sit down with students to review their worksheet portfolios, so they can see and measure their own progress.

Literacy students are unaccustomed to keeping papers organized. The Extra Practice Worksheets can be their first foray into maintaining an organized notebook. Conveniently, the worksheets are already numbered, so students just need to keep them in numerical order, reinforcing a numeracy concept taught in *Literacy Plus*. Occasionally check students' folders to see how well they are keeping their papers in order.

Flashcards

Black line masters permit a constant variety of presentation and reinforcement of vocabulary, letters, and numbers. Lively games and other activities for use of the Flashcards are included in the lesson plans of this Teacher's Edition. The Flashcards are provided free of charge with the Teacher's Edition.

Guide for Native Language Tutors

The *Guide for Native Language Tutors* provides suggestions for native language tutors and aides in the ESL and literacy classroom. The text helps simplify and expand students' understanding of the civics concepts in *Literacy Plus* by conducting discussions in the students' own language.

Table of Contents

Joan Saslow

Joan Saslow has taught English as a second language and English as a foreign language to adults and young adults in the United States and Chile. She taught workplace English at the General Motors auto assembly plant in Tarrytown, NY; and Adult ESL at Westchester Community College and at Marymount College in New York. In addition, Ms. Saslow taught English and French at the Binational Centers of Valparaíso and Viña del Mar, Chile, and the Catholic University of Valparaíso.

Ms. Saslow is the coauthor of the *Workplace Plus* and *Ready to Go* series for adult ESL students. She is the series director of Longman's popular five-level adult course *True Colors, an EFL Course for Real Communication* and of *True Voices*, a five-level video course. She is also author of *English in Context: Reading Comprehension for Science and Technology*, a three-level series for English for special purposes. In addition, Ms. Saslow has been an editor of language teaching materials, a teacher trainer, and a frequent speaker at gatherings of ESL and EFL teachers for over thirty years.

Sarah Lynn

Sarah Lynn has taught Literacy, English as a second language, and English as a foreign language to adults in the United States and Spain.

Ms. Lynn received her Masters in Teaching with a concentration in the teaching of reading from Teacher's College, Columbia University. Over the last eleven years she has taught literacy skills to adult immigrants enrolled in the publicly funded SCALE program in Somerville, Massachusetts. She has also taught at the University of Massachusetts and Harvard University Extension and at the Institute of North American Studies in Barcelona.

She co-authored the book *Business Across Cultures*, a case study approach to cross-cultural communication. In addition, she has written 15 teacher's manuals for such publications as *Word by Word Basic, Focus on Grammar, Side by Side,* and *NorthStar.*

Laura Brooks

Laura Brooks has taught English as a second language, ESL literacy, and workplace ESL in the Boston, Massachusetts, area for eight years. She received her Masters of Education in TESOL from Boston University and has a Certificate in Adult Reading and Learning Disabilities from the Community Learning Center in Cambridge, Massachusetts. In addition, Ms. Brooks holds a Level 1 Certification in the Wilson Reading System.

Series advisor
Edwina Hoffman

Edwina Hoffman has taught English for speakers of other languages in South Florida and at the Miccosukee Tribe of Indians, and English as a foreign language in Venezuela. She provided teacher training in a seven-state area for federally funded multi-functional resource centers serving the southeastern part of the United States. Dr. Hoffman taught English composition at Florida International University and graduate ESOL methods at the University of Miami.

Dr. Hoffman is an instructional supervisor with the adult and vocational programs of Miami-Dade County Public Schools in Miami, Florida. She has acted as a consultant, reviewer, and author of adult ESOL materials for over twenty years. A graduate of Middlebury College, Dr. Hoffman's doctoral degree is from Florida International University.

Scope and sequence

Unit	Literacy	Survival Language	Civics Concepts	Vocabulary
1 page 7	• Recognize and trace triangle, circle, square. • Recognize left-to-right and top-to-bottom directionality.	• Make informal introductions. • Express and acknowledge thanks. • Give and accept a compliment. • Talk about first and last names. • Use titles Mr. and Ms. • Discuss occupations. • Ask about another's state of health and tell about one's own.	• Shake hands, exchange names, and express friendliness upon meeting someone new. • It's polite to express gratitude for a compliment. • Jobs are not determined by gender. • It's polite to ask about another's occupation. • It's polite to ask about another's health. It's important to say thanks when someone asks about your health.	• Occupations.
2 page 25	• Recognize numbers 1–30 as symbols that represent quantities as well as sequences.	• Ask for and give directions to a place. • Confirm information. • Offer help. • Ask for, state, and confirm telephone numbers. • Ask for and give zip code and area code.	• Wait on line to board a bus. • Park within the lines in a parking lot. • It's OK to ask a stranger for directions. • It's polite to offer assistance to a stranger. • It's OK to give a public official your phone number.	• Places in the community. • Types of housing.
3 page 43	• Trace and write numbers 1–10. • Recognize numbers on telephone key pad. • Recognize "0" as a number. • Recognize that the number system repeats in sets of 10. • Write the missing numbers on a grid from 1 to 50. • Recognize that buildings are numbered consecutively on alternating sides of the street. • Fill in missing building numbers on a neighborhood diagram.	• Ask for and give directions for public transportation. • Ask for walking or driving directions. • Report a fire or an accident to 911. • Ask someone to call. • Get a telephone number and area code from Directory Assistance.	• Public transportation is named and numbered. • In the U.S. emergency services are provided to the public. • 911 can help you in an emergency. • You can call 411 to get a phone number you need. • You can ask for directions over the phone.	• Means of transportation. • Emergencies and emergency vehicles.
4 page 61	• Recognize and trace capital E, F, T, I, L, A, H, Y, N, Z, K, X.	• Ask for and express location of items in a store. • Talk about clothes and sizes. • Apologize.	• It's OK to point at a place or a thing, though not at a person. • Expect to find prices on price tags. • Salespeople expect you to ask them where to find things. • Salespeople expect you to ask them to get you a size. • It's OK to tell a salesperson that something's wrong with merchandise or that it's too expensive.	• Types of stores. • Clothing. • Sizes.
5 page 79	• Recognize and trace capital M, W, V, U, J, S, C, O, G, Q, D, B, P, R.	• Exchange appropriate greetings and leave-takings. • Ask for and give the time. • Talk about work and school schedules. • Talk about arrival time at work. • Talk about business hours.	• It's polite to greet people with "Good morning," etc. • Work and school occur in regular schedules. • It's good to be on time. It's not good to be late. • Public offices and businesses keep regular hours.	• Times of day and clock times. • Days of the week. • Months of the year. • Places in the community.

Unit	Literacy	Survival Language	Civics Concepts	Vocabulary
6 page 97	• Understand concept that letters represent sounds. • Recognize sound-symbol correspondence of M, B, P, F, V, and H as initial sound of known words. • Trace first letter of known words.	• Ask for the location of foods. • Order in fast-food restaurant or cafeteria. • Order food items by size from a menu. • Talk about meals. • Politely express likes and dislikes. • Agree and disagree.	• Supermarkets are organized by categories. Salespeople can tell you where each food is. • It's expected that people's tastes vary. It's OK to compare tastes.	• Common foods and drinks. • Meals.
7 page 115	• Recognize that the alphabet has an "order" and that each letter has a name. • Recognize, read, and trace all lowercase letters. • Differentiate between upper and lowercase letters. • Write one's own name on a form, using capital and lowercase letters.	• Ask for and spell names. • State the age of another person. • Politely introduce people. • Provide marital status and spouse's name in an official setting. • Discuss national origin.	• Parents take their children to school in order to register them. The school will ask for the child's age. • It's friendly to ask where someone is from and to offer the same information about oneself. • It's OK to ask questions about a person's marital status. • It's OK to provide the names of people in one's family.	• Family and social relationships. • Marital status.
8 page 133	• Recognize sound-symbol correspondence of D, Z, S, T, N, and J as initial sound of known words. • Trace initial consonant of known words in both capital and lowercase letters.	• Report an injury. • Express concern. • Offer to get help. • Decline help. • Ask for and give directions. • Recognize common street signs. • Recognize basic safety signs and symbols. • Warn someone about a danger.	• You're expected to offer help to someone who is hurt or injured. • Signs protect your safety and that of others. Obey them. • The law requires safety restraints. You must obey the law.	• Parts of the body. • Places within buildings. • Directions within buildings. • Passenger restraints.
9 page 151	• Recognize sound-symbol correspondence of C, G, and K. • Read, say, listen to, and write dollar and cent amounts. • Recognize correct combinations of bills and coins to achieve a specified amount. • Recognize and discriminate between symbols as numbers, letters, words, or sentences.	• Recognize U.S. bills and coins and understand their monetary value. • Ask for change. • Pay for food. • Ask for prices. • Ask and answer questions about payment.	• It's OK to ask a stranger for change. • It's OK to ask salespeople for a price. • A sales tax is charged on many items. • Payment can be made with a variety of devices other than money. • It's OK to ask for a receipt. • Salespeople expect you to ask them about the products they sell.	• Coin and bill names. • Forms of payment.
10 page 169	• Recognize sound-symbol correspondence of L, Y, R, and W. • Recognize rhyming words, associate them with printed words, and read them. • Leave a space between words. • Leave a space between first and last names. • Demonstrate ability to write capital and lowercase letters on lines. • Write name, phone number, and area code on a form.	• Describe one's work skills. • Describe work experience in the U.S. • Provide information about past jobs and experience. • Provide references.	• Each work skill has a name. Speaking English is considered a work skill. • Potential employers ask about prior work experience. It's important to give correct information. • Ability to drive and to use machines and equipment is valuable in life and work. • It's important to bring references to a job interview.	• Work skills. • Occupations. • Machines, vehicles, and equipment.

WELCOME

LESSON PLAN FOR STUDENT'S PAGE 1

TEACHER

Survival: Introduce self with first name.
Civics concepts: Shake hands on greeting. Introduce yourself with your first name in an informal setting. Make eye contact.
New language: I'm [Maria]. / Nice to meet you [too].

⌒ Look and listen.

➤ With their books open to page 1, have students point to the first picture on the left to indicate they are ready to listen.

➤ Read the tapescript or play the cassette. Have students point to each person as they listen. Circulate around the classroom to make sure students are following along.

Note: The tone on the cassette indicates that students are to move to the next picture. The arrow on the page reinforces the left-to-right progression.

Option: To give students visual cues to the dialogue, mime the conversation as the class listens to the cassette or read the conversation aloud, acting out the parts and changing positions as you speak for each person. Extend your hand with the phrase *Nice to meet you.* Demonstrate a handshake with a student.

➤ Have students listen again.

⌒ Listen again and repeat.

➤ Read the tapescript or play the cassette. If you are reading aloud, be sure to pause after each utterance. Have students listen and repeat the lines as they point to the appropriate person.

➤ Have students listen and repeat the conversation until you detect error-free repetitions.

Additional Activities

Activity 1: Check comprehension. With students' books open to page 1, hold up your book for the class to see. Point to the woman in the illustration and say with a rising intonation *Ted? Maria?* Point to the man and say *Ted? Maria?* Have students respond by pointing to each person in the picture and saying the name.

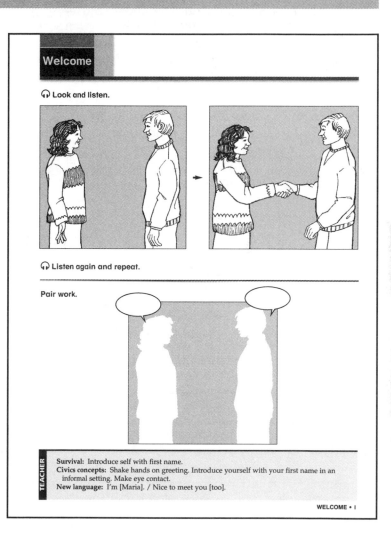

Welcome

⌒ Look and listen.

⌒ Listen again and repeat.

Pair work.

TEACHER

Survival: Introduce self with first name.
Civics concepts: Shake hands on greeting. Introduce yourself with your first name in an informal setting. Make eye contact.
New language: I'm [Maria]. / Nice to meet you [too].

WELCOME • 1

Activity 2: Practice new language. Say *Nice to meet you.* Hold up four fingers and say the sentence again. Touch a finger for each word. Repeat, but omit saying one word. Point to the finger that represents the missing word. Have students tell you the missing word. Repeat this procedure, omitting different words from the sentence.

(Continued on page T1b.)

Tapescript

A: I'm Maria.
B: I'm Ted.

A: Nice to meet you.
B: Nice to meet you too.

Pair work.

➤ Model the Pair work. Invite an advanced student to stand next to you. Face the student and say I'*m [name]** and extend your hand. The student can respond with his own words. If the student is confused, repeat the prompt. After the student responds, say *Nice to meet you* and shake hands. Then invite two other students to model the conversation for the class.

Option: Present the gestures that accompany introductions. Gesture to yourself by placing your hand lightly on your chest as you say *I'm [name]*. Then extend your hand for a handshake as you say *Pleased to meet you*. Have students imitate you.

➤ Divide the class into pairs. Students introduce themselves to a partner. Circulate around the classroom, offering help as needed and encouraging students to practice shaking hands.

➤ Have the whole class stand up and circulate around the room, performing introductions with handshakes. Offer help as needed.

Pair work (possible student responses)

A: I'm [Kim]. **B:** I'm [Maria]. **A:** Nice to meet you.
B: Nice to meet you too.

NOTES

_____

_____

_____

_____

_____

_____

_____

_____

_____

_____

_____

_____

*Here and throughout the Teacher's Edition, text within brackets [ ] indicates one possibility for speech. It is suggested that you use other possibilities as well for more input.

TEACHER

Literacy: Hold pencil or pen in preferred hand. See left-to-right directionality.
New language: Look, listen, write.

For general suggestions on the teaching of writing, see *Introduction*, page iv.

Look.

➤ Hold a pencil up for the class to see. Place it in writing position in your right hand. Then place the pencil in writing position in your left hand.

➤ Have students look at the top two pictures. These are models for a right-handed person. Indicate this by standing with your back to the class and lifting your right hand. Draw a line (from left to right) across the board. Point to the two corresponding pictures.

Then have students look at the second row of pictures modeling the left-handed writer. Stand with your back to the class. With your left hand, draw a line (from left to right) on the board. Point to the two corresponding pictures.

➤ Distribute pencils to the class. Show the class again the way to hold a pencil. Have students imitate you.

Note on holding a pencil: The pencil should be held between the thumb and first two fingers, about an inch above the point. The index finger, which controls the pressure on the pencil, should rest on top of the pencil. The pencil rests against the first (small) knuckle of the middle finger. The top of the pencil should point toward the shoulder of the writing arm. The first (small) knuckle of the index finger should be bent slightly upward as the student writes. If the knuckle is bent downward, the writer is applying too much pressure and will tire quickly.

Trace.

➤ On the board, model writing long horizontal lines from the left to the right. Have students follow along with their fingers in the air while watching you.

Option: Emphasize the left-to-right directionality of these lines with large gestures. Contrast this motion to a right-to-left directionality. Say *No!* and shake your head as you model a right-to-left directionality. Say *Yes!* and nod your head as you model the left-to-right directionality.

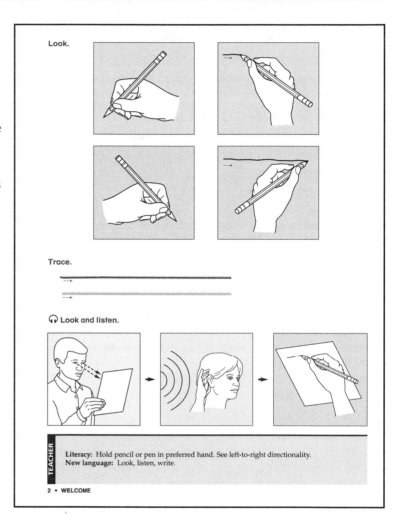

Look.

Trace.

🎧 Look and listen.

TEACHER **Literacy:** Hold pencil or pen in preferred hand. See left-to-right directionality.
New language: Look, listen, write.

2 • WELCOME

➤ Have students practice writing horizontal lines with their fingers on their desktops. Circulate around the classroom to assist with left-to-right directionality.

Note on paper position: Show students how to position the paper properly. The proper paper position for a right-handed student is perpendicular to the edge of the desk. The left-handed paper position rests at a 45-degree acute angle from the edge of the desk. You may want to place a strip of tape on each student's desk to establish the bottom line of the paper.

Note on posture: Make sure students' posture is forward facing and relaxed. Both arms should rest lightly on the edge of the desk. In this position the

(Continued on page T2b.)

large muscle in the forearm can move easily as the student writes.

➤ Have students complete the exercise. Circulate around the classroom, checking their work.

🎧 Look and listen.

➤ Read the tapescript or play the cassette. Have students point to each picture as they listen.

Option: Give students visual cues with gestures. Point to your eye with *look*. Cup your ear with *listen* and mime writing with *write*.

➤ Have students listen twice. Circulate around the classroom to make sure students are pointing to the correct picture.

Option: Test students' comprehension. Say one of the words and have students make the appropriate gesture.

Tapescript
Look.
Listen.
Write.

NOTES

_____

_____

_____

_____

_____

_____

_____

_____

_____

_____

_____

_____

_____

_____

_____

_____

_____

TEACHER

Literacy: Practice tracing lines from left to right and top to bottom.
More practice: Units 1-3 (Student's Book), Worksheet 1 (Teacher's Edition CD-ROM).*

Note: Note the name line at the top of the page. This line will appear on every right-hand literacy page throughout the book. Students are not expected to write their names correctly at this point. Its presence is meant to accustom students to the standard worksheet-like placement of a name line and to provide a space for students to identify their work should you wish them to hand in the literacy pages. By the end of *Literacy A,* students will have learned how to write their names in capital and lowercase letters, and to write their names on a line.

Trace.

For general suggestions on the teaching of writing, see *Introduction,* page iv.

➤ On the board, model drawing short horizontal lines with a left-to-right directionality. Have students follow along with their fingers in the air while watching you.

➤ Lightly draw several short horizontal lines on the board. Invite students to the board to practice tracing the lines. Have the rest of the class follow along with fingers in the air.

➤ Have students complete the horizontal lines exercise in their books. Circulate around the classroom, checking their work. Pay special attention to students' posture and paper position.

➤ On the board, model drawing vertical lines with a top-to-bottom directionality. Have students follow along with their fingers in the air.

Option: Emphasize the top-to-bottom directionality of these lines with large gestures, bending your knees deeply as you draw the line down the board. Contrast this motion to a bottom-to-top directionality. Say *No!* and shake your head as you model a bottom-to-top directionality. Say *Yes!* and nod your head as you model the top-to-bottom directionality.

➤ Lightly draw several vertical lines on the board. Invite students to the board to practice tracing the lines. Have the rest of the class follow along with fingers in the air.

➤ Have students complete the vertical lines exercise. Circulate around the classroom, checking their

TEACHER

Literacy: Practice tracing lines from left to right and top to bottom.
More practice: Units 1-3 (Student's Book), Worksheet 1 (Teacher's Edition CD-ROM).

WELCOME • 3

work. Pay special attention to students' posture and paper position.

Worksheet Link: Worksheet I
Assign the worksheet for in-class independent work. Circulate around the room, observing students' writing position and grip. Make sure that they know how to hold a pencil properly before going on to the next literacy lesson.

*Here and throughout the Student's Book and Teacher's Edition, the Teacher's Resource Kit CD-ROM is referred to as the Teacher's Edition CD-ROM.

TEACHER

Survival: Use first names in class. Understand concept that names are represented with written symbols. Trace own name.
More practice: Worksheet 2 (Teacher's Edition CD-ROM).

Look.

➤ Hold the book up for the class to see. Point to the man in the picture and say *Jose.* Point to the name card and say *Jose.*

Trace.

Note: You need to prepare the student name cards before class. Make copies of the name card template on Worksheet 2. Cut out along the outer lines and fold on the dashed line. Write the name of each student lightly on the bottom portion of each card so that students may trace over the letters. Make a card with your own name to use as a model.

➤ Show the class your name card. With a pencil, trace over your lettering to make your name more visible. Place your card on your desk.

➤ Distribute students' pre-folded name cards. Show each student how to correctly trace each stroke in the letters of their name in order to avoid bad handwriting habits later. The correct stroke directionality and stroke sequence of letters will begin to be taught in Unit 4.

➤ Have students trace their names with pencils. Circulate around the classroom, checking their work.

Option: After tracing their names with pencils, some students may want to use colored markers to make their names more colorful and bold.

Note: You may want to have several extra templates available. Students may want to start over after a mistake, or they may want to make two cards and choose one to show to the class. These name cards are the students' first public presentation of their writing. It's important that they feel comfortable with their final product.

Worksheet Link: Worksheet 2
The worksheet is a template of the name cards. Make copies of the worksheet to make students' name cards.

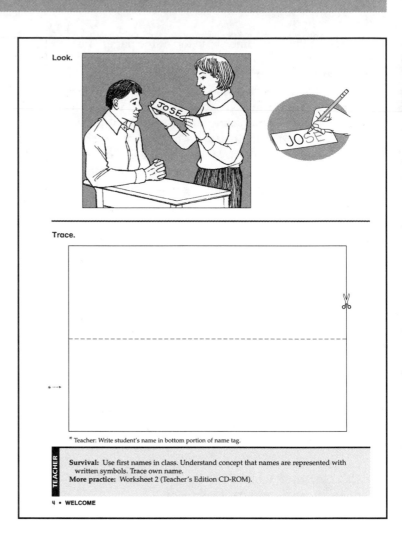

Look.

Trace.

* Teacher: Write student's name in bottom portion of name tag.

TEACHER

Survival: Use first names in class. Understand concept that names are represented with written symbols. Trace own name.
More practice: Worksheet 2 (Teacher's Edition CD-ROM).

4 • WELCOME

TEACHER

Literacy: Copy circling, crossing out, and tracing lines from left to right.

Circle.

Note: This exercise introduces students to concept of "same," which is used in this book to teach students to recognize symbols as individual letters and numbers.

➤ Model the exercise. Have students open their books to page 5 and look at the pictures. Hold your book up for the class to see. If possible, cover the other rows of the exercise with a blank sheet of paper so students see only the first row. Point to the mailbox on the left and then point to the next item (book). Shake your head to indicate they are different and say *No!* Continue in the same manner, comparing the target item on the left with the items on the right. When you come to the mailbox, nod your head, say *Yes!* to indicate it is the same, and circle it. Repeat with the next line of the exercise.

Option: You may want to introduce how to draw a circle now. Encourage all students to draw the circle around the whole object (rather than inside it). Make sure all students draw the circle in a counterclockwise motion, starting at the top. To give students practice, have them practice drawing circles with their fingertips on the board.

➤ Have students do the exercise without a pencil. Holding your book up for the class to see, point to the mailbox on the left, and then point to the first item on the right for comparison. Have students copy your motions in their own books. Continue modeling the first line as students follow in their books. When students come to the mailbox, have them trace a circle around it with their fingers. Have students continue with the second line. Watch to make sure students understand the instructions and can discriminate the items.

Option: Some students may not be accustomed to following the page top-to-bottom and left-to-right and thereby might wander over to another line to cross out a shape. Distribute blank sheets of paper for students to place over the portion of the page on which they are not working. As they complete the first line, show them how to move their sheets down to work on the next. As students work independently, circulate around the room, helping them to adjust their sheets.

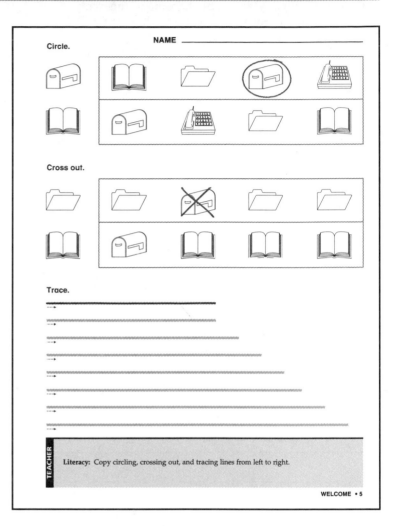

➤ Have students pick up their pencils and complete the exercise on their own. Circulate around the classroom, checking their work.

Cross out.

Note: This exercise introduces students to the concept of "different," which is used in this book to teach students to recognize symbols as individual letters and numbers.

➤ Hold your book up for the class to see. Point to the folder on the left and then point to the next item (folder). Nod your head and say *Yes!* to indicate they are the same. Continue in the same manner,

(Continued on page T5b.)

comparing the target item on the left with the items on the right. When you come to the mailbox, shake your head and say *No!* to indicate it is not the same and cross it out.

➤ Have students do the exercise without a pencil. Have them point to the folder and compare it to the other items. When students come to the mailbox, have them trace an X over it with their fingers. Have students do the next line as you watch to make sure they are recognizing the difference in items.

➤ Have students pick up their pencils and complete the exercise on their own. Circulate around the classroom, checking their work.

Trace.

For general suggestions on the teaching of writing, see *Introduction,* page iv.

➤ On the board, model drawing long horizontal lines from the left to the right. Have students follow along with their fingers in the air while watching you.

➤ Have students practice writing horizontal lines with their fingers on their desktops. Circulate around the classroom to assist with left-to-right directionality.

➤ Make sure students' posture and grip are appropriate and that each book is properly aligned with each writer.

➤ Have students complete the exercise. Circulate around the classroom, checking their work and grip on the pencil.

NOTES

_____

_____

_____

_____

_____

_____

_____

_____

_____

_____

_____

_____

_____

_____

_____

_____

_____

TEACHER

Survival: Say goodbye when departing another's company.
Civics concepts: Saying goodbye before leaving is good manners. It's OK to wave
   to say goodbye.
New language: Bye. / See you later.

🎧 Look and listen.

➤ With their books open to page 6, have students point to the woman in the picture to indicate they are ready to listen.

➤ Read the tapescript or play the cassette. Have students point to each person as they listen. Circulate around the classroom to make sure students are following along.

Option: To give students visual cues to the dialogue, mime the conversation as the class listens to the cassette. Wave your hand to accompany the word *bye*.

➤ Have students listen again.

🎧 Listen again and repeat.

➤ Read the tapescript or play the cassette. If you are reading aloud, be sure to pause after each utterance. Have students listen and repeat the words as they point to the appropriate person.

➤ Have students listen and repeat the conversation until you detect error-free repetitions.

Additional Activity

Practice new language. Say the phrase *See you later.* Hold up three fingers and say the phrase again. Touch a finger for each word. Make sure to touch your fingers in sequence from the students' left to right. Repeat, but omit saying one word. Point to the finger that represents the missing word. Have students tell you the missing word. Repeat this procedure, omitting different words from the sentence.

Tapescript
A: Bye!
B: Bye! See you later.

Pair work.

➤ Model the Pair work. Invite an advanced student to stand next to you. Say *Bye* and wave your hand. The student can respond with his own words. If the student is confused, repeat the prompt. Then invite two other students to model the conversation for the class.

🎧 Look and listen.

🎧 Listen again and repeat.

Pair work.

TEACHER

Survival: Say goodbye when departing another's company.
Civics concepts: Saying goodbye before leaving is good manners. It's OK to wave
   to say goodbye.
New language: Bye. / See you later.

6 • WELCOME

Option: Present the gestures that accompany leavetaking. Hold your hand up, facing the other person, and wiggle your fingers or wave side-to-side to say good-bye. Have students imitate you.

➤ Divide the class into pairs. Students practice saying good-bye to each other. Circulate around the classroom, offering help as needed and encouraging students to practice waving good-bye.

➤ Have the whole class stand up and circulate around the room, practicing leave-taking. Offer help as needed.

Pair work (possible student responses)
A: Bye! See you later! **B:** Bye! See you later!

LESSON PLAN FOR STUDENT'S PAGE 7

TEACHER

Literacy: Recognize triangle. Demonstrate recognition of difference in shapes.
More practice: Worksheet 3 (Teacher's Edition CD-ROM).

Cross out.

➤ Model the exercise. Copy the model on the board. Point to the triangle on the left and then point to the next shape (triangle). Nod your head and say *Yes!* to indicate they are the same. Continue in the same manner, comparing the target shape on the left with the shapes on the right. When you come to the circle, shake your head and say *No!* to indicate it is not the same and cross it out.

➤ Have students do the first row of shapes without a pencil. Model the first line as students follow in their books. When students come to the circle shape, trace a cross over it with your fingers. Model the action of crossing out a few times if necessary. You may need to walk around the room, modeling for individual students in their books. Students do the next few lines as you watch to make sure they are recognizing the different shapes.

Option: Some students may not be accustomed to following the page top-to-bottom and left-to-right and thereby might wander over to another line to cross out a shape. Show the class your book. Cover all but the first line of the page with a blank sheet of paper, as you model the exercise. Distribute blank sheets of paper for students to place over their pages. Model covering the exercise with your paper again, helping individual students as necessary. As students complete the first line, show them how to move their sheets down to work on the next exercise.

➤ Have students pick up their pencils and complete the exercise on their own. Circulate around the classroom, checking their work.

Option: The purpose of this activity is to teach students to recognize difference in shapes. You may choose to teach the names of the shapes as well.

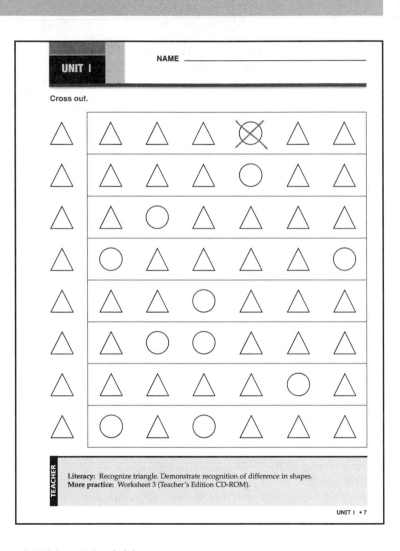

TEACHER

Literacy: Recognize triangle. Demonstrate recognition of difference in shapes.
More practice: Worksheet 3 (Teacher's Edition CD-ROM).

UNIT I • 7

Additional Activities

Activity 1: Draw similar sequences of triangles and circles on the board. Have students take turns coming up to the board and crossing out the different shapes.

Activity 2: Cut triangle and circle shapes out of blank paper. Have students work in pairs to sort them into two piles.

Worksheet Link: Worksheet 3

Assign the worksheet for in-class independent work. Follow the procedures above. Make sure that students have mastered the concept of difference in shapes before going on to the next literacy lesson.

TEACHER

Literacy: Recognize circle. Demonstrate recognition of difference in shapes.
More practice: Worksheet 4 (Teacher's Edition CD-ROM).

Cross out.

➤ Model the exercise. Copy the first row of shapes on the board. Point to the circle on the left, and then point to the next shape (circle). Nod your head and say *Yes!* to indicate they are the same. Continue in the same manner, comparing the target shape on the left with the shapes on the right. When you come to the triangle shape, shake your head and say *No!* to indicate it is not the same and cross it out.

➤ Have students complete the model line without a pencil. Have them point to the circle and compare it to the other shapes. When students come to the triangle shape, have them trace a cross over it with their fingers. Have students do the next line(s) as many times as necessary as you watch to make sure they are discriminating the shapes.

➤ Have students pick up their pencils and complete the exercise on their own. Circulate around the classroom, checking their work.

Option: Some students may not be accustomed to following the page top-to-bottom and left-to-right and thereby might wander over to another line to cross out a shape. To focus students on each line, you can distribute blank sheets of paper to place over the rest of the page. As students complete a line, they can move their sheets down to work on the next exercise.

Additional Activities

Activity 1: Draw similar sequences of triangles and circles on the board. Have students take turns coming up to the board and crossing out the different shapes. Make sure students always move from the left to the right.

Activity 2: Cut triangle and circle shapes out of blank paper. Have students work in pairs to sort them into two piles.

Worksheet Link: Worksheet 4

Assign the worksheet for in-class independent work. Follow the procedures above. Review students' work before going on to the next lesson.

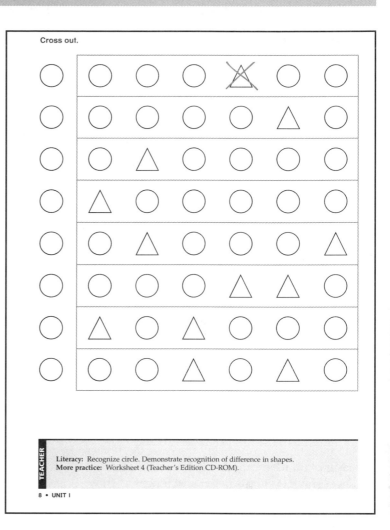

Cross out.

TEACHER

Literacy: Recognize circle. Demonstrate recognition of difference in shapes.
More practice: Worksheet 4 (Teacher's Edition CD-ROM).

8 • UNIT I

TEACHER

Survival: Introduce oneself in an informal setting.
Civics concepts: Shake hands, exchange names, and express friendliness upon
meeting someone new. Use first names in informal settings.
New language: Hi. I'm [Nick].

🎧 Look and listen.

➤ With their books open to page 9, have students
point to the first picture on the left to indicate they
are ready to start.

➤ Read the tapescript or play the cassette. Have students point to each person in the picture as they
listen. Circulate around the classroom to make
sure students are following along.

   Option: To give students visual cues to the dialogue, mime the conversation as the class listens to
   the cassette, or read the conversation aloud, acting
   out the parts.

➤ Have students listen as many times as necessary.

Additional Activity
Check comprehension. Hold up your book for the
class to see. Point to one of the characters in the illustration and say with a rising intonation *Nick? Yes?
No?* Elicit students' response. Repeat the procedure
for Nina.

🎧 Listen again and repeat.

➤ Read the tapescript or play the cassette. If you are
reading aloud, be sure to pause after each sentence. Have students listen and repeat as they
point to the appropriate person in the picture.

➤ Have students listen and repeat the conversation
until you detect repetitions free of major errors.

Additional Activity
Practice new language. Say *Hi! I'm Nick.* Hold up
three fingers and say the sentence again, touching a
finger for each word. Make sure to touch the fingers
in sequence from the students' left to right. Repeat.
Repeat once more, but omit saying one word. For example, *Hi! ____ Nick.* Touch the finger that represents
the missing word (*I'm*). Have students say the missing word. Repeat the procedure, omitting a different
word each time. Follow the same procedure for the
sentences *Nice to meet you* and *Nice to meet you too.*

🎧 Look and listen.

🎧 Listen again and repeat.

Pair work.

TEACHER

Survival: Introduce oneself in an informal setting.
Civics concepts: Shake hands, exchange names, and express friendliness upon
meeting someone new. Use first names in informal settings.
New language: Hi. I'm [Nick].

UNIT I • 9

Tapescript
A: Hi. I'm Nick.
B: Hi, Nick. I'm Nina.

A: Nice to meet you, Nina.
B: Nice to meet you too. |

Pair work.

➤ Model the Pair work. Invite an advanced student to stand next to you. Turn to the student and say *Hi. I'm [name]*.* Let the student use his own words to respond and then say *Nice to meet you, [name]* and shake hands. Then have two other students model the conversation for the class. Make sure that students understand that this is not a test of their memory—they should feel free to change the conversation and use their own words. The goal is for students to become comfortable using the language they have learned in an unscripted setting.

➤ Divide the class into pairs. Have students introduce themselves to each other. Circulate around the classroom, offering help as needed and encouraging students to practice shaking hands.

➤ Have the entire class stand up and circulate around the room, performing introductions with handshakes. Offer help as needed. If you prefer, have students stand in two lines and move down the line, introducing themselves.

If your students are ready . . .

Civics enrichment: Demonstrate appropriate handshaking with a student volunteer. Begin by showing inappropriate handshaking practices. First shake hands vigorously for more than the customary two shakes. Feel free to exaggerate the motions. Then shake your head to indicate that this was not correct. You can also demonstrate a limp and motionless handshake and then shake your head after to indicate it was not appropriate. Finally, demonstrate the customary firm handshake with one or two shakes, including the appropriate eye contact. Before and after this handshake, nod your head to indicate it was correct. Circulate around the classroom, shaking hands with students. Give feedback with frowns and head shaking, smiles and head nodding.

Pair work (possible student responses)
A: Hi. I'm [Nick]. **B:** Hi, [Nick]. I'm [Nina].
A: Nice to meet you, [Nina]. **A:** Nice to meet you too, [Nick].

NOTES

_____

_____

_____

_____

_____

_____

_____

_____

_____

_____

_____

_____

*Here and throughout the Teacher's Edition, text within brackets [ ] indicates one possibility for speech. It is suggested that you use other possibilities as well for more input.

TEACHER

Survival: Ask about names. Express and acknowledge thanks.
Civics concept: Give first and last name in formal settings.
New language: What's your name? / Thank you. / You're welcome.

🎧 Look and listen.

➤ With their books open to page 10, have students point to the picture on the left to indicate they are ready to start.

➤ Identify the setting by using an office name with which students are familiar (the school office, a Social Security office, an INS office, a customs office).

➤ Play the cassette or read the tapescript aloud. As students listen, have them point to the appropriate person in the picture. Circulate around the classroom to make sure students are following along.

➤ Have students listen as many times as necessary.

Additional Activity

Check comprehension. Point to the woman in the picture and ask with a rising intonation *Dan? Yes? No?* Elicit students' responses.

🎧 Listen again and repeat.

➤ Read the tapescript or play the cassette. If you are reading aloud, be sure to pause after each utterance. Have students listen and repeat as they point to the appropriate person in the picture.

➤ Have students listen and repeat as many times as necessary.

Additional Activities

Activity 1: Practice new language. Ask *What's your name?* Hold up three fingers and ask the question again, touching a finger for each word. Make sure to touch the fingers in sequence from the students' left to right. Repeat twice. On the third repeat, omit saying one word. For example, point to each finger as you ask *What's ____ name?* Point to the finger that represents *your*. Students say the missing word. Repeat the procedure, omitting a different word each time.

Activity 2: Test students' memory. Point to the woman in the picture and elicit the question *What's your name?* Point to the man and elicit the response. Continue with the next scene. Accept speech that makes sense but may vary slightly from the tapescript.

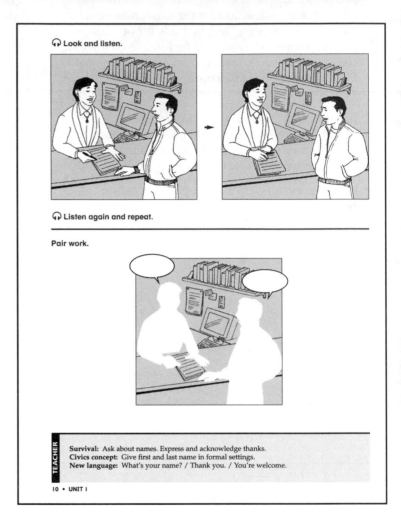

🎧 Look and listen.

🎧 Listen again and repeat.

Pair work.

TEACHER
Survival: Ask about names. Express and acknowledge thanks.
Civics concept: Give first and last name in formal settings.
New language: What's your name? / Thank you. / You're welcome.

10 • UNIT 1

Activity 3: You may want to work on students' pronunciation of *Thank you* and *You're welcome*. Call on students to repeat after you. The /θ/ sound of *thank* and the /w/ of *welcome* may be challenging. To help students approximate the sound, encourage them to look at your mouth as you utter the sounds. For the /θ/ sound, the tongue is visible. The /w/ sound has the lips puckered as in a kiss.

Activity 4: Focus on intonation. Demonstrate with hand motions the rising/falling intonation pattern of the *wh–* question *What's your name?* Move your hand upward through the question and bring it swiftly down on the end sound of *name*. Have students mirror the hand motions to reinforce the learning.

Tapescript

A: What's your name?
B: Dan Bass.

A: Thank you.
B: You're welcome.

Pair work.

➤ Model the Pair work. Invite an advanced student to stand next to you. Turn to the student and ask *What's your name?* Listen to the student's response. Say *Thank you* and wait for the student to say *You're welcome.* Then invite two other students to model the conversation for the class.

➤ Divide the class into pairs. Students ask for and give their names. Circulate around the classroom, offering help as needed.

➤ Have the entire class stand up and circulate around the room, asking for and giving their names. Offer help as needed.

Pair work (possible student responses)

A: What's your name? B: [Nick Jones] / I'm [Nick Jones]. A: Thank you. B: You're welcome.

If your students are ready . . .

Civics enrichment: These conversations are not introductions; rather they are exchanges of information. In this context, it is not appropriate to shake hands after giving your name. With a student volunteer, you can demonstrate this by offering a handshake after giving your name. Shake your head to indicate that this scene was not correct. Then demonstrate an appropriate response with hands at your side or in your pockets as you say your name. You may also want to model an introduction again (as on page 9) to reinforce the concept of when handshakes are appropriate.

NOTES

TEACHER

Literacy: Recognize square. Demonstrate recognition of difference in shapes.
More practice: Worksheet 5 (Teacher's Edition CD-ROM).

Cross out.

➤ Model the exercise. Copy the first row of shapes on the board. Point to the square on the left and then point to the next shape (square). Nod your head to indicate they are the same. Continue in the same manner, comparing the target shape on the left with the shapes on the right. When you come to the circle, shake your head to indicate it is not the same and cross it out.

➤ Have students do the model line without a pencil. Have them point to the square and compare it to the other shapes. When students come to the circle, have them trace an X over it with their fingers. Have students do the next few lines as many times as necessary as you watch to make sure they are discriminating the shapes.

➤ Have students pick up their pencils and complete the exercise on their own. Circulate around the classroom, checking their work.

Option: Some students might wander over to another line to cross out a shape. To focus students on each line, you can distribute blank sheets of paper to place over the rest of the page. As students complete a line, they can move their sheets down to work on the next.

Additional Activities

Activity 1: Draw similar sequences of squares, triangles, and circles on the board. Have students take turns coming up to the board and crossing out the different shapes. Make sure students always move from the left to the right.

Activity 2: Cut triangle, circle, and square shapes of varying sizes out of blank paper. Have students sort them into three piles.

Worksheet Link: Worksheet 5

Assign the worksheet for in-class independent work. Follow the procedures above. Review students' work before going on to the next lesson.

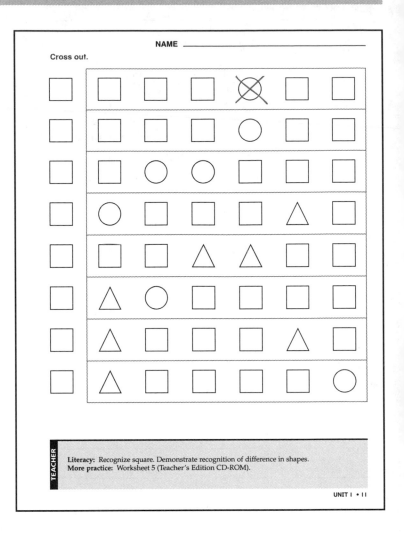

NAME _____

Cross out.

TEACHER

Literacy: Recognize square. Demonstrate recognition of difference in shapes.
More practice: Worksheet 5 (Teacher's Edition CD-ROM).

UNIT 1 • 11

Literacy: Recognize triangle, square, and circle. Demonstrate recognition of sameness in shapes.
More practice: Worksheet 6 (Teacher's Edition CD-ROM).

Circle.

➤ Model the exercise. Copy the first row of shapes on the board. Point to the triangle on the left and then point to the next shape (circle). Shake your head and say *No!* to indicate they are different. Continue in the same manner, comparing the target shape on the left with the shapes on the right. When you come to the triangle, nod your head and say *Yes!* to indicate it is the same and circle it.

Option: You may want to focus on how to draw a circle now. Demonstrate drawing a circle around the entire shape (rather than inside it). To give students practice, have them practice drawing circles around shapes with their fingertips on the board. Make sure all students draw the circle in a counterclockwise motion, starting at the top.

➤ Have students do the model line without a pencil. Have them point to the triangle and compare it to the other shapes. When students come to another triangle shape, have them trace a circle over it with their fingers. Have students do the next few lines as many times as necessary, as you watch to make sure they understand the instructions and can discriminate the shapes.

➤ Have students pick up their pencils and complete the exercise on their own. Circulate around the classroom, checking their work.

Option: Some students might wander over to another line to circle a shape. To focus students on each line, you can distribute blank sheets of paper to place over the rest of the page. As students complete a line, they can move their sheets down to work on the next line.

Additional Activity
Draw similar sequences of squares, triangles, and circles on the board. Have students take turns coming up to the board and circling similar shapes. Make sure students always move from the left to the right.

Worksheet Link: Worksheet 6
Assign the worksheet for in-class independent work. Follow the procedures above. Review students' work before going on to the next lesson.

Circle.

Literacy: Recognize triangle, square, and circle. Demonstrate recognition of sameness in shapes.
More practice: Worksheet 6 (Teacher's Edition CD-ROM).

12 • UNIT I

TEACHER

Survival: Talk about last names. Give and accept a compliment.
Civics concept: It is polite to express gratitude for a compliment.
New language: What's your last name? / That's a nice name. / Thanks!

🎧 Look and listen.

➤ With their books open to page 13, have students point to the first picture on the left to indicate they are ready to start.

➤ Read the tapescript or play the cassette. Have students point to the appropriate person in the picture as they listen. Circulate around the classroom to make sure students are following along.

➤ Have students listen as many times as necessary.

Additional Activity
Test comprehension. Hold the book up for the class to see. Point to the character of Nick and say with a rising intonation *Nick Smith? Yes? No?* Elicit students' response.

🎧 Listen again and repeat.

➤ Read the tapescript or play the cassette. If you are reading the tapescript aloud, pause after each utterance. Have students listen and repeat as they point to the appropriate person in the picture.

➤ Have students listen and repeat as many times as necessary.

Additional Activities
Activity 1: Practice new language. Ask the question *What's your last name?* Hold up four fingers and ask the question again, touching a finger for each word. Make sure to touch the fingers in order from the students' left to right. Repeat twice. On the third repeat, omit saying one word. Point to the finger that represents the missing word. Have students say the missing word. Repeat the procedure, omitting a different word each time.

Activity 2: Test students' memory. Point to Nina in the first picture and elicit the question. Point to Nick and elicit the response. Continue with the next scene. Accept speech that makes sense but may vary slightly from the tapescript.

Activity 3: If you worked on the rising/falling intonation of *wh–* questions on page 10, reinforce your instruction with the *wh–* question *What's your last name?* Remember to have students mirror the hand motions to reinforce the learning.

🎧 Look and listen.

🎧 Listen again and repeat.

Pair work.

TEACHER
Survival: Talk about last names. Give and accept a compliment.
Civics concept: It is polite to express gratitude for a compliment.
New language: What's your last name? / That's a nice name. / Thanks!

UNIT I • 13

Activity 4: If you focused on the pronunciation of the /w/ and /θ/ sounds in previous lessons, reinforce your instruction with the utterances *What's your name? Thanks.* Remember to encourage students to look at your mouth as you speak.

Tapescript
A: What's your last name, Nick?
B: Jones.

A: Nick Jones. That's a nice name.
B: Thanks.

Pair work.

➤ Model the Pair work. Invite an advanced student to stand next to you. Turn to the student and ask *What's your last name, [student's name]?* After the student responds, repeat his first and last name and then say *That's a nice name.* Wait for the student's response. (*Thanks!*) Then invite two other students to model the conversation for the class.

➤ Divide the class into pairs. Have students ask about last names. Circulate around the classroom, offering help as needed and encouraging students to say *Thanks!* in response to the compliment.

➤ Have the entire class stand up and circulate around the room, asking about last names. Offer help as needed.

If your students are ready . . .

Civics enrichment: Demonstrate that it is appropriate in English to acknowledge a compliment. Invite a student volunteer to present the conversation with you. Have the students initiate the conversation. After you receive the compliment, do something "inappropriate," such as looking down or away. Shake your head to indicate your response was not correct. Then repeat the conversation. This time give the appropriate response, *Thanks,* to the compliment. Before and after this scene, nod your head to indicate it was correct.

Pair work (possible student responses)

A: What's your last name, [Nick]? **B:** [Jones].
A: [Nick Jones]. That's a nice name. **B:** Thank you. / Thanks!

Your students can also say . . .

A: Hi. **B:** Hi. **A:** What's your name? **B:** [Nick]. / I'm [Nick]. **A:** I'm [Nina]. Nice to meet you, [Nick]. **B:** Nice to meet you too.

NOTES

_____
_____
_____
_____
_____
_____
_____
_____
_____
_____
_____
_____
_____
_____

TEACHER

Survival: Talk about first and last names. Use Ms. or Mr. with last (not first) name.
Civics concepts: Use a title in formal settings. The last name is the family name.
New language: Ms. [Brown] / Mr. [Smith] / What's your first name?

🎧 Look and listen.

➤ Identify the setting by using an office name with which students are familiar (the school office, a Social Security office, an INS office, a customs office).

➤ With their books open to page 14, have students point to the first picture on the left to indicate they are ready to start.

➤ Read the tapescript or play the cassette. Have students point to the correct person in the picture as they listen. Circulate around the classroom to make sure students are following along. Note that this is the first time that students have to move from the second conversation picture, on the upper right, to the third picture, at the beginning of the second row. You may need to work on the concept of moving from the end of one row to the beginning of the next row.

➤ Have students listen as many times as necessary.

Additional Activity
Test comprehension. Hold the book up for the class to see. Point to Kim Jones and say with a rising intonation *Mr. Jones? Yes? No?* Elicit students' response. Repeat with Mr. Smith.

🎧 Listen again and repeat.

➤ Read the tapescript or play the cassette. If you are reading aloud, be sure to pause after each utterance. Have students listen and repeat as they point to the appropriate person in the picture.

➤ Have students listen and repeat as many times as necessary. Circulate around the classroom to make sure students are pointing to the correct person as they repeat.

Additional Activities
Activity 1: Drill the concept of *Mr.* and *Ms.* Ask a student *What's your last name?* Then say *Thank you, [title and last name].* After several examples, motion for students to help you choose *Mr.* or *Ms.* after you say *Thank you.*

🎧 Look and listen.

🎧 Listen again and repeat.

Pair work.

TEACHER
Survival: Talk about first and last names. Use Ms. or Mr. with last (not first) name.
Civics concepts: Use a title in formal settings. The last name is the family name.
New language: Ms. [Brown] / Mr. [Smith] / What's your first name?

14 • UNIT 1

Activity 2 (Challenge): Cut out pictures of famous people from newspapers and magazines. Show the class a picture and give students the celebrity's first and last name. Have students repeat the last name with a title.

Activity 3 (Challenge): Have students try to recreate the conversations in this activity without a listening prompt. After modeling for the class, have pairs of students point to each person in the pictures and say an appropriate phrase. Circulate around the classroom, offering help when needed. This challenge prepares students for the Pair work.

Tapescript

Conversation 1

A: What's your last name?
B: Brown.

A: What's your first name, Ms. Brown?
B: Kim.

A: Thank you.
B: You're welcome.

Conversation 2

A: What's your last name?
B: Smith.

A: What's your first name, Mr. Smith?
B: Tom.

Pair work.

➤ Model the Pair work. Invite a student to the front of the class to model the dialogue. Ask *What's your last name?* After the student responds, ask *What's your first name, [Ms. Nguyen]?* Repeat the conversation again in order to present the class with more natural-sounding speech. Then invite another student to the front of class to model the conversation. This time have the student ask you the questions.

➤ Divide the class into pairs. Have students ask about first and last names. Circulate around the classroom, offering help as needed.

➤ Have the entire class stand up and circulate around the room, asking for last and first names. Offer help as needed.

Additional Activity

Have students present themselves to the class by saying their first and last name and then repeating their last name with a title. For example, *Song Lee. Mr. Lee.*

Pair work (possible student responses)

A: What's your last name? **B:** [Brown]. **A:** What's your first name, [Ms. Brown]? **B:** [Kim]. **A:** Thank you. / Thanks. **B:** You're welcome.

Your students can also say . . .

1. **A:** What's your name? **B:** [Tom]. / I'm [Tom].
   A: What's your last name? **B:** [Smith].
2. **A:** What's your first name, [Mr. Smith]?
   B: [Tom].

TEACHER

Literacy: Observe and recognize left-to-right and top-to-bottom directionality. Trace a line from left to right and top to bottom.
More practice: Worksheet 7 (Teacher's Edition CD-ROM).

Trace.

➤ Model horizontal lines. On the board, model writing short horizontal lines from the left to the right. Have students follow along with their fingers in the air while watching you.

➤ Have students practice writing horizontal lines with their fingers on their desktops. Circulate around the classroom to check for correct left-to-right directionality.

➤ Model vertical lines. On the board, model writing short vertical lines from the top to bottom. Have students follow along with their fingers in the air while watching you.

➤ Have students practice writing vertical lines with their fingers on their desktops. Circulate around the classroom to check for correct top-to-bottom directionality.

➤ Have students complete the exercise. Circulate around the classroom, checking their work.

Option: You may want students to complete the exercise one time through without a pencil so they can focus on their strokes. Circulate around the classroom to check their strokes.

Note: This is the time to establish good writing practices. Make sure students' posture is forward facing and relaxed. Both arms should rest lightly on the edge of the desk. Show students how to position the paper properly, according to whether they are right- or left-handed. Make sure students are holding the pencil correctly and with appropriate pressure. (For more specific suggestions, see handwriting instructions on page iv of the *Introduction*.)

Worksheet Link: Worksheet 7
Assign the worksheet for in-class independent work. Follow the procedures above. Review students' work before going on to the next lesson.

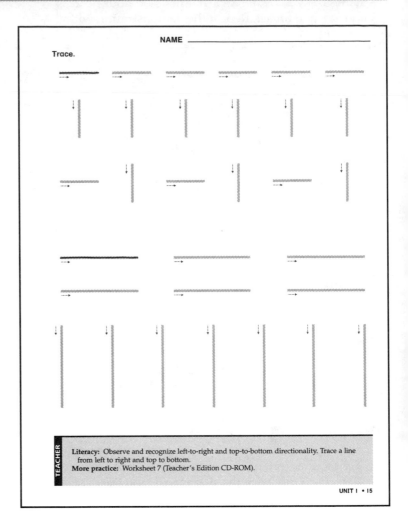

TEACHER

Literacy: Observe and recognize left-to-right and top-to-bottom directionality. Trace a line from left to right and top to bottom.
More practice: Worksheet 7 (Teacher's Edition CD-ROM).

UNIT 1 • 15

TEACHER

Literacy: Trace horizontal and vertical lines to complete square, using left-to-right and top-to-bottom directionality.
More practice: Worksheet 8 (Teacher's Edition CD-ROM).

Trace.

➤ On the board, model the four strokes necessary to complete a square. Draw the strokes in the order presented in the Student's Book: left vertical, top horizontal, right vertical, and finally, bottom horizontal. Use left-to-right and top-to-bottom directionality. Have students follow along with their fingers in the air while watching you.

➤ Draw several incomplete (three-sided) squares on the board. Draw some with missing vertical lines and some with missing horizontal lines. Invite students to the board to practice completing the squares. Have the rest of the class follow along with fingers in the air.

➤ Have students complete the exercise. Students trace only along the light gray lines. Circulate around the classroom, checking their work. Pay special attention to the sequence of strokes as students trace the entire squares in the last two rows.

Option: You may want students to complete the exercise one time through without a pencil. For students not accustomed to holding a writing instrument, this frees them to focus only on the strokes.

Note: This is the time to establish good writing practices. Make sure students' posture is forward facing and relaxed. Both arms should rest lightly on the edge of the desk. Show students how to position the paper properly, according to whether they are right- or left-handed. Make sure students are holding the pencil correctly and with appropriate pressure. (For more specific suggestions, see handwriting instructions on page iv of the *Introduction*.)

Worksheet Link: Worksheet 8
Assign the worksheet for in-class independent work. Follow the procedures above. Review students' work before going on to the next lesson.

Trace.

TEACHER

Literacy: Trace horizontal and vertical lines to complete square, using left-to-right and top-to-bottom directionality.
More practice: Worksheet 8 (Teacher's Edition CD-ROM).

16 · UNIT 1

Survival: Learn names of occupations.
Civics concept: Jobs are not determined by gender.
New language: Teacher, student, housekeeper, cook, mechanic, babysitter.

🎧 Look and listen.

➤ Point to yourself and say *Teacher*. Point to a student and say *Student*. Repeat with another student.

➤ With their books open to page 17, have students point to the left picture on the first line to indicate they are ready to start.

➤ Read the tapescript or play the cassette. Have students point to each picture as they listen. Circulate around the classroom to make sure students are following along.

➤ Have students listen two more times or as many times as necessary.

Additional Activity
Test students' comprehension. Say a vocabulary word and have students point to the picture in the book.

🎧 Listen again and repeat.

➤ Read the tapescript or play the cassette. Have students listen and repeat the words as they point to the appropriate picture.

➤ Have students listen and repeat the vocabulary until you detect repetitions free of major errors.

Additional Activities
Activity 1: Provide listening practice. Place Vocabulary Cards 4–9 on the board rim. Invite a student volunteer to the front of the class. Say a word and have the student point to the correct Vocabulary Card. Repeat the process with several words and students. Then have students open their books to page 17 to do this activity in pairs.

Activity 2: Provide speaking practice. Place Vocabulary Cards 4–9 on the board rim. Point to a Vocabulary Card and gesture for students to supply the word. Repeat the process with several words. Then have students open their books to page 17 to do this activity in pairs, using the pictures in the book.

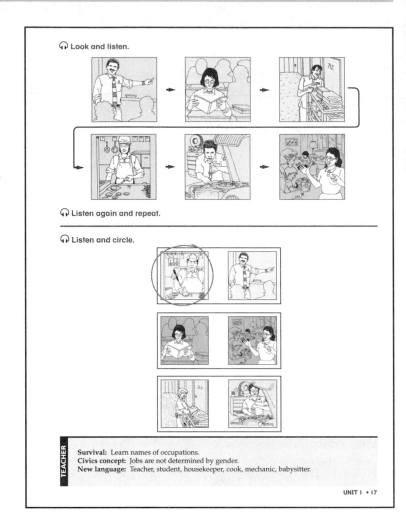

Survival: Learn names of occupations.
Civics concept: Jobs are not determined by gender.
New language: Teacher, student, housekeeper, cook, mechanic, babysitter.

UNIT 1 • 17

Tapescript

teacher / student / housekeeper / cook / mechanic / babysitter

🎧 Listen and circle.

➤ Model the exercise. Hold the book up for the class to see. Point to the cook in the first item and say *Cook*. Point to the teacher and say *Teacher*. Read the tapescript for the first item aloud or play the first item on the cassette. With your finger, trace the circle around the cook.

➤ Read the tapescript or play the cassette. Have students listen and circle what they hear.

Option: Before listening, hold up the Student's Book for the class to see. Point to each picture and have students identify the vocabulary words. This helps prepare students for the listening exercise.

Note: To focus students on one line at a time, you can distribute blank sheets of paper to cover the rest of the page. After students listen to the tape and circle the picture, they can move their sheets down to work on the next item.

Additional Activities

Activity 1: Students work with a partner. Student A says one of the vocabulary words, and Student B points to the correct picture. Partners take turns speaking and pointing.

Activity 2: Give each student a set of Vocabulary Cards 4–9. Pairs of students sit facing each other. Student A chooses a card and says its word without showing the card to Student B. B listens and finds the card in his own set. The two students then check their cards to make sure they match. Students take turns speaking and holding up cards.

Tapescript
cook / student / mechanic

NOTES

TEACHER

Survival: Discuss occupations.
Civics concept: It's OK to ask another's occupation.
New language: I'm a [student]. / What about you? / What do you do? / And you? /
A [babysitter]?

🎧 Look and listen.

➤ With their books open to page 18, have students point to the first picture on the page to indicate they are ready to start.

➤ Play the cassette or read the tapescript aloud. As students listen, have them point to the appropriate person in the picture. Circulate around the classroom to make sure students are following along.

➤ Have students listen as many times as necessary.

Additional Activity
Check comprehension. Point to one of the people in the picture and say with a rising intonation *Teacher?* Gesture for students to correct you. Pointing to the other person, say *Cook?* Have students correct you. Students may simply answer *No.* You may wish to encourage them to go further and say *No. Student.*

🎧 Listen again and repeat.

➤ Read the tapescript or play the cassette. Have students listen and repeat as they point to the appropriate person. Circulate around the classroom to check pronunciation.

➤ Have students listen and repeat as many times as necessary.

Additional Activities
Activity 1: Practice new language. Say *I'm a student.* Hold up three fingers and say the sentence again, touching a finger for each word. Make sure to touch the fingers in order from the students' left to right. Repeat twice. On the third repeat, omit saying one word. Point to the finger that represents the missing word. Have students say the missing word. Repeat the procedure, omitting other words in the sentences *What about you? I'm a student, too.*

Activity 2: If you have worked on the rising/falling intonation of *wh–* questions in previous lessons, reinforce your instruction with the *wh–* question *What about you?* Remember to have students mirror the hand motions to reinforce the learning.

Activity 3 (Challenge): Have students try to recreate the conversations in this activity without a listening prompt. After modeling for the class, have pairs of

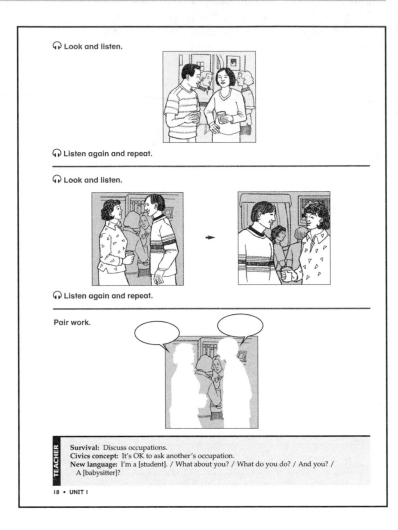

🎧 Look and listen.

🎧 Listen again and repeat.

🎧 Look and listen.

🎧 Listen again and repeat.

Pair work.

TEACHER
Survival: Discuss occupations.
Civics concept: It's OK to ask another's occupation.
New language: I'm a [student]. / What about you? / What do you do? / And you? /
A [babysitter]?

18 • UNIT I

students point to each person in the pictures and say an appropriate phrase. Circulate around the classroom, offering help when needed. This challenge prepares students for the Pair work.

Tapescript
A: I'm a student. What about you?
B: I'm a student too.

🎧 Look and listen.

➤ Have students point to the first picture of this exercise to indicate they are ready to listen.

➤ Play the cassette or read the tapescript aloud. As students listen, have them point to the appropriate person in the picture. Circulate around the classroom to make sure students are following along.

➤ Have students listen as many times as necessary.

Additional Activity

Check comprehension. Hold the book up for the class to see. Point to the man in the picture and say with a rising intonation *Teacher?* Students can say *No*, or they may say *Cook*. You may need to model the first response and say *No. Cook.* Point to the woman and say *Student?* Have students correct you.

🎧 Listen again and repeat.

➤ Read the tapescript or play the cassette. Have students listen and repeat as they point to the appropriate person. Circulate around the classroom to check pronunciation.

➤ Have students listen and repeat as many times as necessary.

Additional Activities

Activity 1: Practice new language. Ask the question *What do you do?* Hold up four fingers and repeat the question, touching a finger for each word. Make sure to touch the fingers in order from the students' left to right. Repeat twice. On the third repeat, omit saying one word. Point to the finger that represents the missing word. Have students say the missing word. Repeat the procedure, omitting other words in the sentences *And you? I'm a cook. I'm a babysitter.*

Activity 2: If you have worked on the rising/falling intonation of *wh–* questions in previous lessons, reinforce your instruction with the *wh–* question *What do you do?*

Activity 3: Introduce the concept of repetition of a word with rising intonation to ask for feedback. Use hand motions to illustrate the rise in pitch at the end of the word *babysitter* in the line *A babysitter?* Then have students practice. Hold up a Vocabulary Card (of an occupation) and say the name of the occupation with a rising intonation. Students respond *Yes* or *No*. For example, hold up the card for *cook* and say *A teacher?* Students reply *No*. After several examples, students can continue the activity in small groups.

Tapescript

A: What do you do?
B: I'm a cook. And you?
A: I'm a babysitter.

B: A babysitter?
A: Yes.

Pair work.

➤ Model the Pair work. Have an advanced student join you in front of the class. Ask *What do you do?* Have the student respond. *(I'm a student).* Prompt the student to ask you a question by pointing to yourself. *(What about you? / And you?)* Repeat the conversation again in order to present the class with more natural-sounding speech. Then invite another student to the front of class. This time say *I'm a teacher. What about you?* After the student responds correctly, repeat the exchange.

➤ Divide the class into pairs. Students discuss occupations. Circulate around the classroom, offering help as needed.

Option: Find out your students' occupations. Introduce those occupations to the class before students do the Pair work.

Option: You can assign occupation Vocabulary Cards to students so they can practice talking about different occupations.

Option: If students have difficulty remembering the words in the conversation, use finger counting to remind them of the words in each utterance.

➤ Have several volunteer pairs act out their conversations in front of the class.

Pair work (possible student responses)
A: What do you do? **B:** I'm a mechanic / teacher / housekeeper / cook / student / babysitter. **A:** [A mechanic]? **B:** Yes. What about you? / And you? **A:** I'm a [mechanic] too. / I'm a [student].

Your students can also say . . .
A: Hi. I'm [Kim Brown]. What's your name? **B:** [Nick Jones]. / I'm [Nick Jones]. **A:** Nice to meet you, [Nick]. **B:** Nice to meet you too, [Kim].

TEACHER

Literacy: Trace diagonal lines to complete triangle, using top-to-bottom and left-to-right directionality.
More practice: Worksheet 9 (Teacher's Edition CD-ROM).

Trace.

➤ On the board, model writing the forward slant. Have students follow along with their fingers in the air while watching you.

Option: Slants can be challenging for literacy students. You may want to give students time to practice the large arm movements before working on the paper.

Option: Emphasize the top-to-bottom directionality of these lines, with large gestures, bending your knees deeply as you draw the line diagonally across the board.

➤ Lightly write several forward slants on the board. Invite students to the board to practice tracing the lines. Have the rest of the class follow along with fingers in the air.

Option: Students can practice writing the slants with their fingers on their desks.

➤ Repeat the above procedure to introduce the backward slant.

➤ On the board, model the three strokes used to draw a triangle. Draw the strokes in the order presented on the Student's Book page: left slant, right slant, and finally, bottom horizontal. Have students follow along with their fingers in the air while watching you.

➤ Draw several incomplete (two-sided) triangles on the board. Invite students to the board to practice completing the triangles. Have the rest of the class follow along with fingers in the air. You may want to review using left-to-right directionality to draw horizontal lines.

➤ Have students complete the exercise. Note: Students trace only along the light gray lines. Circulate around the classroom, checking their work. Pay special attention to students' posture and paper position. The tendency is to twist the body or angle the paper rather than draw the line at a diagonal. Also, pay attention to the sequence of strokes as students trace the entire triangles in the last two rows.

Option: You may want students to complete the exercise one time through without a pencil. For students

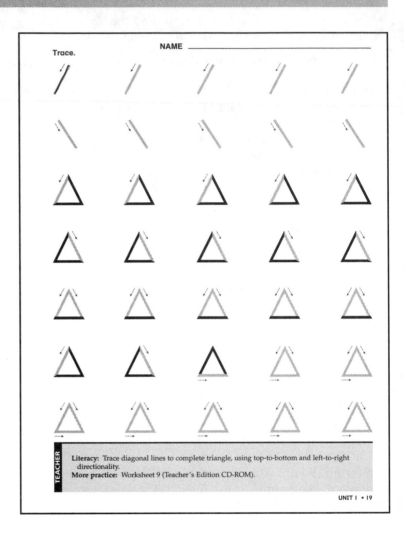

Trace. NAME _____

Literacy: Trace diagonal lines to complete triangle, using top-to-bottom and left-to-right directionality.
More practice: Worksheet 9 (Teacher's Edition CD-ROM).

UNIT I • 19

not accustomed to holding a writing instrument, this frees them to focus only on the strokes.

Option: Emphasize the importance of correct posture and paper position. As you demonstrate the correct way, say *Yes!* and nod your head. Contrast this to a slouching posture or angling of the paper. Say *No!* and shake your head.

Worksheet Link: Worksheet 9
Assign the worksheet for in-class independent work. Follow the procedures above. Review students' work before going on to the next lesson.

TEACHER

Literacy: Trace and complete square, triangle, and circle.
More practice: Worksheet 10 (Teacher's Edition CD-ROM).

Trace.

➤ On the board, lightly draw the shapes of triangles and squares. Invite students to the board to trace the shapes with the correct stroke sequences.

➤ On the board, model drawing a circle. Emphasize the counter-clockwise motion of the circle stroke. Have the rest of the class follow along with fingers in the air.

Option: Students can practice drawing circles with their fingers on their desktops.

➤ Lightly draw several circles on the board. Invite students to the board to practice tracing the circles. Have the rest of the class follow along with fingers in the air.

➤ Have students complete the exercise. Note: Students trace only along the light gray lines. Circulate around the classroom, checking their work. Also, pay attention to the sequence of strokes as students trace the complete triangles and squares.

Option: You may want students to complete the exercise one time through without a pencil. For students not accustomed to holding a writing instrument, this frees them to focus only on the strokes.

Additional Activities

Activity 1: Lightly draw triangles, squares, and circles on the board. Have students take turns coming up to the board and tracing the shapes.

Activity 2 (Challenge): Provide additional tracing practice. Using the cut-out shapes from previous activities, have students trace along their edges with a pencil onto paper. This is a good activity to focus on handwriting pressure and the proper way to hold the pencil.

Worksheet Link: Worksheet 10

Assign the worksheet for in-class independent work. Follow the procedures above. Review students' work before going on to the next lesson.

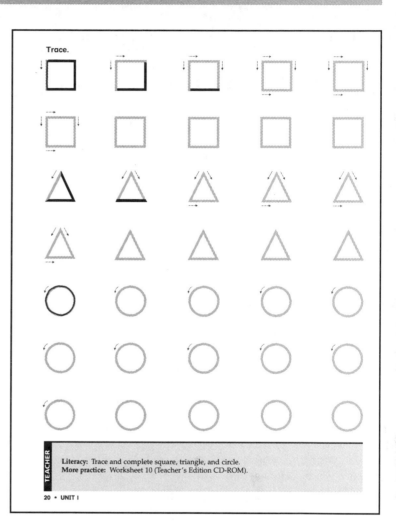

Trace.

Literacy: Trace and complete square, triangle, and circle.
More practice: Worksheet 10 (Teacher's Edition CD-ROM).

20 • UNIT I

TEACHER

Survival: Ask how someone is. Tell about oneself.
Civics concepts: It's polite to ask how someone is. It's important to say thanks when someone asks about your health.
New language: How are you? / [I'm] fine, thanks.

🎧 Look and listen.

➤ With their books open to page 21, have students point to the picture on the left to indicate they are ready to start.

➤ Play the cassette or read the tapescript aloud as many times as necessary. As students listen, have them point to the appropriate person in the picture.

🎧 Listen again and repeat.

➤ Read the tapescript or play the cassette. If you are reading the tapescript aloud, pause after each utterance. Have students listen and repeat as they point to the appropriate person in the picture.

➤ Have students listen and repeat as many times as necessary.

Additional Activities

Activity 1: Practice new language. Ask the question *How are you?* Hold up three fingers and repeat the question, touching a finger for each word. Repeat twice. On the third repeat, omit saying one word. Point to the finger that represents the missing word. Have students say the missing word. Repeat the procedure, omitting other words in the sentences *Fine, thanks. / And you? / I'm fine.*

Activity 2 (Challenge): Have students try to recreate the conversations in this activity without a listening prompt. After modeling for the class, have pairs of students point to each person in the pictures and say an appropriate phrase. This challenge prepares students for the following Pair work.

Tapescript

A: Hi. Nick. How are you?
B: Fine, thanks. And you?

A: I'm fine.

Pair work.

➤ Model the Pair work. Have an advanced student join you in front of the class. Say *Hi, [student's name]. How are you?* Have the student respond. Prompt the student to ask you a question by

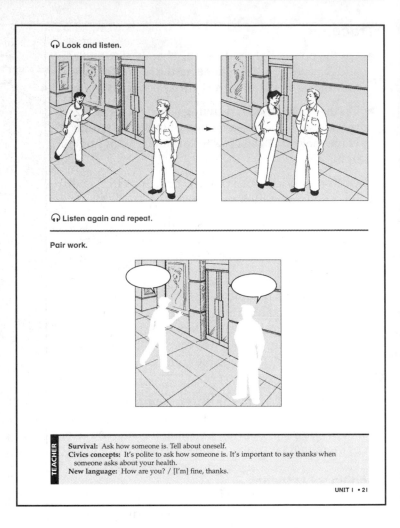

🎧 Look and listen.

🎧 Listen again and repeat.

Pair work.

TEACHER
Survival: Ask how someone is. Tell about oneself.
Civics concepts: It's polite to ask how someone is. It's important to say thanks when someone asks about your health.
New language: How are you? / [I'm] fine, thanks.

UNIT I • 21

pointing to yourself. (*And you?*) Repeat the conversation. Then invite pairs of students to the front of the class to model the conversation.

➤ Have students circulate around the classroom, greeting one another. Offer help as needed.

Pair work (possible student responses)

A: Hi, [Nick]. How are you? **B:** Fine, thanks / thank you. And you? **A:** I'm fine.

If your students are ready . . .

Civics enrichment: You may want to model that in the United States culture, an appropriate distance for conversation is an arm's length.

TEACHER

Authentic practice: Students listen to an authentic conversation in a public office and then complete listening and speaking tasks, providing true information about themselves.
New language: Good morning.

🎧 Look and listen.

Note: This conversation is a model for the authentic "Listen and respond" exchange that follows.

➤ Play the cassette or read the tapescript aloud. As students listen, have them point to the appropriate person in the pictures. As there are four pictures to follow, pay special attention to students' orientation to the pictures. You may need to direct attention to the tone on the cassette, which indicates to students to move to the next picture. You may also need to remind students to move from the second picture, at the end of the first row, to the third picture, at the beginning of the next row.

➤ Have students listen as many times as necessary.

Tapescript

A: Good morning. Your last name, please?
B: Chu.

A: And your first name, Mr. Chu?
B: Martin.

A: What do you do?
B: Oh, I'm a student.

A: Thank you, Mr. Chu.
B: You're welcome.

🎧 Listen and circle.

➤ Hold the book up for the class to see. Point to each illustration and elicit the occupations (student, cook).

➤ Play the cassette or read the tapescript aloud. Then point to each illustration again and ask *Mr. Chu?* After students indicate the correct illustration (the first picture), trace a circle around the picture with your finger. Have students draw a circle around that illustration in their books.

🎧 Listen and respond.

Note: The goal of this activity is to give students practice responding to authentic prompts, using the language they have learned so far, thus building confidence. Different students will say different things.

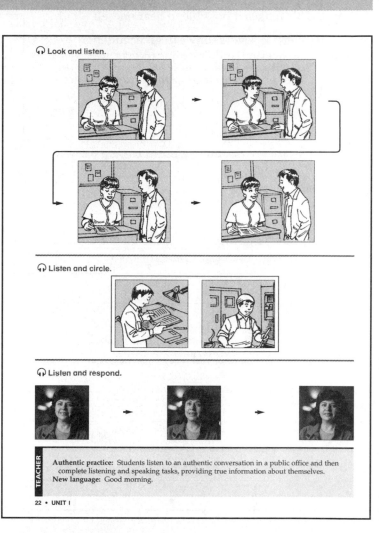

🎧 Look and listen.

🎧 Listen and circle.

🎧 Listen and respond.

Authentic practice: Students listen to an authentic conversation in a public office and then complete listening and speaking tasks, providing true information about themselves.
New language: Good morning.

22 • UNIT 1

➤ Model the exercise with a student volunteer. Say *Good morning. Your last name, please?* If the student responds appropriately, give a big smile and ask another student the question. If the student is confused, give the answer and repeat the exchange for practice.

➤ In the same manner, model the questions *What's your first name? What do you do?*

➤ If you are using the cassette, you may first want to read the tapescript aloud once, pausing for the class to respond, to give students practice before they respond to the prompts on the cassette.

(Continued on page T22b.)

➤ Play the cassette or read the tapescript aloud. Have all students respond to the questions at the same time. This gives them the opportunity to build confidence as they practice, without being watched by the class. To help students focus on their own speech, have them cover one ear as they speak. This makes it possible to hear oneself.

➤ Do this exercise several times to give students practice answering authentic questions.

➤ Finally, ask individual students the three question prompts.

Tapescript

Prompt 1: Good morning. Your last name, please?

Prompt 2: What's your first name?

Prompt 3: What do you do?

**Listen and respond
(possible student responses)**

Prompt 1: [last name].

Prompt 2: [first name].

Prompt 3: I'm a student / teacher / cook / housekeeper / mechanic / babysitter.

NOTES

_____
_____
_____
_____
_____
_____
_____
_____
_____
_____
_____
_____
_____
_____
_____
_____
_____
_____
_____
_____
_____

Literacy review: Review left-to-right and top-to-bottom directionality. Trace square, triangle, circle.
More practice: Worksheet 11 (Teacher's Edition CD-ROM).
Literacy test: Teacher's Edition CD-ROM.

Trace.

➤ Model the exercise. Draw horizontal, vertical, and forward and backward slants on the board. Emphasize correct directionality. Lightly draw squares, triangles, and circles on the board. Trace the shapes, emphasizing correct directionality and stroke sequences.

➤ Have students trace the lines and shapes in the book without a pencil. Check for correct directionality and stroke sequence.

➤ Have students pick up their pencils and complete the exercise on their own. Circulate around the classroom, checking their work. Pay special attention to the sequencing of strokes as students trace the entire shapes.

Additional Activities

Activity 1: Have students trace similar shapes on the board.

Activity 2: Test students' knowledge of the strokes. Draw a shape on the board correctly. As you draw, nod your head and say *Yes!* Then draw the shape incorrectly with a stroke out of sequence or an incorrect right-to-left motion. As you draw, shake your head and say *No!* Then invite students to say *Yes!* or *No!* as you draw shapes correctly and incorrectly. This activity builds students' confidence as they get to correct the teacher and assert their own knowledge.

Worksheet Link: Worksheet 11

Assign the worksheet for in-class independent work. Follow the procedures above. Review students' work before going on to the next lesson.

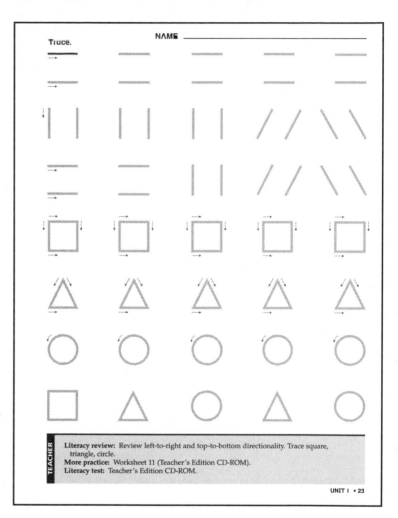

Literacy review: Review left-to-right and top-to-bottom directionality. Trace square, triangle, circle.
More practice: Worksheet 11 (Teacher's Edition CD-ROM).
Literacy test: Teacher's Edition CD-ROM.

UNIT I • 23

TEACHER

Survival / civics review: Point and name things in the pictures. Make statements about the pictures. Role-play conversations based on the pictures.
Tests: Teacher's Edition CD-ROM.

For general suggestions on the survival language review page, see *Introduction*, page iv.

Talk about the pictures.

➤ With students' books open, name occupations and have students point to a person in the picture who has that occupation (*babysitter, cook*).

➤ Hold up the picture for the class to see and point to people in the picture. Have students name the occupations as you point. Have students practice pointing and naming occupations with a partner.

Possible student responses
student / teacher / housekeeper / cook / mechanic / babysitter

Role-play conversations.

➤ Point to one of the scenes—for example, the man and the woman shaking hands. Point to the woman and say *Hi, I'm [name].* Then point to the man and elicit a student's response (*Hi, [name]. I'm [name].*) Repeat with another scene.

➤ Students work with a partner to practice conversations appropriate to the contexts in the picture.

➤ Ask pairs of students to present one or two of their conversations to the class.

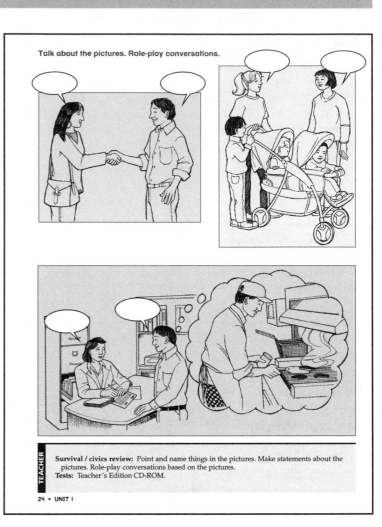

Talk about the pictures. Role-play conversations.

TEACHER Survival / civics review: Point and name things in the pictures. Make statements about the pictures. Role-play conversations based on the pictures.
Tests: Teacher's Edition CD-ROM.

24 • UNIT I

Role-play conversations **(possible student responses)**
(Picture of woman and man shaking hands)
A: Hi. I'm [Kim]. **B:** Nice to meet you, [Kim]. I'm [Nick]. **A:** Nice to meet you too, [Nick]. **B:** What's your last name? **A:** [Brown]. **B:** [Kim Brown]. That's a nice name. **A:** Thanks. / Thank you. **B:** You're welcome.
(Picture of two women talking)
A: Hi / Good morning. How are you? **B:** [I'm] fine, thanks / thank you. And you? **A:** [I'm] fine. **B:** Bye! See you later. **A:** Bye!

(Picture of woman and man in an office)

A: Good morning. What's your last name, please?
B: [Jones]. **A:** And your first name, [Mr. Jones]?
B: [Nick]. **A:** Thank you. / Thanks. **B:** You're welcome. **A:** What do you do, [Mr. Jones]? **B:** I'm a student / teacher / housekeeper / cook / mechanic / babysitter.

LESSON PLAN FOR STUDENT'S PAGE 25

TEACHER

Literacy: Recognize sameness in quantity.
More practice: Worksheet 12 (Teacher's Edition CD-ROM).

Option: If you wish to provide a review / confidence-builder before proceeding with Unit 2, print out a worksheet from Unit 1 and have students complete part or all of it.

Circle.

See "Circle" on page T12.

➤ This activity teaches students to recognize sameness in quantity in preparation for page 26, where they begin to learn the concept of numbers representing quantity.

➤ As you present the target shapes on the left and the shapes within the boxes, tap your finger or pen on each triangle in each group. For example, in the first row, tap each triangle on the left once (2 taps total). Then tap each triangle in the box, pausing between groups. (1 tap [pause], 2 taps [pause], 3 taps [pause].) This auditory aid will help students recognize which group matches the target group on the left.

Option: You may wish to review drawing a circle at this point.

Additional Activity

For further practice, draw shapes in groups of 1, 2, and 3 on the board. Have students take turns coming up to the board. Call out a number and ask students to circle the corresponding groups of shapes.

Worksheet Link: Worksheet 12

Assign the worksheet for homework or for in-class independent work. Review students' work before going on to the next lesson.

TEACHER

Literacy: Understand that quantity can be represented by a symbol. Identify and understand meaning of numbers 1, 2, 3.
More practice: Worksheet 13 (Teacher's Edition CD-ROM).

🎧 Look and listen.

New concept: Note that this is the first time a written symbol is used to represent something other than itself. You may need to take some time with this presentation, until students understand the concept.

➤ Read the tapescript or play the cassette. Have students point to each number as they listen.

➤ Draw groups of 1, 2, and 3 triangles on the board, with the numbers 1, 2, and 3 under them, as on Student's Book page 26. Point to the number 1, say *One,* and clap your hands once. Point to the number 2, say *Two,* and clap you hands twice. Repeat for 3. Repeat several times.

Additional Activity
Test students' comprehension. Say a number and have students point to the number in their books.

🎧 Listen again and repeat.

➤ Read the tapescript or play the cassette. Have students listen and repeat the numbers as they point in their books.

➤ Have students listen and repeat the numbers until you detect repetitions free of major errors.

➤ After students repeat, have them say each number and clap the correct number of times. This activity reinforces the meaning of numbers for quantity.

Additional Activities
Activity 1: Write the numbers 1, 2, and 3 on the board. Have students individually say a number as you point to it. Repeat several times. Then have students do this activity in pairs, using the numbers in the book.

Activity 2: You may want to work on students' pronunciation of numbers. Call on students to repeat after you. The /θ/ sound in *three* may be challenging. To help students approximate the sound, encourage them to look at your mouth as you utter the word. For the /θ/ sound, the tongue is visible.

🎧 Look and listen.

△ ➤ △△ ➤ △△△
1   2   3

🎧 Listen again and repeat.

Circle.

○	①	2	3
□□□	1	2	③
○○	1	2	3
△△△	1	2	3
□□	1	2	3
△△	1	2	3
○	1	2	3
○○○	1	2	3
△	1	2	3

TEACHER
Literacy: Understand that quantity can be represented by a symbol. Identify and understand meaning of numbers 1, 2, 3.
More practice: Worksheet 13 (Teacher's Edition CD-ROM).

26 • UNIT 2

Tapescript
one
two
three

Circle.

See also "Circle" on page T12.

➤ Instead of comparing shapes with shapes, students compare shapes with numbers. Point to the shape or group of shapes on the left, say the number (or elicit the number from the class), and then say each number in the box as you point to it.

➤ You may need to demonstrate several times, as the concept of number symbols for quantity may be new and difficult to grasp.

Additional Activities

Activity 1: On the board, draw shapes in groups of 1, 2, and 3. Point to each and have students say the number.

Activity 2 (Challenge): Have students draw shapes in groups of 1, 2, and 3 on the board freehand and then elicit the number from the class.

Worksheet Link: Worksheet 13

Assign the worksheet for homework or for in-class independent work. Review students' work before going on to the next lesson.

NOTES

TEACHER

Survival: Learn names for number symbols 1-5. Understand that numbers represent quantity.
New language: One, two, three, four, five.

🎧 Look and listen.

See "Look and listen" on page T26a.

🎧 Listen again and repeat.

See "Listen again and repeat" on page T26a.

Additional Activities

Activity 1: Repetition of the following number chant will help your students learn to say the numbers in order. Demonstrate several times and then have the class perform the chant with you.

One, two, three, [CLAP]
Four, five, [CLAP]

Activity 2: Provide listening practice. Place Number Cards 1–5 on the board rim. Have students take turns calling out a number, while other students listen and take turns coming up to the board to point to the number.

Activity 3: Provide speaking practice. Draw shapes (squares, circles, triangles) on the board in groups of 1, 2, 3, 4, and 5. Point to a group of shapes and call on individual students to say the number. Students then do the activity in pairs, using the pictures in the book.

Activity 4 (Challenge): Play a memory game. Briefly (for two or three seconds) show students a few (1 to 5) classroom items on a tray. Cover the tray and then elicit the number of items on the tray. Repeat with different objects and different quantities.

Tapescript
one / two / three / four / five

🎧 Listen and circle.

See also "Listen and circle" on page T17a–b.

➤ This minimal-pairs exercise practices recognition of number symbols.

➤ To prepare students for the listening, you may want to point to each number in the exercise and have students say the numbers before completing the activity.

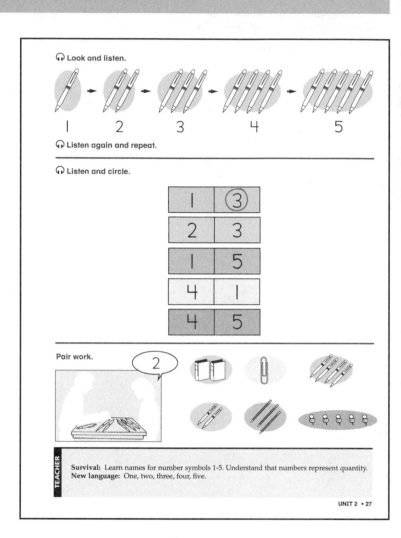

Tapescript
three / two / one / four / five

Pair work.

➤ Model the Pair work. Have a student join you in front of the class. Hold up the book for the class to see. Point to one of the groups of objects in this activity and have the student say the number.

➤ In pairs, students take turns pointing to the groups of objects and saying the numbers.

➤ You may wish to have students cover the group of four pens and the group of five pushpins with a blank piece of paper at first, so they concentrate on the more familiar 1, 2, and 3.

Additional Activity

(Challenge): Demonstrate how Americans count to five with fingers. Hold up your index finger to start with *1*. Continue raising fingers, ending with your thumb for *5*. After you model several times, have students practice in pairs. For further number practice, students can hold up fingers to prompt their partner to say a number.

Pair work (possible student responses)
two / one / four / two / three / five

NOTES

_____

_____

_____

_____

_____

_____

_____

_____

_____

_____

_____

_____

_____

_____

_____

_____

_____

_____

_____

_____

_____

_____

TEACHER

Survival: Learn names for places in the community.
Civics concepts: Wait on line to board a bus. Park within the lines in a parking lot.
New language: House, apartment, bus stop, supermarket, school, restaurant, hotel, parking lot.

🎧 Look and listen.

See "Look and listen" on page T17a.

Option: Provide examples in your community of *hotel, supermarket, school,* and *restaurant.* Have students name more examples. This connects students' knowledge of their community to the material taught in the classroom.

🎧 Listen again and repeat.

See "Listen again and repeat" on page T17a.

Option: Have students tap out the syllables as they say each word. This will help them manage the long words like *restaurant* or *supermarket.* For the monosyllabic words, focus their attention on the length of the sound. The sound *house* is long, but the sounds in *bus stop* are short. To illustrate the length of a long sound, draw your hand evenly from your mouth to the air as you say the word. To illustrate the brevity of the short words, make a chopping motion with your hand as you say them.

Additional Activities

Activity 1: Provide speaking practice. Point to a Vocabulary Card (10–17), and have the entire class say its name. Repeat with several other Vocabulary Cards. Then have students do the same activity in pairs.

Activity 2 (Challenge): Concentration. Photocopy Vocabulary Cards 10–17. Give each pair of students two sets of the Vocabulary Cards. Students place the cards face down on a desk. Student A flips over a card, says the place name, and then flips over another card and says the place name. If the cards match, A removes the cards from the game. If the cards do not match, A flips the cards over face down in their original position. Then Student B turns over two cards. Students take turns until all cards are matched. Make sure that students say the vocabulary word every time they flip over a card and that they keep the cards in their original positions. This game develops memory skills and reviews the vocabulary.

Tapescript
house / apartment / bus stop / supermarket / school / restaurant / hotel / parking lot

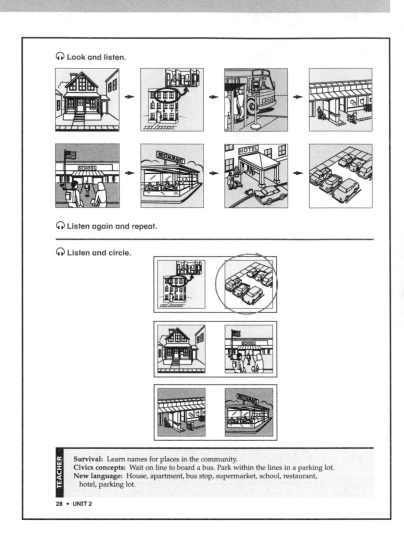

🎧 Look and listen.

🎧 Listen again and repeat.

🎧 Listen and circle.

TEACHER
Survival: Learn names for places in the community.
Civics concepts: Wait on line to board a bus. Park within the lines in a parking lot.
New language: House, apartment, bus stop, supermarket, school, restaurant, hotel, parking lot.

28 • UNIT 2

🎧 Listen and circle.

See "Listen and circle" on page T17a–b.

Additional Activity
Give each student a set of Vocabulary Cards 10–17. Pairs of students sit facing each other. Student A chooses a card and says its word, without showing the card to Student B. B finds the card in his own set. The two students then check their cards to make sure they match.

Tapescript
parking lot / school / supermarket

TEACHER

Literacy: Recognize and differentiate numbers 1-5 as symbols. Associate quantity with number.
More practice: Worksheet 14 (Teacher's Edition CD-ROM).

Circle.

See "Circle" on page T12.

Additional Activity

For further practice, write similar rows of numbers on the board. Have students take turns coming up to the board and circling the numbers that are the same as the number to the left of the row. Make sure students always move from the left to the right.

🎧 Look and listen.

See "Look and listen" on page T26a.

Note: This presentation reinforces the concept, presented on page 27, of numbers as symbols that represent quantity.

Additional Activity

Test comprehension. Say one of the numbers and have students point to the picture in their books.

🎧 Listen again and repeat.

See "Listen again and repeat" on page T17a.

Option: Work on students' pronunciation of numbers. Call on students to repeat after you.

Tapescript
one / two / three / four / five

Circle.

See "Circle" on page T12.

Additional Activities

Activity 1: Play a memory game. Make copies of Number Cards 1–5. Tape one set of cards to the board, in sequence, and give one set to each pair of students. Have students put the cards in the correct sequence on their desks. Then model the memory game. Invite two students to the board. Student A faces the class, with his back to the board. Student B removes one card from the sequence on the board. A turns around and says the missing number. Students then play the game in pairs, taking turns removing a

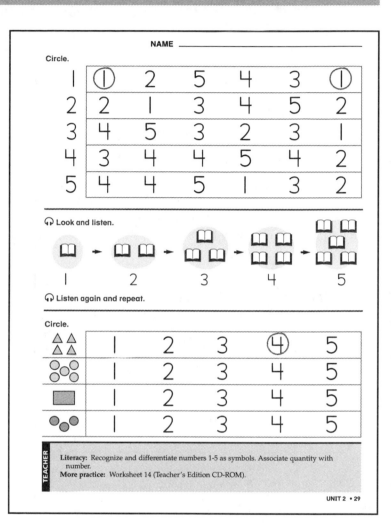

card while their partner covers his eyes and then identifies the missing number.

Activity 2: Call out numbers 1–5 in sequence. Call out the numbers again, but clap instead of saying one number. Motion for students to say the missing number. Repeat, omitting a different number each time. (Note that the concept of numbers as representing sequence is implicit in the presentation of numbers in order. If your students are ready, this activity reinforces this concept.)

Worksheet Link: Worksheet 14

Assign the worksheet for homework or for in-class independent work. Review students' work before going on to the next lesson.

TEACHER

Literacy: Recognize, understand, and differentiate numbers 6, 7, 8, 9, 10.
More practice: Worksheet 15 (Teacher's Edition CD-ROM).

🎧 Look and listen.

See "Look and listen" on page T26a.

🎧 Listen again and repeat.

See "Listen again and repeat" on page T26a.

Additional Activities

Activity 1: Repetition of the following number chant will help your students learn to say the numbers in order. Demonstrate several times and then have the class perform the chant with you.

Six, seven, eight, [CLAP]
Nine, ten, [CLAP]

Activity 2 (Challenge): Demonstrate how Americans count to ten with fingers. Hold up your index finger to start with number 1. Continue raising fingers, holding up your thumb for number 5, then the index finger of your other hand for number 6. After you model several times, have students practice in pairs.

Tapescript
six / seven / eight / nine / ten

Circle.

See "Circle" on page T12.

Additional Activity

(Challenge): Make multiple copies of Number Cards 6–10. Individually or in pairs, have students sort the numbers into five piles, with all number 6 cards in one pile, all number 7 cards in another pile, etc. Note: Students need to find the number's correct orientation before they can sort it.

Cross out.

See "Cross out" on page T7.

Additional Activities

Activity 1: Sit with the class in a circle. Start by saying *one* and hold up one finger. Then hold up two fingers to prompt the student beside you to say *two*.

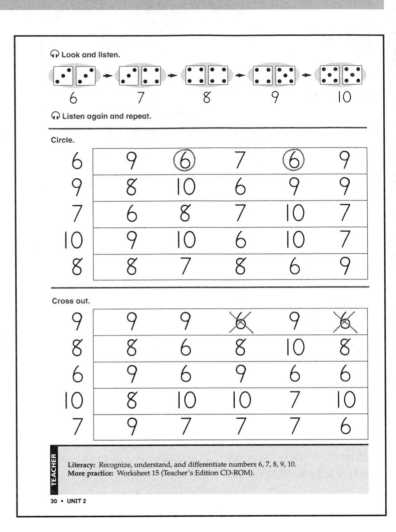

Continue around the circle until the class has recited numbers 1–10 several times.

Activity 2 (Challenge): Call out numbers 1–10 in sequence. Call out the numbers again, but clap in place of one number. Motion for students to say the missing number. Repeat, omitting a different number each time.

Activity 3 (Challenge): Concentration. Photocopy Number Cards 6–10. Follow the directions for Activity 2 on page T28. This game develops memory skills and reviews the numbers.

Worksheet Link: Worksheet 15

Assign the worksheet for homework or for in-class independent work. Review students' work before going on to the next lesson.

Survival: Ask for and give directions to a place. Confirm information.
Civics concepts: It's OK to ask a stranger for directions.
New language: Excuse me. / Where's the [school]? / It's on [Main Street]. / [Right] over there.

🎧 Look and listen.

See also "Look and listen" on page T9a.

➤ Hold up Vocabulary Card 14 (school) and have students identify it.

➤ Play the cassette or read the tapescript aloud.

Option: To get students to focus on the intonation patterns of English, demonstrate with hand motions the rising/falling intonation pattern of the *wh–* question *Where's the school?*

🎧 Listen again and repeat.

See "Listen again and repeat" on page T9a.

Additional Activity
Check comprehension. Ask *Where is the school?* Allow for variations in the basic response *On Main Street.*

If your students are ready . . .

Civics enrichment: You may want to teach students the hand gesture for *right over there.* Have them practice saying the phrase and making the pointing gesture.

Tapescript

A: Excuse me. Where's the school?
B: The school? It's on Main Street.
A: Main Street?
B: Yes. Right over there.

Pair work.

➤ Model the Pair work. Place Vocabulary Cards 13 and 14 *(supermarket, school)* on the board rim. Invite an advanced student to join you in front of the class to practice the model conversation. Then invite another student to the front of the class to practice the model conversation with *supermarket.*

➤ Divide the class into pairs. Students ask for directions. Circulate around the classroom, offering help as needed.

Option: Encourage students to make eye contact and use the hand gesture for *right over there.*

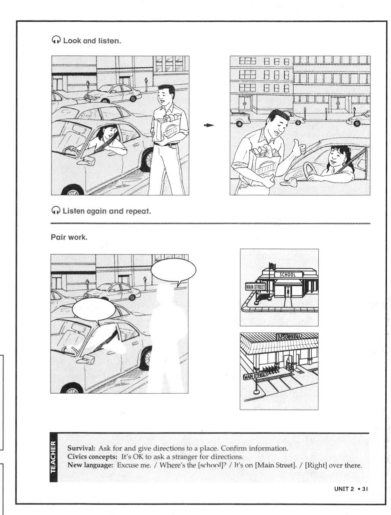

🎧 Look and listen.

🎧 Listen again and repeat.

Pair work.

TEACHER **Survival:** Ask for and give directions to a place. Confirm information.
Civics concepts: It's OK to ask a stranger for directions.
New language: Excuse me. / Where's the [school]? / It's on [Main Street]. / [Right] over there.

UNIT 2 • 31

➤ Have several volunteer pairs act out their conversations in front of the class.

Additional Activity
(Challenge): Distribute Vocabulary Cards 10–17 to students to prompt other *where* questions.

Pair work (possible student responses)

A: Excuse me. Where's the school / supermarket?
B: The [school]? It's on Main Street. **A:** Main Street? **B:** Yes. [Right] over there.

Your students can also say . . .

Where's the house / apartment / bus stop / hotel / restaurant / parking lot?

Survival: Offer help. Ask for directions. Confirm information.
Civics concept: It's polite to offer assistance to a stranger.
New language: Can I help you? / Yes, please. / It's next to [the school].

🎧 Look and listen.

See also "Look and listen" on page T9a.

➤ Place Vocabulary Cards 17 (*parking lot*) and 14 (*school*) next to each other on the rim of the board. Draw your finger from one to the other as you say *Next to. The parking lot is next to the school.* If two students are sitting next to each other, gesture to them and say *[Student's name] is next to [student's name].*

➤ Play the cassette or read the tapescript aloud.

🎧 Listen again and repeat.

See "Listen again and repeat" on page T9a.

Additional Activities

Activity 1: Check comprehension. Ask *Where's the parking lot?* Allow for variations in student response.

Activity 2: Practice new language. Ask *Can I help you?* Hold up four fingers and ask the question again, touching a finger for each word. Repeat twice. On the third repeat, omit saying one word. For example, *Can I ____ you?* Point to the finger that represents the missing word (*help*). Have students say the missing word. Repeat the procedure, omitting other words, in the sentences *Yes, please. / Where's the parking lot? / It's next to the school.*

Activity 3 (Challenge): Have students re-create the conversations. After modeling for the class, have pairs of students point to each person in the pictures and say an appropriate phrase. Circulate around the classroom, offering help when needed. This challenge prepares students for the following Pair work.

Survival: Offer help. Ask for directions. Confirm information.
Civics concept: It's polite to offer assistance to a stranger.
New language: Can I help you? / Yes, please. / It's next to [the school].

32 • UNIT 2

Tapescript

A: Can I help you?
B: Yes, please. Where's the parking lot?

A: The parking lot? It's next to the school.
B: Oh. Thanks!

Pair work.

➤ Along the board rim, place the Vocabulary Cards 13 and 14 (*supermarket, school*). Say *The school is next to the supermarket.* Then place Vocabulary Cards 15 and 17 (*restaurant, parking lot*) on the rim. Say *The parking lot is next to the restaurant.*

➤ Model the Pair work. Invite a student to the front of the class. Hand the student Vocabulary Card 13 (*supermarket*). Begin the model conversation by asking *Can I help you?* Prompt the student when necessary, using the Vocabulary Card and your fingers to represent the words in the question *Where's the supermarket?* Complete the conversation and repeat, in order to present the class with more natural-sounding speech. Be sure to make eye contact and use hand gestures as you speak. Then invite two students up to the front of the class to model the conversation, using Vocabulary Cards 15 and 17 (*restaurant, parking lot*).

➤ Along the board rim, place Vocabulary Cards 12–14 and 16–17 (*bus stop, supermarket, school, hotel, parking lot*). Distribute another set of the same Vocabulary Cards to students to prompt other *where* questions. Divide the class into pairs. Students ask for and give directions. Circulate around the classroom, offering help as needed and encouraging students to use gestures.

Option: You may want students to stand as they speak, which will encourage use of hand gestures, eye contact, and body orientation to communicate.

➤ Have several volunteer pairs act out their conversations in front of the class.

Pair work (possible student responses)

A: Can I help you? **B:** Yes, please. Where's the school / supermarket / restaurant / parking lot?
A: The [school]? It's next to the [supermarket].

Your students can also say . . .

A: Excuse me. Where's the house / apartment / bus stop / hotel? **B:** It's on [Main Street]. [Right] over there. **A:** (Unit 1:) Oh. Thanks. / Thank you.
B: You're welcome.

NOTES

Literacy: Recognize and understand symbols 1–10. Understand that large numbers are made up of combinations of smaller numbers.
More practice: Worksheet 16 (Teacher's Edition CD-ROM).

Circle.

See "Circle" on page T12.

Option: You may want students to count out the number of dots in each pair of dice before practicing. Make sure students focus on the number of dots rather than the number of dice.

Additional Activities

Activity 1: Distribute ten dried beans to each pair of students. Student A shows Student B a quantity of beans. B counts the beans and says the number. Students should take turns counting.

Activity 2: Play a memory game. Copy Number Cards 1–10. Tape one set of cards to the board, in sequence, and give one set to every pair of students. Have students put the cards in the correct sequence on their desks. Then model the memory game. Invite two students to the board. Student A faces the class, with his back to the board. Student B removes one card from the sequence on the board. A turns around and says the missing number. Students then play the game in pairs, taking turns removing a card while their partner covers his eyes and then identifies the missing number.

Activity 3 (Challenge): Concentration. Photocopy Number Cards 6–10. Give each pair of students two copies of the Number Cards. Follow the directions for Activity 2 on page T28.

Activity 4 (Challenge): Photocopy Number Cards 6–10. Invite five students to the front of the room. Hand each student one card. Have the students arrange themselves in the correct sequence. When students are correctly lined up, have each student say aloud the number on his Number Card. Repeat with another group of students. This activity can also be done as a game. Give two groups the cards and see which group arranges itself in the correct sequence first.

Note: The concept of numbers as representing sequence is implicit in the presentation of numbers in order. This Challenge activity practices this concept and will ready students for the activity on page 34.

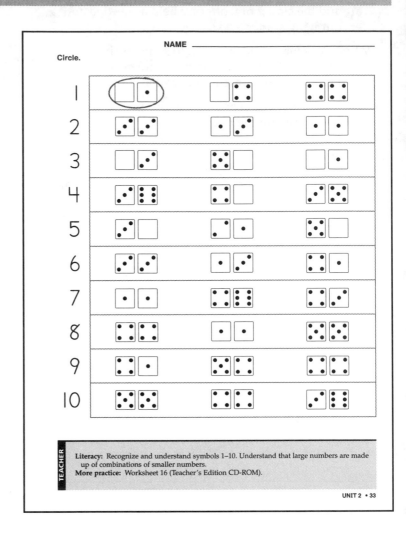

Worksheet Link: Worksheet 16

Assign the worksheet for homework or for in-class independent work. Review students' work before going on to the next lesson.

TEACHER

Literacy: Recognize numbers 1-20 in sequence.
More practice: Worksheet 17 (Teacher's Edition CD-ROM).

🎧 Look and listen.

See also "Look and listen" on page T26a.

➤ Read the tapescript or play the cassette. Have students point to each number as they listen. Make sure students are moving from left to right and top to bottom through the grid of numbers.

Additional Activities

Activity 1: You may want to reinforce the notion of a number representing a quantity. Bring a bag of dried beans to class. Give each student twenty beans. Have students count the beans as you say the numbers aloud.

Activity 2: Test comprehension. Say a number and have students point to the number in their books.

🎧 Listen again and repeat.

See "Listen again and repeat" on page T26a.

Option: Have students tap out the syllables as they say each word. This will help them manage the three-syllable numbers like *eleven*. Also encourage students to emphasize and lengthen the last syllable of all of the –*teen* numbers (thir*teen,* for example).

Additional Activity

Hold up a Number Card (1–20) and call on a student to say the number. Repeat several times with different numbers and students. Then copy and distribute Number Cards 11–20. Students continue the activity with a partner.

Tapescript
11 / 12 / 13 / 14 / 15 / 16 / 17 / 18 / 19 / 20

Cross out.

➤ Model the exercise. Copy the first two rows of numbers on the board. Point to each number as you say it. When you come to a number out of sequence, say it again with rising intonation, say *No!* and shake your head. (Note that the incorrect number is one of the numbers on the color background.) Cross out the incorrect number. Then read the entire sequence again, omitting the

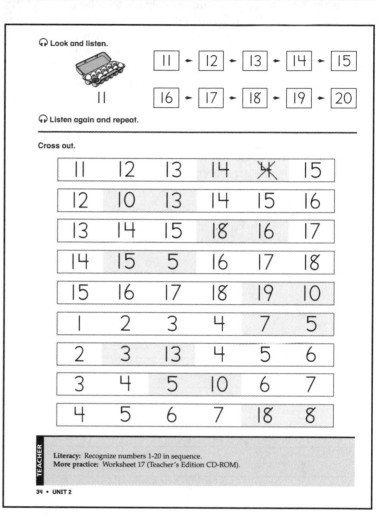

🎧 Look and listen.

11 → 12 → 13 → 14 → 15
11
16 → 17 → 18 → 19 → 20

🎧 Listen again and repeat.

Cross out.

11	12	13	14	⧓	15
12	10	13	14	15	16
13	14	15	18	16	17
14	15	5	16	17	18
15	16	17	18	19	10
1	2	3	4	7	5
2	3	13	4	5	6
3	4	5	10	6	7
4	5	6	7	18	8

TEACHER

Literacy: Recognize numbers 1-20 in sequence.
More practice: Worksheet 17 (Teacher's Edition CD-ROM).

34 • UNIT 2

crossed-out number, so students can hear the correct sequence. Repeat for the second line.

➤ Have students point to each number in the next line as they say it. When they come to a number out of sequence, have students trace an x over it with their fingers and read the corrected sequence again. Have students do the next line(s) as many times as necessary as you watch to make sure they understand the correct sequences.

➤ Have students complete the exercise.

Option: You may want to do this exercise as a class. Students are likely to *hear* the numbers out of sequences better than *see* them. Lead a choral reading of the number sequences and let students indicate when a number is out of sequence.

(Continued on page T34b.)

Additional Activities

Activity 1: Play a memory game. Copy Number Cards 11–20. Tape one set of cards to the board, in sequence, and give one set to every pair of students. Have students put the cards in the correct sequence on their desks. Then model the memory game. Invite two students to the board. Student A faces the class, with his back to the board. Student B removes one card from the sequence on the board. A turns around and says the missing number. Students then play the game in pairs, taking turns removing a card while their partner covers his eyes and then identifies the missing number.

Activity 2: Distribute a pair of dice to every pair of students. Have students take turns throwing the dice and saying the number. You may need to model the action of jiggling the dice in your hand and gently tossing them on the desk.

Activity 3 (Challenge): Concentration. Photocopy Number Cards 11–20. Give each pair of students two sets of the Number Cards. Follow the directions for Activity 2 on page T28.

Activity 4 (Challenge): Review number sequencing. Copy Number Cards 11–15. Invite five students to the front of the room. Hand each student one card. Have the students arrange themselves in the correct sequence. When students are correctly lined up, have each student say aloud the number on his Vocabulary Card. Repeat with another group of students. You may choose to repeat with Number Cards 16–20. This activity can also be done as a game. Give two groups five consecutive cards and see which group arranges itself in the correct sequence first.

Worksheet Link: Worksheet 17

Assign the worksheet for homework or for in-class independent work. Review students' work before going on to the next lesson.

NOTES

_____

_____

_____

_____

_____

_____

_____

_____

_____

_____

_____

_____

_____

_____

_____

TEACHER

Survival: Confirm addresses.
Civics concept: Houses have numbered addresses. Multi-digit numbers can be stated as individual digits.
New language: Where / What's the address? / Number [125].

🎧 Look and listen.

See "Look and listen" on page T9a.

Option: To get students to focus on the intonation patterns of English, demonstrate with hand motions the rising/falling intonation pattern of the *wh–* questions *Where's the house?* and *What's the address?*

🎧 Listen again and repeat.

See "Listen again and repeat" on page T9a.

Additional Activities

Activity 1: Practice new language. Ask *What's the address?* Hold up three fingers and ask the question again, touching a finger for each word. Repeat twice. On the third repeat, omit saying one word. Point to the finger that represents the missing word. Have students say the missing word. Repeat the procedure, omitting other words, in the sentences *Where's the house?* and *On Main Street.*

Activity 2 (Challenge): Have students try to re-create the conversations in this activity without a listening prompt. After modeling for the class, have pairs of students point to each person in the pictures and say an appropriate phrase. Circulate around the classroom, offering help when needed. This challenge prepares students for the following Pair work.

Tapescript

A: Where's the house?
B: On Main Street.

A: What's the address?
B: Number 1-2-5.
A: 1-2-5 Main Street. Thanks.

Pair work.

➤ Set the scene. Draw a simple outline of a house on the board. Draw a street sign with *Main Street.* Point to the sign and say *Main Street.* Write a number on the house and say the number (367, for example). Say the complete address: *[3-6-7] Main Street.*

🎧 Look and listen.

🎧 Listen again and repeat.

Pair work.

TEACHER

Survival: Confirm addresses.
Civics concept: Houses have numbered addresses. Multi-digit numbers can be stated as individual digits.
New language: Where / What's the address? / Number [125].

UNIT 2 • 35

➤ Model the Pair work. Invite a student to join you in front of the class. Ask *Where's the house?* and *What's the address?* Have the student respond, according to your cues on the board. Repeat the conversation again in order to present the class with more natural-sounding speech. Then change the number on the house on the board and invite pairs of students to the front of the class to model the conversation, using the new cue.

➤ Draw several houses on the board with number addresses on them. Students work with a partner to ask and answer questions about one of the house addresses or another address.

(Continued on page T35b.)

Pair work (possible student responses)

A: Where's the house? **B:** On [Main Street].
A: What's the address? **B:** Number [2-3-5] Main Street. [numbers 1–20]

Your students can also say . . .

A: Excuse me. Where's the supermarket / apartment / school / hotel / restaurant / bus stop?
B: It's next to the [parking lot]. [Right] over there.
A: (Unit 1:) Thanks. / Thank you. **B:** You're welcome.

If your students are ready . . .

Civics enrichment: To teach students that houses and buildings have number addresses, go for a walk with your class. Walk down one block. Have students read the number addresses on the buildings. Cross the street, if possible, and repeat the activity up the other side of the street. If students are ready, you can show how numbers ending in 0, 2, 4, 6, and 8 are one side of the street and numbers ending with 1, 3, 5, 7, and 9 are on the other side of the street. Say an address and have students point to which side of the street that address belongs.

NOTES

TEACHER

Survival: Ask for, state, and confirm telephone numbers.
Civics concepts: Telephones have numbers. It's OK to give a public official your phone number. Telephone numbers can be stated as individual digits.
New language: What's your telephone number? / [238-5803] / ["Oh" for "zero" in phone numbers].

🎧 Look and listen.

See also "Look and listen" on page T9a.

➤ Write a telephone number that includes the number 0 on the board. Elicit the numbers from the students by pointing to the board. When you come to 0, say *oh*. Have students repeat after you several times. Repeat the modeling procedure with a different telephone number.

➤ Play the cassette or read the tapescript aloud.

Option: You may want students to cover the second conversation with a blank paper as they listen to the first.

🎧 Listen again and repeat.

See "Listen again and repeat" on page T9a.

Additional Activities

Activity 1: Check comprehension. For each conversation, ask *What's the telephone number?*

Activity 2: If you have worked on the rising/falling intonation of *wh*– questions in previous lessons, reinforce your instruction with the *wh*– question *What's your telephone number?*

Activity 3: Practice new language. Ask *What's your telephone number?* Hold up four fingers and ask the question again, touching a finger for each word. Repeat twice. On the third repeat, omit saying one word. Point to the finger that represents the missing word. Have students say the missing word. Repeat the procedure, omitting other words, in the sentence *Excuse me?*

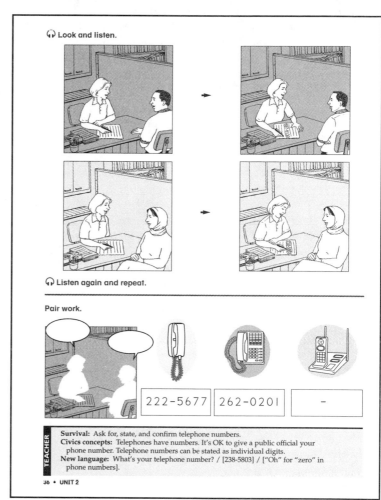

🎧 Look and listen.

🎧 Listen again and repeat.

Pair work.

222-5677   262-0201   –

TEACHER
Survival: Ask for, state, and confirm telephone numbers.
Civics concepts: Telephones have numbers. It's OK to give a public official your phone number. Telephone numbers can be stated as individual digits.
New language: What's your telephone number? / [238-5803] / ["Oh" for "zero" in phone numbers].

36 • UNIT 2

```
                  Tapescript
Conversation 1
A: What's your telephone number?
B: 597–6130.

A: Excuse me?
B: 597–6130.


Conversation 2
A: What's your telephone number?
B: 238–5803.

A: Excuse me?
B: 238–5803.
```

Pair work.

➤ Prior to doing this activity, prepare several index cards with fictitious phone numbers. Keep these on hand to pass out to any students who do not have phone numbers.

➤ Model the Pair work. Invite an advanced student to stand next to you. Turn to the student and ask *What's your telephone number?* After the student responds, say *Excuse me?* Then invite two other students to model the conversation for the class.

➤ Divide the class into pairs. Students ask about each other's phone numbers.

(Continued on page T36b.)

➤ Have the entire class stand up and circulate around the room, asking each other for their phone numbers.

Additional Activity

(Challenge): Give each pair of students three sets of Number Cards 0–9. Have students take turns telling each other their telephone numbers. While Partner A gives his number, Partner B selects the correct number cards and displays the telephone number on the desk. Partner B then says his number for A.

Pair work (possible student responses)

A: What's your telephone number? **B:** [telephone number, numbers 1–9, 0]. **A:** Excuse me? **B:** [Repeats telephone number].

Your students can also say . . .

A: (Unit 1:) Good morning. What's your name / first name / last name, please? **B:** [first name, last name]. **A:** And what do you do, [Ms. / Mr. Miller]? **B:** I'm a student / teacher / housekeeper / cook / mechanic / babysitter. **A:** Thanks. / Thank you. **B:** You're welcome.

NOTES

_____

_____

_____

_____

_____

_____

_____

_____

_____

_____

_____

_____

_____

_____

_____

_____

_____

_____

_____

_____

TEACHER

Literacy: Recognize numbers 21-30 in sequence. Understand that items can be counted individually or in groups.
More practice: Worksheets 18–19 (Teacher's Edition CD-ROM).

🎧 Look and listen.

See also "Look and listen" on page T26a.

➤ Bring a calendar to class. Hold up the calendar for the class to see. Point to today's date.

🎧 Listen again and repeat.

See "Listen again and repeat" on page T26a.

Additional Activities

Activity 1: Give each pair of students a pile of dried beans. Have students work together to count out thirty beans. Students can either count together or count alternating numbers.

Activity 2: Have students tap out the syllables as they say each word. This will help them enunciate the often forgotten second syllable of numbers twenty and above (for example, twen-*ty*-three).

Activity 3 (Challenge): Give individual students two sets of Number Cards 0–9. Call out a number between 10 and 30. Have students create the number, using two of their cards. You may need to model this activity a few times. Say the number 21. Hold up a 2 card and a 1 card. Hold or tape them to the board to make the number 21. Repeat with other numbers until students get the idea. Repeat many times. If students are ready, have them take turns calling out numbers for their classmates to create. This activity gets students to identify the place value for ones and the place value for tens. It also highlights the importance of reading left to right (for example, 12 is different from 21).

Tapescript
21 / 22 / 23 / 24 / 25 / 26 / 27 / 28 / 29 / 30

Circle.

See also "Circle" on page T12.

➤ Model the exercise. Copy the model on the board. Point to the target grouping on the left. Count the shapes aloud and say the total number. Point to the number 21 on the right. Nod your head and say *21—Yes* to indicate that it is the same quantity and circle it. Say the next number on the right.

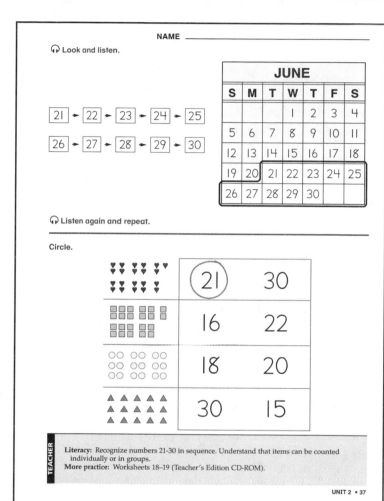

Literacy: Recognize numbers 21-30 in sequence. Understand that items can be counted individually or in groups.
More practice: Worksheets 18–19 (Teacher's Edition CD-ROM).

UNIT 2 • 37

Shake your head and say *No* to indicate it is not the same quantity.

➤ Have students complete the exercise in their books.

Additional Activities

Activity 1: Play a memory game. Copy Number Cards 21–30. Follow the directions for Activity 1 on page T29.

Activity 2: Concentration. Give each pair of students two sets of Number Cards 21–30. Follow the directions for Activity 2 on page T28.

Worksheet Link: Worksheets 18–19

Assign the worksheets for homework or for in-class independent work. Review students' work before going on to the next lesson.

TEACHER

Literacy: Numbers indicate sequence as well as quantity. Trace numeral 1 and all 1's in numbers from 1 to 31, using top-to-bottom directionality.

Trace

See also "Trace" on page T15.

➤ Model the exercise. Draw vertical lines on the board. Trace the lines with the correct top-to-bottom directionality. Lightly write on the board the numbers 1, 10, 11, 12, 13, 14, 15, 16, 17, 18 , 19, and 21. Trace the numeral 1 in each number, emphasizing top-to-bottom directionality.

Option: Emphasize the top-to-bottom directionality of the lines with large gestures, bending your knees deeply as you draw the line down the board. Contrast this motion to a bottom-to-top directionality. Say *No!* and shake your head as you model a bottom-to-top directionality. Say *Yes!* and nod your head as you model the top-to-bottom directionality.

Option: Invite students to the board to trace the numeral 1 in the numbers 1, 10, 12, 13, 14, 15, 16, 17, 18, 19, and 21.

➤ Have students complete the exercise in their books.

Note: This is the time to review good writing practices. Make sure students' posture is forward facing and relaxed. Both arms should rest lightly on the edge of the desk. Have students establish the proper paper position according to whether they are right- or left-handed. Make sure students are holding the pencil correctly and with appropriate pressure. (For more specific suggestions, see handwriting instructions on page iv of the *Introduction*.)

Additional Activity

Bring a wall calendar to class and show students a month with 31 days. You can photocopy the month and distribute to pairs of students. Students circle all numbers that contain 1.

Trace.

S	M	T	W	T	F	S
			1	2	3	4
5	6	7	8	9	10	11
12	13	14	15	16	17	18
19	20	21	22	23	24	25
26	27	28	29	30	31	

TEACHER

Literacy: Numbers indicate sequence as well as quantity. Trace numeral 1 and all 1's in numbers from 1 to 31, using top-to-bottom directionality.

38 • UNIT 2

TEACHER

Survival: Ask for and give zip code and area code.
Civics concepts: Addresses have zip codes. Phone numbers have area codes. Zip codes and area codes can be stated as individual digits.
New language: Sure. / What's your zip code? / phone number / area code.

🎧 Look and listen.

For both "Look and listen" activities on this page, see also "Look and listen" on page T9a.

➤ Make multiple enlarged photocopies of an identification card and distribute to the class. Show the class the identification card and the photocopy. Point to the *name, address, zip code, phone number,* and *area code* on the card. Repeat, naming the items several times. When you introduce *phone number,* also say *telephone number.* Repeat several times to illustrate that the two phrases mean the same thing.

➤ To establish the concept of street naming, say several street names with which students are familiar and have them repeat after you.

🎧 Listen again and repeat.

For both "Listen again and repeat" activities on this page, see "Listen again and repeat" on page T9a.

Additional Activities

Activity 1: Check comprehension. To check students' understanding of the first conversation, point to the second picture and ask *What's the zip code?* For the second conversation, point and ask *What's the area code?*

Activity 2 (Challenge): Have students re-create the conversations. After modeling for the class, have pairs of students point to each person in the pictures and say an appropriate phrase. Circulate around the classroom, offering help when needed. This challenge prepares students for the following Pair work.

Tapescript

A: Hello. Your name and address please?
B: Sure. Lisa Mendes. 32 State Street.

A: What's your zip code?
B: 87121.

Tapescript

A: What's your phone number?
B: 555–6588.

A: What's your area code?
B: 305.

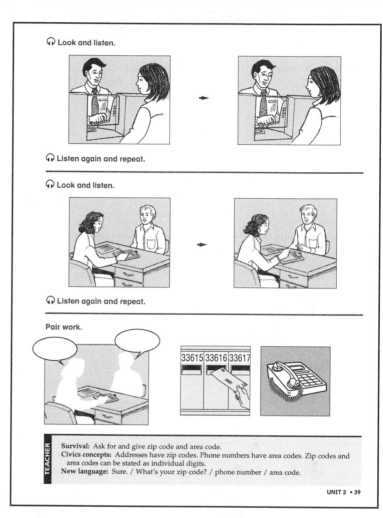

🎧 Look and listen.

🎧 Listen again and repeat.

🎧 Look and listen.

🎧 Listen again and repeat.

Pair work.

33615 33616 33617

TEACHER

Survival: Ask for and give zip code and area code.
Civics concepts: Addresses have zip codes. Phone numbers have area codes. Zip codes and area codes can be stated as individual digits.
New language: Sure. / What's your zip code? / phone number / area code.

UNIT 2 • 39

Pair work.

➤ Model the Pair work. Have an advanced student join you in front of the class. Ask *Your name and address please?* You may need to prompt an answer. Then ask *And what's your zip code?* After the student answers, call on another student. Ask *What's your phone number?* Again, you may need to prompt a response. Then ask *What's your area code?* After the student answers, repeat the conversation to present the class with more natural-sounding speech.

➤ Divide the class into pairs. Students ask each other for their names, addresses, zip codes, and phone numbers, or area codes.

(Continued on page T39b.)

➤ Have students circulate around the classroom, asking for and giving information.

Note: Students need not ask for *all* of the information. This Pair work combines practice of the two previous conversations. This is not a test of their memory—they should feel free to change the previous two conversations and use their own words. The goal is for students to become comfortable using the language in an unscripted setting.

Option: Encourage students to ask for clarification by saying *Excuse me?*

Pair work (possible student responses)

A: Hello. Your name and address, please? **B:** Sure. [name and address]. **A:** What's your zip code? **B:** [zip code].

Your students can also say . . .

A: Good morning. / Hi. **B:** Good morning. / Hello. / Hi. **A:** What's your phone number / telephone number / area code? **B:** [telephone number and area code]. **A:** (Unit 1:) And what do you do, [Ms. / Mr. Miller]? **B:** Excuse me? **A:** [Repeats]. **B:** I'm a student / teacher / housekeeper / cook / mechanic / babysitter. **A:** (Unit 1:) Thank you. / Thanks. **B:** You're welcome.

NOTES

TEACHER

Authentic practice: Students listen to authentic questions and answers about name, address, zip code, and phone number, and then complete listening and speaking tasks, providing true information about themselves.

🎧 Look and listen.

See "Look and listen" on page T22a.

Tapescript

A: Hello. Name and address?
B: Sam Harris. 4501 Mason Street.

A: Your zip code, please?
B: 78523.

A: That's 78523. Thanks . . . Oh! What's your area code and phone number?

A: 813-555-6200. [sixty-two hundred]
B: Thank you very much. Next?

🎧 Listen and circle.

See also "Listen and circle" on page T22a.

➤ Play the cassette several times if necessary. Students circle the correct zip code.

🎧 Listen and respond.

See also "Listen and respond" on page T22a.

Note: The goal of this activity is to give students practice responding to authentic prompts, using the language they have learned so far, thus building confidence. Different students will say different things.

➤ Prepare index cards with fictitious phone numbers for students who do not have phone numbers.

➤ Model the exchange. Invite a student volunteer to the front of the classroom. Say *Hello. Name and address?* If the student responds appropriately, give a big smile and continue with the remaining questions. If the student is confused, call on another student for his information, then give the volunteer another chance. Repeat the conversation once for practice.

➤ Play the cassette or read the tapescript aloud. Have all students respond to the questions at the same time. This gives them the opportunity to build confidence as they practice, without being watched by the class. To help students focus on their own speech, have them cover one ear as they speak. This makes it possible to hear oneself.

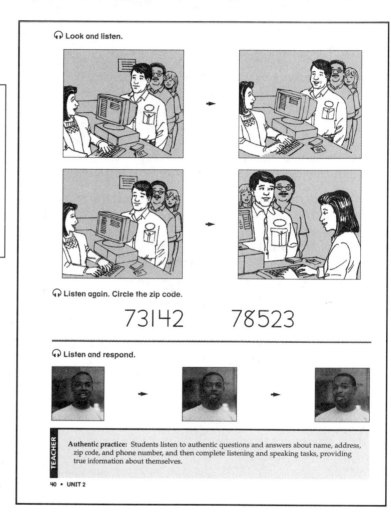

🎧 Look and listen.

🎧 Listen again. Circle the zip code.

73142   78523

🎧 Listen and respond.

TEACHER

Authentic practice: Students listen to authentic questions and answers about name, address, zip code, and phone number, and then complete listening and speaking tasks, providing true information about themselves.

40 • UNIT 2

➤ Do this exercise several times to give students practice answering authentic questions.

Tapescript

Prompt 1: Hello. Name and address?

Prompt 2: Your zip code, please?

Prompt 3: Thanks . . . Oh! What's you're area code and phone number?

**Listen and respond
(possible student responses)**

Prompt 1: [student's first name, last name, address]. **Prompt 2:** [student's zip code]. **Prompt 3:** [student's area code and phone number].

Literacy review: Numbers are symbols that represent quantity and sequence.
More practice: Worksheet 20 (Teacher's Edition CD-ROM).
Literacy test: Teacher's Edition CD-ROM.

Circle.

See also "Circle" on page T12.

➤ Model exercise. Copy the model on the board. Point to the target grouping on the left. Count the shapes aloud and say *4*. Point to the number 14 on the right. Shake your head and say *Fourteen—No* to indicate that it is not the same quantity. Point to the next number, 4. Nod your head and say *Four — Yes* to indicate it is the same quantity and circle it.

➤ Have students practice without pencils and then complete the exercise in their books.

Additional Activities

Activity 1: On the board, draw groups of shapes. Point to each and have students say the number.

Activity 2 (Challenge): In pairs, students drill each other on numbers with their flashcards.

Activity 3 (Challenge): Give individual students two sets of Number Cards 0–9. Call out a number between 10 and 30. Have students create the number, using two of their cards. You may need to model this activity a few times. Repeat many times. If students are ready, have them take turns calling out numbers for their classmates to create.

Cross out.

See "Cross out" on page T34a.

Option: You may want to do this exercise as a class. Students are likely to *hear* the numbers out of sequences better than *see* them. Lead a choral reading of the number sequences and let students indicate when a number is out of sequence.

Additional Activities

Activity 1: Play a memory game. Copy Number Cards 1–15 or 16–30. Tape one set of cards to the board, in sequence, and give one set to every pair of students. Follow the directions for Activity 1 on page T29.

Activity 2: Call out numbers in a sequence. Clap instead of saying one number. Have students say the missing number. Individual students can take turns calling out numbers and clapping for the class.

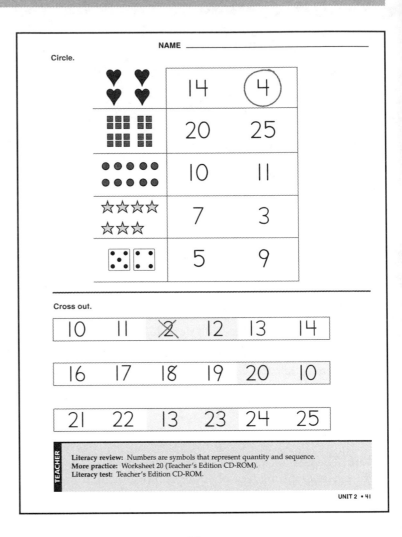

Literacy review: Numbers are symbols that represent quantity and sequence.
More practice: Worksheet 20 (Teacher's Edition CD-ROM).
Literacy test: Teacher's Edition CD-ROM.

UNIT 2 • 41

Activity 3: Copy a group of five consecutive Number Cards. Invite five students to the front of the room. Hand each student one card. Have the students arrange themselves in the correct sequence. When students are correctly lined up, have each student say the number on his or her card. Repeat with another group of students. This activity can also be done as a game. Give two groups the cards and see which group arranges itself in the correct sequence first.

Worksheet Link: Worksheet 20

Assign the worksheet for homework or for in-class independent work. Review students' work before going on to the next lesson.

TEACHER

Survival / civics review: Point and name things in the pictures. Make statements about the pictures. Role-play conversations based on the pictures.
Tests: Teacher's Edition CD-ROM.

Talk about the pictures.

➤ With students' books open, say the place names and have students point to an illustration of that place (school, restaurant, bus stop, parking lot).

➤ Say *zip code* and have students point to the zip code on the mailboxes.

➤ Hold up the picture for the class to see and point to locations in the illustrations. Have students name the place names. Have students practice pointing and saying place names with a partner.

Possible student responses

house / apartment / parking lot / restaurant / telephone

Your students can also say . . .

school / hotel / bus stop / supermarket

Role-play conversations.

➤ Point to one of the scenes (for example, the woman and man in front of the post office). Point to the woman on the left and ask *Excuse me. Where's the school?* Then point to the man and elicit a student response. Gesture to reverse roles so the student asks you the question. Invite two other students to come to the front of the class to model a conversation for the same two people. Continue in the same manner, modeling the two other conversations.

➤ Have students work in pairs to practice conversations appropriate to the contexts in the picture.

➤ Ask pairs of students to present one or two of their conversations to the class.

Talk about the pictures. Role-play conversations.

TEACHER

Survival / civics review: Point and name things in the pictures. Make statements about the pictures. Role-play conversations based on the pictures.
Tests: Teacher's Edition CD-ROM.

42 • UNIT 2

**Role-play conversations
(possible student responses)**

(Picture of woman and man in front of the post office)

A: Excuse me. Where's the school? **B:** The school?
A: Yes. **B:** It's on [Main Street]. **A:** [Main Street]?
B: Yes. [Right] over there. It's next to the [supermarket]. **A:** (Unit 1:) Oh. Thanks. / Thank you.
B: You're welcome.

Your students can also say . . .

Where's the bus stop / hotel / restaurant / parking lot? What's the address?

(Continued on page T42b.)

**Role-play conversations
(possible student responses)**

(Picture of two men talking on the street)

A: Can I help you? **B:** Yes, please. Where's the bus stop? **A:** The bus stop? It's on [Main Street]. [Right] over there. It's next to the [parking lot]. **B:** (Unit 1:) Oh. Thanks. / Thank you. **A:** You're welcome.

Your students can also say . . .

Excuse me. Where's the hotel / supermarket / restaurant / school? What's the address?

**Role-play conversations
(possible student responses)**

(Picture of woman and man in an office)

A: Good morning. / Hello. / Hi. **B:** Good morning. / Hello. / Hi. **A:** Your name, please? **B:** Excuse me? **A:** [Repeats]. **B:** Sure. [first name, last name]. **A:** What's your phone number / telephone number / area code? **B:** [numbers 1–9, 0]. **A:** What's your address / zip code? **B:** [address and zip code]. **A:** (Unit 1:) Thank you. / Thanks. **B:** You're welcome.

Your students can also say . . .

A: What's your name? / What's your last name? / What's your first name, [Mr. Black]? **B:** [first name, last name]. **A:** (Unit 1:) And what do you do, [Mr. Black]? **B:** I'm a student / teacher / housekeeper / cook / mechanic / babysitter.

NOTES

_____
_____
_____
_____
_____
_____
_____
_____
_____
_____
_____
_____
_____
_____
_____
_____
_____
_____
_____

LESSON PLAN FOR STUDENT'S PAGE 43

TEACHER

Literacy: Trace numbers 1-5, using top-to-bottom and left-to-right directionality in sequential strokes.
More practice: Worksheet 21 (Teacher's Edition CD-ROM).

Option: If you wish to provide a review/confidence-builder before proceeding with Unit 3, print out a worksheet from a previous unit and have students complete part or all of it.

Trace.

Follow these steps for each number.

➤ Say the number. Then on the board, model the strokes of the number. To instruct students on the correct sequence of strokes, count aloud as you do each stroke. Then have students follow along with their fingers in the air while watching you. Have the class count the strokes aloud. By using kinesthetic and verbal modalities (large arm movements and stroke counting), students are more likely to remember the shape and sequence of strokes used to form each number.

➤ Have students practice tracing the strokes of the number with large movements with their fingers on their desktops. Circulate around the classroom to correct strokes. Pay attention to the correct sequence of strokes.

➤ Lightly write several examples of the number on the board. Invite students to the board to practice tracing them. Have the rest of the class follow along with fingers in the air.

➤ Have students trace the numbers. Note: students trace only along the light gray lines. Circulate around the classroom, checking student work.

Note: This is the time to review good writing practices. Make sure students' posture is forward facing and relaxed. Both arms should rest lightly on the edge of the desk. Show students how to position the paper properly, according to whether they are right- or left-handed. Make sure students are holding the pencil correctly and with appropriate pressure.

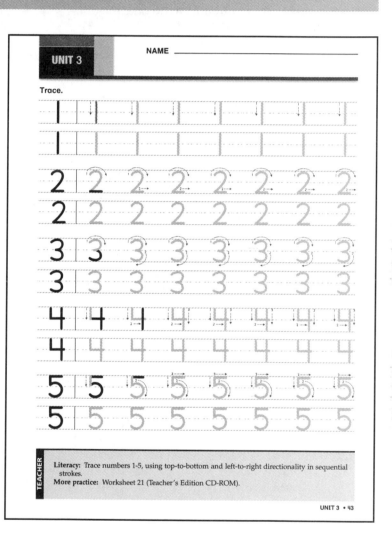

UNIT 3

NAME

Trace.

TEACHER
Literacy: Trace numbers 1-5, using top-to-bottom and left-to-right directionality in sequential strokes.
More practice: Worksheet 21 (Teacher's Edition CD-ROM).

UNIT 3 • 43

Note: The directional arrows on the gray numbers are numbered in sequence from here on, because students now know the <u>meaning</u> of numbers.

Worksheet Link: Worksheet 21

Assign the worksheet for homework or for in-class independent work. Review students' work before going on to the next lesson to make sure that students can trace numbers 1–5.

TEACHER

Literacy: Trace and write numbers 1-5 freehand, based on model and prior tracing practice.
More practice: Worksheet 22 (Teacher's Edition CD-ROM).

Trace and write.

See "Trace" on page T43.

Option: You may want students to do one line of each number without a pencil first.

Option: To develop students' awareness of well-formed numbers, have them evaluate their work after each line of freehand practice. Have them circle their best number and mark a small x below any numbers that need improvement.

Additional Activities

Activity 1: Draw shapes in groups of 1, 2, 3, 4, and 5 on the board. Have students write the correct number next to each group. Students can then do this activity in pairs on the board or on paper at their desks. This practices writing of numbers and reviews meaning of numbers.

Activity 2: Number dictation. Copy and distribute Worksheet 0 (blank primer rules). Place a pile of Number Cards 1–5 face down in the front of the class. Have students take turns picking a card and dictating the number to the class. Have students write the number they hear.

Activity 3: Test students' knowledge of the strokes used to form each number. Write a number on the board correctly. As you write, nod your head and say *Yes!* Then write the number incorrectly with a stroke out of sequence or an incorrect bottom-to-top motion. As you write, shake your head and say *No!* Then invite students to say *Yes!* or *No!* as you write numbers 1–5 correctly and incorrectly.

Worksheet Link: Worksheet 22

Assign the worksheet for homework or for in-class independent work. Review students' work before going on to the next lesson to make sure that students can trace and write numbers 1–5.

Worksheet option: If students didn't evaluate their own work, mark each freehand line with circles for best-written numbers and Xs for numbers that need improvement. Return the marked-up sheet for students to redo the numbers that need improvement.

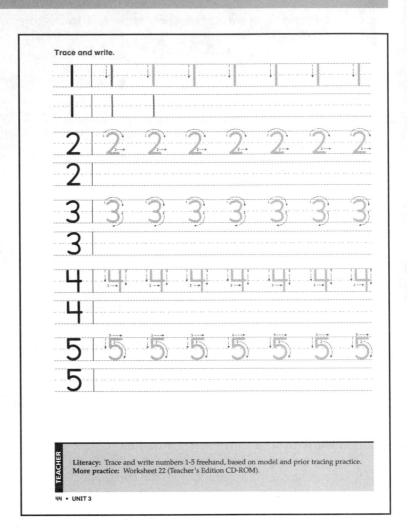

Trace and write.

TEACHER

Literacy: Trace and write numbers 1-5 freehand, based on model and prior tracing practice.
More practice: Worksheet 22 (Teacher's Edition CD-ROM).

44 • UNIT 3

TEACHER

Survival: Learn means of transportation. Ask for and give directions for public transportation.
Civics concept: Public transportation is named and numbered.
New language: Bus, car, train, subway, taxi, street, corner, highway / How do I get to the [supermarket]? / Take the [bus]. / Which one? / The number [104].

🎧 Look and listen.

See also "Look and listen" on page T17a.

➤ Point to the pictures. See if students can identify any vocabulary they already know.

➤ Play the cassette or read the tapescript aloud.

Option: You may want to give students the local name for a subway or bus system (for example, Metro, El, BART, etc.). You can point to the subway picture and say *New York City—subway; [your city]— [local designation]*.

Option: When you present pictures 6 and 8, you may want to give students several examples of street and highway names in your community.

Note: From here on, vocabulary pictures are numbered sequentially.

Additional Activity
Provide listening practice. Give each student a set of Vocabulary Cards 19–26. Have students lay the cards out face up on their desks. Call out a vocabulary word and have students select the card and hold it up.

🎧 Listen again and repeat.

See "Listen again and repeat" on page T17a.

Option: Work on students' pronunciation. The /tr/ sound of *train* can be particularly challenging. Call on students to repeat after you.

Additional Activities
Activity 1: Provide listening practice. Say a vocabulary word and have students point to the picture in their books. Circulate around the room to check student responses. Give several other examples. Then have students do this activity in pairs.

Activity 2: Provide speaking practice. Hold up a Vocabulary Card (19–26) and have the class as a whole say the vocabulary word. Repeat with several other Vocabulary Cards. Then have students do the same activity in pairs, using Vocabulary Cards or pointing to the pictures on page 45.

Activity 3: Concentration. Photocopy Vocabulary Cards 19–26. Give each pair of students two copies

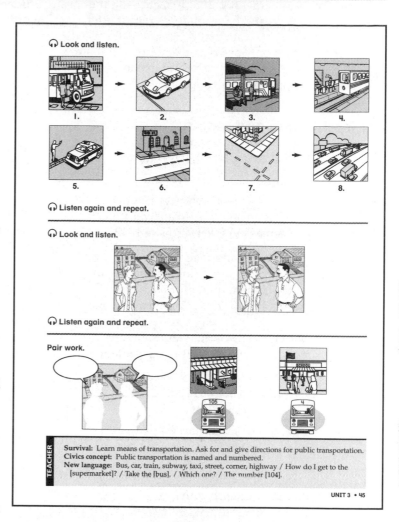

of the Vocabulary Cards. Follow the directions for Activity 2 on page T28.

Tapescript

1. bus 2. car 3. train 4. subway 5. taxi 6. street
7. corner 8. highway

🎧 Look and listen.

See also "Look and listen" on page T9a.

➤ Place Vocabulary Cards 13 and 19 (*supermarket, bus*) on the board rim for reference. Call on students to identify the pictures.

(Continued on page T45b.)

➤ Play the cassette or read the tapescript aloud. Write the number 104 on the board to illustrate the line *The 104.*

Additional Activity

Have students practice saying numbers containing 0. Write several numbers—102, 103, 105, etc.—on the board. Point to each and have students repeat after you—*One-oh-two*, etc. Note that the numeral 0 is used in the conversation only as vocabulary, not as a math concept. You may wish to explore and expand on the concept of 0 in appropriate groups.

🎧 Listen again and repeat.

See "Listen again and repeat" on page T9a.

Additional Activities

Activity 1: Check comprehension. Ask *How do I get to the supermarket?* Call on students to answer you. (Take the bus.) Then ask *Which bus?* (The 104.)

Activity 2: Practice new language. Ask *How do I get to the supermarket?* Hold up seven fingers and ask the question again, touching a finger for each word. Repeat twice. On the third repeat, omit saying one word. Point to the finger that represents the missing word. Have students tell you the missing word. Repeat the procedure with the following sentence: *Take the bus.*

Tapescript

A: How do I get to the supermarket?
B: Take the bus.

A: Which one?
B: The number 104. [one-oh-four]

Pair work.

➤ Model the Pair work. Place Vocabulary Cards for *supermarket* and *school* (13–14) on the board rim. Point to the card for *supermarket* and ask *How do I get to the supermarket?* Ask the question again, holding up a finger for each word. Repeat twice. Repeat the modeling with *school.*

➤ Invite students to join you in front of the class to practice the model conversation. Use the Vocabulary Cards.

➤ Divide the class into pairs. Have students ask for directions.

➤ Have several volunteer pairs act out their conversations in front of the class.

Additional Activity

(Challenge): Put Vocabulary Cards 19–23 (*bus, car, train, subway, taxi*) along the rim of the board. Ask the class *How do you get to school?* Point to each mode of transportation. Say each vocabulary word. Then ask *Which one?* Call on individual students to respond. Students may respond with only the vocabulary word, not a complete sentence.

Pair work (possible student responses)

A: How do I get to the supermarket / school?
B: Take the bus. **A:** Which one? **B:** The 105 / 4.

Your students can also say . . .

A: (Unit 2:) Excuse me. Where's the parking lot / restaurant / bus stop / (Unit 3:) bus / car / train / subway / taxi / street / corner / highway? **B:** The [subway]? **A:** Yes. **B:** (Unit 2:) It's on [Main Street]. It's next to the [hotel]. [Right] over there. **A:** (Unit 1:) Thanks. / Thank you. **B:** You're welcome.

If your students are ready . . .

Civics enrichment: Public transportation is named and numbered. If appropriate, ask the class *How do you get to school? Which bus? Which subway?* Have students identify the numbers of the buses and subways. Write the numbers on the board. Then ask *Where's the bus stop for the [104]? Where's the subway stop?* Go outside with the class and visit the bus stops and the subway stop. Point to the number of the bus on the bus stop sign. Point to the numbers of the subways at the subway entrance.

If possible, distribute schedules of the buses and subways to students. Interpreting a schedule is a challenging reading task. Do NOT try to explain the schedule in class. Let the students take the schedules home and look at them. If they are ready, they will ask questions.

TEACHER

Survival: Ask for walking or driving directions.
Civics concepts: It's polite to be helpful to strangers. It's OK to ask strangers for help.
New language: Turn [right] at the corner. / I need directions. / Where are you going? /
Here's the address.

🎧 Look and listen.

See also "Look and listen" on page T9a.

➤ Place Vocabulary Cards 25–26 (*corner, highway*) on the board rim for reference. Call on students to identify the pictures.

➤ Present the language *right* and *left*. With your back to the class, hold up your right arm and say *right*. Then hold up your left arm and say *left*. Have students mimic your movements as you say the words.

➤ Play the cassette or read the tapescript aloud. Use gestures to convey the meaning of *turn left at the corner*.

🎧 Listen again and repeat.

See "Listen again and repeat" on page T9a.

Additional Activities
Activity 1: Test comprehension. Point to the first picture. Ask *How do I get to the highway?* Call on students to answer you. (Turn left at the corner.)

Activity 2: Use Vocabulary Cards 12–17 (*bus stop, supermarket, school, restaurant, hotel, parking lot*) for students to practice composing new questions. They can do this in pairs, or you can hold up the cards and call on students.

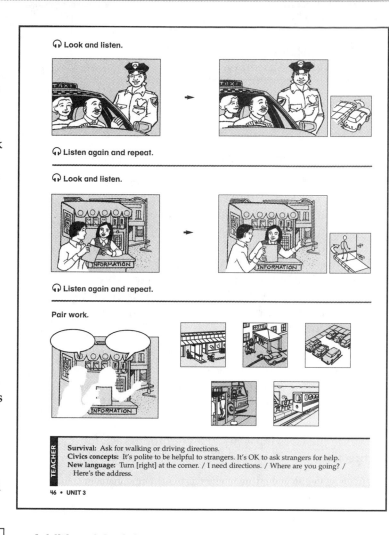

🎧 Look and listen.

🎧 Listen again and repeat.

🎧 Look and listen.

🎧 Listen again and repeat.

Pair work.

TEACHER
Survival: Ask for walking or driving directions.
Civics concepts: It's polite to be helpful to strangers. It's OK to ask strangers for help.
New language: Turn [right] at the corner. / I need directions. / Where are you going? /
Here's the address.

46 • UNIT 3

Tapescript
A: How do I get to the highway?
B: The highway?
A: Yes.
B: Turn left at the corner.
A: Thanks.
B: You're welcome.

🎧 Look and listen.

See "Look and listen" on page T9a.

➤ Use gestures to convey the meaning of *turn right at the corner*.

Additional Activity
Drill the concepts of *right* and *left* with the class. Call out *Right* or *Left* and have students raise the appropriate arm to indicate they understood. Repeat many times.

🎧 Listen again and repeat.

See "Listen again and repeat" on page T9a.

Additional Activity
Practice new language. Say *I need directions.* Hold up three fingers and say the sentence again, touching a finger for each word. Repeat twice. On the third repeat, omit saying one word. Point to the finger that

(Continued on page T46b.)

represents the missing word. Have students tell you the missing word. Repeat the procedure with the sentences *Here's the address. Turn right at the corner.*

Tapescript

A: I need directions.
B: Sure. Where are you going?

A: Here's the address.
B: Turn right at the corner.

Pair work.

Follow these steps for each model conversation:

➤ Identify the place names of all the illustration cues.

➤ Model the first conversation. Place Vocabulary Cards 12–17 and 26 (*bus stop, supermarket, school, restaurant, hotel, parking lot, highway*) on the board rim. Invite an advanced student to join you in front of the class. Hand the student a Vocabulary Card to elicit the question *How do I get to the ____?* If the student is confused, provide the question and begin the conversation again. Repeat the conversation in order to present the class with more natural-sounding speech.

➤ Model the second conversation. Invite another student to the front of the class. Approach the student and say *I need directions.* Show the class a Vocabulary Card as you explain where you are going.

➤ Divide the class into pairs. Have students ask for directions.

➤ Have several volunteer pairs act out their conversations in front of the class.

Additional Activity

Use the classroom furniture to set up a simple obstacle course. Divide the class into teams. Blindfold one student on each team. The goal is for each team to direct their blindfolded student through the obstacle course to the other side of the room, saying only *Turn right* or *Turn left.* (Note: You may want to adjust the blindfolds so students can see out the bottom to prevent collisions.)

Pair work (possible student responses)

A: How do I get to the supermarket / hotel / parking lot / bus stop / subway? **B:** Turn right / left at the corner.

Your students can also say . . .

A: (Unit 2:) Excuse me. (Unit 3:) I need directions. **B:** Sure. Where are you going? **A:** Here's the address. **B:** Take the bus / train / subway / a taxi. **A:** The [bus]? Which one? **B:** The [105]. (Unit 2:) It's on [Main Street]. It's next to the [hotel]. [Right] over there. **A:** (Unit 1:) Thanks. / Thank you. **B:** You're welcome.

If your students are ready . . .

Civics enrichment: It's polite to be helpful to strangers. It's OK to ask strangers for help. Identify landmarks for your students to find within a block of the school (for example, a bus stop, subway station, parking lot, hotel, supermarket). Send each student out with the assignment to ask a stranger for directions to one landmark. They must then find the landmark and return to the class.

TEACHER

Literacy: Trace numbers 6-10, using top-to-bottom and left-to-right directionality in sequential strokes.
More practice: Worksheet 23 (Teacher's Edition CD-ROM).

Trace.

See "Trace" on page T43.

Option: You may want students to do the exercise one time through without a pencil so they focus only on the strokes.

Note: This is the time to review good writing practices. Make sure students' posture is forward facing and relaxed. Both arms should rest lightly on the edge of the desk. Show students how to position the paper properly according to whether they are right- or left-handed. Make sure students are holding the pencil correctly and with appropriate pressure. (For more specific suggestions, see handwriting instructions on page iv.)

Additional Activity
If the board is dusty with chalk, trace the number in the dust. Have students follow your movements with their fingers in the air, counting their strokes aloud. This is good practice for students unaccustomed to holding a writing instrument.

Worksheet Link: Worksheet 23
Assign the worksheet for homework or for in-class independent work. Review students' work before going on to the next lesson to make sure that students can trace numbers 6–10.

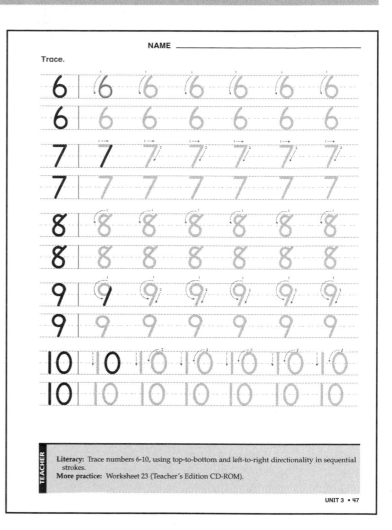

NAME

Trace.

6 6 6 6 6 6 6
6 6 6 6 6 6
7 7 7 7 7 7 7
7 7 7 7 7 7
8 8 8 8 8 8 8
8 8 8 8 8 8
9 9 9 9 9 9 9
9 9 9 9 9 9
10 10 10 10 10 10 10
10 10 10 10 10 10 10

TEACHER

Literacy: Trace numbers 6-10, using top-to-bottom and left-to-right directionality in sequential strokes.
More practice: Worksheet 23 (Teacher's Edition CD-ROM).

UNIT 3 • 47

TEACHER

Literacy: Trace and write numbers 6-10 freehand, based on model and prior tracing practice.
More practice: Worksheet 24 (Teacher's Edition CD-ROM).

Trace and write.

See "Trace" on page T43.

Option: You may want students to do the exercise one time through without a pencil first so they focus only on the strokes.

Option: To develop students' awareness of well-formed numbers, you can have them evaluate their work after each line of practice. Have them circle their best number and mark a small x below any numbers that need improvement.

Additional Activities

Activity 1: Draw shapes in groups of 1, 2, 3, 4, and 5 on the board. Have students write the correct number next to each group. Students can then do this activity in pairs on the board or on paper at their desks.

Activity 2: Review hand gestures for numbers. Copy and distribute Worksheet 90 (blank primer rules). Hold up 1 to 10 fingers. Have students write the number they see. Repeat several times, holding up a different number of fingers each time. Students can then take turns doing the activity with a partner.

Activity 3: Test students' knowledge of the strokes used to form each number. Write a number on the board correctly. As you write, nod your head and say *Yes!* Then write the number incorrectly with a stroke out of sequence or an incorrect bottom-to-top motion. As you write, shake your head and say *No!* Invite students to say *Yes!* or *No!* as you write numbers 6–10 correctly and incorrectly.

Worksheet Link: Worksheet 24

Assign the worksheet for homework. Review students' work to make sure that students can trace and write numbers 6–10.

Worksheet option: If students didn't evaluate their own work, mark each freehand line with circles for well-written numbers and Xs for numbers that need improvement. Return the sheet for students to redo the letters that need improvement.

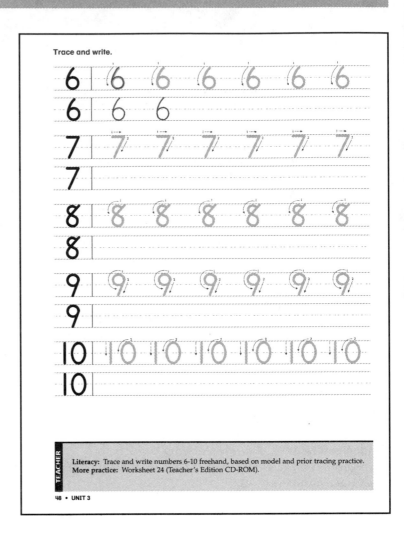

TEACHER

Survival: Learn vocabulary for emergencies and emergency vehicles.
Civics concept: In the U.S., emergency services are provided to the public.
New language: Accident, fire, fire truck, ambulance, hospital, telephone, call, press.

🎧 Look and listen.

See also "Look and listen" on page T17a.

➤ Point to the pictures. See if students can identify any vocabulary they already know.

➤ Play the cassette or read the tapescript aloud.

Option: You can mime the words *press* and *call* to illustrate they are actions.

Additional Activities

Activity 1: Test comprehension. Say a word and have students point to the picture in their books.

Activity 2: Reinforce comprehension of numbers and vocabulary. Place Vocabulary Cards 27–34 *(accident, fire, fire truck, ambulance, hospital, telephone, call, press)* on the board rim. Write a number above each picture. (Numbers should be consecutive.) Have students take turns calling out the name of the picture while other students listen and then call out the picture number.

🎧 Listen again and repeat.

See "Listen again and repeat" on page T17a.

Option: Work on pronunciation. Have students tap out the syllables as they say each word. This will help them manage the long words like *ambulance* or *telephone*. For the monosyllabic words, focus their attention on the length of the sound. The sound *fire* is long but *press* is short.

Additional Activities

Activity 1: Provide speaking practice. Hold up a Vocabulary Card (27–34) and have the entire class say the vocabulary word. Repeat with several other Vocabulary Cards. Then have students do the same activity in pairs, using Vocabulary Cards or pointing to the pictures on page 49.

Activity 2: Concentration. Photocopy Vocabulary Cards 27–34 *(accident, fire, fire truck, ambulance, hospital, telephone, call, press).* Follow the instructions for Activity 2 on page T28.

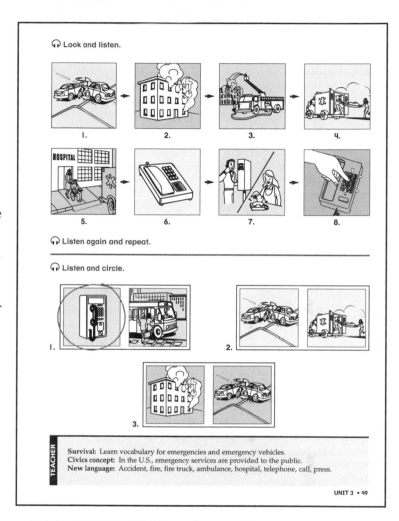

Tapescript
1. accident 2. fire 3. fire truck 4. ambulance
5. hospital 6. telephone 7. call 8. press

🎧 Listen and circle.

See "Listen and circle" on page T17a–b.

Option: To prepare students for the listening, point to each picture. Ask students to say the word for each picture.

Option: To help students focus on each set, you can distribute blank white sheets of paper to cover over the rest of the page.

(Continued on page T49b.)

Additional Activity

Give each student a set of Vocabulary Cards 27–34. Students work with a partner. Student A chooses a card and says its name without showing the card to Student B. B finds the card in his own set. The two students then check their cards to make sure they match.

Tapescript

1. telephone 2. accident 3. fire

If your students are ready . . .

Civics enrichment: In the U.S., emergency services are provided to the public. To help students understand how to get emergency services, you may want to introduce the telephone number *911*. (The concept of 911 is more fully presented on Student's Book page 50.) Point to the corresponding pictures on Student's Book page 49, as you say *accident, call 911; fire, call 911; ambulance, call 911; fire truck, call 911.* If you have a dummy telephone or cell phone (make sure it is turned off), show students the numbers *911* on the phone. You can also show the class the front page of a phone book where the emergency numbers are listed.

NOTES

Survival: Report a fire or an accident to 911. Request a fire truck or an ambulance.
Civics concept: 911 can help you in an emergency.
New language: Oh, no! / Call 911. / OK. / What's the problem? / There's [a fire]. / At [22 Main Street]. / Do you need [an ambulance]? / Please send [a fire truck].

🎧 Look and listen.

See also "Look and listen" on page T9a.

➤ Point to the fire in the first picture and say *Fire*. Repeat with the accident in the second picture.

Option: Explain that *OK* is similar in meaning to *Sure*. Say the two words several times to demonstrate they are similar.

🎧 Listen again and repeat.

See "Listen again and repeat" on page T9a.

Option: Show students the most common gesture (hands held up to the face) accompanying the phrase *Oh, no!*

Additional Activity

Bring in pictures of different types of accidents—at home, on the street, at school, etc. Hold up each picture and say *Accident*. Distribute pictures to pairs of students and have them practice the conversation.

Tapescript

Conversation 1
A: Oh, no! A fire.
B: Call 911.
A: OK.

Conversation 2
A: Oh, no! An accident.
B: Call 911.
A: OK.

🎧 Look and listen.

See also "Look and listen" on page T9a.

➤ To illustrate the cause and effect of calling *911*, show the class Vocabulary Card 28 *(fire)* and say *Fire*. Then say *911* and mime calling 911. Hold up Vocabulary Card 29 *(fire truck)* along with the picture of fire. Move the fire truck toward the picture of the fire and say *Fire truck*. Repeat.

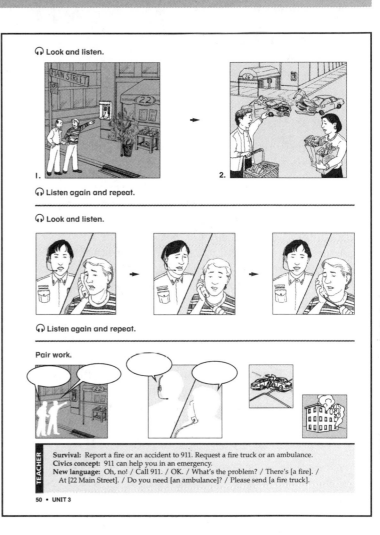

🎧 Look and listen.

🎧 Listen again and repeat.

🎧 Look and listen.

🎧 Listen again and repeat.

Pair work.

Survival: Report a fire or an accident to 911. Request a fire truck or an ambulance.
Civics concept: 911 can help you in an emergency.
New language: Oh, no! / Call 911. / OK. / What's the problem? / There's [a fire]. / At [22 Main Street]. / Do you need [an ambulance]? / Please send [a fire truck].

50 • UNIT 3

🎧 Listen again and repeat.

See "Listen again and repeat" on page T9a.

Additional Activity

Practice new language. Ask *What's the problem?* Hold up three fingers and ask the question again, touching a finger for each word. Repeat twice. On the third repeat, omit saying one word. Point to the finger that represents the missing word. Have students tell you the missing word. Repeat the procedure with the sentences *There's a fire. Please send a fire truck.*

(Continued on page T50b.)

Tapescript

A: 911. What's the problem?
B: There's a fire.

A: Where?
B: At 22 Main Street.

A: Do you need an ambulance?
B: No. Please send a fire truck.

Pair work.

Follow these steps for each model conversation:

➤ Point to the illustration cues on the right and say *Accident. Fire.*

➤ Model the first conversation. Place Vocabulary Cards 27–28 on the board rim. Invite a student to join you in front of the class. Hand the student a Vocabulary Card and say *Oh, no! An [accident].* Gesture for the student to respond. If the student is confused, provide the response, *Call 911,* and begin the conversation again. Repeat with another student.

➤ Model the second conversation. Place Vocabulary Cards 27–28 side by side on the board rim. Hold up Vocabulary Card 28 (*fire*) as you say *There's a fire.* Repeat. Then substitute *an accident* for *a fire.* Have students practice both sentences with a partner. Repeat this procedure with Vocabulary Cards 29–30 (*fire truck, ambulance*) for the sentences: *Do you need an ambulance? Do you need a fire truck?*

➤ Divide the class into pairs. Students practice reporting emergencies.

➤ Have several volunteer pairs act out their conversations in front of the class.

Pair work (possible student responses)

1. A: Oh, no! An accident. / A fire. **B:** Call 911. **A:** OK.

2. A: 911. What's the problem? **B:** There's an accident / a fire. **A:** Where? **B:** [any number] Main Street. **A:** Do you need a fire truck / an ambulance? **B:** Yes. Please send an ambulance / a fire truck.

Your students can also say . . .

(Unit 2:) What's the address?

If your students are ready . . .

Civics enrichment: You may want to refine the idea of an emergency. Mime various mishaps and emergencies, and after each scene ask *911?* Have students say *Yes!* or *No!* For example, mime losing your keys and not being able to get in the house. Ask *911?* The students should say *No!* Mime a terrible fight and then ask *911?* Students should say *Yes!*

Literacy: Recognize numbers on telephone key pad. Recognize "0" as a number.
Write numbers 0–9 on "buttons."
More practice: Worksheet 25 (Teacher's Edition CD-ROM).

Look.

➤ Hold up the Student's Book for the class to see. Point to each button on the keypad and say the number. Repeat several times.

Option: Introduce the words *star* for the asterisk (*) and *pound* for the number sign (#).

➤ Have students point to each number in their books and say its name.

Write.

➤ Have students point to each button on the blank keypad and say its number.

➤ Have students write the numbers on the keypads. Note that students have learned to write the numeral 0. It is not necessary at this point for them to understand the concept of "zero."

Additional Activity

Call out single numbers and have students touch that button in the illustration. Then call out strings of three or four numbers and have students repeat the numbers aloud as they touch the buttons on the keypad. This activity prepares students to listen and comprehend phone numbers.

Worksheet Link: Worksheet 25

Assign the worksheet for homework or for in-class independent work. Review students' work before going on to the next lesson.

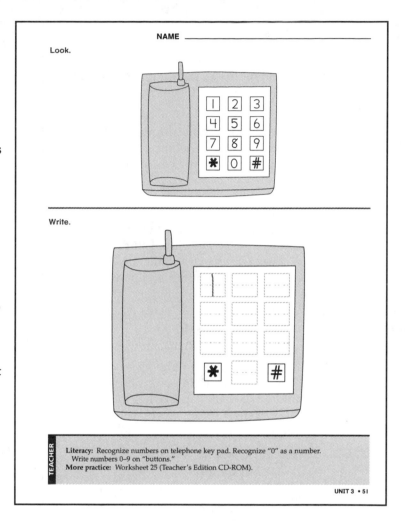

NAME _____

Look.

Write.

Literacy: Recognize numbers on telephone key pad. Recognize "0" as a number.
Write numbers 0–9 on "buttons."
More practice: Worksheet 25 (Teacher's Edition CD-ROM).

UNIT 3 • 51

TEACHER

Literacy: Write down phone numbers as if hearing them socially or from Information.
More practice: Worksheets 26–27 (Teacher's Edition CD-ROM).

🎧 Listen and write.

➤ Play the cassette or read the tapescript aloud. Have students follow along, pointing to each number with their pencils as they listen. Students fill in the missing numbers.

➤ Have students read these phone numbers aloud to their partner. If necessary, model the correct way to say a phone number, with the pause in the correct spot.

Additional Activities

Activity 1: Number recitation. Call out strings of three or four numbers. Have individual students recite them back to you. For an extra challenge, students recite seven-digit phone numbers, always pausing between the third and fourth digit. This activity helps develop students' recall skills while reviewing the pronunciation of numbers.

Activity 2: Number dictation. Distribute sheets of paper with lists of a few phone numbers and copies of Worksheet 27. Students work in pairs. Student A reads a number aloud. B listens and writes the number down on the worksheet. After several sets of numbers, the students switch roles.

Tapescript

1. 222–3315 **2.** 711–3434 **3.** 881–6677 **4.** Hold for that number, please. That's 222–7578.

Pair work.

➤ Note that students may be reluctant to reveal their personal phone numbers. Prior to doing this activity, prepare index cards with fictitious phone numbers to give to students if necessary.

➤ Model the Pair work. Invite a student to stand next to you. Turn to the student and ask *What's your telephone number?* As the student tells you, write the number on the board. Encourage the student to tell you the numbers in groupings of three and then four.

➤ Divide the class into pairs. Students ask each other for their phone numbers and write them down. Circulate around the classroom, offering help as needed.

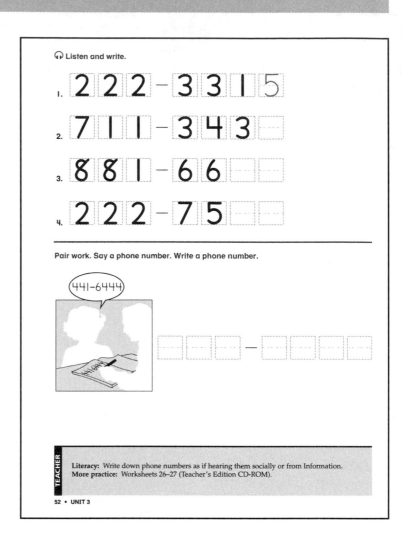

Additional Activities

Activity 1: Photocopy Worksheet 27 and distribute. Students circulate around the classroom, asking for and giving phone numbers and writing them down.

Activity 2: Copy Worksheet 27 and distribute. Have students take turns saying their phone numbers for the class to write down.

Worksheet Link: Worksheets 26–27

Assign Worksheet 26 for homework or for in-class independent work.

Note that Worksheet 27 is designed for in-class practice of writing down phone numbers, either through group work or as a class dictation.

TEACHER

Survival: Ask someone to call. Provide and verify a phone number.
Civics concepts: Telephones are used for social calls. It's OK to give a friend your phone number.
New language: Please call me. / What's your number? / Yes, that's right. / I've got it.

🎧 Look and listen.

See also "Look and listen" on page T9a.

➤ Explain that the following sentences have the same meaning: *What's your telephone number? What's your phone number? What's your number?* Say the three questions in a row to demonstrate they are similar. Repeat several times.

➤ Play the cassette or read the tapescript aloud. Use a phone gesture (hand to the ear) for the phrase *Please call me.*

Option: You may want students to cover the second conversation with a blank paper as they listen to the first.

🎧 Listen again and repeat.

See "Listen again and repeat" on page T9a.

Option: If you have worked on the rising/falling intonation of *wh–* questions in previous lessons, reinforce your instruction with the *wh–* question *What's your number?*

Additional Activities

Activity 1: Check comprehension. Ask *What's the phone number?*

Activity 2: Provide speaking practice. Distribute telephone numbers to students. Have students take turns telling each other their numbers, always pausing after the first three digits. Have students ask for clarification as they retell the numbers.

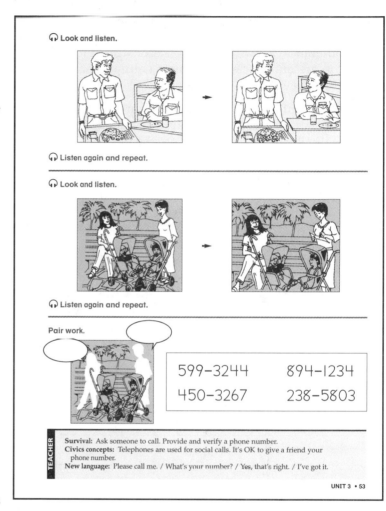

UNIT 3 • 53

Tapescript
A: Please call me.
B: OK. What's your number?
A: 322–4599.
B: 322–4599?
A: Yes, that's right. Bye!

🎧 Look and listen.

Follow the procedures for the above activity.

🎧 Listen again and repeat.

Follow the procedures for the above activity.

Tapescript
A: Please call me.
B: OK. What's your number?
A: 456–7765.
B: 456–7655?
A. No. 456–7765.
B: Thanks. I've got it.

(Continued on page T53b.)

Pair work.

➤ Again, have index cards with fictitious phone numbers on hand for any students who do not wish to reveal their personal phone numbers.

➤ Model the Pair work. Invite a student to the front of the class. Begin the model conversation by saying *Please call me.* Prompt the student, when necessary, using your fingers to represent the words in each utterance. Repeat the conversation again in order to present the class with more natural-sounding speech.

Option: If you live in an area in which area codes are always required in dialing, model the phone number with its area code in the model conversation.

➤ Divide the class into pairs. Have students ask for and give the phone numbers. Circulate around the classroom, offering help as needed.

➤ Have several volunteer pairs act out their conversations in front of the class.

Additional Activity
Distribute telephone numbers to students. Have students recite their numbers to you, always pausing after the first three digits. Recite back the numbers, sometimes correctly, sometimes incorrectly. Encourage students to correct you.

Pair work (possible student responses)

A: Please call me. **B:** OK. / Sure. What's your number? / What's your phone number? / What's your telephone number? **A:** [telephone number]. **B:** [telephone number]? **A:** Yes, that's right. / No. [Repeats number]. **B:** Thanks. I've got it.

Your students can also say . . .

A: (Unit 1:) Hi. **B:** Hi. How are you? **A:** Fine, thanks. And you? **B:** I'm fine. **A:** (Welcome unit:) Bye! See you later. **B:** Bye!

NOTES

TEACHER

Survival: Get a telephone number and area code from Information.
Civics concept: You can call 411 to get a phone number you need.
New language: What [city], please? / What listing? / One moment, please. / The number is (713) 555-1748.

🎧 Look and listen.

See also "Look and listen" on page T9a.

➤ Show the class Vocabulary Card 31 *(hospital)* and ask *What's the phone number?* Hold your hands up with a shrug. Then say *Aha! 411! Call 411.*

Option: Give students visual cues to the dialogue by miming the dialing, showing Vocabulary Card 31 *(hospital)* when you say the listing, and making a *hold on* gesture (one finger up) when the operator says *One moment, please.*

🎧 Listen again and repeat.

See "Listen again and repeat" on page T9a.

Additional Activity

Give context to the conversation. Show students Vocabulary Cards 13–16 (places in the community). As you show each Vocabulary Card, give a local example of the place. (For example, *restaurant:* Sam's Restaurant). Elicit several more examples of local restaurant names. Then say the name of a restaurant and ask *What's the phone number? Call 411.* Act out the phone call with a student. Begin the call by saying *411. What city, please?*

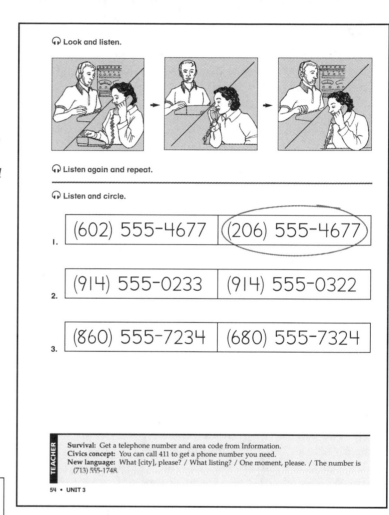

🎧 Look and listen.

🎧 Listen again and repeat.

🎧 Listen and circle.

1. (602) 555-4677   **(206) 555-4677**
2. (914) 555-0233   (914) 555-0322
3. (860) 555-7234   (680) 555-7324

TEACHER
Survival: Get a telephone number and area code from Information.
Civics concept: You can call 411 to get a phone number you need.
New language: What [city], please? / What listing? / One moment, please. / The number is (713) 555-1748.

54 • UNIT 3

Tapescript
A: 411. What city, please?   **B:** Houston.   **A:** What listing?   **B:** Central Hospital.   **A:** One moment, please . . . The number is area code (713) 555–1748.

If your students are ready . . .
Civics enrichment: You can call 411 to get a phone number you need. Have students identify local restaurants, hotels, supermarkets. Assign the name of one business to each student. As a class, go to a room with a phone (or use a cell phone). Rehearse the call with the class. Have each student call Information and ask for the number of his or her business. Make sure students write down the

number they hear. Some students may need to call several times.

🎧 Listen and circle.

See also "Listen and circle" on page T17a–b.

➤ When presenting the example, hold up a Student's Book and point to each numeral in the correct phone number as you say it. Be sure to say *oh* for the numeral 0.

Tapescript
1. The number is . . . area code (206) 555–4677.   2. The number is . . . area code (914) 555–0233.   3. The number is . . . area code (860) 555–7234.

TEACHER

Literacy: Recognize that the number system repeats in sets of 10. Trace missing numbers from 1 to 50.
More practice: Worksheets 28–29 (Teacher's Edition CD-ROM).

Trace.

➤ Students may not be familiar with the sounds of numbers 31–50. Write the numbers 20–50 on a grid on the board. Point to each number and say its name. Say the numbers again, having students repeat after you. You may want to point out that numbers 31–50 are formed in the same way as numbers 21–30. Point to 21 and say the number. Then point to 31 and 41, saying each number. Repeat with 22, 32, 42, and other numbers if necessary.

Option: Give each pair of students a pile of dried beans. Have students work together to count out 50 beans. Students can either count together or count alternating numbers. Have students count them in groups of 10.

➤ Model the exercise. Write the first line of the exercise on the board. Lightly write the numbers students are to trace. Say each number as you point. When you come to the gray number 5, emphasize the strokes as you trace it on the board. Remind students of the correct sequence of strokes in writing the number.

Option: You may want to do this exercise one time through as a class and without pencils. Have the class read the numbers aloud as they point to each one. When you come to a tracing number, have students say the number as they trace it with their fingers.

➤ Have students trace the numbers.

Additional Activities

Activity 1: Have students tap out the syllables as they say each word. This will help them enunciate the often forgotten second syllable of numbers *twenty* to *fifty* (for example, thir-*ty*-three).

Activity 2: Practice the concept that numbers come in groups of 10. Photocopy and distribute Number Cards 20–49. Tape Number Cards 20, 30, and 40 on the board. Show the class several other cards, say the numbers, and tape them under the correct 20, 30, or 40 card on the board. Students then work in pairs to sort their number cards in groups of 10.

Activity 3: Number dictation. Give individual students two sets of Number Cards 0–9. Call out a num-

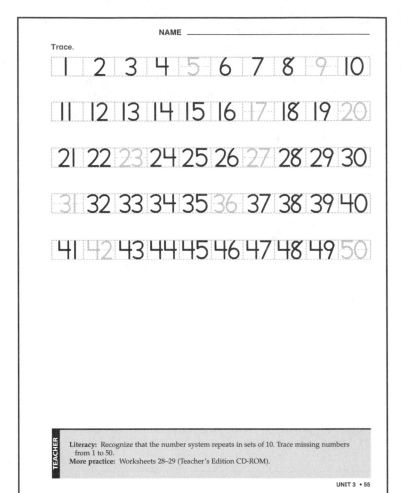

NAME _____

Trace.

1 2 3 4 5 6 7 8 9 10

11 12 13 14 15 16 17 18 19 20

21 22 23 24 25 26 27 28 29 30

31 32 33 34 35 36 37 38 39 40

41 42 43 44 45 46 47 48 49 50

TEACHER

Literacy: Recognize that the number system repeats in sets of 10. Trace missing numbers from 1 to 50.
More practice: Worksheets 28–29 (Teacher's Edition CD-ROM).

UNIT 3 • 55

ber between 10 and 50. Have students create the number with their cards. Repeat many times. If students are ready, have them take turns calling out numbers.

Activity 4: Round robin. Sit with the class in a circle. Start by saying *One,* and then, with the gesture of two fingers up, prompt a student to say *Two.* Continue around the circle, again and again, until the class has counted to 50.

Worksheet Link: Worksheets 28–29

You can assign both worksheets for homework or for in-class independent work. Review students' work before going on to the next lesson.

TEACHER

Literacy: Recognize that buildings are numbered consecutively on alternating sides of the street. Trace missing address numbers on a neighborhood diagram.
More practice: Worksheet 30 (Teacher's Edition CD-ROM).

Look.

➤ Before doing this exercise, you may want to accustom students to the idea of alternating numbers. Photocopy Student's Book page 55 or Worksheets 28–29. Give each student two copies. First, demonstrate circling alternating numbers, starting with 1. Do one row as a class and then let students do the remaining rows individually or in pairs. Then, on the next sheet, repeat the procedure with alternating numbers, starting with 2.

➤ Count out the consecutive addresses, pointing to the houses on alternating sides of the street as you say the numbers. Then count out the addresses on each side of the street (for example, 1, 3, 5). Then ask 7? and point to both sides of the street. Have students point to the correct side. Repeat with 8.

Additional Activity
Hand out Number Cards 1–10. Students work in pairs to place the numbers on the correct side of the picture in the Student's Book.

Trace.

➤ Look at the picture with the class. Count out the consecutive addresses, pointing to the houses on alternating sides of the street. When you come to a gray number, look to the class and gesture for a student to call it out.

➤ Have students pick up their pencils and complete the addresses. Go over the answers with the class, pointing to each house and saying the address number.

Additional Activity
Go for a walk with your class. Walk down one block. Have students read the number addresses on the buildings. Cross the street and repeat the activity up the other side of the street. Say an address and have students point to which side of the street that address belongs.

Worksheet Link: Worksheet 30
Assign the worksheet for homework or for in-class independent work. Review students' work before going on to the next lesson.

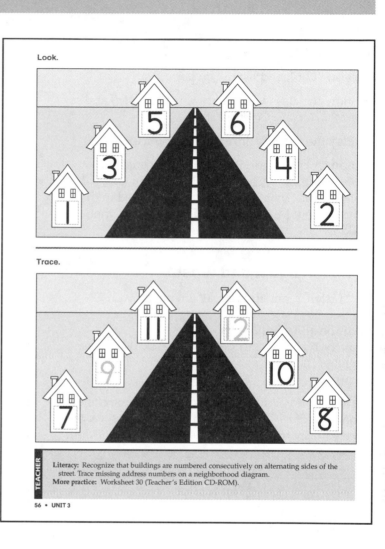

Look.

Trace.

TEACHER **Literacy:** Recognize that buildings are numbered consecutively on alternating sides of the street. Trace missing address numbers on a neighborhood diagram. **More practice:** Worksheet 30 (Teacher's Edition CD-ROM).

56 • UNIT 3

TEACHER

Survival: Ask for and give directions for public transportation.
Civics concept: It's OK to ask for directions over the phone.
New language: [Bus] or [subway]? / Where do I get off? / Get off [in front of] [the hospital]. /
[The hotel] is [on the corner].

🎧 Look and listen.

See also "Look and listen" on page T9a.

➤ Show the class Vocabulary Card 16 (hotel) and say *I need directions. Call the hotel!*

➤ Play the cassette or read the tapescript aloud.

Option: As the students listen, give visual cues. Show Vocabulary Cards 19, 22, 25, 31, 16 (bus, subway, corner, hospital, hotel) as they are mentioned in the conversation. Mime getting off the bus and then walking.

🎧 Listen again and repeat.

See "Listen again and repeat" on page T9a.

Additional Activities

Activity 1: Check comprehension. Ask *Which bus?* (Number 3). *Where do I get off?* (In front of the hospital).

Activity 2: If you have worked on the rising/falling intonation of *wh–* questions in previous lessons, reinforce your instruction with the *wh–* question *Where do I get off?*

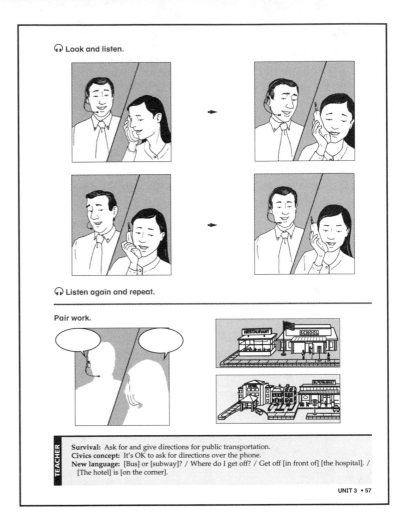

🎧 Look and listen.

🎧 Listen again and repeat.

Pair work.

Survival: Ask for and give directions for public transportation.
Civics concept: It's OK to ask for directions over the phone.
New language: [Bus] or [subway]? / Where do I get off? / Get off [in front of] [the hospital]. /
[The hotel] is [on the corner].

UNIT 3 • 57

Tapescript

A: Hotel 7. Can I help you?
B: Yes. I need directions.

A: Sure. Bus or subway?
B: Bus, please.

A: OK. Take the number 3 bus.
B: Where do I get off?

A: Get off in front of the hospital. The hotel is on the corner.
B: Thanks.

Pair work.

➤ Set the scene. Have students look at the illustration cues on the right. Say *The school is next to the restaurant. The restaurant is on the corner. The house is next to the hotel. The hotel is on the corner.*

➤ Practice the directions. Put Vocabulary Cards 13–16 and 31 (supermarket, school, restaurant, hotel, hospital) on the rim of the board. Say *Get off in front of the supermarket.* Hold up seven fingers and say the sentence again, touching a finger for each word. Repeat, but omit saying *supermarket.* Instead, point to a different Vocabulary Card. Have students practice substituting different place names in the sentence. Repeat this procedure with the sentence *Take the number 3 bus.* Substitute different bus numbers. (Write them on the board.)

- ➤ Model the Pair work. Invite an advanced student to sit next to you. Give the student Vocabulary Card 15 *(restaurant)*. Hold a phone in your hand and say *[Tony's] Restaurant. Can I help you?* If the student responds appropriately, give a big smile and continue with the conversation. *(Bus or subway?)* If the student is confused, provide the line *I need directions* and begin the conversation again.

- ➤ Divide the class into pairs. Have students ask for and give directions, using the Vocabulary Cards.

- ➤ Have several volunteer pairs act out their conversations in front of the class.

Pair work (possible student responses)

A: [Hotel 7]. Can I help you? **B:** Yes. / Yes, please. I need directions. **A:** OK. Bus or subway? **B:** Bus, please. **A:** Take the number [number] bus. **B:** Where do I get off? **A:** Get off in front of the hotel / restaurant / school / supermarket. It's on the corner. **B:** Thanks.

Your students can also say . . .

1. A: How do I get to the hospital / subway / train / (Unit 2:) parking lot / house / apartment? / Where's the [hospital]? **B:** It's on [Main Street]. [Right] over there.

2. A: Where are you going? / (Unit 2:) What's the address? **B:** [any number 0–9] [Main Street] / (Unit 3:) Here's the address. **A:** Turn right / left at the corner. It's [right] next to the [hotel]. **B:** (Unit 1:) Thank you. **A:** You're welcome.

NOTES

Authentic practice: Students listen to an authentic conversation about directions and then complete listening and speaking tasks, providing true information.

🎧 Listen and circle.

Option: To prepare students for the listening, have them point and say all four telephone numbers before completing the exercise.

➤ Play the cassette or read the tapescript aloud once. Students listen only, pencils on desk.

➤ Play the cassette or read the tapescript aloud. Students circle the number they hear in each conversation.

Tapescript

Conversation 1
A: What's the phone number? **B:** It's 264–6701.
A: I didn't get that. Could you say it again?
B: Sure 2-6-4 6-7-0-1. **A:** Thanks.

Conversation 2
A: What's your phone number? **B:** 345–6722.
A: 345–6272? **B:** No. 345–6722. **A:** Oh. Thanks.

🎧 Look and listen

See also "Look and listen" on page T22a.

➤ Show the class Vocabulary Card 14 (*school*). Point to the picture of the man and say *He needs directions*.

Option: Check comprehension. Ask *Which bus?* (Number 3.) *Where's the school?* or *What's the address?* (35 Main Street.)

Tapescript

A: Can I help you? **B:** Yes, please. I need directions.
A: Are you taking the bus or the train? **B:** The bus.
A: OK. Take the number 3 to Main Street. Get off there. Turn right at the corner. The school is right there. The address is number 35. **B:** Excuse me?
A: Bus 3 to Main. Turn right at the corner.
B: Thanks.

🎧 Listen and respond.

See also "Listen and respond" on page T22a.

➤ Model the exchange with a student volunteer.

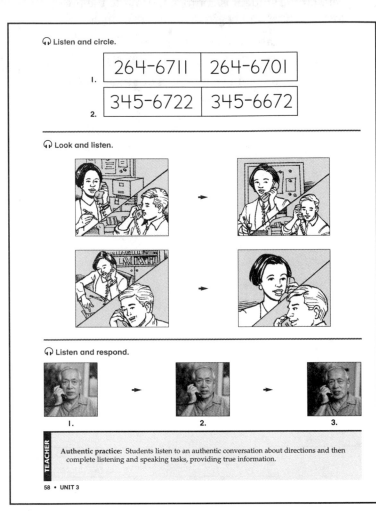

1.	264-6711	264-6701
2.	345-6722	345-6672

🎧 Look and listen.

🎧 Listen and respond.

1.　　　　2.　　　　3.

Authentic practice: Students listen to an authentic conversation about directions and then complete listening and speaking tasks, providing true information.

58 • UNIT 3

➤ Play the cassette or read the tapescript aloud. Have all students respond to the questions at the same time.

➤ Do this exercise several times to give students practice answering authentic questions.

Tapescript

Prompt 1: Are you taking the train or the bus?
Prompt 2: Take the number 5. Get off at Main Street. The school is right there.
Prompt 3: Bye!

Listen and respond (possible responses)

Prompt 1: The bus / train. **Prompt 2:** OK / I've got it. **Prompt 3:** (Unit 1:) Thanks. / Thank you. / (Welcome unit:) Bye.

TEACHER

Literacy review: Review concepts of address numbers and telephone key pads. Fill in missing numbers.
More practice: Worksheet 31 (Teacher's Edition CD-ROM).
Literacy test: Teacher's Edition CD-ROM.

Trace and write.

➤ Look at the top picture with the class. Count out the consecutive addresses, pointing to the houses on alternating sides of the street. When you come to a gray number, look at the class and gesture for someone to call it out.

➤ Look at the bottom picture with the class. Point to the number 1 and say *1.* Then point to the next blank button and gesture for someone to call out the number. Repeat with the remaining buttons.

➤ Have students trace and write the missing numbers.

Worksheet Link: Worksheet 31

Assign the worksheet for homework or for in-class independent work. Review students' work before going on to the next review lesson.

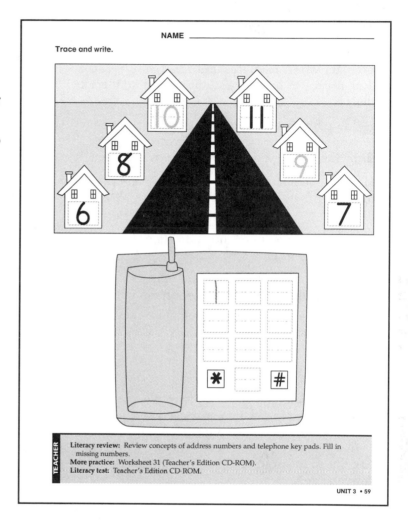

NAME _____

Trace and write.

TEACHER

Literacy review: Review concepts of address numbers and telephone key pads. Fill in missing numbers.
More practice: Worksheet 31 (Teacher's Edition CD-ROM).
Literacy test: Teacher's Edition CD-ROM.

UNIT 3 • 59

TEACHER

Survival / civics review: Point and name things in the pictures. Make statements about the pictures. Role-play conversations based on the pictures.
Tests: Teacher's Edition CD-ROM.

Talk about the pictures.

➤ With Students' Books open, say the following vocabulary words from this unit: *street, corner, accident, phone, car,* and have students point to them in their books.

➤ Hold up the picture for the class to see and point to vocabulary items *(street, corner, accident, phone, car).* Have students name the items as you point.

➤ Hold up the picture for the class to see and point to the building. Ask *What's the address?* (33 [Main Street].)

➤ Have students point to and name items in the picture with a partner.

Possible student responses

telephone / corner / street / accident / car / (Unit 2:) house

Role-play conversations.

➤ Point to one of the scenes (for example, the large picture). Point to the man on the left and say *Oh no! An accident!* Continue creating a conversation between the two men. Then invite two students to come to the front of the class to model the conversation.

➤ Have students work in pairs to practice conversations appropriate to the contexts in the pictures.

➤ Ask pairs of students to present one or two of their conversations to the class.

Talk about the pictures. Role-play conversations.

TEACHER

Survival / civics review: Point and name things in the pictures. Make statements about the pictures. Role-play conversations based on the pictures.
Tests: Teacher's Edition CD-ROM.

60 • UNIT 3

**Role-play conversations
(possible student responses)**

(Two men talking near the accident)
A: Oh, no! An accident. **B:** Call 911. **A:** OK. / (Unit 2:) Sure.

(The 911 operator and the man talking on the phone.)
A: 911. What's the problem? **B:** There's an accident. **A:** Where? / (Unit 2:) What's the address?
B: [In front of] 33 Main Street. **A:** Do you need a fire truck? **B:** No. Please send an ambulance.

LESSON PLAN FOR STUDENT'S PAGE 61

TEACHER

Literacy: Recognize capital E and F.
More practice: Worksheet 32 (Teacher's Edition CD-ROM).

Cross out.

➤ Model the exercise. Copy the first row of letters on the board. Point to the letter E on the left, say *E* and then point to the next letter (E). Nod your head and say *Yes!* to indicate they are the same. Continue in the same manner, comparing the target letter on the left with the letters on the right. When you come to the letter F, shake your head and say *No!* to indicate it is not the same, and cross it out.

➤ Have students do the first row of letters without a pencil. Holding a book up for the class to see, model the first line as students follow in their books. When you come to the F, trace an X over it with your fingers. You may need to walk around the room, modeling for individual students in their books. Have students do the next few lines without pencils.

➤ Have students pick up their pencils and complete the exercise on their own. Circulate around the classroom, checking their work.

Option: Go over the answers as a class. After each line is completed, have students count the number of crossed-out items per line. This activity reinforces deliberate and careful letter discrimination and reviews numbers.

➤ Repeat the above steps for the F exercise.

Additional Activities

Activity 1: Write similar sequences of E and F on the board. Have students take turns coming up to the board and crossing out the letters that are different from the target letter.

Activity 2: For further letter discrimination practice, make multiple copies of the E and F Letter Cards and distribute. Individually or with a partner, students sort the E and F letters into two piles.

Note: Students need to find the letter's correct orientation before they can sort each letter.

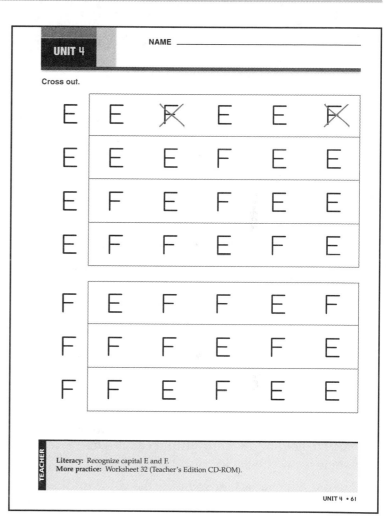

Worksheet Link: Worksheet 32

Assign the worksheet for homework or for in-class independent work. Follow the procedures above. Review students' work before going on to the next lesson to make sure that students can distinguish between E and F.

TEACHER

Literacy: Trace capital E and F, using classic uppercase penmanship.
More practice: Worksheet 33 (Teacher's Edition CD-ROM).

Trace.

Follow these steps for each letter.

➤ Model the writing of the letter E. Say *E*. On the board, model the strokes of the letter. To instruct students on the correct sequence of strokes, count aloud as you do each stroke. When you have completed the letter, point to it and say *E* again. Then have students follow along with their fingers in the air while watching you model the stroke again. Have everyone count the strokes aloud. By using kinesthetic and verbal modalities (large arm movements and stroke counting), students are more likely to remember the shape and sequences of strokes used to form each letter.

➤ Have students practice tracing the strokes of the letter, with their fingers on their desktops. Circulate around the classroom to correct strokes. Pay attention to the correct sequence of strokes.

➤ Lightly write several examples of the letter on the board. Invite students to the board to practice tracing them. Have the rest of the class follow along with fingers in the air.

➤ Have students trace the letters in their books. Note: Students trace only along the light gray tracing lines. Circulate around the classroom, checking student work.

➤ You may want students to do the exercise one time through without a pencil. For students not accustomed to holding a writing instrument, this frees them to focus only on the strokes.

➤ Observe students as they complete the last two lines on their own.

Note: Review good writing practices. Make sure students' posture is forward facing and relaxed. Both arms should rest lightly on the edge of the desk. Show students how to position the paper properly, according to whether they are right- or left-handed. Make sure students are holding the pencil correctly and with appropriate pressure.

Additional Activities

Activity 1: If the board is dusty with chalk, trace the letters E and F in the dust. Have students follow your

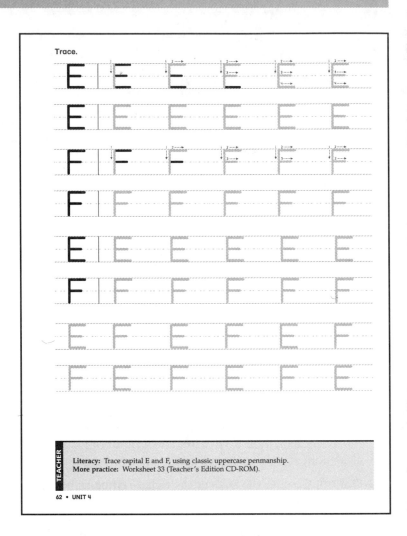

Trace.

TEACHER

Literacy: Trace capital E and F, using classic uppercase penmanship.
More practice: Worksheet 33 (Teacher's Edition CD-ROM).

62 • UNIT 4

marks with their fingers, counting their strokes aloud.

Activity 2: Make sure students have their name cards from the Welcome unit on their desks. Hold up the E Letter Card. Have students raise their hand if they have E in their name. Repeat with F.

Worksheet Link: Worksheet 33

Assign the worksheet for in-class independent work. Circulate around the room, observing students' strokes. Review students' work before going on to the next lesson to make sure that they have mastered the strokes for E and F.

TEACHER

Survival: Learn vocabulary for types of stores.
Civics concept: Stores sell specific types of merchandise.
New language: Discount store, restaurant, supermarket, grocery store, drugstore, hardware store, bakery, mall.

🎧 Look and listen.

See "Look and listen" on page T17a.

Option: Give students local examples of each type of store. Elicit several other examples from students. This activity connects students' knowledge of their neighborhoods to the material taught in the classroom.

Option: Bring in ads with pictures for local stores. Hold up each ad and say the corresponding vocabulary word.

Additional Activity

Provide listening practice. Give each student or pair of students a set of Vocabulary Cards 35–42 (stores). Students lay the cards out face up on their desks. Call out a vocabulary word and have students select the corresponding card and hold it up for you to see.

🎧 Listen again and repeat.

See "Listen again and repeat" on page T17a.

Additional Activities

Activity 1: Provide speaking practice. With books open, call out a picture number and have students say the word. Repeat several times. Then have students do this activity in pairs.

Activity 2: Bring to class several daily articles (fruit, soap, bread, masking tape, etc.) or picture cut-outs of these items from newspaper advertising fliers. Place Vocabulary Cards 35–42 on 8 desks, one card per desk. Have students circulate around the classroom to sort the items by placing them with the type of store where they can be purchased. This activity links students' personal knowledge of these items with the new vocabulary in the lesson.

Tapescript

1. discount store 2. restaurant 3. supermarket
4. grocery store 5. drugstore 6. hardware store
7. bakery 8. mall

🎧 Listen and circle.

See "Listen and circle" on page T17a-b.

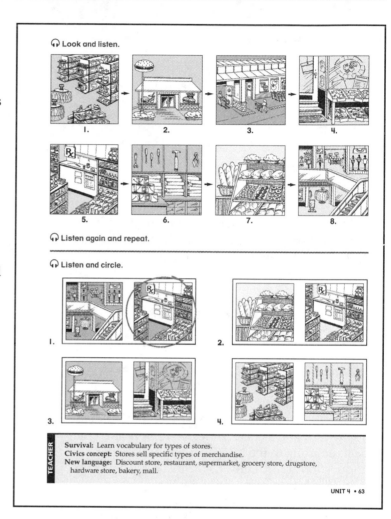

🎧 Look and listen.

1. 2. 3. 4.
5. 6. 7. 8.

🎧 Listen again and repeat.

🎧 Listen and circle.

1. 2.
3. 4.

TEACHER
Survival: Learn vocabulary for types of stores.
Civics concept: Stores sell specific types of merchandise.
New language: Discount store, restaurant, supermarket, grocery store, drugstore, hardware store, bakery, mall.

UNIT 4 • 63

Additional Activities

Activity 1: With books open, call out one of the two words (*mall* or *drugstore*) in item 1. Have students point to the correct picture. Repeat this process with all 4 items. Then students do this activity in pairs.

Activity 2: Give each student a set of Vocabulary Cards 35–42. Pairs of students sit facing each other. Student A chooses a card and says its name without showing the card to Student B. B finds the card in his own set. The two students then check their cards to make sure they match.

Tapescript

1. drugstore 2. bakery 3. grocery store
4. hardware store

TEACHER

Survival: Ask for and give directions to places in the neighborhood.
Civics concept: It's OK to point at a place or a thing, though not at a person.
New language: Is there a [bakery] near here? / around the corner /
across from [the parking lot].

🎧 Look and listen.

See also "Look and listen" on page T9a.

➤ Place Vocabulary Cards 38, 39, and 41 *(grocery store, drugstore, bakery)* on the board rim for reference. Call on students to identify the pictures.

➤ Play the cassette or read the tapescript aloud.

Option: Use gestures to convey the meaning of the prepositional phrases *around the corner* and *across from.*

Option: Demonstrate with hand motions the rising intonation of the *yes/no* question *Is there a grocery store near here?* Move your hand sharply upward on the end sound of *here.*

🎧 Listen again and repeat.

See "Listen again and repeat" on page T9a.

Additional Activities

Activity 1: Practice forming questions. Place Vocabulary Cards 38, 39, and 41 *(grocery store, drugstore, bakery)* on the rim of the board. Point to the *grocery store* card and ask *Is there a grocery store near here?* Repeat, pointing to the *bakery* card and changing your question accordingly. *(Is there a bakery near here?)* Call on students to practice asking the question, substituting other types of stores. You may need to point to the Vocabulary Cards as a prompt. This activity prepares students for the following Pair work.

Activity 2: Test comprehension. Pointing to the man in picture 1, ask *Where is the grocery store?* Then point to the woman to elicit the response. (On Main Street.) Continue with picture 2: *Where is the bakery?* (Around the corner.) And picture 3: *Where is the drugstore?* (Across from the parking lot.) This activity recycles language learned in Unit 2.

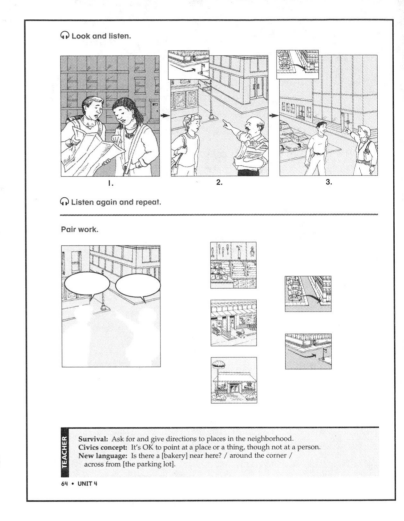

🎧 Look and listen.

1.   2.   3.

🎧 Listen again and repeat.

Pair work.

TEACHER

Survival: Ask for and give directions to places in the neighborhood.
Civics concept: It's OK to point at a place or a thing, though not at a person.
New language: Is there a [bakery] near here? / around the corner /
across from [the parking lot].

64 • UNIT 4

Tapescript

Conversation 1
A: Is there a grocery store near here?
B: Yes. On Main Street.

Conversation 2
A: Is there a bakery near here?
B: Yes. Around the corner.

Conversation 3
A: Is there a drugstore near here?
B: Yes. Across from the parking lot.

Pair work.

➤ Review the language. Hold the book up for the class to see. Point to each small picture cue on the right and identify the type of store and the directions *across the street* and *around the corner.*

➤ Model the Pair work. Invite a student to the front of the class. Begin the model conversation by asking *Is there a restaurant near here?* Give the student a moment to respond, using his own words. If the student responds appropriately, give a big smile and end the conversation with *Thank you.* If the student is confused, give a possible response and repeat the conversation for practice. Be sure to make eye contact and use hand gestures as you speak. Then invite two other students to model the conversation for the class, using another Vocabulary Card.

➤ Divide the class into pairs. Have students ask for and give directions to places in the neighborhood. Circulate around the classroom, offering help as needed.

Option: As you circulate around the classroom, pay attention to students' intonation of *yes/no* questions. Remind them of the correct intonation by using an upward hand motion.

➤ Have several volunteer pairs act out their conversations in front of the class.

Additional Activity

For further conversation practice, distribute Vocabulary Cards 15–16, 35–42 (*restaurant, hotel, stores*) to students. Using the Vocabulary Cards as prompts, have students circulate around the classroom, asking for and giving directions to places in the neighborhood.

Pair work (possible student responses)

A: Is there a hardware store / supermarket / restaurant near here? **B:** Yes. Around the corner. / Across from the parking lot.

Your students can also say . . .

1. A: (Unit 3:) I need directions. How do I get to (Unit 4:) a discount store / grocery store / drugstore / bakery / mall / (Unit 3:) bus / train / subway / highway / telephone / hospital / (Unit 2:) school / supermarket / bus stop / restaurant / hotel? **B:** (Unit 3:) Turn left / right at the corner. **A:** (Unit 1:) Thanks. / Thank you. **B:** You're welcome.

2. A: (Unit 2:) Where's [the school]? **B:** [It's] next to [the hotel]. / [It's] on [Main Street]. / [Right] over there.

If your students are ready . . .

Civics enrichment: It is appropriate to point at a place or thing. It is not polite to point at people. You can demonstrate this concept by pointing at an object or place in the classroom and nodding your head. Then point at a student and shake your head. Repeat as necessary with various objects and people.

TEACHER

Literacy: Recognize capital T, I, and L.
More practice: Worksheet 34 (Teacher's Edition CD-ROM).

Circle.

➤ Model the exercise. Copy the first row of letters on the board. Point to the T on the left, say *T*, and then point to the next letter (T). Nod your head and say *T, yes!* to indicate it is the same, and circle it. When you get to the I, shake your head and say *No!* to indicate they are different. Continue in the same manner, comparing the target letter on the left with the letters on the right.

➤ Have students do the model line without a pencil. Have students trace the circles with their fingers. Students do the next few lines as many times as necessary, as you watch to make sure they understand the instructions and can discriminate the letters.

➤ Have students pick up their pencils and complete the exercise on their own. Circulate around the classroom, checking their work.

➤ Repeat the steps for the I and L exercises.

Note: Say the name of the target letter on the left each time you point to it.

Option: Distribute blank sheets of paper for students to place over the portion of the page on which they are not working.

Option: Go over the answers as a class. Have students count the number of circled items per line. This activity reinforces deliberate and careful letter discrimination practice (always checking back with the target letter) and reviews numbers.

Additional Activities

Activity 1: Write similar sequences of T, I, and L on the board, occasionally adding E and F from the previous lesson. Have students take turns coming up to the board and crossing out the letters that are different from the target letter. Make sure students always move from the left to the right.

Activity 2: Make multiple copies of the T, I, and L Letter Cards. Individually, or with a partner, students sort the letters into three piles. Note: Students need to find the letter's correct orientation before they can sort each letter. Add multiple copies of the E and F Letter Cards and have students repeat the activity, now sorting the letters into five piles.

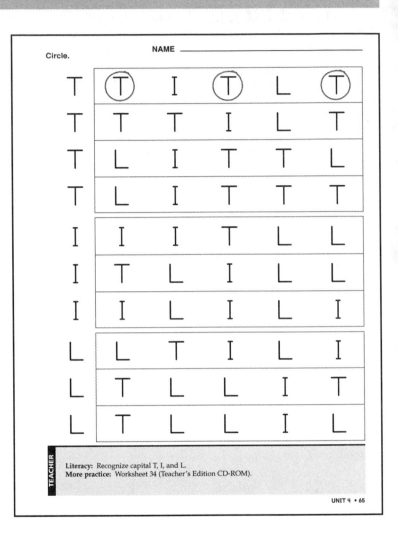

Worksheet Link: Worksheet 34

Assign the worksheet for homework or for in-class independent work. Follow the procedures above. Review students' work to make sure that students can distinguish between T, I, and L before going on to the next literacy lesson.

TEACHER

Literacy: Trace capital T, I, and L, using classic uppercase penmanship.
More practice: Worksheet 35 (Teacher's Edition CD-ROM).

Trace.

See also "Trace" on page T62.

➤ As you model the writing of letter T, give special emphasis to the first stroke, as all the letters on this page begin with that downward stroke.

Option: You may want students to do the exercise one time through without a pencil so they can focus only on the strokes.

➤ Repeat each procedure for the I and L exercises.

➤ Observe students as they complete the last two lines on their own.

Note: Review good writing practices. Make sure students' posture is forward facing and relaxed. Both arms should rest lightly on the edge of the desk. Show students how to position the paper properly, according to whether they are right- or left-handed. Make sure students are holding the pencil correctly and with appropriate pressure.

Additional Activities

Activity 1: Give students the opportunity to correct you. Write the letter T on the board correctly. As you write, nod your head and say *Yes!* Then write the letter incorrectly, with a stroke out of sequence or an incorrect right-to-left motion. As you write, shake your head and say *No!* Then invite students to say *Yes* or *No* as you write other letters correctly and incorrectly. Repeat the activity several times, reviewing the writing of the letters E, F, T, I, and L. This activity inspires students' confidence as they get to correct the teacher and assert their own knowledge.

Activity 2: Make sure students have their name cards from the Welcome unit on their desks. Hold up the T Letter Card. Have students raise their hand if they have T in their name. Repeat with I and L.

Worksheet Link: Worksheet 35

Assign the worksheet for in-class independent work. Circulate around the room, observing students' strokes. Review students' work before going on to the next literacy lesson to make sure that they have mastered the strokes for these letters.

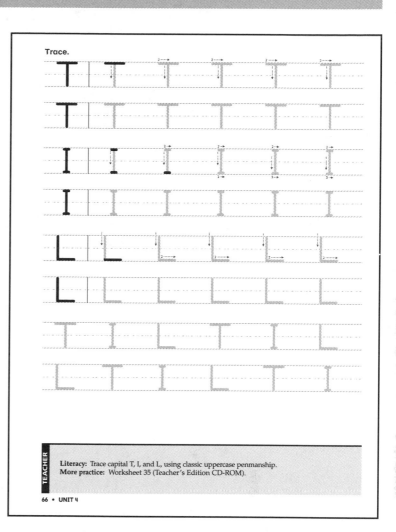

Trace.

TEACHER

Literacy: Trace capital T, I, and L, using classic uppercase penmanship.
More practice: Worksheet 35 (Teacher's Edition CD-ROM).

66 • UNIT 4

Survival: Learn vocabulary for types of clothing.
Civics concept: Look for prices on price tags.
New language: Shirt, skirt, dress, uniform, jacket, pants, shoes, socks, stockings, cheap, expensive.

🎧 Look and listen.

See "Look and listen" on page T17a.

Option: To anticipate the following lesson in plurals, emphasize that these vocabulary items are singular. Point to picture 1 and say *Shirt. One shirt.* You can hold up one finger as you say *One shirt.* Repeat with the other vocabulary items.

Additional Activity

Test comprehension. Point to an article of your own clothing and say with a rising intonation *Shirt?* Students respond *Yes* or *No.* Repeat the procedure, pointing to other articles of your own clothing, or pictures of clothing cut out from magazines or in Vocabulary Cards 43–47.

🎧 Listen again and repeat.

See "Listen again and repeat" on page T17a.

Option: Work on students' pronunciation. The /dr/ sound is challenging. Pay attention to how the tongue pulls back slightly from the back of the teeth to form the /r/ sound. Use your hand to illustrate that motion.

Additional Activities

Activity 1: To discriminate between the words *skirt* and *shirt,* hold up Vocabulary Cards 43 and 44 several times as you say the corresponding word. Then have students say the word as you hold up a card.

Activity 2: Provide speaking practice. Call out a picture number and have students say the word. Repeat the process with several words. Then have students do this activity in pairs.

Tapescript
1. shirt 2. skirt 3. dress 4. uniform 5. jacket

🎧 Look and listen.

See "Look and listen" on page T17a.

Option: Use gestures or dollar bills to convey the meaning of *cheap* and *expensive.*

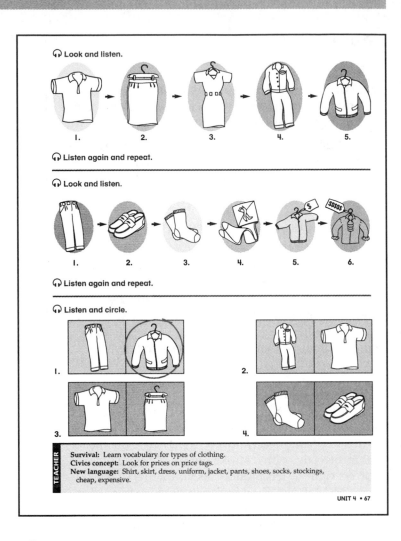

🎧 Listen again and repeat.

See "Listen again and repeat" on page T17a.

Option: Work on students' pronunciation. Have students tap out the syllables as they listen to each word. This will help underscore that the final plural sound in this vocabulary set is a phoneme, not a syllable.

Contrast the soft and long /ʃ/ sound with the plosive and short sound /tʃ/. To demonstrate the plosion of a /tʃ/ sound, hold a strip of paper in front of your mouth as you say *cheap.* Contrast it with *shoes.*

Additional Activities

Activity 1: Copy and distribute one set of Vocabulary Cards 43–53 to each student. Say a word, and have the class hold up the correct Vocabulary Card. Repeat the process with several words. Then have students do this activity in pairs.

Activity 2: Play a memory game. Photocopy Vocabulary Cards 43–53 and give each student one set. Have students close their eyes. Call out four vocabulary items in a row. Have students open their eyes and find the items in their Vocabulary Card sets. Repeat with different vocabulary items. This game reviews vocabulary and develops memory recall in English.

Activity 3: Concentration. Photocopy Vocabulary Cards 43–53. Follow the instructions for Activity 2 on page T28.

> **Tapescript**
> 1. pants 2. shoes 3. socks 4. stockings 5. cheap 6. expensive

🎧 Listen and circle.

See also "Listen and circle" on page T17a-b.

➤ Model the exercise. Hold the book up for the class to see. Point to the pants and say *pants*. Point to the jacket and say *jacket*. Read the tapescript or play the first item on the cassette. With your finger, trace a circle around the jacket.

Option: To prepare students for the listening, review the vocabulary in the pictures.

➤ Continue as on page T17b.

Additional Activity

Review *cheap* and *expensive*. Bring to class cut-outs of items from advertising fliers and magazines. On one desk, place the Vocabulary Card for *expensive* and on another desk, place the card for *cheap*. Have students circulate around the classroom to sort the items, placing the expensive items on one table and the cheap items on the other.

> **Tapescript**
> 1. jacket 2. uniform 3. skirt 4. socks

NOTES

_____

_____

_____

_____

_____

_____

_____

_____

_____

_____

_____

_____

_____

Survival: Learn plural forms of known clothing items.
New language: Shirts, skirts, jackets, uniforms, dresses.

🎧 Look and listen.

See "Look and listen" on page T17a.

Option: To make explicit the notion of plurals, point to the single shirt in picture 1 and say *A shirt. One shirt.* Then point to the plural form and say *Shirts. Two shirts.* Use your fingers, if necessary, to make clear the numbers. Repeat with pictures 2, 3, 4, and 5. For pictures 6, 7, and 8, gesture by putting your hands side by side to suggest a pair.

Additional Activity

Test comprehension. Have students open their books to page 68. Say one of the words, in either singular or plural form and have students point to the one they hear.

🎧 Listen again and repeat.

See "Listen again and repeat" on page T17a.

Option: Work on students' pronunciation. Have students tap out the syllables as they say each word. This will help underscore that only the word *dress* adds a new syllable in its plural form.

Additional Activity

Provide speaking practice. Call out a picture number 1–5 and have students say the word in singular and plural form. You will need to demonstrate this first. Repeat the process with several words. Then have students do this activity in pairs.

Tapescript

1. a shirt, shirts 2. a skirt, skirts 3. a jacket, jackets
4. a uniform, uniforms 5. a dress, dresses
6. socks 7. shoes 8. stockings

🎧 Listen and circle.

See "Listen and circle" on page T17a-b.

Additional Activities

Activity 1: Play a memory game. Photocopy Vocabulary Cards 43–51 and 54–58 (singular and plural vocabulary on this page) and give each student one set. Have students close their eyes. Call out four

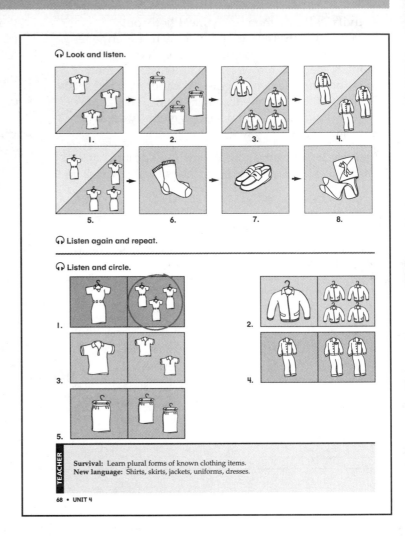

🎧 Look and listen.

1. 2. 3. 4. 5. 6. 7. 8.

🎧 Listen again and repeat.

🎧 Listen and circle.

1. 2. 3. 4. 5.

Survival: Learn plural forms of known clothing items.
New language: Shirts, skirts, jackets, uniforms, dresses.

68 • UNIT 4

vocabulary items in a row. Have students open their eyes and find the items in their Vocabulary Card sets. Repeat with different vocabulary items.

Activity 2: Concentration. Photocopy Vocabulary Cards 43–51 and 54–58 (singular and plural clothing items). Follow the instructions for Activity 2 on page T28.

Tapescript

1. dresses 2. a jacket 3. shirts 4. a uniform
5. a skirt

TEACHER

Literacy: Recognize capital A, H, and Y.
More practice: Worksheet 36 (Teacher's Edition CD-ROM).

Cross out.

See "Cross out" on page T61.

Option: Distribute blank sheets of paper for students to place over the portion of the page on which they are not working.

Option: Go over the answers as a class by holding up the book for the class to see. On each line, compare the target letter with each letter on the right. After each line is completed, have students count the number of crossed-out items per line. This activity reinforces deliberate and careful letter discrimination practice (always checking back with the target letter) and reviews numbers.

Additional Activities

Activity 1: For further practice, write similar sequences of A, H, and Y on the board, occasionally including the capital letters E, F, T, I, and L. Have students take turns coming up to the board and crossing out the letters that are different from the target letter.

Activity 2: Make multiple copies of the A, H, and Y Letter Cards and distribute. Individually, or with a partner, students sort the letters into three piles. To review previous letter discrimination work, add multiple copies of any of the letters E, F, T, I, and L, and have students repeat the activity, now sorting the letters into multiple piles. Review with the class. Hold up each card in each pile and say its name.

Worksheet Link: Worksheet 36

Assign the worksheet for in-class independent work. Follow the procedures above. Review students' work to make sure that students can distinguish between A, H, and Y before going on to the next literacy lesson.

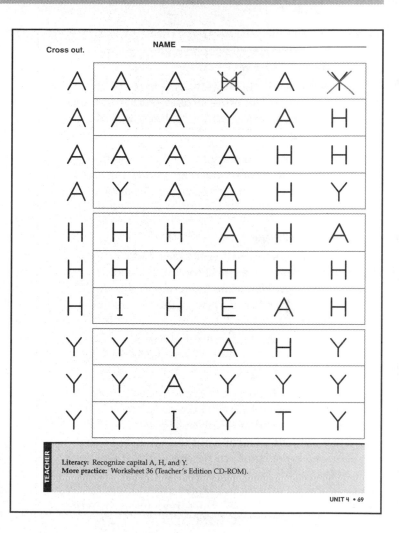

TEACHER

Literacy: Trace A, H, and Y, using classic uppercase penmanhsip.
More practice: Worksheet 37 (Teacher's Edition CD-ROM).

Trace.

See "Trace" on page T62.

Option: Some students may struggle with the forward and backward slanting strokes required for the A and Y. To prepare these students, have them do Worksheet 9 again.

Option: You may want students to do the exercise one time through without a pencil so they can focus on their strokes. Circulate around the classroom to check their strokes.

Additional Activities

Activity 1: Bring some salt to the classroom and shake some over a broad desktop or on a cookie sheet. In large strokes, write the letters A, H, and Y. Have students take turns tracing your letters in the salt. (A similar activity can be done with a damp sponge and a dusty chalkboard.) This is good practice for students unaccustomed to holding a writing instrument.

Activity 2: Give students the opportunity to correct you. Write the letter A on the board correctly. As you write, nod your head and say *Yes!* Then write the letter incorrectly with a stroke out of sequence or an incorrect right-to-left motion. As you write, shake your head and say *No!* Then invite students to say *Yes* or *No* as you write other letters correctly and incorrectly. Repeat the activity several times, reviewing the writing of the letters E, F, T, I, and L.

Activity 3: Make sure students have their name cards from the Welcome unit on their desks. Hold up the A Letter Card. Have students raise their hand if they have A in their name. Repeat with H and Y.

Worksheet Link: Worksheet 37

Assign the worksheet for in-class independent work. Follow the procedures above. Make sure that students have mastered the strokes for A, H, and Y before going on to the next literacy lesson.

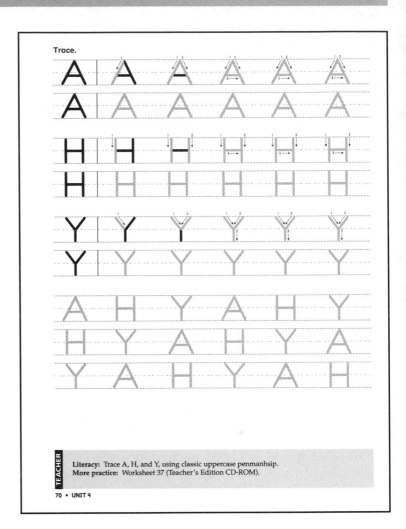

TEACHER

Literacy: Trace A, H, and Y, using classic uppercase penmanhsip.
More practice: Worksheet 37 (Teacher's Edition CD-ROM).

70 • UNIT 4

TEACHER

Survival: Ask for and express location of items in a store.
Civics concept: Salespeople expect you to ask them where to find things.
New language: May I help you? / Where are the [jackets]? / The [jackets] are next to the [pants].

🎧 Look and listen.

See also "Look and listen" on page T9a.

➤ Set the scene. Hold the book up for the class to see. Point to the pictures and say *Discount store.*

➤ Continue as on page T9a.

Option: Use gestures such as a shrug for *Where are the pants?* and a pointing motion for *Right over there.*

Option: If you have worked on the rising intonation of *yes/no* questions in previous lessons, reinforce your instruction with the question *May I help you?* You may want to contrast this pattern with the rising/falling intonation pattern of the *wh*– question *Where are the pants?*

🎧 Listen again and repeat.

See "Listen again and repeat" on page T9a.

Additional Activity

Practice forming questions. Place Vocabulary Cards 48–51 and 54–58 on the rim of the board. Point to the *pants* card and ask *Where are the pants?* Ask the question again. Then repeat, pointing to a new Vocabulary Card and changing your question accordingly. Call on students to practice the question, substituting other clothing items. You may need to point at Vocabulary Cards as a prompt.

Repeat this procedure with the statement *The jackets are right over there.* This activity prepares students for the following Pair work.

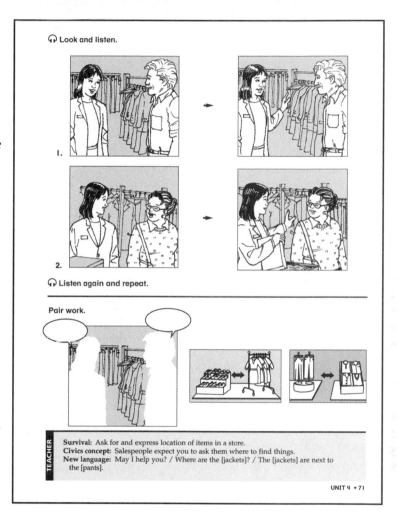

🎧 Look and listen.

🎧 Listen again and repeat.

Pair work.

TEACHER

Survival: Ask for and express location of items in a store.
Civics concept: Salespeople expect you to ask them where to find things.
New language: May I help you? / Where are the [jackets]? / The [jackets] are next to the [pants].

UNIT 4 • 71

Pair work.

➤ Review *next to* and *across from.* Hold the book up for the class to see. Point to the picture cues on the right. Say *The shoes are next to the dresses. The pants are across from the shirts.*

➤ Model the Pair work. Invite a student to join you in front of the class. Give the student the *pants* Vocabulary Card. Ask *May I help you?* To prompt the student's question, point to the Vocabulary Card. Wait for the student to compose a question. (Where are the pants?) If the student is confused, provide the question. Point to the cues in the Student's Book and answer *The pants are right over there* or *The pants are across from the shirts.* Then

---

Tapescript

Conversation 1
A: May I help you?
B: Yes, please. Where are the pants?

A: The pants are right over there.
B: Thanks.
A: You're welcome.

Conversation 2

A: May I help you?
B: Yes, please. Where are the jackets?

A: The jackets are next to the pants.
B: Thanks.
A: You're welcome.

(Continued on page T71b.)

T71a

invite two other students to model the conversation for the class, using another Vocabulary Card.

➤ Divide the class into pairs. Have students ask for the location of clothes. Circulate around the classroom, offering help as needed.

➤ Have several volunteer pairs act out their conversations in front of the class.

Additional Activity

Create a store scene in your classroom. Use Vocabulary Cards 43–58 (clothing items) or bring to class cut-outs of those clothing items from magazines. Place the pictures in an area of the classroom. Say *This is (school name)'s Discount Store.*

Using the classroom store setting, distribute different Vocabulary Cards to several students. Have them practice asking for the items in the classroom store.

Pair work (possible student responses)

A: May I help you? **B:** Yes, please. Where are the shoes / dresses? Where are the pants / shirts?
A: The shoes [dresses] are right over there / next to the dresses [shoes]. The pants / shirts are across from the shirts / pants. **B:** Thanks. / Thank you.
A: You're welcome.

Your students can also say . . .

Where are the skirts / uniforms / jackets / pants / socks / stockings?

NOTES

TEACHER

Survival: Ask for a size in a store.
Civics concept: Salespeople expect you to ask them to get you a size.
New language: I need [a uniform/pants]. / What size? / small, medium, large.

🎧 Look and listen.

See also "Look and listen" on page T9a.

➤ Hold the book up for the class to see. Point to the pictures and say *Discount store*. Introduce the vocabulary *small*, *medium*, and *large* by drawing three squares in graduated sizes on the board. Point to the small square, draw an *S* on it, and say *small*. Repeat with the medium and large squares. Then hold up the Student's Book and point to the small, medium, and large uniforms next to the second picture.

➤ Continue as on page T9a.

Option: Give students visual cues to the dialogue by pointing to the size models in the Student's Book as they listen.

Additional Activity
Provide listening practice. For further practice, distribute the Letter Cards S, M, L to each student. Call out a size and have students hold up the corresponding letter card.

🎧 Listen again and repeat.

See "Listen again and repeat" on page T9a.

Additional Activities
Activity 1: Talk about sizes. Point to yourself and say your size (small, medium, or large). Gesture to a student and ask *What size?* If the student doesn't understand, ask someone else. Continue around the room until all students have identified their sizes. Note: You may want to discuss this individually with each student or in small groups of two or three students. Be sensitive to the fact that some students may not be comfortable discussing their sizes.

Activity 2: Illustrate that the article is omitted when using plurals. Hold up four fingers and say *I need a jacket*, touching a finger for each word. Repeat several times so students associate each finger with a word. Point to the third finger and say the word *a*.

Then say *I need jackets*. Emphasize the /s/ sound at the end of *jackets*. Hold up your four fingers as you say *I need jackets* again, but curl down the third finger to show the absence of *a*. Contrast the sentences again and then give other examples.

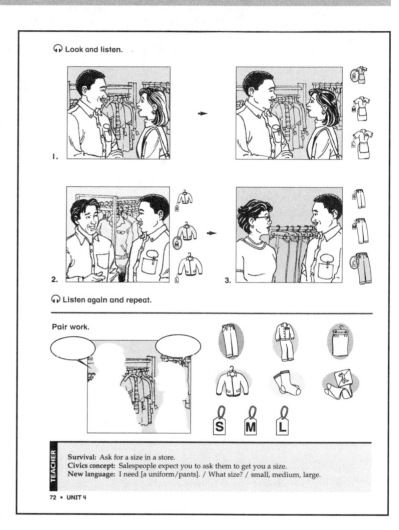

Tapescript

Conversation 1
A: May I help you?
B: Yes, please. I need a uniform.
A: What size?
B: Small.

Conversation 2
A: I need a jacket.
B: What size?
A: Medium.

Conversation 3
A: I need pants.
B: What size?
A: Large.

(Continued on page T72b.) **T72a**

Pair work.

➤ Review students' knowledge of the clothing vocabulary, using Vocabulary Cards 43–58. Prompt students to say *small, medium,* and *large* by pointing to the size cues *S, M,* and *L* on the board.

➤ Model the Pair work. Have an advanced student join you in front of the class. Ask *Can I help you?* Point to the first cue to the right of the Pair work picture. Wait for the student to respond. *(I need pants.)* If the student is confused, provide a possible response. Point to the size cues and ask *What size?* Repeat the conversation in order to present the class with more natural-sounding conversation. Then invite two other students to model the conversation, using some of the other cues.

➤ Students work with a partner to ask for clothing items in their size. Circulate around the classroom, offering help as needed.

➤ Have several volunteer pairs act out their conversations in front of the class.

Pair work (possible student responses)

A: May I help you? **B:** Yes, please. I need pants / a uniform / a skirt / a jacket / socks / stockings.
A: What size? **B:** Small. / Medium. / Large.

Your students can also say . . .

A: Where are the shirts / dresses / shoes? **B:** [The shirts] are across from the [dresses] / (Unit 2:) right over there / next to the [shoes]. **A:** (Unit 1:) Thanks. / Thank you. **B:** You're welcome.

NOTES

_____

_____

_____

_____

_____

_____

_____

_____

_____

_____

_____

_____

_____

_____

_____

_____

_____

_____

TEACHER

Literacy: Recognize capital N, Z, K, and X.
More practice: Worksheet 38 (Teacher's Edition CD-ROM).

Circle.

See "Circle" on page T65.

Option: After they have finished, have students work with a partner to compare their answers. Together they count the number of circled items per line. Circulate around the classroom, checking their work.

Additional Activities

Activity 1: For further practice, write similar sequences of N, Z, K, and X on the board, occasionally including other capital letters with slants such as A and Y. Have students take turns coming up to the board and crossing out the letters that are different from the target letter.

Activity 2: For further letter discrimination practice, make multiple copies of the N, Z, K, and X Letter Cards. Individually or with a partner, students sort the letters into four piles. To review previous letter discrimination work, add multiple copies of any of the following letters: E, F, T, I, L, A, H, or Y. Have students repeat the activity, now sorting the letters into multiple piles.

Worksheet Link: Worksheet 38

Assign the worksheet for homework or for in-class independent work. Follow the procedures above. Review students' work to make sure that students can distinguish between N, Z, K, and X before going on to the next literacy lesson.

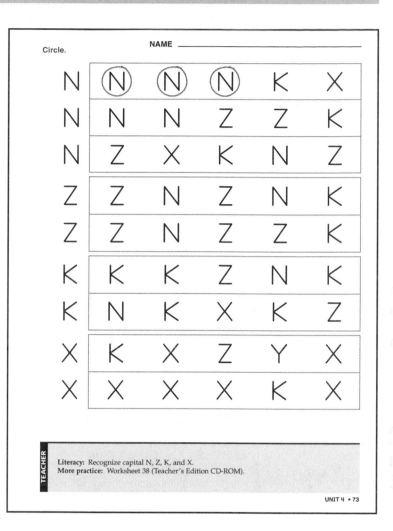

Circle.   NAME _____

N	Ⓝ	Ⓝ	Ⓝ	K	X
N	N	N	Z	Z	K
N	Z	X	K	N	Z
Z	Z	N	Z	N	K
Z	Z	N	Z	Z	K
K	K	K	Z	N	K
K	N	K	X	K	Z
X	K	X	Z	Y	X
X	X	X	X	K	X

TEACHER

Literacy: Recognize capital N, Z, K, and X.
More practice: Worksheet 38 (Teacher's Edition CD-ROM).

TEACHER

Literacy: Trace N, Z, K, and X, using classic uppercase penmanship.
More practice: Worksheet 39 (Teacher's Edition CD-ROM).

Trace.

See "Trace" on page T62.

Option: Some students may struggle with the forward and backward slanting strokes required for the N, Z, K, and X. To prepare these students, have them do Worksheet 9 again.

Option: You may want students to do the exercise one time through without a pencil so they can focus only on the strokes.

Additional Activities

Activity 1: Give students the opportunity to correct you. Write the letter N on the board correctly. As you write, nod your head and say *Yes!* Then write the letter incorrectly, with a stroke out of sequence or an incorrect bottom-to-top motion. As you write, shake your head and say *No!* Then invite students to say *Yes* or *No* as you write letters correctly and incorrectly. Repeat the activity several times, reviewing the writing of the letters E, F, T, I, L, A, Y, and H. This activity inspires students' confidence, as they get to correct the teacher and assert their own knowledge.

Activity 2: Make sure students have their name cards from the Welcome unit on their desks. Hold up the N Letter Card. Have students raise their hand if they have N in their name. Repeat with Z, K, and X.

Worksheet Link: Worksheet 39

Assign the worksheet for in-class independent work. Circulate around the room, observing students' strokes. Review students' work to make sure that they have mastered the strokes for N, Z, K, and X before going on to the next literacy lesson.

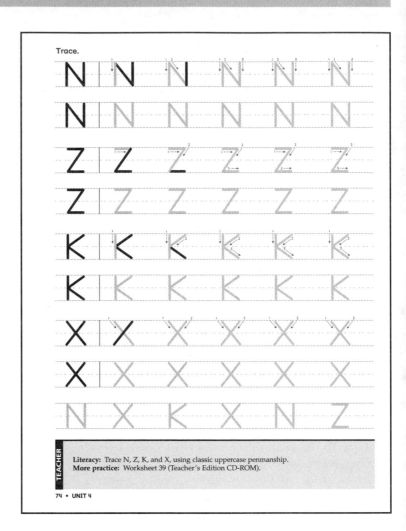

Trace.

TEACHER

Literacy: Trace N, Z, K, and X, using classic uppercase penmanship.
More practice: Worksheet 39 (Teacher's Edition CD-ROM).

74 • UNIT 4

TEACHER

Survival: Decide to buy or decline because of poor fit or price. Apologize.
Civics concept: It's OK to tell a salesperson that something's wrong with merchandise or that it's too expensive.
New language: How are they? / They're [fine]. / too large / too small / I'm sorry.

Look and listen.

See also "Look and listen" on page T9a.

➤ Set the scene. Hold the book up for the class to see. Point to the pictures and say *shoe store.*

Option: Use gestures and exaggerated mime to convey the concepts *too large, too small,* and *too expensive.*

Option: To check students' understanding of the four conversations, point to each picture and ask *OK?* with a rising intonation. Students can answer *Yes* or *No.* (Picture 1: Yes. Picture 2: No. Picture 3: No. Picture 4: No.)

Listen again and repeat.

See "Listen again and repeat" on page T9a.

Additional Activities

Activity 1: Practice new language. Hold up three fingers and say *They're too large,* touching a finger for each word. Repeat but change the last word to *small.* Repeat once more, changing the last word to *expensive.* Then have students practice with a partner.

Activity 2: Test comprehension. Point to the salesman in each picture and ask *How are they?* Elicit student responses.

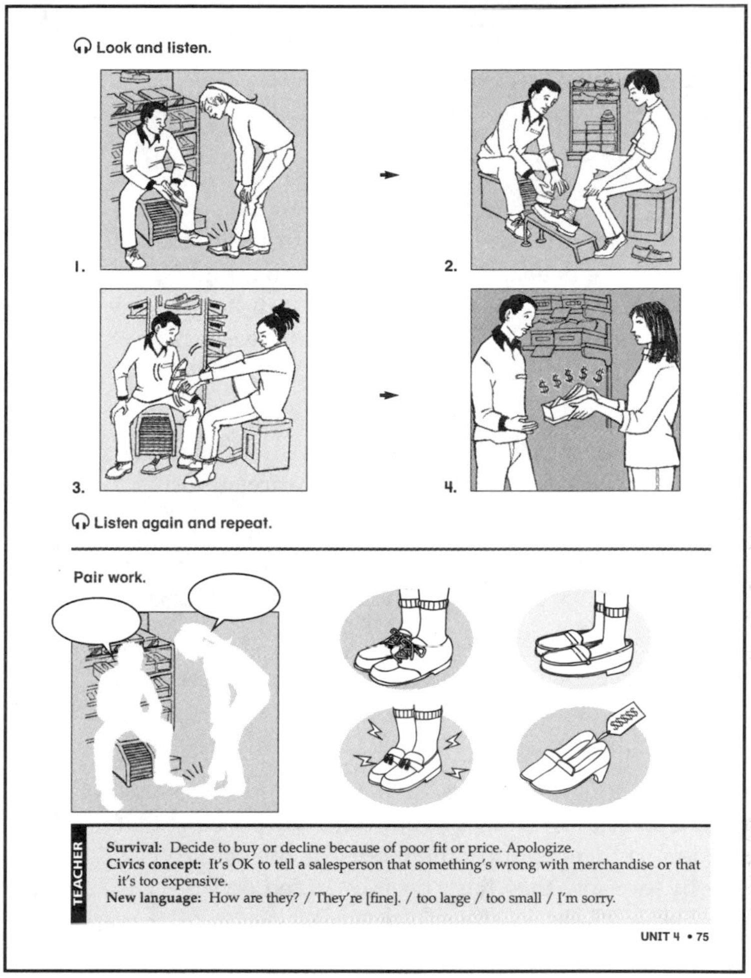
Look and listen.
1. 2. 3. 4.
Listen again and repeat.
Pair work.
TEACHER
Survival: Decide to buy or decline because of poor fit or price. Apologize.
Civics concept: It's OK to tell a salesperson that something's wrong with merchandise or that it's too expensive.
New language: How are they? / They're [fine]. / too large / too small / I'm sorry.
UNIT 4 • 75

Tapescript

Conversation 1
A: How are they?
B: They're fine.

Conversation 2
A: How are they?
B: They're too large.
A: I'm sorry.

Conversation 3
A: How are they?
B: They're too small.
A: I'm sorry.

Conversation 4
A: How are they?
B: They're too expensive.
A: I'm sorry.

Pair work.

➤ Review the language. Point to the picture cues to the right of the Pair work picture and have students say the appropriate phrase for each.

Option: Bring clothing items such as a pair of shoes, a pair of pants, and a pair of socks to class. Use these items to practice the conversation.

➤ Model the Pair work. Have an advanced student join you in front of the class. Hand the student a pair of shoes or Vocabulary Card 49 *(shoes).* Ask *How are they?* Make sure that students understand that this is not a test of their memory—they should feel free to change the conversation and use their own words.

➤ Students work with a partner. Have students decide or decline to buy something.

➤ Have several volunteer pairs act out their conversations in front of the class.

Pair work (possible student responses)

A: How are they? **B:** They're fine / too large / too small / too expensive. **A:** OK. / I'm sorry.

TEACHER

Authentic practice: Students listen to an authentic conversation with a salesperson and then complete listening and speaking tasks, providing their own information.

🎧 Listen and circle.

See also "Listen and circle" on page T58.

➤ Show the class Vocabulary Cards 45, 49, and 46 (*dress, shoes, uniform*). Gesture as you show each one to elicit the word.

➤ Write the numbers 12, 8, 10, 1, etc. from the exercise on the board. Point to each number and have students say it. Then point to each number and say *Size [number]*, so students understand these numbers represent sizes.

➤ Have students listen once with visual cues. Hold up the Vocabulary Cards as the class listens to the cassette or as you read the conversation aloud.

➤ Model the exercise. Read the tapescript or play the cassette for Conversation 1 again. Hold up the Student's Book and trace the circle around 8. Say *Size 8.*

➤ Play the cassette or read the tapescript aloud. Students circle the size they hear in each conversation.

Note: Although numbers have not been used to represent sizes previously in this book, it is possible that students will encounter them outside the classroom. For this reason, they have been included on the Authentic Practice page.

Additional Activity
Place Vocabulary Cards 45, 49, and 46 (*dress, shoes, uniform*) on the board rim. After each conversation, point to the cards and gesture to have students identify the clothing item mentioned in the conversation.

If your students are ready . . .

Civics enrichment: Students may want to know (or confirm) their sizes in the U.S. system. Approach one student, point to a clothing item (dress, pants, or shoes) the student is wearing, and ask *What size?* If the student is unable to respond, point to the clothing item again and give an estimate. (*Hmm. Size [8] or Size [10].*) Repeat with other students. Some students may be eager to help estimate each other's sizes too. However, be sensitive to the fact that some students may not be comfortable discussing their sizes.

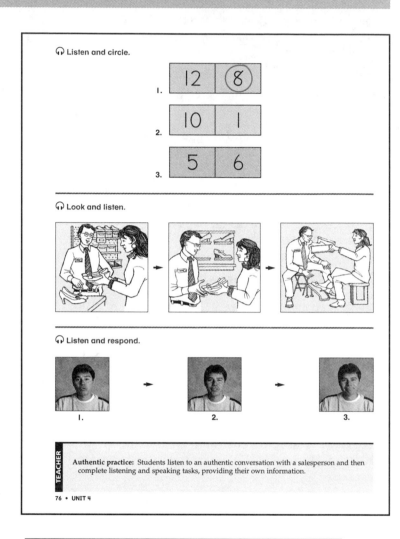

🎧 Listen and circle.

1. 12 (8)
2. 10 1
3. 5 6

🎧 Look and listen.

🎧 Listen and respond.

1.   2.   3.

TEACHER — **Authentic practice:** Students listen to an authentic conversation with a salesperson and then complete listening and speaking tasks, providing their own information.

76 • UNIT 4

Tapescript

Conversation 1
A: Do you have this dress in size 8?
B: Size 8? Hmm. Yes. Here you go. Size 8.

Conversation 2
A: Can I help you?
B: Yes, please. I need a pair of shoes.
A: Certainly. What size?
B: 10, please.

Conversation 3
A: Can you help me? I need a uniform.
B: Sure! What size do you need?
A: Small.
B: Small? Hmm. Small is size 6.

🎧 Look and listen.

See also "Look and listen" on page T22a.

➤ Set the scene. Hold the book up for the class to see. Point to the pictures and say *Shoe store*.

➤ Continue as on page T22a.

Additional Activity

(Challenge): Have students try to recreate the conversations in this activity without a listening prompt. After modeling for the class, have pairs of students point to each person in the picture and say an appropriate phrase. Circulate around the classroom, offering help when needed. This challenge prepares students for the "Listen and respond" activity.

Tapescript

A: May I help you with those shoes?
B: Yes, thanks.

A: What size do you need?
B: Size 9, please.

A: Well, how are they?
B: They're fine. But they're too expensive.

🎧 Listen and respond.

Note: The goal of this activity is to give students practice responding to authentic prompts, using the language they have learned so far, thus building confidence. Different students will say different things.

➤ Model the exercise. Hand a student Vocabulary Card 49 *(shoes)* and ask *May I help you with shoes?* If the student responds appropriately, give a big smile and move on to another student. If the student is confused, give a possible response and then repeat the prompt.

➤ Ask other students the remaining two questions: *What size?* and *How are they?* You may want to write numbers on the board to indicate sizes.

➤ If you are using the cassette, you may first want to read the tapescript aloud once, pausing for the class to respond, to give students practice before they respond to the prompts on the cassette.

➤ Play the cassette or read the tapescript aloud. Have all students respond to the question at the same time. This gives them the opportunity to build confidence as they practice, without being watched by the class. To help students focus on their own speech, have them cover one ear as they speak. This makes it possible to hear oneself.

➤ Do this exercise several times to give students practice answering authentic questions.

➤ Have the class listen as you ask individual students the three question prompts.

Tapescript

Prompt 1: May I help you with shoes?

Prompt 2: What size?

Prompt 3: Well, how are they?

**Listen and respond
(possible student responses)**

Prompt 1: Yes, please.
Prompt 2: Small. / Medium. / Large. / [any number 1–50].
Prompt 3: They're fine / too large / too small / too expensive.

TEACHER

Literacy review: Recognize and trace capital E, F, T, I, L, A, H, Y, N, Z, K, and X.
More practice: Worksheet 40 (Teacher's Edition CD-ROM).
Literacy test: Teacher's Edition CD-ROM.

Circle and trace.

➤ Model the exercise. Copy the first line on the board. Point to the Z on the left and compare it to the letters on the right. When you come to the letter Z on the right, nod your head, say *Yes,* and circle it.

Model tracing the letter Z on the board. Count aloud as you trace each stroke. Then have students follow along with their fingers in the air while watching you. Have everyone count the strokes aloud.

➤ Have students practice circling and tracing with their fingertips before completing the exercise with pencils.

Option: Distribute blank sheets of paper for students to place over the portion of the page on which they are not working.

Option: Review the answers as a class by holding up Student's Book page 77. On each line, compare the target letter with each letter on the right. Then have students count aloud the number of strokes to write the letter at the end of the line.

Additional Activities

Activity 1: Have students sort the letters learned so far. Make five sets of the A, E, F, H, I, K, L, N, T, X, Y, and Z Letter Cards. Place one set on 12 desks—one card per desk. Deal out the remaining cards. Students move around the classroom, placing matching cards on the correct desks. Then review with the class. Hold up each card in each pile and say its name.

Activity 2: Review the writing of the letters E, F, T, I, L, A, H, Y, N, Z, and K. Follow the instructions for Activity 1 on page T66.

Worksheet Link: Worksheet 40

Assign the worksheet for homework or for in-class independent work. Follow the procedures above. Review students' work to make sure that students can distinguish between E, F, T, I, L, A, H, Y, N, Z, K, and X before finishing this unit.

TEACHER

Literacy review: Recognize and trace capital E, F, T, I, L, A, H, Y, N, Z, K, and X.
More practice: Worksheet 40 (Teacher's Edition CD-ROM).
Literacy test: Teacher's Edition CD-ROM.

UNIT 4 • 77

TEACHER

Survival / civics review: Point and name things in the pictures. Make statements about the pictures. Role-play conversations based on the pictures.
Tests: Teacher's Edition CD-ROM.

Talk about the picture. (top picture)

➤ Name places or things in the picture (*bus stop, restaurant, bakery, parking lot, drug store, street, corner, bus*) and have students point to their location.

➤ Hold up the picture and point to the places in the picture. Have students say the words.

➤ Have students point and name places and things in the picture with a partner.

> **Possible student responses**
>
> drugstore / bakery / (Unit 3:) street / bus / corner / car / (Unit 2:) restaurant / bus stop / house / parking lot
>
> **Your students can also say . . .**
>
> discount store / grocery store / hardware store / mall / (Unit 3:) train / subway / taxi / highway / (Unit 2:) school / hotel / apartment / supermarket

Role-play conversations.

➤ Point to one of the two people talking on the street and ask *Is there a bakery near here?* Then point to the other person to elicit a student's response. (*Yes. Across from the parking lot.*) Gesture to reverse roles and have the student ask you for directions.

➤ Students work with a partner to practice asking for and giving directions to places in the picture.

➤ Ask pairs of students to present some of their conversations to the class.

> **Role-play conversations
> (possible student responses)**
>
> **A:** Is there a bakery near here? **B:** It's around the corner / across from the parking lot / (Unit 2:) next to the drugstore / [right] over there / on Main Street. **A:** (Unit 3:) OK. (Unit 1:) Thanks. / Thank you. **B:** You're welcome.
>
> **Your students can also say . . .**
>
> **1. A:** (Unit 3:) How do I get to the (Unit 4:) drugstore / discount store / grocery store / hardware store / mall / (Unit 3:) train / subway / taxi /

Talk about the pictures. Role-play conversations.

TEACHER **Survival / civics review:** Point and name things in the pictures. Make statements about the pictures. **Tests:** Teacher's Edition CD-ROM.

78 • UNIT 4

> bus / highway / (Unit 2:) school / hotel / supermarket / restaurant / bus stop? **B:** (Unit 3:) Turn right / left at the corner.
>
> **2. A:** (Unit 2:) I need directions. Where's the [bakery]?

Talk about the picture. (bottom picture)

➤ Name clothing or vocabulary items in the picture (*jackets, shirts, uniforms, shoes, expensive, cheap*) and have students point to them.

➤ Hold up the picture and point to the items in the picture. Have students say the words.

(Continued on page T78b.)

➤ Have students point and name items in the picture with a partner.

Possible student responses

shirt / skirt / dress / uniform / jacket / pants / shoes

Role-play conversations.

➤ Point to the female shoe clerk and male customer. Point to the woman and ask *May I help you with shoes?* Then point to the man to elicit a student's response. Continue in the same manner, modeling the two other conversations in the picture.

➤ In pairs, have students practice conversations appropriate to the contexts in the picture.

➤ Ask pairs of students to present some of their conversations to the class.

Role-play conversations
(possible student responses)

(Shoe clerk and female customer)

A: How are they? **B:** They're fine / too large / too small / too expensive. **A:** (Unit 3:) OK. / (Unit 4:) I'm sorry.

(Shoe clerk and male customer)

A: May I help you? **B:** Yes, please. I need shoes. **A:** What size? **B:** Small. / Medium. / Large. / [any number 1–50].

Your students can also say . . .

I need pants / socks / stockings / a shirt / skirt / dress / uniform / jacket.

Role-play conversations
(possible student responses)

(Female customer and male store clerk)

A: Where are the jackets? **B:** The jackets are across from the shoes / (Unit 2:) right over there / next to the shirts.

Your students can also say . . .

Where are the skirts / dresses / uniforms / shirts / pants / shoes / socks / stockings?

NOTES

_____

_____

_____

_____

_____

_____

_____

_____

_____

_____

_____

LESSON PLAN FOR STUDENT'S PAGE 79

TEACHER

Literacy: Recognize capital M, W, and V.
More practice: Worksheet 41 (Teacher's Edition CD-ROM).

Circle.

See "Circle" on page T65.

Note: Say the name of the target letter on the left each time you point to it.

Option: Distribute blank sheets of paper for students to place over their pages. Remind them how to move their sheets down to work on the next line.

Option: Go over the answers as a class. Have students count the number of circled items per line. This activity reinforces deliberate and careful letter discrimination practice (always checking back with the target letter) and reviews numbers.

Additional Activities

Activity 1: Write similar sequences of M, W, and V on the board, occasionally including other capital letters with slants such as A and Y. Have students take turns coming up to the board and crossing out the letters that are different from the target letter. Make sure students always move from the left to the right.

Activity 2: Make ten sets of the M, W, and V Letter Cards. Place one set on three desks—one card per desk. Deal out the remaining cards. Students move around the classroom, placing matching cards on the correct desks. Then review with the class. Hold up each card in each pile and say its name.

Activity 3: Concentration. Photocopy Letter Cards A, H, M, V, W, and Y. Follow the directions for Activity 2 on page T28.

Worksheet Link: Worksheet 41

Assign the worksheet for homework or for in-class independent work. Follow the procedures above. Review students' work to make sure that students can distinguish between M, V, and W before going on to the next literacy lesson.

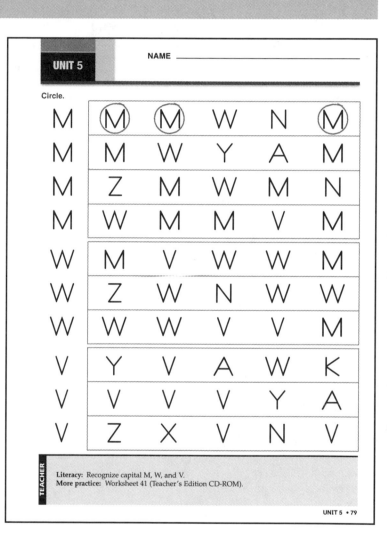

UNIT 5

NAME

Circle.

Literacy: Recognize capital M, W, and V.
More practice: Worksheet 41 (Teacher's Edition CD-ROM).

UNIT 5 • 79

TEACHER

Literacy: Trace capital M, W, and V, using classic uppercase penmanship.
More practice: Worksheet 42 (Teacher's Edition CD-ROM).

Trace.

See "Trace" on page T62.

Option: Some students may struggle with the forward and backward slanting strokes required for the M, W, and V. To give students extra practice on slants, copy and distribute Worksheet 9.

Option: You may want students to do the exercise one time through without a pencil. For students not accustomed to holding a writing instrument, this frees them to focus only on the strokes.

Additional Activities

Activity 1: Lightly draw Ms, Ws, and Vs on the board. Invite individual students to the board to trace the letters with the correct stroke sequences.

Activity 2: Have students evaluate your handwriting. Write several examples of the letter M in a line on the board. Include one or two examples of a malformed M (for example, inverted, or with one hump much larger than the other). Have students take turns coming up to the board to cross out the incorrectly formed letters. Repeat this procedure with the letters W and V. You may also choose to have students erase the malformed letters and write them correctly.

Activity 3: Give students the opportunity to correct you. Write the letter M on the board correctly. As you write, nod your head and say *Yes!* Then write the letter incorrectly with an incorrect bottom-to-top motion. As you write, shake your head and say *No!* Then invite students to say *Yes* or *No* as you write other letters correctly and incorrectly.

Activity 4: Make sure students have their name cards from the Welcome unit on their desks. Hold up the M Letter Card. Have students raise their hand if they have M in their name. Repeat with W and V.

Worksheet Link: Worksheet 42

Assign the worksheet for in-class independent work. Circulate around the room, observing students' strokes. Review students' work to make sure that they have mastered the strokes for these letters before going on to the next literacy lesson.

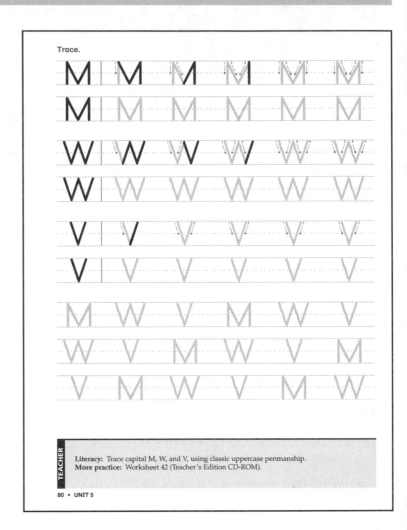

TEACHER

Literacy: Trace capital M, W, and V, using classic uppercase penmanship.
More practice: Worksheet 42 (Teacher's Edition CD-ROM).

80 • UNIT 5

TEACHER
Survival: Learn vocabulary for times of day and clock times.
Civics concept: Time is represented by a numbering system on a clock.
New language: Morning, afternoon, night / It's [8:00].

🎧 Look and listen.

See also "Look and listen" on page T17a.

➤ Tell the class what time of day it is. Say *It's [after-noon].* Gesture to indicate that you are referring to current time, not a picture in the book.

Additional Activity
Place Vocabulary Cards 62–64 *(morning, afternoon, night)* on the board rim. Mime the actions of waking up and ask *Morning? Night?* Mime the actions of going to sleep and ask *Morning? Night?*

🎧 Listen again and repeat.

See "Listen again and repeat" on page T17a.

Additional Activity
Bring travel magazines (or *National Geographic*) to class. Show pictures of people outdoors. Ask *Morning? Afternoon? Night?* and gesture for student response.

Tapescript
1. morning **2.** afternoon **3.** night

🎧 Listen and circle.

See "Listen and circle" on page T17a–b.

Tapescript
1. afternoon **2.** night **3.** morning

🎧 Look and listen.

See "Look and listen" on page T17a.

🎧 Listen again and repeat.

See "Listen again and repeat" on page T17a.

Option: Demonstrate that it is not correct to say *o'clock* when mentioning the hour and the minutes. Say *seven-fifteen. Yes!* Say *seven-fifteen o'clock. No!*

Additional Activities
Activity 1: Practice new language. First present how to say the top of the hour. Write many clock times on the board (7:00, 9:00, 12:00, 2:00). Point to a time and say *It's [seven] o'clock.* Hold up three fingers and repeat the sentence, touching a finger for each word. Then point to another time on the board and say the sentence

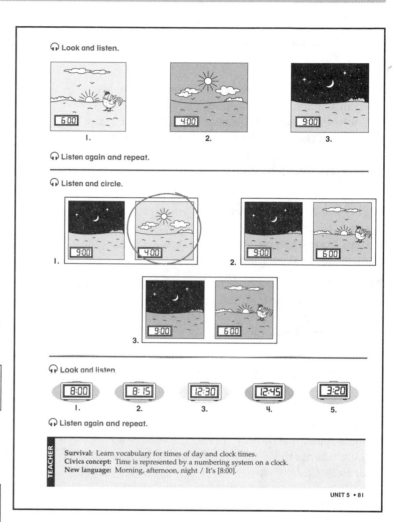

again, but omit the hour (*It's _____ o'clock*). Have students say the missing word. Repeat again, this time omitting just the word *o'clock*.

Activity 2: Repeat Activity 1, above, with times containing minutes (7:15, 7:30, 7:45).

Activity 3: Concentration. Use Vocabulary Cards 65–69 or create a set of cards, each with a different time written on it. Photocopy so you have two matching sets for each pair of students. Follow the instructions for Activity 2 on page T28.

Tapescript
1. It's eight o'clock. **2.** It's eight fifteen. **3.** It's twelve thirty. **4.** It's twelve forty-five. **5.** It's three twenty.

T81

TEACHER

Survival: Exchange appropriate greetings and leave-takings. Ask for and give the time.
Civics concept: It's polite to greet people with "Good morning," etc.
New language: Good morning. / Good afternoon. / Good evening. / Good night. /
What time is it?

⌒ Look and listen.

See also "Look and listen" on page T9a.

➤ Hold the Student's Book up for the class to see. Point to each picture and identify the time of day (Picture 1: morning. Picture 2: afternoon. Picture 3: evening. Picture 4: night.) Note that the phrase *Good evening* is presented in Conversation 3. The context of the picture will provide meaning for the word *evening*.

➤ Play the cassette or read the tapescript aloud as many times as necessary. Students follow along in their books. Gesture to your watch to convey the meaning of *What time is it?*

Option: Focus on intonation. If you have worked on the rising/falling intonation pattern of *wh–* questions in previous lessons, reinforce your instruction with the question *What time is it?*

⌒ Listen again and repeat.

See "Listen again and repeat" on page T9a.

Option: Teach students the *time* gesture of pointing to one's watch (or bare wrist if not wearing a watch). Teach students the gesture as they ask the question *What time is it?*

Additional Activities

Activity 1: Practice forming greetings. Put Vocabulary Cards 62–64 (*morning, afternoon, night*) on the rim of the board. Say *Good morning* and point to the appropriate card. Hold up two fingers and repeat the greeting, touching a finger for each word, but omit the word *morning* and allow students to say it. Repeat, pointing at the *night* card to elicit a new greeting (*Good night*). Repeat until students can easily produce greetings for different times of the day.

Activity 2: Test comprehension. Point to each picture and ask *What time is it?*

Activity 3: Provide more practice giving the time. Write various times on the board. Ask *What time is it?* Point to one of the times on the board to elicit a student response. Repeat with several different times. Students then work with a partner to practice asking for and giving the time.

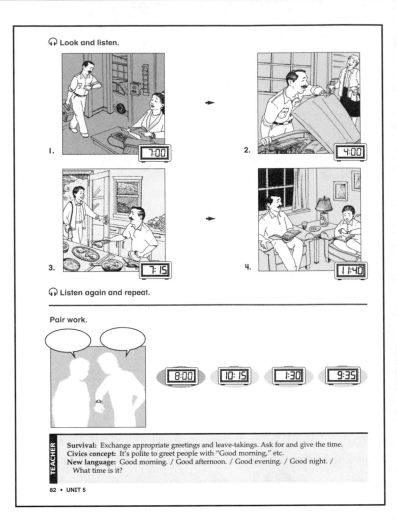

Activity 4: Use Vocabulary Cards 65–69 or create a set of cards, each with a different time written on it. Photocopy so you have two matching sets. Give each student one card. The goal is for students to circulate around the classroom, asking for the time until they find the person with their matching card. To demonstrate, hold a card in your hand. Approach a student and say *Good [afternoon]. What time is it?* Point to the student's card to elicit the response. Show the class your card. If the cards are the same, nod your head and say *Yes!* If they are different, say *No!* and ask another student the time. Repeat the modeling until everyone understands the object of the game. Then have students do the activity.

Tapescript

Conversation 1
A: Good morning.
B: Good morning. What time is it?
A: It's 7 o'clock.

Conversation 2
A: Good afternoon.
B: Good afternoon. What time is it?
A: It's 4 o'clock.

Conversation 3
A: Good evening.
B: Good evening. What time is it?
A: It's 7:15.

Conversation 4
A: What time is it?
B: It's 11:40.
A: 11:40? Good night!

Pair work.

➤ Model the Pair work. Write a time on the board. Approach a student and say *Good [morning]. What time is it*? Point to a time written on the board to prompt the student. Repeat this procedure with another student.

➤ Students work with a partner to ask for and give the time. Circulate around the classroom, offering help as needed.

➤ Have several volunteer pairs act out their conversations in front of the class.

Pair work (possible student responses)

A: Good morning / afternoon / evening. What time is it? **B:** It's 8:00 / 10:15 / 1:30 / 9:35.

Your students can also say . . .

[All clock times] / **A:** It's [eleven o'clock]? Good night! / (Unit 1:) Bye! See you later!

If your students are ready . . .

Civics enrichment: *Good morning, Good afternoon,* and *Good evening* are greetings. They are all similar in meaning to *Hello. Goodnight,* however, means *good-bye.* You can demonstrate this notion by saying *Hello! Good morning!* and *Hello! Good afternoon!* and *Hello! Good evening!* as you repetitively enter the room. Then say *Good night! Bye!* and leave the room. Repeat this contrast several times.

NOTES

TEACHER

Literacy: Recognize capital U, J, and S.
More practice: Worksheet 43 (Teacher's Edition CD-ROM).

Cross out.

See "Cross out" on page T61.

Option: Have students compare their work in pairs and count the number of circled items per line.

Additional Activities
Activity 1: For further practice, write similar sequences of letters on the board. Students take turns coming up to the board and circling the letters that are the same as the target letter.

Activity 2: Give each student a set of M, W, V, U, J, and S Letter Cards. Have students lay the cards out face up on their desks. Show the class a card and call out its name. Have students select the card from their own sets and hold it up for you to see.

Worksheet Link: Worksheet 43
Assign the worksheet for homework or for in-class independent work. Follow the procedures above. Review students' work to make sure that students can recognize the difference between U, J, and S before going on to the next literacy lesson.

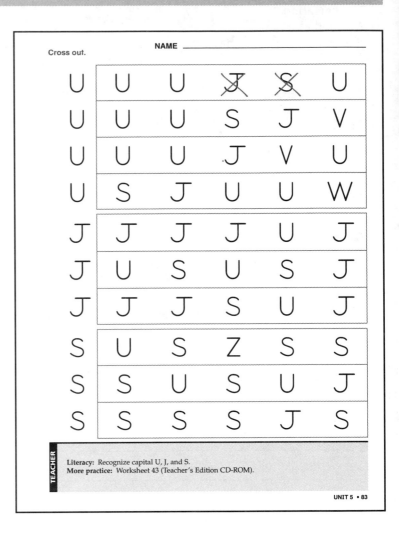

Cross out.

NAME _____

U	U	U	X	X	U
U	U	U	S	J	V
U	U	U	J	V	U
U	S	J	U	U	W
J	J	J	J	U	J
J	U	S	U	S	J
J	J	J	S	U	J
S	U	S	Z	S	S
S	S	U	S	U	J
S	S	S	S	J	S

TEACHER
Literacy: Recognize capital U, J, and S.
More practice: Worksheet 43 (Teacher's Edition CD-ROM).

UNIT 5 • 83

TEACHER

Literacy: Trace capital U, J, and S, using classic uppercase penmanship.
More practice: Worksheet 44 (Teacher's Edition CD-ROM).

Trace.

See "Trace" on page T62.

Option: You may want students to do the exercise one time through without a pencil so they can focus only on the strokes.

Additional Activities

Activity 1: Lightly draw multiple letters U, J, and S on the board. Invite individual students to the board to trace the letters with the correct stroke sequences.

Activity 2: Have students evaluate your handwriting. Write several examples of the letter U in a line on the board. Include one or two examples of a malformed U (for example, with one vertical line shorter than the other). Have students take turns coming up to the board to cross out or erase and rewrite the incorrectly formed letters. Repeat this procedure with the letters J and S. You may also choose to have students erase the malformed letters and write them correctly.

Activity 3: Give students the opportunity to correct you. Write the letter U on the board correctly. As you write, nod your head and say *Yes!* Then write the letter incorrectly, with an incorrect right-to-left motion. As you write, shake your head and say *No!* Then invite students to say *Yes* or *No* as you write the letters U, J, and S correctly and incorrectly.

Activity 4: Make sure students have their name cards from the Welcome unit on their desks. Hold up the U Letter Card. Have students raise their hand if they have U in their name. Repeat with J and S.

Worksheet Link: Worksheet 44

Assign the worksheet for in-class independent work. Circulate around the room, observing students' strokes. Review students' work to make sure that they have mastered the strokes for these letters before going on to the next literacy lesson.

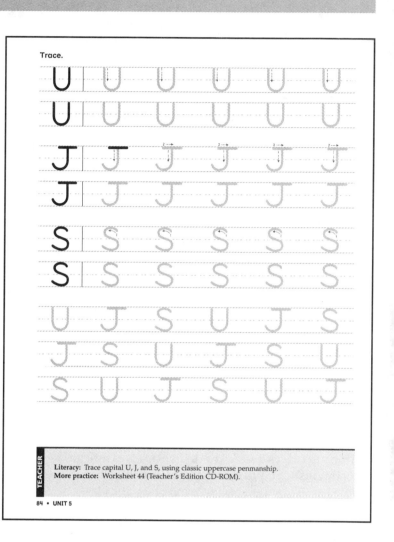

Trace.

TEACHER

Literacy: Trace capital U, J, and S, using classic uppercase penmanship.
More practice: Worksheet 44 (Teacher's Edition CD-ROM).

84 • UNIT 5

TEACHER

Survival: Learn days of the week.
Civics concept: There are 7 days in a week. Each day has its own name.
New language: Day, week, Sunday, Monday, Tuesday, Wednesday, Thursday, Friday, Saturday /
What day is today? / What day is tomorrow?

🎧 Look and listen.

See also "Look and listen" on page T17a.

➤ Hold a monthly calendar up for the class to see. Point to the first day and say *Day*. Repeat with several more days. Then point to the length of a week and say *Week*. As a class, count the days in a week. Say *A week—seven days*.

➤ Play the cassette or read the tapescript aloud as many times as necessary. As students listen to the days of the week, point to the days on a monthly calendar.

Additional Activity

Test comprehension. Hold up a monthly calendar. Make sure that the week on your calendar begins on Sunday, not Monday. Point to a day of the week and say with a rising intonation *Monday?* Students respond *Yes* or *No*. Repeat with other days. Be sure to include more correct statements than incorrect at this point.

🎧 Listen again and repeat.

See "Listen again and repeat" on page T17a.

Option: The days *Tuesday* and *Thursday* are difficult to distinguish. Emphasize the hard T in Tuesday. Isolate the /θ/ sound of *Thursday*. Show the class how your tongue rests between your teeth as you blow. /θ/ is a long and voiceless sound. The length of the sound can be illustrated by drawing your hand evenly from your mouth to the air as you say it. To help students identify the voiceless quality of /θ/, have them place their hands on their throats as they say /θ/. Have students contrast this voiceless sound to the voiced /d/ of *day*.

The /θ/ may be embarrassing for students to produce. Try to relieve some of the anxiety and embarrassment by hamming up the absurdity of the tongue-blowing sound. Encourage everyone to practice the sound at home in front of a mirror.

Option: It is easier to remember the days of the week if they are first introduced as a sequence. Chant the sequence (all days have two syllables except Saturday) with the class several times. Or set the days of the week to the score of "Twinkle Twinkle Little Star" (also used for the alphabet song in Unit 7).

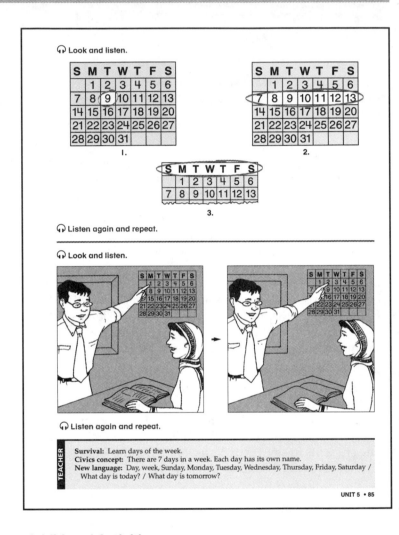

TEACHER

Survival: Learn days of the week.
Civics concept: There are 7 days in a week. Each day has its own name.
New language: Day, week, Sunday, Monday, Tuesday, Wednesday, Thursday, Friday, Saturday /
What day is today? / What day is tomorrow?

UNIT 5 • 85

Additional Activities

Activity 1: Round robin. Sit with the class in a circle. Start by saying *Sunday* and point to a Sunday on a monthly calendar. Then point to the next day of the week on the calendar to prompt the student beside you to say *Monday*. Continue around the circle, again and again, until the class has recited the days of the week several times.

Activity 2: Call out the days of the week in sequence, but clap in place of saying one day. Students say the missing day. Repeat, omitting a different day of the week each time.

Tapescript

1. day **2.** week **3.** Sunday, Monday, Tuesday, Wednesday, Thursday, Friday, Saturday

---

🎧 Look and listen.

See also "Look and listen" on page T9a.

➤ As students listen to the exchange in the first picture, hold a monthly calendar up for the class to see and point to Monday. As they listen to the exchange in the second picture, point to Tuesday.

🎧 Listen again and repeat.

See "Listen again and repeat" on page T9a.

Additional Activity

Hold up a current monthly calendar. Ask *What day is today?* and point to today's date on the calendar to elicit students' response. Ask *What day is tomorrow?* and point to tomorrow's date. Photocopy the calendar page and have students practice with a partner.

Tapescript

A: What day is today?
B: Monday.

A: What day is tomorrow?
B: Tuesday.

NOTES

TEACHER

Survival: Talk about work and school schedules.
Civics concept: Work and school occur in regular schedules.
New language: When is [school/work]? / [School] is [Monday].

🎧 Look and listen.

See also "Look and listen" on page T17a.

➤ Gesture around you and say *school*. Show Vocabulary Cards 4–9 (occupations) and say *work*.

🎧 Listen again and repeat.

See "Listen again and repeat" on page T17a.

Tapescript
1. work 2. school

🎧 Look and listen.

See also "Look and listen" on page T9a.

➤ Gesture around you and say *School. School is [list the days of the week the class meets]*. Repeat.

Additional Activity
Test comprehension. Hold the book up for the class to see. Point to the man in the first picture and ask *When is school?* Point to the woman to elicit students' response. Repeat with the second picture.

🎧 Listen again and repeat.

See "Listen again and repeat" on page T9a.

Additional Activity
Place Vocabulary Cards 73 and 72 (*school, work*) on the rim of the board. Point to Picture Card 73 (*school*) and ask *When is school?* Gesture for students to repeat the question. Then point to the card for *work* to elicit a new question.

Tapescript
A: When is school?
B: School is Monday, Wednesday, and Friday.
A: And when is work?
B: Work is Tuesday and Saturday.

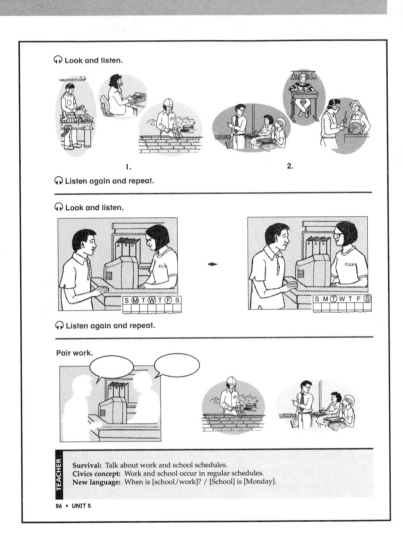

TEACHER

Survival: Talk about work and school schedules.
Civics concept: Work and school occur in regular schedules.
New language: When is [school/work]? / [School] is [Monday].

86 • UNIT 5

Pair work.

➤ Model the Pair work. Gesture around you and ask *When is school?* Hold up a current monthly calendar and point to the days of the week as students call out the days the class meets. Then approach a student who works and ask *When is work?* Always point to the days of the week on the calendar as the student answers.

➤ Students talk with a partner about their work and school schedules. Circulate around the classroom, offering help as needed.

Option: Hand out copies of a current monthly calendar. As students speak to one another, they can point to the days they work and study.

➤ Have several volunteer pairs act out their conversations in front of the class.

NOTES

TEACHER

Literacy: Recognize capital C, O, G, and Q.
More practice: Worksheet 45 (Teacher's Edition CD-ROM).

Cross out.

See "Cross out" on page T61.

Additional Activities
Activity 1: Make multiple copies of the C, G, O, and Q Letter Cards. Begin by lining up several of the same Letter Cards (five C cards, for example) on the board rim, but turn some of the cards on their sides or upside down. Invite students to come to the board to correct the orientation of each card. For a greater challenge, combine different Letter Cards in the same line-up.

Activity 2: Make multiple copies of the C, G, O, and Q Letter Cards. Individually, or with a partner, students sort the letters into four piles. To review previous letter discrimination work, add multiple copies of any of the letters J, S, and U, and have students repeat the activity, now sorting the letters into multiple piles. Review with the class. Hold up each card in each pile and say its name.

Worksheet Link: Worksheet 45
Assign the worksheet for homework or for in-class independent work. Follow the procedures above. Review students' work to make sure that students can recognize the difference between C, O, G, and Q before going on to the next literacy lesson.

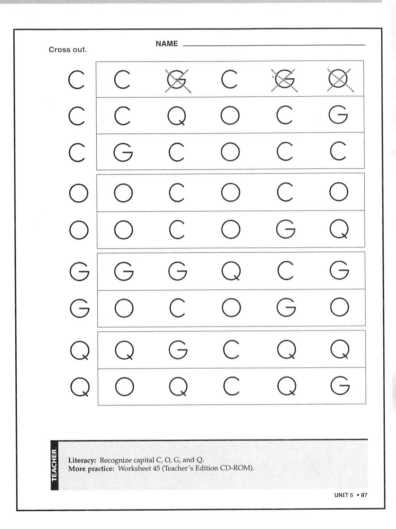

TEACHER

Literacy: Trace capital C, O, G, and Q, using classic uppercase penmanship.
More practice: Worksheet 46 (Teacher's Edition CD-ROM).

Trace.

See "Trace" on page T62.

Note: Emphasize the right-to-left motion of the curve in the letter C. This directionality of the first stroke is shared by all letters on this page.

Additional Activities

Activity 1: Lightly draw Cs, Os, Gs, and Qs on the board. Invite individual students to the board to trace the letters with the correct stroke motions and sequences.

Activity 2: Give students the opportunity to correct you. Write the letter C on the board correctly. As you write, nod your head and say *Yes!* Then write the letter incorrectly with a bottom-to-top motion. As you write, shake your head and say *No!* Then invite students to say *Yes* or *No* as you write other letters correctly and incorrectly. Repeat the activity several times, reviewing the writing of the letters C, O, G, and Q.

Activity 3: Make sure students have their name cards from the Welcome unit on their desks. Hold up the C Letter Card. Have students raise their hand if they have C in their name. Repeat with O, G, and Q.

Worksheet Link: Worksheet 46

Assign the worksheet for in-class independent work. Follow the procedures above. Review students' work to make sure that students have mastered the strokes for these letters before going on to the next literacy lesson.

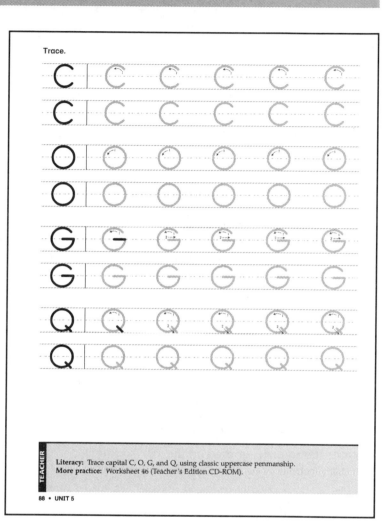

Trace.

TEACHER

Literacy: Trace capital C, O, G, and Q, using classic uppercase penmanship.
More practice: Worksheet 46 (Teacher's Edition CD-ROM).

88 • UNIT 5

LESSON PLAN FOR STUDENT'S PAGE 89

Survival: Learn months of the year. Talk about school schedules.
Civics concept: There are 12 months in a year. Each month has its own name.
New language: January, February, March, April, May, June, July, August, September, October, November, December / in your country / From [September] to [June].

🎧 Look and listen.

See also "Look and listen" on page T17a.

Note: *Day* and *week* are reviewed here to give context to the presentation of *month* and *year*.

➤ Hold a monthly calendar up for the class to see. Point to a day and say *Day*. Then point to the length of a week and say *Week*. Circle the whole month and say *Month*. Flip through all twelve months of the calendar and say *Year*.

➤ Play the cassette or read the tapescript aloud as many times as necessary.

Option: As students listen to the months of the year, show them on a calendar.

**Additional Activity
(Challenge):** Ask *What day is today? What month?* Write several year numbers on the board (2003, 2004, 2005) and ask students *What year?*

🎧 Listen again and repeat.

See "Listen again and repeat" on page T17a.

Option: If you have worked on the /θ/ sound in *Thursday*, repeat your drill with the /θ/ sound in *month*.

Additional Activities

Activity 1: Sit with the class in a circle. Start by saying *January,* and point to the first month in a yearly calendar. Then point to the next month on the calendar to prompt the student beside you to say *February.* Continue with *March* and *April.* Continue around the circle, again and again, until the class has recited the group of four months several times. Repeat with the remaining months, in groups of four.

Activity 2: Call out the months of the year in sequence. Clap in place of saying one month. Students say the missing month. Have students take turns leading the activity. You may want to do this activity with groups of three or four months, rather than all twelve at once.

Activity 3: Give students the opportunity to correct you. Say a correct sequence of four months in a row. After you speak, nod your head and say *Yes!* Then

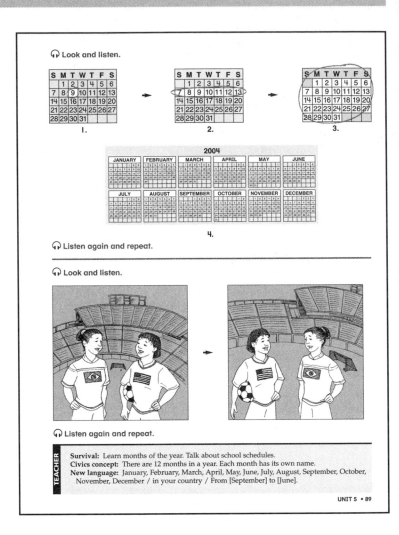

say an incorrect sequence of four months. After you speak, shake your head and say *No!* Then invite students to say *Yes* or *No* as you call out correct and incorrect sequences of the months.

Activity 4: The following activity helps students encode and memorize words by connecting kinesthetic activity (left/right) with words. Model the activity with a student volunteer. You and the student stand face-to-face, holding your hands out with palms up. Cross your right hand over to tap the student's opposing (right) hand and say the first month of the year (*January*). Then cross your left hand over to tap the student's left hand and say the next month (*February*). Then invite the student to do the speaking and tapping (*March, April*). Practice the sequence of all months of the year in this manner. You may want to do this activity with groups of three or four months.

T89a

🎧 Look and listen.

See also "Look and listen" on page T9a.

➤ Gesture around the room, say *School*, and then name the months your class is in session.

➤ Introduce the word *country*. Say *Country,* and then name the U.S. and other country names students recognize. Elicit from the students additional examples of country names.

➤ Play the cassette or read the tapescript aloud as many times as necessary.

Option: Give visual cues as students listen. Use gestures to contrast the meaning of *this country* and *your country*. As students listen, hold a yearly calendar up for the class to see and point to the months mentioned in the conversation.

🎧 Listen again and repeat.

See "Listen again and repeat" on page T9a.

Additional Activities

Activity 1: Test comprehension. Say *School in this country is from September to June. Hmmm. One month? Two months?* Start counting out the months and then shrug your shoulders. Have students figure out how many months of school there are from September to June. Repeat this procedure with the statement *School is from March to December.*

Activity 2: Practice new language. Ask *When is school in this country?* Hold up six fingers and ask the question again, touching a finger for each word. Repeat, but omit saying one word. Point to the finger that represents the missing word. Have students say the missing word. Then change the question to *When is school in your country?* Repeat the procedure.

Tapescript

A: When is school in this country?
B: From September to June.

A: And when is school in your country?
B: From March to December.

NOTES

_____

_____

_____

_____

_____

_____

_____

_____

_____

_____

_____

_____

_____

TEACHER

Survival: Talk about arrival time at work. Recognize importance of being on time.
Civics concepts: It's good to be on time. It's not good to be late.
New language: Early, on time, late / Oh good. / I'm [on time].
Sight word: Hours

🎧 Look and listen.

See also "Look and listen" on page T17a.

➤ Write the time 9:00 on the board. Point to it and say *School is at 9:00.*

➤ Play the cassette or read the tapescript aloud as many times as necessary.

Option: Give visual cues as students listen. Write the clock times 8:30 and 9:15. Point to the appropriate time when the words *early* and *late* are mentioned.

🎧 Listen again and repeat.

See "Listen again and repeat" on page T17a.

Option: Work on students' pronunciation. The glide from /ər/ to /l/ in the word *early* can be challenging. Pay attention to how the tongue moves up to touch the back of the front teeth as it glides from an /ər/ sound to an /l/ sound. Try to emphasize the open mouth on the /ər/ sound and the tongue touching the back of the upper front teeth on the /l/.

Additional Activity

Test comprehension. Write the two times on the board (8:30 and 9:15). Say *School is at 9:00.* Point to each time and ask *Early?* Invite a student to come up and point to the early time (8:30). Repeat the question for *late.* Repeat this procedure, using your class time to set the context.

Tapescript
1. early **2.** late

🎧 Look and listen.

See also "Look and listen" on page T9a.

➤ Set the scene. Write the hours 9:00–3:00 on the board. Hold the book up for the class to see. Point to the first picture and say *Hours: 9:00 to 3:00.*

➤ Play the cassette or read the tapescript aloud as many times as necessary.

Option: Give visual cues as students listen. Use mime and facial expressions to contrast the meaning of *Oh, good!* and *Oh, no!*

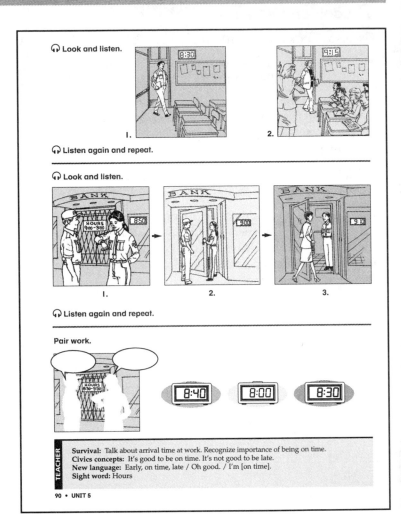

🎧 Look and listen.

🎧 Listen again and repeat.

🎧 Look and listen.

🎧 Listen again and repeat.

Pair work.

TEACHER

Survival: Talk about arrival time at work. Recognize importance of being on time.
Civics concepts: It's good to be on time. It's not good to be late.
New language: Early, on time, late / Oh good. / I'm [on time].
Sight word: Hours

90 • UNIT 5

Additional Activity

Test comprehension. Write the three times on the board (8:50, 9:00, and 9:10). Say *Hours 9:00–3:00.* Point to the three times and ask *Early?* Invite a student to come up and point to the early time (8:50). Repeat the question for *on time* and *late.* (You can repeat this procedure, using other business or store hours to set the context.)

🎧 Listen again and repeat.

See "Listen again and repeat" on page T9a.

Option: Focus on intonation. If you have worked on the repetition of a word with rising intonation to ask for feedback in previous lessons, reinforce your instruction with the question *8:50?*

Option: Focus on pronunciation. The /m/ sound in *I'm* often gets lost. Emphasize the sound by pressing your lips together. Have the class repeat after you several times.

Additional Activities

Activity 1: Practice new language. Put Vocabulary Cards 76–77 *(early, late)* on the rim of the board. Point to the *late* card and say *I'm late.* Hold up two fingers and repeat the sentence, touching a finger for each word. Then say, *I'm _____,* and point to the *early* card to elicit a new sentence *(I'm early).* Repeat until students can easily produce both sentences. There is no Vocabulary Card for *on time,* but the sentence *I'm on time* can be practiced in a similar manner.

Activity 2: Write several times on cards and distribute to students. Have students tell you the times on their cards. Recite back the time, sometimes correctly, sometimes incorrectly. Have students correct you when you are incorrect. *(No. It's [8:30].)* Have students practice this activity in pairs.

Tapescript

Conversation 1
A: What time is it?
B: It's 8:50.
A: 8:50? I'm early.

Conversation 2
A: What time is it?
B: 9:00.
A: 9:00? Oh, good! I'm on time.

Conversation 3
A: What time is it?
B: 9:10.
A: 9:10? Oh, no! I'm late.

Pair work.

➤ Model the Pair work. Point to the picture in the book and say *Hours: 8:30–5:30.* Write 8:40 on the board. Invite a student to the front of the class. Say *Excuse me. What time is it?* Point to the time on the board to elicit an answer. Then say *Oh, no! I'm late.* Repeat the conversation with 8:00 on the board. Then invite two other students to model the conversation for the class.

➤ Students talk about the time with a partner. Circulate around the classroom, offering help as needed.

Option: You may want to hand out cards with different times on them. Have students use these times in their conversations.

➤ Have several volunteer pairs act out their conversations in front of the class.

Pair work (possible student responses)

A: What time is it? **B:** It's 8:40 / 8:00 / 8:30.
A: 8:40 / 8:00 / 8:30? Oh, no! I'm late. / I'm early. / Oh, good! I'm on time.

If your students are ready . . .

Civics enrichment: Sensitize your students to U.S. standards of *early, on time,* and *late.* Place Vocabulary Cards 76 and 77 *(early, late)* on the board rim. Between the two cards, write the time 1:00 and say *School is at 1:00.* Then write some clock times above Picture Card 76 *(early)* to illustrate early times (for example, 12:30, 12:50). Repeat this procedure for *late.* Point to the clock time *(1:00)* and say *On time.* Show the class various clock times written on cards and ask the class to decide if the time is *early, late,* or *on time.* Place the card in the appropriate spot on the board rim. Be sure to include a few difficult ones (1:05, 1:10) to tease out student assumptions of what *on time* really means.

Literacy: Recognize capital D, B, P, and R.
More practice: Worksheet 47 (Teacher's Edition CD-ROM).

Circle.

See "Circle" on page T65.

Option: To focus students on each line as they work, have students place a blank white sheet of paper over the rest of the page.

Option: As students finish, pair them up to compare their answers. Together they can count the number of circled items per line. Circulate around the classroom, checking their work.

Additional Activities

Activity 1: Give each student a set of B, C, D, G, J, M, O, P, Q, R, S, U, V, and W Letter Cards. Have students lay the cards out face up on their desks. Show the class a card and call out its name. Students select the card from their own sets and hold it up for you to see.

Activity 2: Make multiple copies of the B, D, P, and R Letter Cards. Place one set on four desks—one card per desk. Deal out the remaining cards. Have students move around the classroom, placing their cards on the correct desks. Review with the class. Hold up each card in each pile and say its name.

Activity 3: Make multiple copies of the B, D, P, and R Letter Cards. Begin by lining up several of the same Letter Cards on the board rim, but turn some of the cards on their sides or upside down. Invite students to come to the board to correct the orientation of each card. For a greater challenge, combine different Letter Cards in the same line-up.

Worksheet Link: Worksheet 47

Assign the worksheet for homework or for in-class independent work. Follow the procedures above. Review students' work to make sure that students can recognize the difference between D, B, P, and R before going on to the next literacy lesson.

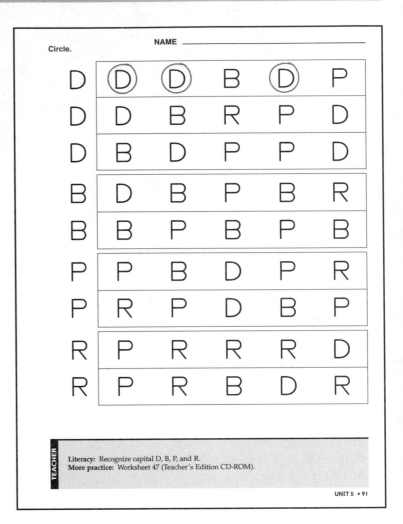

Circle.   NAME _____

Literacy: Recognize capital D, B, P, and R.
More practice: Worksheet 47 (Teacher's Edition CD-ROM).

UNIT 5 • 91

TEACHER

Literacy: Trace capital D, B, P, and R, using classic uppercase penmanship.
More practice: Worksheet 48 (Teacher's Edition CD-ROM).

Trace.

See also "Trace" on page T62.

➤ Model the writing of the letter D. Give special emphasis to the first stroke, as all the letters on this page begin with that first stroke.

Note: Early in learning the alphabet, students reverse their letters. Emphasize that all these capital letters have left vertical lines and curved loops on the right.

➤ You may want students to do the exercise one time through without a pencil so they can focus only on the strokes.

Additional Activities
Activity 1: Lightly draw multiple letters D, B, P, and R on the board. Invite individual students to the board to trace the letters with the correct stroke motions and sequences.

Activity 2: Give students the opportunity to correct you. Write the letter D on the board correctly. As you write, nod your head and say *Yes!* Then write the letter incorrectly with a stroke out of sequence or an incorrect bottom-to-top motion. As you write, shake your head and say *No!* Then invite students to say *Yes* or *No* as you write letters correctly and incorrectly. Repeat the activity several times, reviewing the writing of the letters B, P, and R.

Activity 3: Have students evaluate your handwriting. Write several examples of the letter B in a line on the board. Include one or two examples of a malformed B (for example, reversed, or with the curves not joining to the vertical line). Have students take turns coming up to the board to cross out or erase and rewrite the incorrectly formed letters. Repeat this procedure with the letters D, P, and R.

Activity 4: Make sure students have their name cards from the Welcome unit on their desks. Hold up the D Letter Card. Have students raise their hand if they have D in their name. Repeat with B, P, and R.

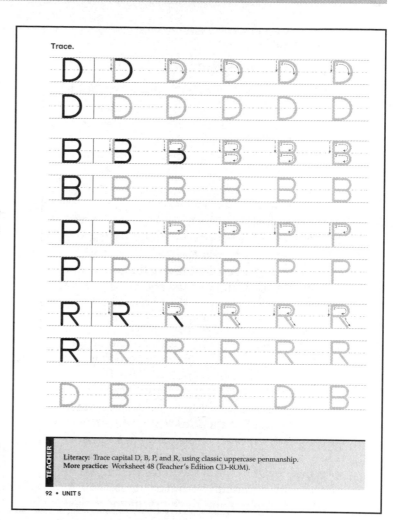

Trace.

Literacy: Trace capital D, B, P, and R, using classic uppercase penmanship.
More practice: Worksheet 48 (Teacher's Edition CD-ROM).

92 • UNIT 5

Worksheet Link: Worksheet 48
Assign the worksheet for in-class independent work. Circulate around the room observing students' strokes. Review students' work to make sure that they have mastered the strokes for these letters before going on to the next literacy lesson.

Survival: Learn vocabulary for places in the community. Talk about business hours.
Civics concept: Public offices and businesses keep regular hours.
New language: Bank, post office, office, factory, garage / the [bank] / open / closed / on [Saturday] / from [Monday] to [Friday].

🎧 Look and listen.

See "Look and listen" on page T17a.

Option: Hold up Vocabulary Card 78 *(bank)*. Say *Bank* and give the name of a common bank in the area. Elicit several other examples from students. Repeat this activity for Vocabulary Cards 80–82 *(office, factory, garage)*. This activity connects students' knowledge of their neighborhoods to the material taught in the classroom.

Additional Activities
Activity 1: Provide listening practice. Give each student a set of Vocabulary Cards 78–82 *(bank, post office, office, factory, garage)*. Have students lay the cards out face up on their desks. Call out a vocabulary word and have students select the card and hold it up for you to see.

Activity 2: Play a memory game. Students can do this activity individually or with a partner. Photocopy Vocabulary Cards 14, 16, 35–41, and 78–82 *(school, hotel, discount store, restaurant, supermarket, grocery store, drugstore, hardware store, bakery, bank, post office, office, factory, garage)*. Give each student or each pair of students one set. Have students close their eyes. Call out four vocabulary items in a row. Have students open their eyes and find the items in their set of cards. Repeat with different vocabulary items. This game reviews vocabulary and develops memory recall in English.

🎧 Listen again and repeat.

See "Listen again and repeat" on page T17a.

Option: Work on stress patterns. Demonstrate with hand motions the high/low pitch of multisyllabic nouns *(post office, office, factory, garage)*. Have students mirror the hand motions to reinforce the learning

Additional Activities
Activity 1: Provide speaking practice. With books open, call out a picture number and have students say the word. Repeat the process with several words. Then have students do this activity in pairs.

Activity 2: Bring to class several daily articles (paper, folders, letter with stamp, money, tools for a car) or

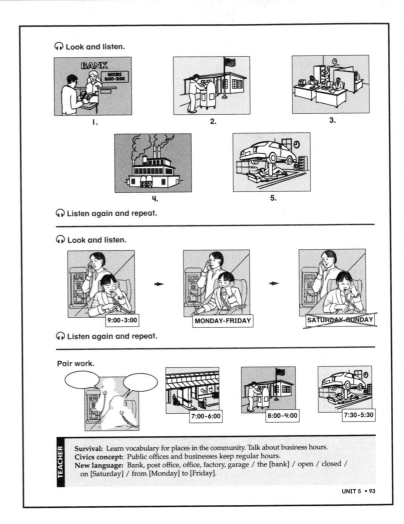

picture cut-outs of these items from magazines. Place one set of Vocabulary Cards 78–82 on 5 desks—one card per desk. Have students sort the items by placing them on the desk of the place they can be found. This activity links students' personal knowledge of these items with the new vocabulary in the lesson.

Tapescript
1. bank **2.** post office **3.** office **4.** factory **5.** garage

🎧 Look and listen.

See also "Look and listen" on page T9a.

➤ Introduce the vocabulary *open* and *closed*. Open the classroom door as you say *Open*. Then shut the door and say *Closed*. Repeat several times.

➤ Review days of the week. Show the class a monthly calendar. Point to each day of the week in order and have students say the days. Then, with your finger or a pen, circle the five days Monday–Friday and say *Monday **to** Friday*.

➤ Play the cassette or read the tapescript aloud as many times as necessary.

🎧 Listen again and repeat.

See "Listen again and repeat" on page T9a.

If your students are ready …

Civics enrichment 1: Take a walk around the block. Have students look at storefronts and try to identify signs with the hours of business. Read the signs aloud to the students.

Civics enrichment 2: Bring advertising fliers to class. Have students find the hours of operation.

Tapescript

A: When is the bank open?
B: It's open from nine to three.

A: From Monday to Friday?
B: Yes. From Monday to Friday.

A: What about Saturday and Sunday?
B: It's closed on Saturday and Sunday.

Pair work.

➤ Model the exercise. Place Vocabulary Cards 13, 79, and 82 (*supermarket, post office, garage*) on the rim of the board. Copy the business hours from the Student's Book onto the board above the corresponding cards. (Note that the Vocabulary Cards and business hours reflect the cues to the right of the Pair work picture.) Invite a student to the front of the class. Ask *When is the supermarket open?* Point to the hours above the Vocabulary Card to elicit an answer. Then ask *What about Saturday and Sunday?* If the student is confused, offer a possible response and repeat the question.

➤ Students talk with a partner about business hours. Circulate around the classroom, offering help as needed.

➤ Have several volunteer pairs act out their conversations in front of the class.

Additional Activity
For further practice, place more Vocabulary Cards of businesses (35–42, 78–82) on the board rim and write business hours above them. Using the information on the board as cues, have students circulate around the classroom, asking about the business hours.

Pair work (possible student responses)

A: When is the supermarket / post office / garage open? **B:** It's open from seven to six / from eight to four / from 7:30 to 5:30. **A:** From Monday to Friday? **B:** Yes. From Monday to Friday. **A:** What about Saturday and Sunday? **B:** The [post office] is open [from nine to three] on [Saturday] and it's closed on [Sunday].

Your students can also say . . .

1. A: (Unit 1:) Hi. / (Unit 2:) Excuse me. / Hello. / (Unit 5:) Good morning / afternoon / evening. When is the (Unit 2:) school / restaurant / parking lot / (Unit 4:) discount store / grocery store / drugstore / bakery / mall / (Unit 5:) bank / office / factory open? **B:** The [factory]? / It's open on [Monday] [from eight to five]. / It's closed on [Sunday].

2. A: (Unit 3:) I need directions. / How do I get to the [hospital]? **B:** Bus or subway? **A:** Bus, please. **B:** Sure. Take the [number 10] bus. **A:** Where do I get off? **B:** Get off in front of the [bank]. Turn right / left at the corner. / The [hospital] is on the corner / (Unit 2:) right there / next to the [parking lot] / (Unit 4:) around the corner / across from the [mall]. **A:** (Unit 1:) Thanks. / Thank you. **B:** You're welcome.

If your students are ready . . .

Civics enrichment: Have students investigate the operating hours of various businesses and public offices. Brainstorm the name and location of supermarkets, discount stores, drugstores, post offices, banks, schools, restaurants, and public offices in the community. Assign each student one place to visit (or call) to find out when it is open. When students report their information, write the hours on the board.

TEACHER

Authentic practice: Students listen to an authentic conversation in a public office and then complete listening and speaking tasks, providing true information about themselves.

🎧 Listen and circle.

See also "Listen and circle" on page T58.

➤ Show the class Vocabulary Card 78 *(bank)* and say *Bank.* Write the two sets of business hours, 9:00–3:00 and 9:00–1:00, on the board. Point to each set and say the hours.

➤ Play the cassette or read the tapescript aloud. Point to the times on the board as they are mentioned.

➤ Play the cassette or read the tapescript aloud again. Students circle the correct business hours.

Tapescript
A: Is the bank open on Saturday?
B: Saturday? Yes. Saturday, we're open from 9 to 1.
A: From 9 to 3?
B: No. On Saturday the bank's open from 9 to 1.

🎧 Look and listen.

See also "Look and listen" on page T22a.

➤ Set the scene. Hold the book up for the class to see. Point to the picture and say *School.*

Tapescript
A: Good morning. Welcome to the Main Street Adult School.
B: Thanks.
A: Please tell me your name and address.
B: Betty Bates. 10 B Street.
A: Could you repeat that please?
B: Yes. 10 B Street.
A: Thanks, Ms. Bates. Do you have any questions about the school?
B: Yes. When is school open?
A: School's open from 8 to 6.
B: Thank you very much.

🎧 Listen and respond.

See "Listen and respond" on page T22a.

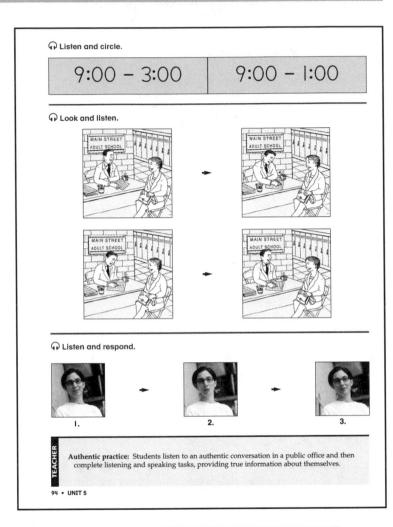

🎧 Listen and circle.

| 9:00 – 3:00 | 9:00 – 1:00 |

🎧 Look and listen.

🎧 Listen and respond.

1.　　2.　　3.

TEACHER **Authentic practice:** Students listen to an authentic conversation in a public office and then complete listening and speaking tasks, providing true information about themselves.

94 • UNIT 5

Tapescript
Prompt 1: Could you please tell me your name and address?
Prompt 2: Could you please repeat that?
Prompt 3: Do you have any questions?

Listen and respond **(possible student responses)**
Prompt 1: (Unit 1:) [student's name and address].
Prompt 2: [student repeats name and address].
Prompt 3: When is school / work? / When is the [factory] open? / (Unit 3:) How do I get to the [hospital]? / (Unit 2:) Where's the [school]? / What's the phone / telephone number / address?

TEACHER

Literacy review: Recognize and trace capital M, W, V, U, J, S, C, O, G, Q, D, B, P, R.
More practice: Worksheet 49 (Teacher's Edition CD-ROM).
Literacy test: Teacher's Edition CD-ROM.

Circle and trace.

See "Circle and trace" on page T77.

Option: To focus students on each line as they work, have students place a blank sheet of paper over the rest of the page. Students can move their sheets down as they finish each line.

Option: Go over the answers as a class. On each line, compare the target letter with each letter on the right. Say the letter names as you compare. Then have students count aloud the number of strokes to write the letter at the end of the line.

Note: Students have now learned to recognize and trace all the uppercase letters of the alphabet. Take some time to review all the letters.

Additional Activities

Activity 1: For review practice, make five sets of the Λ, H, K, M, N, V, W, X, Y and Z Letter Cards. Place one set on ten desks—one card per desk. Deal out the remaining cards. Students move around the classroom, placing matching cards on the correct desks. Review with the class. Hold up each card in each pile and say its name. You can repeat this activity, reviewing the letters E, F, T, I, L, B, D, P, and R.

Activity 2: Concentration. Photocopy multiple sets of any ten Letter Cards. Follow the instructions for Activity 2 on page T28.

Activity 3: Review the writing of any uppercase letter. Follow the instructions for Activity 1 on page T66.

Activity 4: Lightly draw capital letters on the board. Invite individual students to the board to trace the letters with the correct stroke motions and sequences.

Worksheet Link: Worksheet 49

Assign the worksheet for homework or for in-class independent work. Follow the procedures above. Review students' work to make sure that students can recognize the difference between M, W, V, J, U, S, C, O, G, Q, B, D, P, and R and have mastered the strokes for all 26 letters of the alphabet before finishing this unit.

NAME _____

Circle and trace.

M	M	W	Z	N	W	M	M
W	M	Z	W	A	V	W	W
V	A	Y	V	U	X	V	V
U	V	J	U	C	D	U	U
J	T	I	L	J	S	J	J
S	S	Z	C	U	J	S	S
C	D	U	J	C	S	C	C
O	O	G	Q	C	D	O	O
G	Q	O	C	D	G	G	G
Q	O	C	G	Q	D	Q	Q
D	C	B	P	O	D	D	D
B	B	D	P	E	R	B	B
P	D	B	P	R	F	P	P
R	K	P	R	A	B	R	R

Literacy review: Recognize and trace capital M, W, V, U, J, S, C, O, G, Q, D, B, P, R.
More practice: Worksheet 49 (Teacher's Edition CD-ROM).
Literacy test: Teacher's Edition CD-ROM.

UNIT 5 • 95

TEACHER

Survival / civics review: Point and name things in the pictures. Make statements about the pictures. Role-play conversations based on the pictures.
Tests: Teacher's Edition CD-ROM.

Talk about the pictures.

➤ Hold up the Student's Book and point to the places in the pictures. Have students name the places.

➤ Have students point and name places and things in the pictures with a partner.

Possible student responses
garage / house / car / apartment / mechanic

Role-play conversations.

➤ Point to the speech bubble of the woman in the upper left picture and say *Good morning. What time is it?* Then point to the man's speech bubble to elicit a student's response (*It's 8:20.*) Make sure the student's response corresponds to your *Good morning.* Gesture to reverse roles so the student asks you for the time.

➤ Model any of the other scenes.

➤ Students work with a partner to practice conversations appropriate to the contexts in the pictures.

➤ Ask pairs of students to present some of their conversations to the class.

**Role-play conversations
(possible student responses)**

(Woman asking man the time)

A: Good morning / afternoon / evening. / What time is it? **B:** It's 8:20 / 2:45 / 9:00 / 12:00. **A:** OK. (Unit 1:) Thanks. / Thank you.

(Husband and wife at home)

A: What time is it? **B:** It's 6:30. **A:** Oh, no! I'm late.

(Two mechanics)

A: Good morning. **B:** Good morning. / Hello. / Hi. **A:** What time is it? **B:** It's 7:20. **A:** Oh, no! I'm late!

Talk about the pictures. Role-play conversations.

TEACHER

Survival / civics review: Point and name things in the pictures. Make statements about the pictures. Role-play conversations based on the pictures.
Tests: Teacher's Edition CD-ROM.

96 • UNIT 5

LESSON PLAN FOR STUDENT'S PAGE 97

TEACHER

Literacy: Review tracing of capital letters in alphabetical order.
More practice: Worksheet 50 (Teacher's Edition CD-ROM).

Trace.

➤ On the board, model the strokes of each letter in the alphabet. To remind students of the correct sequence of strokes, count aloud as you do each stroke. Then have students follow along with their fingers in the air while watching you. Have everyone count the strokes aloud. When each letter is finished on the board, point to it and say its name.

Note: Since this page is a review, you may want to invite individual students to model the letters.

➤ Lightly write the alphabet on the board. One at a time, invite students to the board to trace the letters. Have the rest of the class follow along by tracing the strokes of the same letters with their fingers on their desktops.

➤ Have students trace each letter in their books. Circulate around the classroom, checking their work.

Option: You may want students to do the exercise one time through without a pencil so they focus only on the strokes.

Note: This is the time to review good writing practices. Make sure students' posture is forward facing and relaxed. Both arms should rest lightly on the edge of the desk. Show students how to position the paper properly, according to whether they are right- or left-handed. Make sure students are holding the pencil correctly and with appropriate pressure.

Additional Activities

Activity 1: Lightly draw sections of the alphabet on the board. Invite individual students to the board to trace the letters with the correct stroke sequences.

Activity 2: Give students the opportunity to correct you. Write any capital letter correctly on the board. As you write, nod your head and say *Yes!* Then write the letter incorrectly with an incorrect stroke direction or sequence. As you write, shake your head and

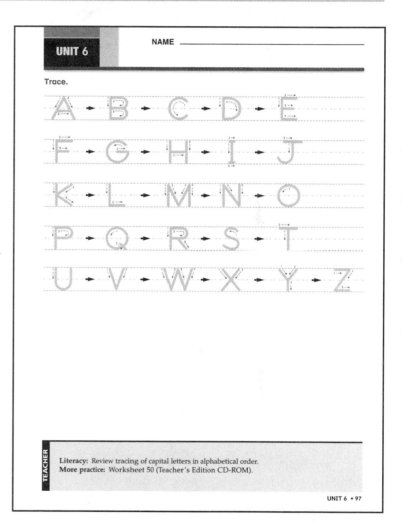

say *No!* Then invite students to say *Yes* or *No* as you write other letters correctly and incorrectly.

Worksheet Link: Worksheet 50

Assign the worksheet for homework or for in-class independent work. Follow the procedures above. Review students' work to make sure they have mastered the tracing of all capital letters before going on to the next lesson.

TEACHER

Literacy: Begin to understand concept that letters represent sounds. Recognize sound-symbol correspondence of M and B as initial sound of known words.

Note: Prior to this unit, students have learned two aspects of letters—that they have "names" to be used in spelling, and that they occur in a sequence—the alphabet. In this unit, students begin associating letters with their sound as opposed to their "names." This can be a difficult concept because these two aspects do not necessarily correspond (W, /w/). To aid in acquisition of this important reading concept, the letters have been associated with words that are known to the students.

🎧 Look and listen.

➤ Write a capital M on the board. Point to it and say *M*. Then make the /m/ sound.

➤ Play the cassette or read the tapescript as many times as necessary. Point to the pictures of *mall* and *medium* as they are spoken.

🎧 Listen again and repeat.

➤ Read the tapescript or play the cassette again. Have students repeat after each sound or word.

Option: Associate each letter sound with a word. Show Letter Card M and Vocabulary Card 60 (*medium*) and say *M, medium, /m/*. Have students repeat the chant. As they progress to reading and writing, these chants will be their mnemonic device for remembering letter sounds. Be certain to use one word for each phoneme you introduce.

If any students in the class have a name beginning with M, say *M, [name], /m/*. Have students repeat.

➤ Have students practice repeating after each sound or word until their pronunciation is error-free.

Option: Make sure students understand the mechanics in forming the /m/ sound. Encourage them to look at your mouth as you say it. Exaggerate the pressing motions of the lips. You can illustrate the length of /m/ by drawing your hand evenly from your mouth to the air as you say it. Have the class imitate you and produce a very long /m/ sound. To help students identify the voiced quality of /m/, have them place their hands on their throats or plug their ears as they say it.

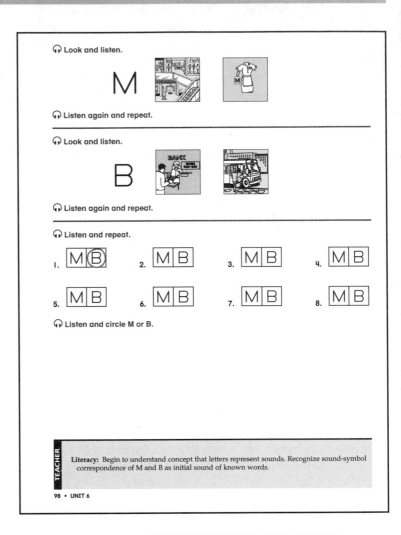

TEACHER **Literacy:** Begin to understand concept that letters represent sounds. Recognize sound-symbol correspondence of M and B as initial sound of known words.

98 • UNIT 6

Tapescript
/m/*, mall, medium

🎧 Look and listen.

➤ Write a capital B on the board. Point to it and say B. Then make the /b/ sound.

➤ Play the cassette or read the tapescript as many times as necessary. Point to the pictures of *bank* and *bus* as they are spoken.

*Here and throughout, initial consonants are vocalized with a schwa-like sound on the cassette so they can be heard and repeated by students. In in-class teacher demonstrations you may wish to eliminate the schwa-like sound and isolate the initial consonants.

🎧 Listen again and repeat.

Follow the procedures for the same type of exercise above.

Option: Associate each letter sound with a word. Show the Letter Card B, Vocabulary Card 78 (bank) and say B, bank, /b/. Have students repeat the chant.

If any students in the class have a name beginning with a B, say B, [name] /b/.

Option: Make sure students understand the mechanics in forming the /b/ sound. Encourage them to look at your mouth as you say it. Exaggerate how both lips meet evenly. You can illustrate the brevity of the /b/ sound by opening your fist quickly as you say it. Have the class imitate you. To help students identify the voiced quality of /b/, have them place their hands on their throats or plug their ears as they say it.

Tapescript
/b/, bank, bus

🎧 Listen and repeat.

➤ Play the cassette once. Students listen and repeat.

🎧 Listen and circle M or B.

➤ Model the exercise. Write the letters M and B on the board. Say *bakery* and then circle the letter B. Erase your circle and model again, this time saying *mechanic*. Circle the letter M.

➤ Read the tapescript or play the cassette. Students listen again and circle the letter that they hear.

Note: Students may have difficulty keeping track of the numbered items. Circulate around the room and check that they are on the right item, or supply students with a blank sheet of paper to cover the portion they are not working on.

Additional Activity

Have students identify letter sounds in words they know. Copy Letter Cards M and B and give to each student. Place on the board rim Vocabulary Cards 8, 9, 19, 41, 42, 62, 74, and 78 (*mechanic, babysitter, bus, bakery, mall, morning, month, bank*). Hold up a Vocabulary Card and say its name. Then ask *M? B?* Have students hold up the letter they hear. Repeat with different words.

Tapescript
1. /b/ 2. /m/ 3. bakery 4. mechanic 5. mall 6. bus 7. babysitter 8. medium

TEACHER

Survival: Learn names of a number of common foods and drinks.
New language: Chicken, meat, fish, cheese, bread, rice, pasta, fruit, milk, coffee, tea, juice, water, oil.

🎧 Look and listen.

See also "Look and listen" on page T17a.

➤ Hold up Vocabulary Cards 83–90 (*chicken, meat, fish, cheese, bread, rice, pasta, fruit*) for the class to see. See if students can identify any vocabulary they already know.

➤ Play the cassette or read the tapescript aloud as many times as necessary.

➤ Test comprehension. Say one of the vocabulary words and have students identify the number of the picture.

Additional Activity
Provide listening practice. Give each student a set of Vocabulary Cards 83–90 (*chicken, meat, fish, cheese, bread, rice, pasta, fruit*). Call out a vocabulary word and have students select the card and hold it up for you to see.

🎧 Listen again and repeat.

See "Listen again and repeat" on page T17a.

Option: Focus on the initial /tʃ/ sound of *chicken* and *cheese*. Illustrate that it is a plosive sound by placing a thin strip of paper in front of your mouth as you say the sound. Show how the paper reacts to the sound. Encourage students to practice with a piece of paper or even with their hands in front of their mouths so they can feel the burst of air.

Option: To get students to fully associate letters with sounds in words they know, place the Letter Cards M and B on the board rim. Say *meat* and point to the letter M. Say *bread* and point to the letter B.

Additional Activity
Provide speaking practice. With books open, call out a picture number and have students say the vocabulary word. Repeat the process with several words. Then have students do this activity with a partner.

Tapescript
1. chicken **2.** meat **3.** fish **4.** cheese **5.** bread **6.** rice **7.** pasta **8.** fruit

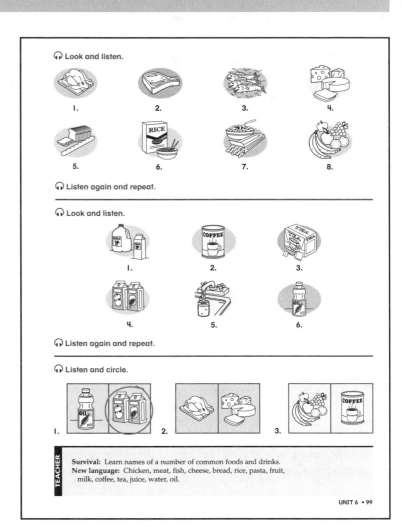

Survival: Learn names of a number of common foods and drinks.
New language: Chicken, meat, fish, cheese, bread, rice, pasta, fruit, milk, coffee, tea, juice, water, oil.

UNIT 6 • 99

🎧 Look and listen.

See also "Look and listen" on page T17a.

➤ Hold up Vocabulary Cards 91–96 (*milk, coffee, tea, juice, water, oil*) for the class to see. See if students can identify any vocabulary they already know.

➤ Play the cassette or read the tapescript aloud as many times as necessary.

Additional Activities
Activity 1: Test comprehension. Say one of the vocabulary words and have students identify the number of the picture.

Activity 2: Play a memory game. Photocopy Vocabulary Cards 83–96 (*chicken, meat, fish, cheese, bread, rice, pasta, fruit, milk, coffee, tea, juice, water, oil*). Give each student one set. Have students close their eyes. Call out four vocabulary items in a row. Have students open their eyes and find the items in their Vocabulary Card sets. Repeat with different vocabulary items. This game reviews vocabulary and develops memory recall in English.

🎧 Listen again and repeat.

See "Listen again and repeat" on page T17a.

Option: To get students to fully associate letters with sounds in words they know, place the Letter Card M on the board rim. Say *milk* and point to the letter M.

Additional Activity

Provide speaking practice. With books open, call out a picture number and have students say the vocabulary word. Repeat the process with several words. Then have students do this activity in pairs.

Tapescript
1. milk 2. coffee 3. tea 4. juice 5. water 6. oil

🎧 Listen and circle.

See "Listen and circle" on page T17a-b.

Additional Activity

Give each student a set of Vocabulary Cards 83–96 (*chicken, meat, fish, cheese, bread, rice, pasta, fruit, milk, coffee, tea, juice, water, oil*). Pairs of students sit facing each other. Student A chooses a card and says its name without showing the card to Student B. B finds the card in his own set. The two students then check their cards to make sure they match.

Tapescript
1. juice 2. cheese 3. fruit

If your students are ready . . .
Civics enrichment: Demonstrate that familiar foods are available in this country. Place on the board rim Vocabulary Cards 83–96. Bring supermarket advertising fliers to class. Have students look through the fliers with a partner. Show the class a Vocabulary Card and say its name. Have students look for that food in the flier and circle it. Repeat with other Vocabulary Cards.

NOTES

_____

_____

_____

_____

_____

_____

_____

_____

_____

_____

_____

_____

TEACHER

Survival: Ask for the location of foods in a grocery or supermarket.
Civics concepts: Supermarkets are organized by categories. Salespeople can tell you where each food is.
New language: Aisle [2].

🎧 Look and listen.

See also "Look and listen" on page T9a.

➤ Set the scene. Say *supermarket* and give several examples of supermarkets in your community. Hold the book up for the class to see. Point to the pictures and say *supermarket*.

➤ Write the numbers 1, 2, 3, 4, 5 on the board to represent the supermarket aisles. Place Vocabulary Card 96 *(oil)* under the number 2 and Vocabulary Card 92 *(coffee)* under number 5.

➤ Play the cassette or read the tapescript aloud as many times as necessary.

🎧 Listen again and repeat.

See "Listen again and repeat" on page T9a.

Additional Activities

Activity 1: Test comprehension. Ask *Where's the oil? Where's the coffee?* Students answer.

Activity 2: Practice forming questions. Put Vocabulary Cards 83–96 (food items) on the rim of the board. Ask *Where's the oil?* and point to the Vocabulary Card for *oil.* Ask the question again, but omit the word *oil* and point to a different Vocabulary Card to elicit a new question. Repeat this procedure until students can easily produce *Where* questions for many food items.

Activity 3: Place Vocabulary Cards 83–96 (food items) in clusters along the board rim. Write an aisle number above each group of food items. Ask *Where's the oil?* Gesture to the Vocabulary Card for *oil* and the aisle number above it to elicit a student response. Repeat this process with many different foods until everyone has had the opportunity to identify the location of a food item.

Tapescript

Conversation 1
A: Excuse me. Where's the oil?
B: The oil? The oil's in aisle 2.
A: Thanks.

Conversation 2
A: Excuse me. Where's the coffee?
B: The coffee's in aisle 5, across from the bread.

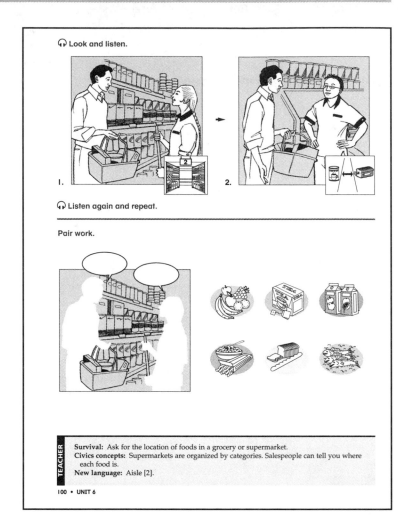

🎧 Look and listen.

🎧 Listen again and repeat.

Pair work.

TEACHER

Survival: Ask for the location of foods in a grocery or supermarket.
Civics concepts: Supermarkets are organized by categories. Salespeople can tell you where each food is.
New language: Aisle [2].

100 • UNIT 6

Pair work.

➤ Model the Pair work. Repeat Activity 3, above.

➤ Hand out copies of Vocabulary Cards 83–96. Students ask a partner for the location of food in a grocery store or supermarket.

➤ Have several volunteer pairs act out their conversations in front of the class.

NOTES

TEACHER

Literacy: Discriminate between M and B as initial sound of known words.
Recognize M and B.

🎧 Look and listen.

➤ Review the sound of the letter B. Write a capital B on the board. Point to it and say *B.* Then make the /b/ sound.

➤ Play the cassette or read the tapescript aloud as many times as necessary. Point to the pictures of *bus* and *bank* as they are spoken.

🎧 Listen again and repeat.

See "Listen again and repeat" on page T98a.

Tapescript
Bus, bank

🎧 Look and listen.

➤ Review the sound of the letter M. Write a capital M on the board. Point to it and say *M.* Then make the /m/ sound.

➤ Play the cassette or read the tapescript aloud as many times as necessary. Point to the pictures of *mall* and *mechanic* as they are spoken.

🎧 Listen again and repeat.

See "Listen again and repeat" on page T98a.

Tapescript
Mall, mechanic

🎧 Listen and repeat.

➤ With books closed, read the tapescript or play the cassette and have students repeat the words.

🎧 Listen and repeat.

➤ Play the cassette once. Students listen and repeat.

🎧 Listen and circle M or B.

See "Listen and circle M or B" on page T98b.

TI0I

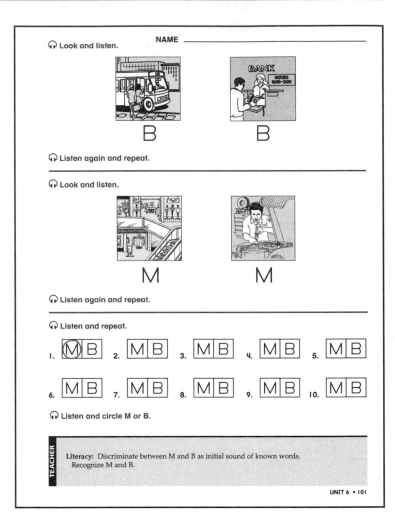

Literacy: Discriminate between M and B as initial sound of known words.
Recognize M and B.

UNIT 6 • 101

Option: To give students visual cues to the tapescript, place Vocabulary Cards 8, 9, 19, 41, 60, 78, 84, 91 (*mechanic, babysitter, bus, bakery, medium, bank, meat, milk*) on the board. Point to each card when its name is mentioned.

Additional Activity

Have students identify letter sounds in words they know. Copy Letter Cards M and B and give a set to each student. Have students hold up the letter they hear as you say the following vocabulary words: *morning, milk, March, May, babysitter, mall, bakery, bus, bus stop, meat, bread, medium,* and any students' names that begin with B or M.

Tapescript
1. March 2. May 3. babysitter 4. bakery 5. meat 6. bus 7. milk 8. bank 9. medium 10. mechanic

TEACHER

Literacy: Discriminate between M and B as initial sound of known words.
More practice: Worksheet 51 (Teacher's Edition CD-ROM).

Say the word. Circle M or B.

➤ Model the exercise. Write giant letters M and B on the board. Hold up Vocabulary Card 19 *(bus)* for the class to see. Point to the picture and say *bus*. Then circle the letter B on the board.

➤ Have students say each word and circle the correct letter.

Additional Activity

Hand out a set of M and B Letter Cards to each student. Hold for yourself a set of Vocabulary Cards 9, 19, 12, 41, 42, 60, 62, 84, 87, 91 *(babysitter, bus stop, bus, bakery, mall, medium, morning, meat, bread, milk).* Hold up a Vocabulary Card and gesture for students to say the word. Then ask *M? B?* Have students hold up the letter they hear.

Circle M and B.

➤ Model the M exercise. Copy the M line on the board. Point to the letter M and say *M*. Gesture to the entire word *MAY* and point to the first letter (M). Say *M* and circle it. Invite a student to come up to the board to circle the letter M in the next word.

Note: This is an opportunity to reinforce the correct counterclockwise direction to draw a circle.

➤ Have students work individually to complete the M line. Circulate around the class to check their work. Make sure students always move from the left to the right.

➤ Repeat each of the above steps for the B exercise.

Worksheet Link: Worksheet 51

Assign the worksheet for in-class independent work. Follow the procedures for the above activities. Circulate around the classroom, observing students as they work to make sure they understand the sound-symbol correspondence for M and B before going on to the next literacy lesson.

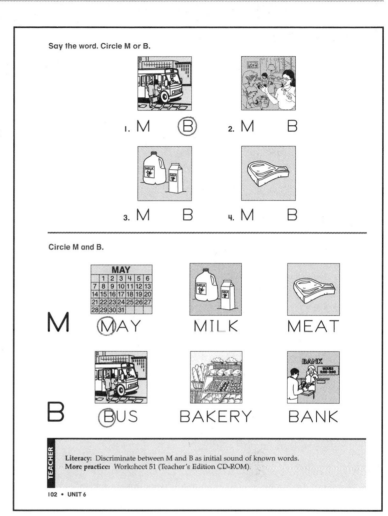

TEACHER

Survival: Order in a fast-food restaurant or cafeteria.
Civics concept: Order fast food from a server at the counter.
New language: Sandwich, cheese sandwich, chicken sandwich, fish sandwich, hamburger, salad, drink / Something to drink?

🎧 Look and listen.

See also "Look and listen" on page T17a.

➤ Before presenting the vocabulary, name several fast food restaurants in the neighborhood whose names students recognize. Then show the class Vocabulary Cards 97–103 *(sandwich, cheese sandwich, chicken sandwich, fish sandwich, hamburger, salad, drink)*. Point to each picture to see if students can identify any vocabulary they already know.

Additional Activity

Test comprehension. Say one of the vocabulary words and have students identify the number of the picture.

🎧 Listen again and repeat.

See "Listen again and repeat" on page T17a.

Option: Have students tap out the syllables of each word. This will help them enunciate all the syllables in *hamburger*.

Option: If you focused on the /tʃ/ sound in chicken and cheese on page 99a, reinforce your instruction with the word *sandwich*.

Option: The /w/ sound in *sandwich* can be challenging. To form the sound, pucker your lips as in a kiss.

Additional Activities

Activity 1: Demonstrate with hand motions the high/low pitch of multisyllabic nouns *(chicken, sandwich, salad, hamburger)*.

Activity 2: Play a memory game. Select ten Vocabulary Cards from the vocabulary presented on pages 99 and 103. (Vocabulary Cards 83–96, 97–103.) Give each student one set of cards. Have students close their eyes. Call out four vocabulary items in a row. Have students open their eyes and find the items in their Vocabulary Card sets.

Activity 3: Provide speaking practice. With books open, call out a picture number and have students say the vocabulary word. Repeat the process with several words. Then have students do this activity in pairs.

T103a

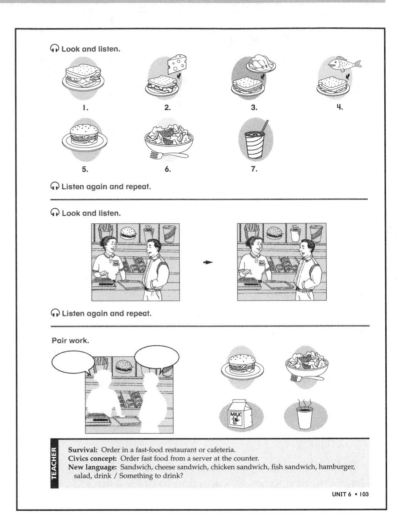

Activity 4: Concentration. Copy Vocabulary Cards 83–96 and 97–103. Follow the instructions for Activity 2 on page T28.

Tapescript
1. sandwich **2.** cheese sandwich **3.** chicken sandwich **4.** fish sandwich **5.** hamburger **6.** salad **7.** drink

🎧 Look and listen.

See also "Look and listen" on page T9a.

➤ Set the scene. Name several fast food restaurants in the neighborhood whose names students recognize.

➤ Play the cassette or read the tapescript aloud as many times as necessary.

🎧 Listen again and repeat.

See "Listen again and repeat" on page T9a.

Additional Activity

Practice new language. Ask the question *Something to drink?* from the conversation. Hold up three fingers and ask the question again, touching a finger for each word. Repeat, but omit saying one word. Point to the finger that represents the missing word. Have students say the missing word. Repeat this procedure, omitting different words from the question.

Tapescript

A: Can I help you?
B: Yes, a hamburger, please.

A: Something to drink?
B: Coffee, please.

Pair work.

➤ Model the Pair work. Place Vocabulary Cards 91–95 and 97–102 (*milk, coffee, tea, juice, water, sandwich, cheese sandwich, chicken sandwich, fish sandwich, hamburger, salad*) on the rim of the board. Group the cards into two groups—foods and drinks. Invite a student to the front of the class. Ask *Can I help you?* Gesture toward the food cards to elicit a response. Then ask *Something to drink?* Then invite two other students to model the conversation for the class.

➤ Copy and distribute Vocabulary Cards 91–95 and 97–102. Students practice ordering food in a fast food restaurant. Circulate around the classroom, offering help as needed.

➤ Have several volunteer pairs act out their conversations in front of the class.

Pair work (possible student responses)

A: Can I help you? **B:** Yes, a hamburger / a salad, please. **A:** Something to drink? **B:** Milk / Coffee, please.

Your students can also say . . .

a cheese sandwich / a chicken sandwich / a fish sandwich / juice / tea / water

---

NOTES

TEACHER

Survival: Order food. Clarify an order in response to questions.
Civics concept: The server wants you to get what you'd like.
New language: Certainly. / What kind of [sandwich]? / Anything else? /That's all.

🎧 Look and listen.

See also "Look and listen" on page T9a.

➤ Set the scene. Hold the book up for the class to see. Point to the pictures and say *restaurant*. Show Vocabulary Cards 98 and 91 *(cheese sandwich, milk)* and say the vocabulary words.

➤ Play the cassette or read the tapescript aloud as many times as necessary.

Option: Introduce the word *certainly*. To illustrate that *certainly* is similar in meaning to *sure* and *OK*, repeat the three expressions in a row. Encourage students to practice pronouncing *certainly*. Have them tap out the syllables.

Additional Activity
Activity 1: Provide speaking practice. Place Vocabulary Cards 98–100 *(cheese sandwich, chicken sandwich, fish sandwich)* on the board rim. Hold up a card and ask *What kind of sandwich?* Elicit the response. Repeat with the other Vocabulary Cards.

Activity 2: Provide more speaking practice. Place Vocabulary Cards 91–95 *(milk, coffee, tea, juice, water)* on the board rim. Ask *Something to drink?* and motion to the Vocabulary Cards to elicit a response.

🎧 Listen again and repeat.

See "Listen again and repeat" on page T9a.

Option: Focus on intonation. If you have worked on the rising intonation of *yes/no* questions in previous lessons, reinforce your instruction with the questions *Can I help you? Something to drink? Anything else?*

Additional Activity
Practice using *please.* Say *A sandwich, please.* Hold up three fingers and say the sentence again, touching a finger for each word, and emphasize the word *please.* Repeat the procedure with the phrases *Milk, please. A Cheese sandwich, please. Yes, please.* Then say one of the phrases again and omit the word *please.* Point to the finger that represents *please.* Have students say *please.*

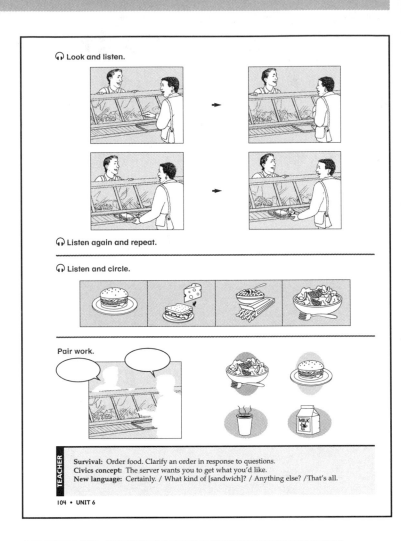

🎧 Look and listen.

🎧 Listen again and repeat.

🎧 Listen and circle.

Pair work.

TEACHER
Survival: Order food. Clarify an order in response to questions.
Civics concept: The server wants you to get what you'd like.
New language: Certainly. / What kind of [sandwich]? / Anything else? /That's all.

104 • UNIT 6

If your students are ready . . .

Civics enrichment: Teach *Yes, please* and *No, thanks.* Shake your head and say *No, thanks.* Have students imitate you. Nod your head and say *Yes, please.* Have students imitate you. Then prompt students to say the phrases by shaking or nodding your head. This exercise helps students associate *yes* with *please* and *no* with *thanks* as it reinforces the accompanying body language.

🎧 Listen and circle.

➤ Review the vocabulary. Tape Vocabulary Cards 101, 98, 89, 102 (*hamburger, cheese sandwich, pasta, salad*) on the board. Point to each Vocabulary Card and have students say the vocabulary word.

➤ Read the tapescript or play the cassette one time. When the conversation has finished, point to the four Vocabulary Cards. Students listen again. Then begin to draw a circle around the first card. Look to the class and ask *Yes? No?* Proceed in the same manner with all four cards. When students have identified the two foods (*cheese sandwich, salad*), have them circle those pictures in the Student's Book.

Additional Activity

Place Vocabulary Cards 89–95, 98–100 (*pasta, fruit, milk, coffee, tea, juice, water, cheese sandwich, chicken sandwich, fish sandwich*) on the board rim. Invite a student to the board. Request food, for example—*A chicken sandwich, a salad, and milk, please*—and have the student pick up the cards that you have requested.

Pair work.

➤ Model the Pair work. Place Vocabulary Cards 91–95, 97–102 (*milk, coffee, tea, juice, water, sandwich, cheese sandwich, chicken sandwich, fish sandwich, hamburger, salad*) on the board. Invite a student to the front of the class and ask *Can I help you?* Gesture toward the food cards to elicit a response. Depending on the student's response, ask *What kind of [sandwich]?* or *Something to drink?* or *Anything else?* When you have finished, invite two other students to model the conversation for the class.

➤ Students use Vocabulary Cards to practice ordering food and clarifying orders with a partner.

➤ Have several volunteer pairs act out their conversations in front of the class.

Additional Activity

Stand in front of the board with all the food item Vocabulary Cards on the rim. Have students take turns coming up to you and requesting the food items on the Cards. Feel free to expand the language as much as possible.

TEACHER

Literacy: Recognize sound-symbol correspondence of P and F as initial sound of known and unknown words.

🎧 Look and listen.

See "Look and listen" on page T98a.

🎧 Listen again and repeat.

See "Listen again and repeat" on page T98a.

Option: Use Letter Card P and Vocabulary Card 48 *(pants)* to present the chant *P, pants, /p/.*

If any students in the class have a name beginning with a P, say *P, [name], /p/.* Have the class repeat.

Option: Exaggerate the popping motion of the lips in forming the /p/ sound. Illustrate the popping sound by opening your fist quickly as you say it. You can also illustrate the sound by placing a thin strip of paper in front of your mouth as you say /p/.

To help students identify the unvoiced quality of /p/, have them place their hands on their throats or cover their ears as they say it. Have students contrast the voiceless /p/ with the voiced /b/.

Tapescript
/p/, pasta, pants

🎧 Look and listen.

See "Look and listen" on page T98a.

🎧 Listen again and repeat.

See "Listen again and repeat" on page T98a.

Option: Use Letter Card F and Vocabulary Card 85 *(fish)* to present the chant *F, fish, /f/.*

If any students in the class have a name beginning with an F, say *F, [name], /f/.* Have the class repeat.

Option: Exaggerate how the top teeth touch the bottom lip when forming the /f/ sound. Have the class imitate you and produce a very long /f/ sound. To help students identify the voiceless quality of /f/, have them place their hands on their throats or cover their ears as they say it.

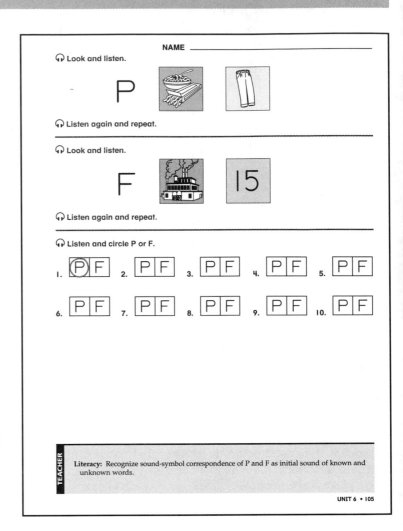

Tapescript
/f/, factory, fifteen

🎧 Listen and circle P or F.

See also "Listen and circle M or B" on page T98b.

➤ Model the exercise with the words *pasta* and *fire.*

Additional Activity

Hand out a set of P and F Letter Cards to each student. Read the tapescript in a scrambled order and have students hold up the letter they hear.

Tapescript
1. /p/ **2.** /f/ **3.** fast **4.** past **5.** pat **6.** fat **7.** fin **8.** pin **9.** pine **10.** fine

TEACHER

Literacy: Discriminate between P and F as initial sound of known words.
Recognize letters P and F.
More practice: Worksheet 52 (Teacher's Edition CD-ROM).

🎧 Listen and repeat.

➤ With books closed, read the tapescript or play the cassette and have students repeat the words.

🎧 Listen and circle P or F.

See "Listen and circle M or B" on page T98b.

➤ Model the exercise with the words *pasta* and *fish*.

Option: To give students visual cues to the tapescript, place Vocabulary Cards 48, 85, 28, 89 *(pants, fish, fire, pasta)* and Number Cards 14 and 15 on the board rim. Point to each card when its name is mentioned.

Additional Activities

Activity 1: Concentration. For each pair of students, photocopy the following two sets of cards:
Set 1: Vocabulary Cards 17, 28, 29, 48, 79, 89 *(parking lot, fire, fire truck, pants, post office, pasta)* and Number Cards 14 and 50. (These numbers begin with the letter F.)
Set 2: Four copies of the Letter Card F and four copies of the Letter Card P.

Give each pair of students Set 1 and Set 2. Students place the cards face down on a desk. Student A flips over a card from Set 1, says the word, and then flips over a card from Set 2 and says the letter. If the cards match, A removes the cards from the game. If the cards do not match, A flips the cards over face down in their original position. The partners take turns. Make sure students say the word, number, or letter every time they flip over a card and that they keep the cards in their original position.

Activity 2: The significant difference between /b/ and /p/ is that the former is voiced and the latter is unvoiced. With students' hands to their throats or their ears covered, drill the pronunciation of the two sounds. Then hold up Vocabulary Cards 9, 17, 19, 48, 78, 89 *(babysitter, parking lot, bus, pants, bank, pasta)* for students to say the words.

Tapescript

1. /p/ **2.** /f/ **3.** pants **4.** fish **5.** fifteen **6.** pasta
7. fourteen **8.** fire

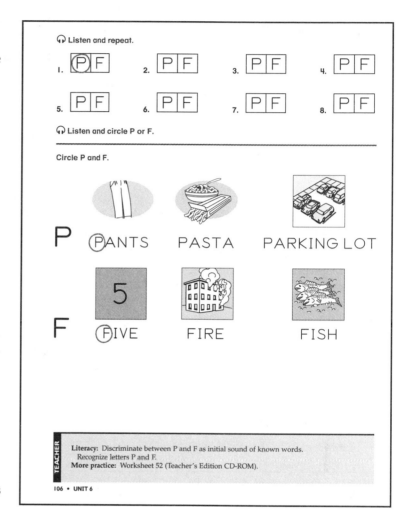

Circle the letters P and F.

See "Circle M and B" on page T102.

Additional Activity

Review letter names. Give each student a set of B, F, M, and P Letter Cards. Have students take turns calling out letter names as the class listens and holds up the corresponding card.

Worksheet Link: Worksheet 52

Assign the worksheet for in-class independent work. Follow the procedures for similar activities on this page and on page T102.

Survival: Order food items by size. Recognize S, M, L as representing *small, medium, large*.
Civics concept: Restaurant food can often be ordered by size.
New language: Fries / small, medium, large (for foods).

🎧 Look and listen.

See also "Look and listen" on page T9a.

➤ Show Vocabulary Card 104 to introduce the new vocabulary item *fries*. With Vocabulary Cards 59–61, review the vocabulary *small, medium,* and *large*.

➤ Hold the Student's Book up for the class to see. Point to items in the menu and say their names. Have students follow along in their books.

➤ Play the cassette or read the tapescript aloud as many times as necessary.

Option: To give students visual cues to the tapescript, place Vocabulary Cards 99, 104, 91, 59–61 (*chicken sandwich, fries, milk, small, medium, large*) on the board rim. Point to each card when its word is mentioned.

Additional Activity

Test comprehension. Pointing to the woman in the picture, ask *Small, medium, or large fries?*

🎧 Listen again and repeat.

See "Listen again and repeat" on page T9a.

Tapescript
A: Can I help you?
B: A chicken sandwich and fries, please.
A: Small, medium, or large fries?
B: Large fries.
A: Something to drink?
B: Milk please.

Pair work.

➤ Model the Pair work. Place Vocabulary Cards 91–95, 98–104 (*milk, coffee, tea, juice, water, cheese sandwich, chicken sandwich, fish sandwich, hamburger, salad, drink, fries*) on the rim of the board. Write the letters S, M, L on the board to represent sizes. Invite a student to the front of the class. Ask *Can I help you?* Gesture toward the food cards to elicit a response. Then ask, if appropriate, *Small, medium, or large _____?* or *What size?* Gesture to the S, M, L letters on the board to elicit a response.

🎧 Look and listen.

🎧 Listen again and repeat.

Pair work.

TEACHER

Survival: Order food items by size. Recognize S, M, L as representing *small, medium, large*.
Civics concept: Restaurant food can often be ordered by size.
New language: Fries / small, medium, large (for foods).

UNIT 6 • 107

➤ Students practice with a partner ordering food items by size. Circulate around the classroom, offering help as needed.

➤ Have several volunteer pairs act out their conversations in front of the class.

Pair work (possible student responses)
A: Can I help you? **B:** Yes, a cheese sandwich / a fish sandwich / a chicken sandwich / a hamburger, please. **A:** Something to drink? **B:** Yes, milk / coffee. **A:** What size? **B:** Small. / Medium. / Large.
Your students can also say . . .
A: Anything else? **B:** A salad / Large fries, please. And juice / tea / water.

TEACHER

Survival: Learn names of meals and foods commonly associated with them.
Civics concept: Certain foods are traditional for meals in this culture.
New language: Breakfast, lunch, dinner, toast, butter, jam, eggs, cereal, soup, vegetables, cake, ice cream.

🎧 Look and listen.

See also "Look and listen" on page T17a.

➤ Write the times *7:30, 12:15*, and *6:45* on the board. Point to each and say the respective time of day: *morning, afternoon, evening.* (Note that *evening* has not yet been taught, but the meaning should be clear from context. The phrase *Good evening* was presented on page 82.)

➤ Play the cassette or read the tapescript aloud as many times as necessary.

🎧 Listen again and repeat.

See "Listen again and repeat" on page T17a.

Option: Work on students' pronunciation. The /br/ consonant blend in *breakfast* can be challenging. Remind students to keep their tongue from touching the back of the teeth by drawing your hand backwards.

Option: If you have worked on the /tʃ/ sound in previous lessons, reinforce your instruction with the pronunciation of the word *lunch*.

Additional Activity

Test comprehension. Place the Vocabulary Cards 62–64 (*morning, afternoon, night*) on the board rim. Point to the night card and ask *Breakfast? Yes? No?* Wait for student response. Repeat this procedure several times, alternating correct matches (*morning/ breakfast*) with incorrect matches (*night/lunch*).

Tapescript
1. breakfast **2.** lunch **3.** dinner

🎧 Look and listen.

See "Look and listen" on page T17a.

Additional Activities

Activity 1: Test comprehension. Say a word and have students tell you the picture number in their books.

Activity 2: Play a memory game. Photocopy Vocabulary Cards 108-116 (all food vocabulary on this page) and give each student one set. Have stu-

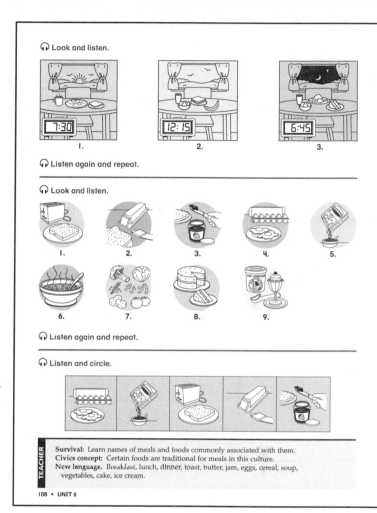

🎧 Look and listen.

1. 2. 3.

🎧 Listen again and repeat.

🎧 Look and listen.

1. 2. 3. 4. 5.

6. 7. 8. 9.

🎧 Listen again and repeat.

🎧 Listen and circle.

TEACHER
Survival: Learn names of meals and foods commonly associated with them.
Civics concept: Certain foods are traditional for meals in this culture.
New language: Breakfast, lunch, dinner, toast, butter, jam, eggs, cereal, soup, vegetables, cake, ice cream.

108 • UNIT 6

dents close their eyes. Call out four vocabulary items in a row. Have students open their eyes and find the items in their Vocabulary Card sets. Repeat with different vocabulary items.

🎧 Listen again and repeat.

See "Listen again and repeat" on page T17a.

Additional Activities

Activity 1: Demonstrate with hand motions the high/low pitch of multisyllabic nouns (*cereal, ice cream, vegetables*). Have students mirror the hand motions to reinforce the learning.

(Continued on page T108b.)

Activity 2: Concentration. Photocopy Vocabulary Cards 108–116. Give each pair of students two sets of Vocabulary Cards. Follow the instructions for Activity 2 on page T28.

Activity 3: Tape Vocabulary Cards 105–107 *(breakfast, lunch, dinner)* on the board. Show the class different food Vocabulary Cards. Have students say the food and indicate which meal to place it under.

> | **Tapescript** |
> | --- |
> | 1. toast 2. butter 3. jam 4. eggs 5. cereal |
> | 6. soup 7. vegetables 8. cake 9. ice cream |

🎧 Listen and circle.

➤ Review the vocabulary. Tape Vocabulary Cards 111, 112, 108, 109, 110 *(eggs, cereal, toast, butter, jam)* on the board. Point to each Vocabulary Card and have students say the word.

➤ Read the tapescript or play the cassette one time. When the conversation has finished, point to the five Vocabulary Cards. Students listen again. Then begin to draw a circle around the first card. Look to the class and ask *Yes? No?* Proceed in the same manner with all five cards. When students have identified the three foods *(eggs, toast, butter),* have them circle those pictures in the Student's Book.

> | **Tapescript** |
> | --- |
> | **A:** Mom. I want eggs for breakfast. |
> | **B:** Anything else? |
> | **A:** Yes. Toast and butter. |
> | **B:** Say please. |
> | **A:** Please, Mom? |
> | **B:** Sure! |

NOTES

_____

_____

_____

_____

_____

_____

_____

_____

_____

_____

_____

_____

_____

_____

_____

_____

_____

TEACHER

Literacy: Recognize sound-symbol correspondence of letter V.
Discriminate between V and F as initial sound of known and unknown words.
More practice: Worksheet 53 (Teacher's Edition CD-ROM).

🎧 Look and listen.

See "Look and listen" on page T98a.

🎧 Listen again and repeat.

See "Listen again and repeat" on page T98a.

Option: Use Letter Card V and Vocabulary Card 114 (*vegetables*) to present the chant *V, vegetables, /v/*.

Option: Exaggerate how the top teeth touch the bottom lip when forming the /v/ sound. The top teeth must be visible to form this sound. Have the class imitate you and produce a very long /v/ sound (as long as your breath). To help students identify the voiced quality of /v/, have them place their hands on their throats or cover their ears as they say it. Have students contrast the /f/ to /v/. The significant difference between these two sounds is that /f/ is unvoiced and /v/ is voiced.

Tapescript
/v/, /v/, vegetables

🎧 Look and listen.

See "Look and listen" on page T98a.

🎧 Listen again and repeat.

See "Listen again and repeat" on page T98a.

Tapescript
/f/, /f/, fifteen

🎧 Listen and circle V or F.

See also "Listen and circle" on page T98b.

Additional Activities:
Activity 1: Provide listening practice. Hand out a set of V and F Letter Cards to each student. Read words from the tapescript in a scrambled order and have students hold up the letter they hear.

Activity 2: Make sure students make the distinction between V and F. Hand each student a V and F Letter

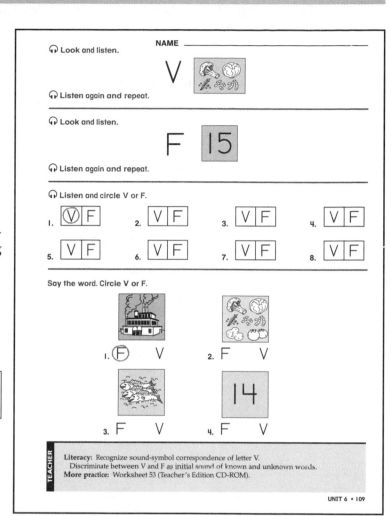

Card. Make the sound of one of the letters. Have students show the letter they hear. Then have students take turns producing the sounds as the rest of class listens and indicates the letter they hear.

Tapescript
1. vat **2.** fat **3.** vine **4.** fine **5.** fan **6.** van **7.** file **8.** vile

Say the word. Circle V or F.

See "Say the word. Circle M or B" on page T102.

Option: Contrast /b/ and /v/. The significant difference between /b/ and /v/ is that /b/ is plosive and

(Continued on page T109b.)

/v/ is continuous. Illustrate the popping sound of /b/ by opening your fist quickly. Contrast this to the long sound of /v/ (as long as your breath).

Additional Activities
Activity 1: Concentration. For each pair of students, photocopy the following two sets of cards:
Set 1: Vocabulary Cards 28, 78, 84, 89, 114 (*fire, bank, meat, pasta, vegetables*).
Set 2: Letter Cards B, F, M, P, and V.

Follow the instructions for Activity 1 on page T106.

Activity 2: Give each student a set of B, F, M, P, and V Letter Cards. Call out a letter sound or a letter name. Have students select the card from their own sets and hold it up for you to see.

Worksheet Link: Worksheet 53
Assign the worksheet for in-class independent work. Follow the procedures for similar activities on this page and on page T106. Circulate around the classroom as students work to make sure they understand the sound-symbol correspondence for V and F.

NOTES

_____

_____

_____

_____

_____

_____

_____

_____

_____

_____

_____

_____

_____

_____

_____

_____

_____

_____

_____

_____

_____

TEACHER

Literacy: Recognize sound-symbol correspondence of letter H. Trace letter H. Discriminate between H, F, and V as initial sound of known words.
More practice: Worksheet 54 (Teacher's Edition CD-ROM).

🎧 Look and listen.

See "Look and listen" on page T98a.

🎧 Listen again and repeat.

See "Listen again and repeat" on page T98a.

Option: Use Letter Card H and Vocabulary Card 31 (*hospital*) to present the chant *H, hospital, /h/.*

Option: Exaggerate how the mouth drops open in a relaxed position when forming the /h/ sound. Have the class imitate you and produce a very long /h/ sound. Have students place their hands in front of their mouths to feel the slow release of air in making the /h/ sound. To help students identify the un-voiced quality of /h/, have them place their hands on their throats or cover their ears as they say it.

Tapescript
/h/, /h/, hotel, highway, hospital

Say the word. Trace the letter.

➤ Count the strokes out loud as you write the letter H on the board.

➤ Have students point to each picture, say its name, and then trace the letter H.

Say the word. Circle the letter.

See "Say the word. Circle M or B" on page T102.

Additional Activities

Activity 1: Have students identify letter sounds in words they know. Hand out a set of B, F, H, M, P, V Letter Cards to each student. Hold for yourself a set of Vocabulary Cards 9, 17, 19, 31, 42, 84, 85, 89, 91, 101, 114 (*babysitter, parking lot, bus, hospital, mall, meat, fish, pasta, milk, hamburger, vegetables*) and Number Cards 5, 14, 40, and 50. (These numbers all begin with the letter F.) Hold up a Vocabulary or Number card. Students say the word and then hold up the letter they hear.

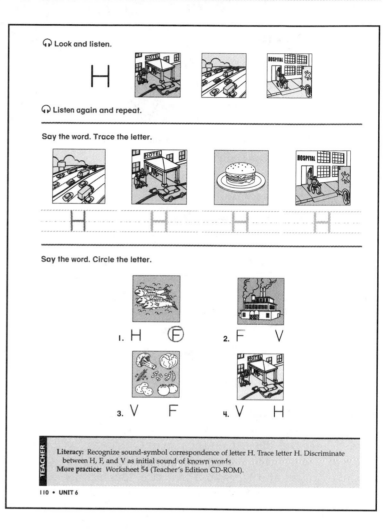

Activity 2: Write known words beginning with H on the board in capital letters (*hotel, highway, hospital, hamburger*). Have students take turns coming up to the board and circling the initial H.

Worksheet Link: Worksheet 54

Assign the worksheet for in-class independent work. Follow the procedures for similar activities on this page and on page T102. Circulate to make sure that students understand the sound-symbol correspondence for the letter H.

Survival: Exchange information about what one eats for various meals. Politely express likes and dislikes. Agree and disagree.
Civics concepts: It's expected that people's tastes vary. It's OK to compare tastes.
New language: What do you eat for [breakfast]? / I eat [eggs]. / I like [coffee]. / Not me. / Me too.

🎧 Look and Listen.

See also "Look and listen" on page T9a.

➤ Hold up a Vocabulary Card of a food you like. Rub your stomach, smile, and say *For breakfast, I eat [cereal].* Give another example.

➤ Play the cassette or read the tapescript aloud as many times as necessary.

Option: Place Vocabulary Cards 111, 108, 110 *(eggs, toast, jam)* on the board rim. Point to the Vocabulary Cards as they are mentioned in the conversation.

Additional Activity
Test comprehension. Hold the Student's Book up for the class to see. Point to one of the people in the picture and ask *Eggs? Yes? No?* Point to the other person and ask *Toast and jam? Yes? No?*

🎧 Listen again and repeat.

See "Listen again and repeat" on page T9a.

Additional Activities
Activity 1: Practice new language. Put Vocabulary Cards 83–90 and 108–116 on the rim of the board. Say *I eat eggs* and point to the *eggs* Vocabulary Card. Hold up three fingers and repeat the sentence, touching a finger for each word. Say the sentence again, but omit *eggs* and point to a different Vocabulary Card to elicit a new food. Repeat this procedure until students can easily produce the sentence with many foods. (Note that the cards used for this activity are noncount or plural count nouns, in order to focus on the conversational language, rather than the grammar of forming plurals.)

Activity 2: Place Vocabulary Cards 83–90, and 108–116 on the board rim. Hold up Vocabulary Card 105 *(breakfast)* and say *For breakfast, I eat [eggs]* and point to the corresponding Vocabulary Card. Repeat the sentence *I eat _____ for all the foods you eat for breakfast. Then ask a student *What about you?* Go around the room, giving every student a chance to say what he or she eats for breakfast. Repeat with the meals *lunch* and *dinner*.

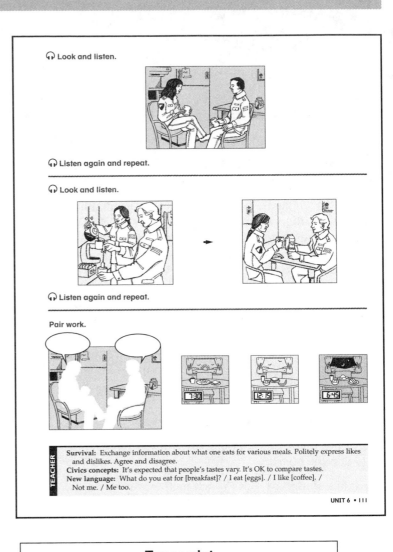

Tapescript
A: What do you eat for breakfast?
B: I eat eggs. What about you?
A: I eat toast and jam.

🎧 Look and listen.

See also "Look and listen" on page T9a.

➤ Hold up a Vocabulary Card of a food you like. Rub your stomach, smile, and say *I like [food].* Give another example.

➤ Play the cassette or read the tapescript aloud as many times as necessary.

Option: Place Vocabulary Cards 92, 93, 91 (*coffee, tea, milk*) on the board rim. Point to the Vocabulary Cards as they are mentioned in the conversation. Nod your head and smile when the speakers mention foods they like. Shake your head and frown when the speaker says *Not me.*

Option: Introduce the downward intonation of *Not me!* Accompany it with a shake of your head and small frown. Introduce the sing-song intonation of *I like coffee!* and *Me too.* Accompany the expressions with a nod of the head and a smile.

🎧 Listen again and repeat.

See "Listen again and repeat" on page T9a.

Additional Activity

Practice new language. Put Vocabulary Cards 83–90 and 108–116 (food items) on the rim of the board. Say *I like milk* and point to the corresponding Vocabulary Card. Hold up three fingers and repeat, touching a finger for each word. Say it again, but omit *milk* and point to a different Vocabulary Card to elicit a new sentence. Repeat this procedure until students can easily produce sentences about many food items.

Tapescript

A: I like coffee.
B: Not me. I like tea.

A: And what about milk?
B: I like milk.
A: Me too.

Pair work.

➤ Model the Pair work. Place Vocabulary Cards 83–90 and 108–116 on the rim of the board. Say *I like [tea]*. Then approach a student and ask *What about you?* Listen to the student's response [Not me./Me too.] Repeat with other students.

➤ Students talk with a partner about what they like to eat. Circulate around the classroom, offering help as needed.

➤ Have several volunteer pairs act out their conversations in front of the class.

Pair work (possible student responses)

A: What do you eat for breakfast? **B:** I eat eggs. What about you? / And you? **A:** I eat cereal. I like coffee. **B:** Me too. / Not me. I like tea.

Your students can also say . . .

A: What do you eat for lunch / dinner? **B:** I eat toast / butter / jam / soup / fruit / bread / rice / pasta / salad / meat / vegetables / small / medium / large fries / a hamburger / a chicken / fish / cheese sandwich. **A:** Anything else? **B:** Cake and ice cream.

Authentic practice: Students listen to an authentic conversation about meals and food and then complete listening and speaking tasks, providing true information about themselves.

🎧 Listen and circle.

See also "Listen and circle" on page T58.

➤ Show the class Letter Cards B and P and say their names. Hold them up when they are mentioned in the conversation.

➤ Students listen and circle the door with the correct letter.

Tapescript
A: Where is lunch?
B: Lunch is in Room B.
A: Room P?
B: No. In room B.
A: Thanks!

🎧 Look and listen.

See also "Look and listen" on page T22a.

➤ Show Vocabulary Cards 83, 89, 102 (*chicken, pasta, salad*). Point to the pasta and salad cards and say *Pasta salad*. Repeat for *chicken salad*.

➤ Play the cassette or read the tapescript aloud as many times as necessary.

Option: Give students visual cues to the dialogue. Place Vocabulary Cards 107, 84, 85, 102, 89, 83, 116, 90. (*dinner, meat, fish, salad, pasta, chicken, ice cream, fruit*) on the board rim. Write the times 6:00 and 7:00 on the board. Point to the Vocabulary Cards and board as these items are mentioned in the conversation.

Tapescript
A: I eat dinner at 6:00. What time do you eat dinner?
B: 7:00.
A: What do you eat for dinner?
B: I eat meat or fish and a salad.
A: Me too. What kind of salad?
B: Well, I like pasta salad.
A: Me too. And I like chicken salad too.
A: And what do you like for dessert?
B: Dessert? Ice cream or fruit.
A: Mmm.

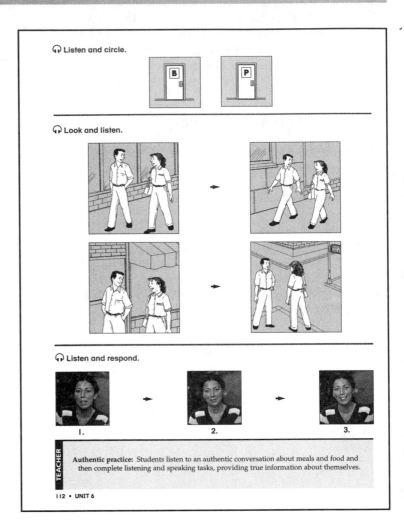

🎧 Listen and circle.

🎧 Look and listen.

🎧 Listen and respond.

1. 2. 3.

Authentic practice: Students listen to an authentic conversation about meals and food and then complete listening and speaking tasks, providing true information about themselves.

112 • UNIT 6

🎧 Listen and respond.

See also "Listen and respond" on page T22a.

➤ Using Vocabulary Cards 83–116, review vocabulary. After students name each card, place it on the board rim.

➤ Model the exercise. Approach a student and say *I eat breakfast at 6:30. What about you? What time do you eat breakfast?* If the student responds appropriately, give a big smile and move on to another student. If the student is confused, give a possible response and then repeat the prompt.

➤ Repeat with other students, asking the questions *What do you eat for breakfast?* and *What do you eat for dinner?*

➤ Continue as on page T22a.

Tapescript

Prompt 1: I eat breakfast at 6:30. What about you? What time do you eat breakfast?

Prompt 2: What do you eat for breakfast?

Prompt 3: And what do you eat for dinner?

Listen and respond
(possible student responses)

Prompt 1: I eat breakfast (Unit 5:) at [time].

Prompt 2: I eat bread / cheese / toast / butter / jam / fruit / eggs / cereal.

Prompt 3: I eat chicken / meat / fish / cheese / bread / rice / pasta / fruit / a sandwich / a cheese sandwich / a chicken sandwich / a fish sandwich / a hamburger / a salad / fries / toast / butter / jam / eggs / cereal / soup / vegetables / cake / ice cream.

NOTES

Literacy review: Trace M, B, F, P, V, and H. Review sounds of initial consonants in known words. Trace first letter of known words.
More practice: Worksheet 55 (Teacher's Edition CD-ROM).
Literacy test: Teacher's Edition CD-ROM.

Trace.

➤ Have students practice writing the letters with their fingers on the desktops.

➤ Students trace each letter. Circulate around the classroom, checking students' work.

Additional Activity

Use this opportunity to review tracing of all capital letters. Lightly draw sections of the alphabet on the board. Invite individual students to the board to trace the letters with the correct stroke sequences.

🎧 Listen and circle.

See "Listen and circle M or B" on page T98b.

Additional Activities

Activity 1: Have students identify letter sounds in words they know. Hand out a set of B, F, H, M, P, and V Letter Cards to each student. Have students hold up the letter they hear as you say any of the following words: *bank, fish, factory, bus, fire, mall, medium, pasta, hospital, hamburger, butter, five, vegetable, breakfast, post office, fifteen.*

Activity 2: Have students sort vocabulary words by initial consonant sound. Make multiple copies of Vocabulary Cards 16, 19, 26, 28, 41, 48, 78, 79, 81, 84, 85, 89, 91, 114 (*hotel, bus, highway, fire, bakery, pants, bank, post office, factory, meat, fish, pasta, milk, vegetables*). Model the activity: Write the letters B, F, H, M P, and V on the board. Pick up a Vocabulary Card. Say the word and place it under the appropriate letter. Hand each student several Vocabulary Cards and have students complete the sorting activity. Review the word piles, picking up each Vocabulary Card, saying its name, and saying its initial letter.

Tapescript

1. meat **2.** bakery **3.** pants **4.** vegetables **5.** fire
6. highway

Say the word. Trace the letter.

See "Say the word. Trace the letter" on page T110.

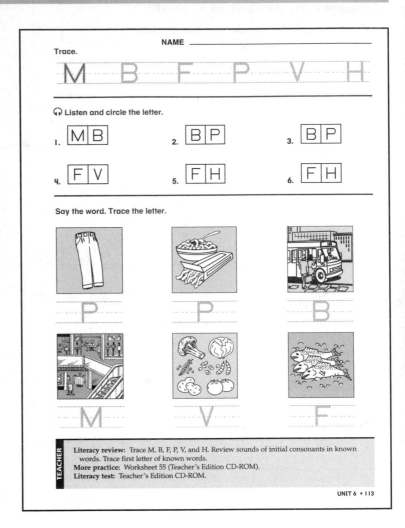

Additional Activity

Concentration. For each pair of students, photocopy the following two sets of cards:

Set 1: Vocabulary Cards 31, 41, 79, 84, 85, 89, 91, 101, 105 (*hospital, bakery, post office, meat, fish, pasta, milk, hamburger, breakfast*) and Number Card 5.

Set 2: Two copies of Letter Cards B, F, H, M, P. Follow the procedure for Activity 1 on page T106.

Worksheet Link: Worksheet 55

Assign the worksheet for in-class independent work. Follow the procedures for similar activities on this page and on pages T106 and T109. Circulate to make sure students understand the sound-symbol correspondence for M; B, F, P, V; and H.

TEACHER

Survival / civics review: Point and name things in the picture. Make sentences about the picture. Role-play conversations based on the picture.
Tests: Teacher's Edition CD-ROM.

Talk about the picture.

➤ Hold up the Student's Book and point to the known items in the picture. (*Vegetables, fruit, cereal, drink, coffee, chicken, fish, meat, cheese, sandwich.*) Students name the words.

➤ Have students point and name items in the picture with a partner.

Possible student responses

chicken / meat / fish / cheese / bread / rice / pasta / fruit / milk / coffee / tea / juice / water / oil / aisle / cheese sandwich / chicken sandwich / fish sandwich / hamburger / salad / fries / toast / butter / jam / eggs / cereal / soup / vegetables / cake / ice cream / (Unit 2:) supermarket

Role-play conversations.

➤ Point to the woman at the end of aisle 5 and ask *Where is the [cereal]?* Then point to the stock clerk to elicit a student's response (It's in aisle 4.) Gesture for the student to ask you a question.

➤ Model any of the other scenes.

➤ Have students work with a partner to practice conversations appropriate to the contexts in the picture.

➤ Ask pairs of students to present some of their conversations to the class.

Talk about the picture. Role-play conversations.

TEACHER **Survival / civics review:** Point and name things in the picture. Make sentences about the picture. Role-play conversations based on the picture.
Tests: Teacher's Edition CD-ROM.

Role-play conversations (possible student responses)

(The customer and the stock clerk)

A: (Unit 2:) Excuse me. Where is (Unit 6:) the chicken / meat / fish / cheese / bread / rice / pasta / fruit / milk / coffee / tea / juice / water / oil / butter / jam / cereal / soup / ice cream / cake? **B:** The [chicken]? It's in aisle [1]. **A:** (Unit 2:) Excuse me? **B:** (Unit 6:) Aisle [1]. / (Unit 4:) Across from the [bread]. / Next to the [vegetables]. / (Unit 2:) Right over there. **A:** (Unit 1:) Thanks. / Thank you. **B:** You're welcome.

(The cashier and the customer)

A: (Unit 2:) Can I help you? **B:** (Unit 6:) Yes, a sandwich, please. **A:** (Unit 2:) Sure. / (Unit 6:) Certainly. What kind of sandwich? **B:** A cheese sandwich / chicken sandwich / fish sandwich. **A:** Something to drink? **B:** Coffee / tea / water / milk / juice, please. **A:** What size? **B:** Small. / Medium. / Large. **A:** Anything else? **B:** Fries / a salad. / No, thanks. That's all.

(Two women at the table)

A: For breakfast I like [eggs and toast]. (Unit 1:) What about you? **B:** (Unit 6:) Me too. / Not me! I like [cereal, fruit, and coffee]. **A:** I eat breakfast / lunch / dinner (Unit 5:) at [time]. (Unit 1:) And you? **B:** (Unit 6:) I eat [breakfast] (Unit 5:) at [time].

LESSON PLAN FOR STUDENT'S PAGE 115

TEACHER

Literacy: Recognize that the alphabet has an order. Learn the the "names" of the letters in a rhythmic chant.

🎧 A. Look and listen.

➤ Have students listen with books closed. Play the cassette or sing the alphabet song (without the rejoinder) for the class. This tunes students into the melody and rhythm of the song before they deal with the printed letters. Most literacy students have very developed oral/aural skills. You may want to practice the song many times before having students look at the printed matter.

➤ Now play the cassette or sing the song with students' books open. Circulate around the room to make sure students are pointing to the correct letter as they listen to the song.

➤ Play the song as many times as needed until students are able to point at each letter as it is sung.

🎧 B. Listen again and repeat.

➤ Read the tapescript or play the cassette. Have students repeat after each string of letters.

➤ Have students practice repeating each string of letters until their pronunciation is error-free.

Option: Some students will find it easier to remember the strings of letters when accompanied with the melody. When students struggle with repetition of the letters, let them sing instead, or sing it for them.

Tapescript
A B C D E F G   H I J K   L M N O P   Q R S T U V   W X   Y Z

Additional Activities

Activity 1: Say the alphabet slowly. Have students raise their hand when a letter in their name is spoken.

Activity 2: Make sure students have their name cards from the Welcome unit on their desks. Have students work in pairs to say the letters in their partner's name.

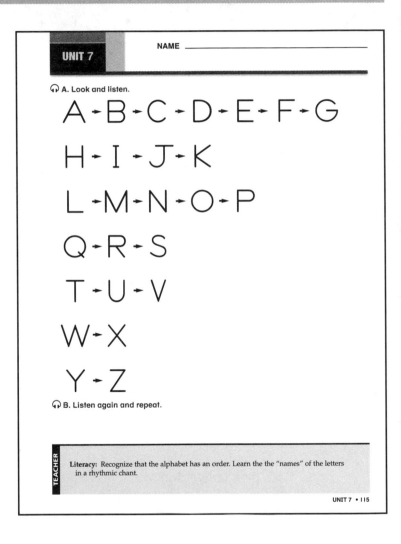

Worksheet Link: Worksheet 50

For additional practice with the complete alphabet, have students do Worksheet 50 from the previous unit. If students do this in class, encourage them to say the name of each letter as they trace it.

TEACHER

Literacy: Read, listen to, and repeat letters that have rhyming or otherwise related sound patterns.

🎧 A. Listen and repeat.

Note: The letters in this activity are grouped to provide practice with the natural rhythm of the spoken alphabet.

➤ Circulate around the room to make sure students are pointing to the correct letter as they listen and repeat.

➤ Repeat the listening as many times as needed until students are able to say each group of letters with ease.

Additional Activity

Use the Letter Cards like flashcards. One by one, show the class each letter and elicit its name. When students can't produce a letter name, model it several times, and then put it aside and return to it later. Have students do this activity in pairs.

Tapescript
A B C   X Y Z   E F G   N O P   R S T
T U V   C D E

🎧 B. Listen and repeat.

Note: These letters are grouped together because they share similar sounds.

➤ Circulate around the room to make sure students are pointing to the correct letter as they listen and repeat.

➤ Repeat the listening as many times as needed until students are able to point to each letter and say its name. Emphasize the sound that each group of letters shares to help students remember the letter names.

Additional Activities

Note: Most students will need more practice learning the names of the letters.

Activity 1: Place sets of three Letter Cards at a time on the board rim. Point to each letter and say the name. Have students individually come up to the board and point and repeat. Slowly try to get students to name the letters without your prior modeling.

🎧 A. Listen and repeat.

```
        A  B  C
        X  Y  Z
        E  F  G
        N  O  P
        R  S  T
        T  U  V
        C  D  E
```

🎧 B. Listen and repeat.

```
  A  J  K
  B  C  D        E  G  P        T  V  Z
  F  L  M        N  S  X
  A  H
  Q  W
  Y  I
```

🎧 C. Listen and circle.

1. B Ⓡ   2. D P   3. H K   4. F L

TEACHER

Literacy: Read, listen to, and repeat letters that have rhyming or otherwise related sound patterns.

116 • UNIT 7

Activity 2: Group Letter Cards on the board rim to duplicate the grouping in the exercise (AJK, BCD, etc.). Point to each letter and say its name. Invite students individually to come up to the board, point to the letter, and say its name. Then have students close their eyes. Change the order of the three letters. Have students open their eyes and try to name the three letters. Repeat this procedure, using different letter sets.

Activity 3: Play a memory game. Give each student a set of Letter Cards. Have students close their eyes. Call out four letters in a row. Have students open their eyes and find the letters in their sets. Repeat with different letters. This game reviews letter names and develops students' visualization of letters.

(Continued on page T116b.)

Activity 4: Concentration. For each pair of students, photocopy two sets of any 6 consecutive capital Letter Cards. Give each pair of students two sets of cards. Follow the instructions for Activity 2 on page T28.

Activity 5: To show students the importance of learning alphabetical order, bring in a local telephone directory and show how last names are grouped alphabetically by letter.

Tapescript

A J K B C D E G P T V Z F L M N S X
A H Q W Y I

⌒ C. Listen and circle.

See "Listen and circle M or B" on page T98b.

Additional Activities

Activity 1: Give each student a set of the first five capital Letter Cards, A–E. Call out a letter name. Have students select the card from their own sets and hold it up for you to see. Repeat this activity with the remaining letters of the alphabet, five or six letters at a time. Then have students take turns calling out letter names as the rest of the class listens and selects the letter card.

Activity 2: Distribute copies of letter cards, one per student, so that each letter has a match somewhere in the class. (If there are 20 students in your class, distribute two copies of the ten letters A–J.) Students circulate to find the person with their matching letter.

Tapescript

1. R **2.** D **3.** K **4.** L

NOTES

_____

_____

_____

_____

_____

_____

_____

_____

_____

_____

_____

_____

_____

_____

_____

_____

_____

_____

Survival: Learn vocabulary for family and social relationships.
Civics concept: Wedding bands are commonly worn on the left hand.
New language: Father, mother, daughter, son, husband, wife, sister, brother, friend.

A. Look and listen.

See "Look and listen" on page T17a.

Option: Test comprehension. Say one of the vocabulary words and have students identify the number.

Additional Activity

Show pictures of nuclear families from magazines or newspapers. Point to each person in the picture and state a family relationship.

B. Listen again and repeat.

See "Listen again and repeat" on page T17a.

Option: Isolate the /ð/ sound in *mother* and *father*. Show the class how your tongue rests between your teeth as you blow. This /ð/ is a voiced sound, unlike the voiceless /θ/ of three or thirteen.

Have students tap out the syllables of each word. This will help them identify the pattern of the –*er* syllable.

Additional Activity

With books open, call out a picture number and have students say the word. Repeat the process with several words. Then have students do this activity in pairs.

Tapescript
1. father   2. mother   3. daughter   4. son

C. Look and listen.

See also "Look and listen" on page T17a.

➤ To illustrate that these vocabulary words designate the relationship between two people, hold up the Student's Book, point to the father and the mother in the top picture, and say *Father, mother.* Then hold your hand over the son and daughter and point back and forth between the man and woman as you say *Husband, wife.* Point to the first picture in Exercise C and repeat *Husband, wife.* Follow the same procedure with *sister* and *brother.*

Option: Gesture to two students who are evident friends. As you gesture, say *friends.*

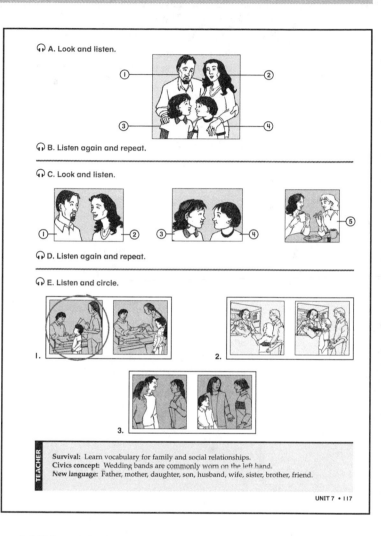

A. Look and listen.

B. Listen again and repeat.

C. Look and listen.

D. Listen again and repeat.

E. Listen and circle.

1.   2.   3.

Survival: Learn vocabulary for family and social relationships.
Civics concept: Wedding bands are commonly worn on the left hand.
New language: Father, mother, daughter, son, husband, wife, sister, brother, friend.

UNIT 7 • 117

Additional Activity

Provide listening practice. Place Vocabulary Cards 117–125 (*father, mother, daughter, son, husband, wife, sister, brother, friend*) on the board rim. Call out the name of the family relationship while students listen and come up to point to the picture.

D. Listen again and repeat.

See "Listen again and repeat" on page T17a.

Option: The /w/ sound in *wife* is challenging. To form the sound, pucker your lips as in a kiss.

Option: To get students to fully associate letters with sounds, place the Letter Cards H and B on the board

(Continued on page T117b.)

T117a

rim. Say *husband* and point to the letter H. Say *brother* and point to the letter B.

If your students are ready . . .

Civics enrichment: Wedding bands signify marriage. Show the class your left hand. Count out your fingers. Identify the ring finger. Place the band of a ring there and say *wife* (or *husband*, if you are male). Look at students' hands. If any students are wearing wedding bands, have them show their rings to the class.

Tapescript

1. husband   2. wife   3. sister   4. brother
5. friend

∩ E. Listen and circle.

See also "Listen and circle" on page T17a–b.

➤ Invite two student volunteers to the front of the class. Introduce them to each other, saying *This is my friend [name]*.

Option: Before listening, have students look carefully at the pictures in the book. Hold your book up for the class to see. Point to the people in the pictures and have students identify the relationships. This helps prepare students for the listening exercise.

➤ Play the cassette or read the tapescript aloud as many times as necessary.

Additional Activity

With books open, call out one of the two relationship words in item 1 (*daughter, son*). Have students point to the correct picture. Repeat this process with items 2 and 3. Then have students do this activity in pairs.

Tapescript

Conversation 1
A: This is my son. His name is Eddie Gomez.
B: Thank you.

Conversation 2
A: This is my daughter. She needs a uniform for school.
B: Certainly. What size?
A: Small.

Conversation 3
A: This is my friend. His name is Richard. He's a mechanic.
B: A mechanic? Great. Nice to meet you, Richard.

NOTES

_____
_____
_____
_____
_____
_____
_____
_____
_____
_____
_____

TEACHER

Survival: Ask for and spell names.
Civics concept: People often ask you to spell a name.
New language: This is my daughter [son]. / What's her [his] name? / How do you spell that?

🎧 A. Look and listen.

See also "Look and listen" on page T9a.

➤ Set the scene. Hold the book up for the class to see and point to the pictures. Say *school*.

➤ Play the cassette or read the tapescript aloud as many times as necessary.

Option: Give students visual cues to the dialogue. For the first conversation, write the letters L-E-E on the board. For the second conversation, write the letters J-O-N S-A-L-I-K. Point to the letters as they are mentioned in the conversation.

🎧 B. Listen again and repeat.

See "Listen again and repeat" on page T9a.

Additional Activities

Activity 1: Test comprehension. Hold the book up for the class to see. Point to the child in the first picture of each conversation and ask *What's her name? / What's his name?*

Activity 2: Present *his* and *her*. Put Vocabulary Cards 121–124 (*husband-wife, sister-brother*) or pictures of famous men and women on the rim of the board. Ask *What's her name?* and point to a girl or woman. Hold up three fingers and repeat the question, touching a finger for each word. Emphasize the middle word *her*. Repeat the question, but change *her* to *his* and point to a boy or man. Emphasize the middle word *his*.

Then ask the question again but omit the middle word and point to a student to elicit the word *her* or *his*. Repeat this procedure until students understand that *her* refers to females and *his* refers to males.

You may also wish to follow this procedure by indicating students rather than people in pictures.

TEACHER

Survival: Ask for and spell names.
Civics concept: People often ask you to spell a name.
New language: This is my daughter [son]. / What's her [his] name? / How do you spell that?

118 • UNIT 7

Tapescript

Conversation 1
A: Good morning. I'm Ann Chung. And this is my daughter.
B: What's her name?
A: Lee.
B: How do you spell that?
A: L-E-E.

Conversation 2
A: Hello. This is my son.
B: What's his name?
A: Jon Salik.
B: How do you spell that?
A: J-O-N S-A-L-I-K.

(Continued on page T118b.) **T118a**

C. Pair work.

➤ Model the Pair work. Invite two students to the front of the class. Write the name of Student A on the board in capital letters. Introduce A to B. Say *This is my daughter / son.* Gesture to elicit the question *What's her name?* Give Student A's name. Gesture for B to respond. If B doesn't ask *How do you spell that?*, offer the spelling on your own. Then switch roles with the same students and repeat the conversation.

➤ Students practice giving and spelling names in groups of three. Make sure students switch roles so that everyone gets a chance to speak. Circulate around the classroom, offering help as needed.

Option: Cut pictures of children from magazines and label each picture with a short name in capital letters. Distribute these pictures so students have the opportunity to practice introducing both boys and girls.

➤ Have several volunteer pairs act out their conversations in front of the class.

Pair work (possible student responses)

A: Good morning. I'm [name]. And this is my daughter / son. **B:** What's her / his name? **A:** [name]. **B:** How do you spell that? **A:** [all alphabet letters].

Your students can also say . . .

A: Good afternoon / Good evening. / (Unit 2:) Excuse me / Hello. **B:** What's your address and zip code? And your telephone number and area code? **A:** [address and zip code, telephone number and area code]. (Unit 5:) Oh, when is school? **B:** School is Monday to Friday, from [hour] to [hour]. **A:** (Unit 3:) Is there a subway / bus / train near here? **B:** Yes, turn left / right at the corner. / It's on [Main Street]. / [Right] over there. / On the corner. **A:** (Unit 1:) Thank you. / Thanks. **B:** You're welcome.

NOTES

_____

_____

_____

_____

_____

_____

_____

_____

_____

_____

_____

_____

_____

_____

_____

_____

TEACHER

Literacy: Recognize, read, and trace lowercase v, w, x, y, z. Match capital
with lowercase letters.
More practice: Worksheets 56–57 (Teacher's Edition CD-ROM).

A. Look at the capital and lowercase letters.

➤ Write a capital and lowercase V on the board.
Point to each and say *large V, small v.* (To facilitate
recognition of the capital and lowercase letters, it
is helpful to use the words *large* and *small,* words
which have meaning and are known to the students. You may also choose to teach the terms *capital* and *lowercase.*) Repeat with the other letters:
W, X, Y, Z.

➤ Have students point to each letter and say its
name, including the words *large* and *small.*
Circulate around the room to check students'
progress.

➤ Have students repeat this activity until they are
able to say all the letter names without errors.

Additional Activities

Activity 1: Write capital and lowercase letters on a
primer-ruled line on the board. Have students take
turns coming up to the board and identifying the
name and size of the letter.

Activity 2: Use capital and lowercase Letter Cards
V, W, X, Y, Z like flashcards. One by one, show the
class each letter and elicit its name and size. When
students can't produce a letter name, model it several
times, and then put it aside and return to it later.
Then have students do this activity with a partner.

Activity 3: Make multiple copies of the capital and
lowercase Letter Cards V, W, X, Y, and Z. Place several of the same lowercase Letter Cards on the board
rim, but turn some of the cards on their sides or upside down. Invite students to come to the board to
correct the orientation of the cards. For more challenge, combine different Letter Cards, both lowercase
and capital, in the same line-up.

B. Match.

➤ Write the first group of letters on the board. Point
to the capital V and say *Large V.* Then point to the
top letter in the right column and say *Small w.*
Shake your head to indicate they are not the same
letter. Continue in the same manner, comparing
the top letter in the left column with the middle
letter on the right (small x). When you point to the

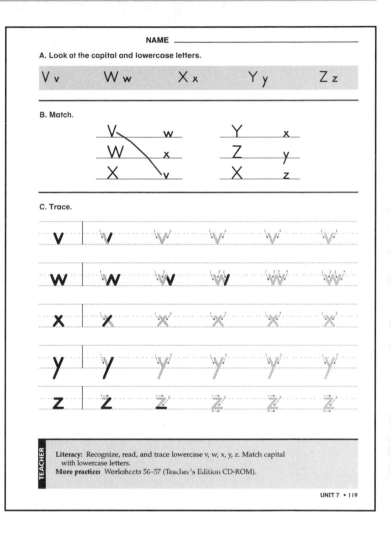

TEACHER

Literacy: Recognize, read, and trace lowercase v, w, x, y, z. Match capital
with lowercase letters.
More practice: Worksheets 56–57 (Teacher's Edition CD-ROM).

UNIT 7 • 119

bottom letter in the right column, say *Small v,* nod
your head, and say *Yes!* to indicate they are the
same letters, and draw a line between them.

➤ Have students do the first column without a pencil
as you watch, to make sure they understand the
activity. Once you see students do it without skip-
ping a letter or misnaming a letter, go on to the
next group of letters.

➤ Have students pick up their pencils and complete
the exercise on their own. Circulate around the
classroom, checking their work.

(Continued on page T119b.)

Additional Activities

Activity 1: Write similar matching exercises on the board. Have students take turns coming up to the board and drawing a line between the matching letters. Make sure students always say the name and size of each letter as they do the exercise.

Activity 2: Copy capital and lowercase Letter Cards V, W, X, Y and Z and give one set of each to each pair of students. Have students work with a partner to match the lowercase and capital letters.

C. Trace.

➤ Model the writing of lowercase letters v, w, x, y, and z. On the board, model the strokes of each letter. To instruct students on the correct sequence of strokes, count aloud as you do each stroke. Then have students follow along with their fingers in the air while watching you. Have everyone count the strokes aloud. When each letter is finished on the board, point to it and say its name and size.

➤ Lightly write the letters v, w, x, y, and z on the board. One at a time, invite students to the board to *trace* the letters. Have students name the letter before they trace it. Have the rest of the class follow along by tracing the strokes of the same letters with their fingers on their desktops. Circulate around the classroom to correct strokes. Pay attention to the correct sequence of strokes.

➤ Have students trace each letter. Circulate around the classroom, checking their work.

Option: You may want students to do the exercise one time through without a pencil.

Additional Activity

Have students evaluate your handwriting. Write several examples of the lowercase letter v in a primer-ruled line on the board. Include one or two examples of a poorly formed V (for example, with one side much longer than the other). Have students take turns coming up to the board to cross out the incorrectly formed letters. You may also choose to have students erase the malformed letters and write them correctly. Repeat this procedure with the letters W, X, Y and Z in lowercase and in capital form.

Worksheet Link: Worksheets 56–57

Assign the worksheets for homework or in-class independent work. For Worksheet 56, follow the above procedures. Worksheet 57 is a repetitive tracing exercise to reinforce students' knowledge of lowercase letters and give students practice placing lowercase letters in relation to capital letters.

Review students' work to make sure that they can recognize, read, and trace these letters before going on to the next literacy lesson.

NOTES

Literacy: Recognize, read, and trace k, l, i, j, t, f. Match capital with lowercase letters.
More practice: Worksheets 58–59 (Teacher's Edition CD-ROM).

A. Look at the capital and lowercase letters.

See "Look at the capital and lowercase letters" on page T119a.

B. Circle.

See "Circle" on page T65.

➤ Students circle the capital letter that matches the target lowercase letter on the left. This activity reinforces the relationship of same capital and lowercase letters.

Additional Activities

Activity 1: Write similar letter sequences on the board. Have students take turns coming up to the board and circling the matching letter. Make sure students always say the name and size of each letter as they do the exercise.

Activity 2: Copy capital and lowercase Letter Cards F, I, J, K, L, and T. Have pairs of students work together to match the lowercase and capital letters.

Activity 3: Concentration. Give each pair of students two copies of lowercase Letter Cards f, i, j, k l, t, v, w, y, and z. Follow the instructions for Activity 2 on page T28.

C. Trace.

See "Trace" on page T119b.

Additional Activities

Activity 1: Have students evaluate your handwriting. Write several examples of the lowercase letter k in a primer-ruled line on the board. Include one or two examples of a poorly formed k (for example, left vertical too short). Have students take turns coming up to the board to cross out the incorrectly formed letters. Repeat this procedure with the letters L, I, J, T and F in lowercase and in capital form.

Activity 2: Give students the opportunity to correct you. Write the lowercase letter k on the board correctly. As you write, nod your head and say *Yes!* Then write the letter incorrectly with an incorrect bottom-to-top motion. As you write, shake your head and say *No!* Then invite students to say *Yes* or *No* as you write other letters correctly and incorrectly.

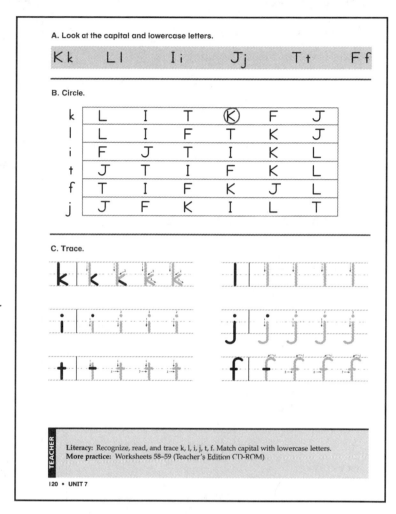

Worksheet Link: Worksheets 58–59

Assign the worksheets for homework or in-class independent work. For Worksheet 58, follow the above procedures. Worksheet 59 is a repetitive tracing exercise to reinforce students' knowledge of lowercase letters and give students practice placing lowercase letters in relation to capital letters.

Review students' work to make sure that they can recognize, read, and trace these letters before going on to the next literacy lesson.

TEACHER

Survival: State the age of another person.
Civics concepts: Parents take their children to school in order to register them. The school will ask for the child's age.
New language: How old is she [he]? / She's [10] years old. / He's [13].

🎧 A. Look and listen.

See also "Look and listen" on page T9a.

➤ Set the scene. Hold the book up for the class to see. Point to the pictures and say *School*.

Additional Activity
Test comprehension. Hold up the book for the class to see. Point to the girl in the picture and ask *How old is she?* Repeat this procedure with the boy.

🎧 B. Listen again and repeat.

See "Listen again and repeat" on page T9a.

Additional Activity
Practice new language. Say *She's ten years old.* Hold up four fingers and repeat the sentence, touching a finger for each word. Fold down the last two fingers to represent the last two words and say *She's ten.* Repeat this contrast with the sentences *He's eight years old* and *He's eight.* This activity will practice the two ways to state an age and will help students understand the meanings of *he* and *she*.

🎧 A. Look and listen.

1. 2003 / 1993   2.

🎧 B. Listen again and repeat.

C. Pair work.

10   4

TEACHER
Survival: State the age of another person.
Civics concepts: Parents take their children to school in order to register them. The school will ask for the child's age.
New language: How old is she [he]? / She's [10] years old. / He's [13].

UNIT 7 • 121

Tapescript

Conversation 1
A: How old is she?
B: She's 10 years old.

Conversation 2
A: How old is he?
B: He's 13.

C. Pair work.

➤ Model the Pair work. Show the class a picture of a child or point to one of the cues to the right of the Pair work picture. Ask *How old is he / she?* Then invite two students to model the conversation for the class.

➤ Divide the class into pairs. Students practice stating the age of another person. Circulate around the classroom, offering help as needed.

➤ Have several volunteer pairs act out their conversations in front of the class.

Pair work (possible student responses)

A: How old is she / he? **B:** She's ten years old. / He's four.

Your students can also say . . .

A: Good morning. / Good afternoon. / Good evening. / (Unit 2:) Excuse me. / Hello. (Unit 7:) I'm [name]. And this is my daughter / son.
B: What's her / his name? **A:** [name]. **B:** How do you spell that? **A:** [all alphabet letters]. **B:** (Unit 2:) What's your address and zip code? And your telephone number and area code? **A:** [address and zip code, telephone number and area code]. (Unit 5:) Oh, when is school? **B:** School is Monday to Friday, from [hour] to [hour].

NOTES

Survival: Politely introduce people. Identify one's home country.
Civics concept: It's friendly to ask where someone is from and to offer the same information about oneself.
New language: Where are you from? / I'm from [Russia]. / [She]'s from [China].

🎧 A. Look and listen.

See also "Look and listen" on page T9a.

➤ Show the class a world map. Say the following place names and point to them on the map: *United States, Russia,* and *China.*

➤ Play the cassette or read the tapescript aloud as many times as necessary.

Additional Activity
Test comprehension. Hold the book up for the class to see. Point to the woman in the second picture and ask *What's her name? Where's she from?* Point to the man and ask the same questions.

🎧 B. Listen again and repeat.

See "Listen again and repeat" on page T9a.

Additional Activities
Activity 1: Practice new language. Ask *Where are you from?* Hold up four fingers and ask the question again, touching a finger for each word. Repeat, but omit saying one word. Point to the finger that represents the missing word. Have students tell you the missing word. Repeat the procedure with the sentence *I'm from China.*

Activity 2: Pointing to a world map, identify the location of students' countries. Tape the name of each student to his country of origin.

If your students are ready . . .

Civics enrichment: Look at page T9b for notes and activities on hand shaking customs.

Tapescript

A: Alice, this is my friend Daniel. Daniel, this is my sister Alice.
B: Nice to meet you, Daniel.
C: Nice to meet you too, Alice.

B: Where are you from?
C: I'm from Russia. And you?
B: I'm from China.

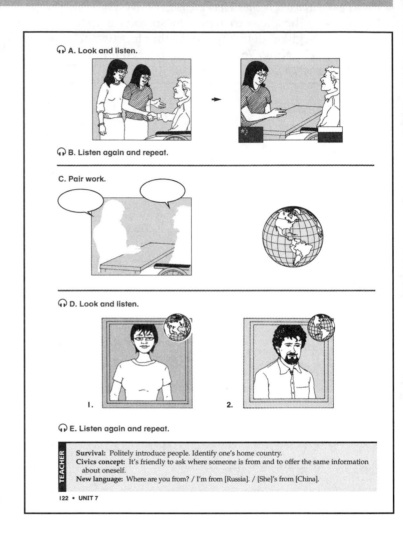

🎧 A. Look and listen.

🎧 B. Listen again and repeat.

C. Pair work.

🎧 D. Look and listen.

1.   2.

🎧 E. Listen again and repeat.

Survival: Politely introduce people. Identify one's home country.
Civics concept: It's friendly to ask where someone is from and to offer the same information about oneself.
New language: Where are you from? / I'm from [Russia]. / [She]'s from [China].

122 • UNIT 7

C. Pair work.

➤ Model the Pair work. Invite two students to the front of the class. Turn to one student and introduce him/her to the other. Point to a world map to prompt the question *Where are you from?* When the students have finished the conversation, invite two other students to the front of the class to model the conversation.

Option: You may want to prepare students for the activity by calling on different students and asking *Where are you from?*

➤ Students practice asking where someone is from in groups of three. Circulate around the classroom, offering help as needed.

Option: You may want students to stand as they speak, which will encourage use of gestures and facial expressions. Encourage students to practice their handshakes as they do their introductions.

➤ Have several volunteer pairs act out their conversations in front of the class.

Pair work (possible student responses)

A: [Name], this is my friend / sister / brother / husband / wife / mother / father / son / daughter, [name]. [Name], this is my [friend, name].
B: Nice to meet you, [name]. **C:** Nice to meet you too, [name]. **B:** Where are you from? **C:** I'm from [place name]. And you? **B:** I'm from [place name].

Your students can also say . . .

B: (Unit 1:) That's a nice name. (Unit 7:) How do you spell that? **C:** Thanks. [all alphabet letters]. **B:** (Unit 1:) What do you do, [name]? **C:** I'm a student / teacher / cook / housekeeper / mechanic / babysitter. What about you? **B:** I'm a [cook] [too]. / (Unit 6:) Me too!

🎧 D. Look and listen.

See also "Look and listen" on page T17a.

➤ Show the class a world map. Say the following place names and point to them on the map: *China, Peru.*

Additional Activity

Test comprehension. Hold the book up for the class to see. Point to the first picture and ask *What's her name? Where's she from?* Point to the second picture and ask *What's his name? Where's he from?*

🎧 E. Listen again and repeat.

See "Listen again and repeat" on page T17a.

Additional Activity

Reinforce *she/he*. Put Vocabulary Cards 121–122 (*husband, wife*) on the rim of the board. Say *He's from [place],* and point to the man in the Vocabulary Card. Repeat the sentence while pointing to a finger for each word. Emphasize the word *he*. Repeat with the woman and *she*. Say the sentence again but omit the subject and point to a person in a Vocabulary Card to elicit *he* or *she*. You may also choose to do this activity by indicating students rather than people in pictures.

Tapescript

1. This is Min Lee. She's from China.
2. This is Ken Cruz. He's from Peru.

TEACHER

Literacy: Recognize, read, and trace lowercase r, n, m, u, h. Match capital with lowercase letters.
More practice: Worksheets 60–61 (Teacher's Edition CD-ROM).

A. Look at the capital and lowercase letters.

See "Look at the capital and lowercase letters" on page T119a.

Additional Activities

Activity 1: Make multiple sets of lowercase and capital Letter Cards H, M, N, R, and U. Place one set of lowercase letters on 5 desks—one card per desk. Deal out the remaining cards. Have students move around the classroom, placing matching cards on the correct desks. Review the piles with the class. Hold up each card and say its name and size.

Activity 2: Test students' knowledge of the letter names. Show students Letter Cards H, M, N, R, and U in both lowercase and capital form. Invite students to say *Yes* or *No* as you call out correct and incorrect names of the letters. Occasionally add in a letter from the previous lessons (F, I, J, K, L, T, V, W, X, Y, Z).

B. Circle.

See "Circle" on page T65.

Additional Activities

Activity 1: Copy capital and lowercase Letter Cards H, M, N, R, and U. Have pairs of students work together to match the lowercase and capital cards.

Activity 2: For further practice, give each student a set of lowercase Letter Cards h, m, n, r, and u. Students work with a partner. Student A chooses a card and says its name without showing the card to B. B finds the card in his own set.

C. Trace.

See "Trace" on page T119b.

Additional Activity

Write several examples of the lowercase letter r in a primer-ruled line on the board. Include one or two examples of a poorly formed r (for example, with the curve on the wrong side). Have students take turns coming up to the board to cross out the incorrectly formed letters. Students can also erase the malformed

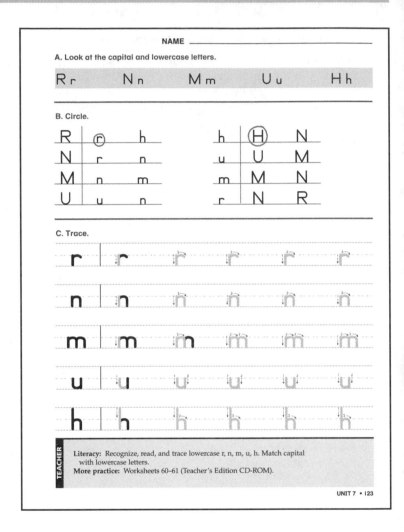

letters and write them correctly. Repeat with the letters h, m, n, and u. Occasionally add in a letter from the previous lessons (f, i, j, k, l, t, v, w, x, y, or z).

Worksheet Link: Worksheets 60–61

Assign the worksheets for homework or in-class independent work. For Worksheet 60, follow the above procedures. Worksheet 61 is a repetitive tracing exercise to reinforce students' knowledge of lowercase letters and give students practice placing lowercase letters in relation to capital letters.

Review students' work to make sure that they can recognize, read, and trace these letters before going on to the next literacy lesson.

TEACHER

Literacy: Recognize, read, and trace lowercase d, p, b, a, q, g. Match capital with lowercase letters.
More practice: Worksheets 62–63 (Teacher's Edition CD-ROM).

A. Look at the capital and lowercase letters.

See "Look at the capital and lowercase letters" on page T119a.

Note: The three most difficult lowercase letters to distinguish are lowercase b, d, and p. As you introduce these, focus on the left or right vertical line when teaching the strokes. Take your time introducing each of these, and be certain students have studied each one before introducing the next.

Additional Activities
Activity 1: Use capital and lowercase Letter Cards A, B, D, G, P, and Q like flashcards. One by one, show the class each letter and elicit its name and size. Occasionally add in a letter from the previous lessons (F, H, I, J, K, L, M, N, R, T, U, V, W, X, Y, or Z). Students can also do this activity with a partner.

Activity 2: Play a memory game. Photocopy lowercase Letter Cards a, b, d, g, m, n, p, q, and r. Give each student one set. Have students lay them out on their desks. Make sure the cards are all correctly oriented, especially the d and p. Have students close their eyes. Call out four letters in a row. Have students open their eyes and find the letters in their Letter Card sets. Repeat, calling out four different letters. This game reviews letter names and develops students' visualization of letters.

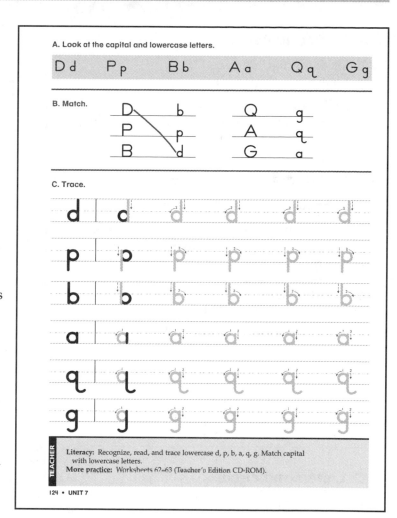

TEACHER

Literacy: Recognize, read, and trace lowercase d, p, b, a, q, g. Match capital with lowercase letters.
More practice: Worksheets 62–63 (Teacher's Edition CD-ROM).

124 • UNIT 7

B. Match.

See "Match" on page T119a.

Additional Activity
Copy capital and lowercase Letter Cards A, B, D, G, and Q. Have pairs of students work together to match the lowercase and capital cards. For more challenge, add in a couple of letters from the previous lessons (F, H, I, J, K, L, M, N, R, T, U, V, W, X, Y, or Z).

C. Trace.

See "Trace" on page T119b.

Additional Activity
Lightly draw lowercase letters d, p, b, a, q, and g on a primer-ruled line on the board. Invite individual students to the board to trace the letters with the correct stroke sequences.

Worksheet Link: Worksheets 62–63
Assign the worksheets for homework or in-class independent work. For Worksheet 62, follow the above procedures. Worksheet 63 is a repetitive tracing exercise to reinforce students' knowledge of lowercase letters and give students practice placing lowercase letters in relation to capital letters.

Review students' work to make sure that they can recognize, read, and trace these letters before going on to the next literacy lesson.

TEACHER

Survival: Learn vocabulary for marital status.
Civics concept: It's OK to ask questions about a person's marital status. Each
status has a name.
New language: Single, married, separated, divorced, widowed.

🎧 A. Look and listen.

See "Look and listen" on page T17a.

Option: Give visual cues to the vocabulary. Show
your (left) hand with no ring. Say *Single*. Place a ring
on your left ring finger and say *Married*. Take the ring
off and set it aside. Say *Divorced*.

🎧 B. Listen again and repeat.

See "Listen again and repeat" on page T17a.

Option: Have students tap out the syllables of each
word. This is especially useful when students try to
pronounce multisyllabic words such as *separated*.

Additional Activity
Provide speaking practice. With books open, call out
a picture number and have students say the word.
Repeat the process with several words. Then have
students do this activity in pairs.

┌───┐
│ **Tapescript** │
│ **1.** single **2.** married **3.** separated **4.** divorced │
│ **5.** widowed │
└───┘

🎧 C. Listen and circle.

See "Listen and circle" on page T17a–b.

Additional Activity
With books open, call out one of the two words in
item 1. Have students point to the correct picture.
Repeat this process with all the exercises. Then have
students do this activity in pairs.

┌───┐
│ **If your students are ready . . .** │
│ **Civics enrichment:** A woman can be addressed │
│ with *Ms.* and her last name whether she is single, │
│ married, divorced, or widowed. A man can be ad- │
│ dressed with *Mr.* and his last name whether he is │
│ single, married, divorced, or widowed. You can il- │
│ lustrate this concept by pointing to students, both │
│ single and married, and saying their names with │
│ the title *Ms.* or *Mr.* │
└───┘

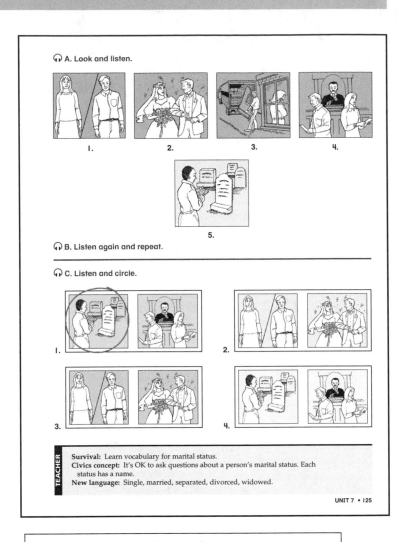

TEACHER

Survival: Learn vocabulary for marital status.
Civics concept: It's OK to ask questions about a person's marital status. Each
status has a name.
New language: Single, married, separated, divorced, widowed.

UNIT 7 • 125

┌──┐
│ **Tapescript** │
│ **Conversation 1** │
│ **A:** Are you married or single? │
│ **B:** I'm widowed. │
│ │
│ **Conversation 2** │
│ **A:** Are you single or married? │
│ **B:** I'm married. │
│ │
│ **Conversation 3** │
│ **A:** Are you single? │
│ **B:** Yes. │
│ │
│ **Conversation 4** │
│ **A:** Are you married? │
│ **B:** No. I'm divorced. │
└──┘

Survival: Provide marital status and spouse's name in an official setting.
Civics concept: It's OK to provide the names of people in one's family.
New language: Are you single or married? / I'm [married]. / What's your [husband]'s name?

∩ A. Look and listen.

See "Look and listen" on page T9a.

∩ B. Listen again and repeat.

See "Listen again and repeat" on page T9a.

Option: Focus on intonation. If you have worked on the rising/falling intonation pattern of *wh–* questions in previous lessons, reinforce your instruction with the question *What's your wife's name?*

Additional Activity

Test comprehension. Point to the person on the right in each picture and ask *Is he / she single or married?*

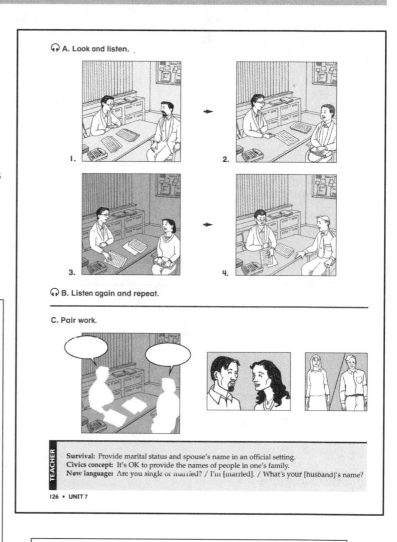

∩ A. Look and listen.

1.   2.

3.   4.

∩ B. Listen again and repeat.

C. Pair work.

TEACHER

Survival: Provide marital status and spouse's name in an official setting.
Civics concept: It's OK to provide the names of people in one's family.
New language: Are you single or married? / I'm [married]. / What's your [husband]'s name?

126 • UNIT 7

Tapescript

Conversation 1
A: Are you single or married?
B: I'm single.

Conversation 2
A: Are you single or married?
B: I'm divorced.

Conversation 3
A: Are you single or married?
B: I'm married.
A: What's your husband's name?
B: Ben Mee.

Conversation 4
A: Are you single or married?
B: I'm married.
A: What's your wife's name?
B: Pam Finn.

C. Pair work.

➤ Model the Pair work. Ask students *Are you single or married?* If the student is married, ask *What is your wife's / husband's name?*

Option: For a challenge, ask the student to spell the spouse's name.

➤ Have students provide marital status to a partner.

➤ Have several volunteer pairs act out their conversations in front of the class.

Pair work (possible student responses)

A: Are you single or married? B: I'm married.
A: What's your husband's name? B: [name].

Your students can also say . . .

B: I'm single / married / separated / divorced / widowed. A: What's your husband's / wife's name? B: [name]. A: How do you spell that? B: [any alphabet letters]. A: (Unit 2:) What's your address and zip code? And your telephone number and area code? B: [address and zip code, telephone number and area code]. A: (Unit 1:) And what do you do, [Ms. / Mr. White]? B: I'm a student / teacher / cook / housekeeper / mechanic / babysitter.

Literacy: Recognize, read, and trace lowercase o, c, e, s. Match capital with lowercase letters.
More practice: Worksheets 64–65 (Teacher's Edition CD-ROM).

A. Look at the capital and lowercase letters.

See also "Look at the capital and lowercase letters" on page T119a.

Additional Activities

Activity 1: Make multiple sets of lowercase Letter Cards c, e, o, s. Place one set on four desks—one card per desk. Deal out the remaining cards. Have students move around the classroom placing matching cards on the correct desks. Review the piles with the class. Hold up each card and say its name.

Activity 2: Play a memory game. Photocopy lowercase Letter Cards a, b, c, d, e, g, o, and s. Give each student one set. Have students lay them out on their desks. Make sure the cards are all correctly oriented, especially the b and d. Have students close their eyes. Call out four letters in a row. Students open their eyes and find the letters in their Letter Card sets. Repeat, calling out different letters. This game reviews letter names and develops students' visualization of letters.

B. Circle.

See "Circle" on page T120.

Additional Activities

Activity 1: Copy capital and lowercase Letter Cards C, E, O, and S. Have pairs of students work together to match the lowercase and capital cards.

Activity 2: Concentration. Photocopy the lowercase and capital Letter Cards C, E, O, S. Follow the instructions for Activity 2 on page T28a.

C. Trace.

See "Trace" on page T119b.

Additional Activities

Activity 1: Give students the opportunity to correct you. Write the letter C on the board correctly. As you write, nod your head and say *Yes.* Then write the letter incorrectly with an incorrect bottom-to-top motion. As you write, shake your head and say *No!* Then invite students to say *Yes* or *No* as you write other letters correctly and incorrectly. Occasionally add in a letter from the previous lessons.

Activity 2: Make sure students have their name cards from the Welcome unit on their desks. Hold up the o Letter Card. Have students raise their hand if they have the letter o in their name. Repeat with c, e, and s.

Worksheet Link: Worksheets 64–65

Assign the worksheets for homework or in-class independent work. For Worksheet 64, follow the above procedures. Worksheet 65 is a repetitive tracing exercise to reinforce students' knowledge of capital letters and give students practice placing lowercase letters in relation to capital letters.

Review students' work to make sure that they can recognize, read, and trace these letters before going on to the next literacy lesson.

A. Look at the capital and lowercase letters.

O o   C c   E e   S s

B. Circle.

O	⊚	c		s	C	Ⓢ
C	e	c		c	O	C
E	s	e		o	E	O
S	s	e		e	E	C

C. Trace.

o

c

e

s

Literacy: Recognize, read, and trace lowercase o, c, e, s. Match capital with lowercase letters.
More practice: Worksheets 64–65 (Teacher's Edition CD-ROM).

TEACHER

Literacy: Write your own name on a form, using capital and lowercase letters.
Sight words: First name, last name.
More practice: Worksheet 66 (Teacher's Edition CD-ROM).

A. Look.

➤ Point to yourself and say *First name, [your name]. Last name, [your name].* Then ask several students *What's your first name? What's your last name?*

➤ Hold the Student's Book up. Point to the name on the first form. Say *First name, Tim. Last name, Baker.* Repeat this several times. Then say *Tim, T– I– M, Tim. Baker, B–A–K–E–R, Baker.* Have students repeat after you. Point out that the first letter of each name is capital (large) and that the other letters are lowercase (small).

➤ Have students practice spelling out the name *Tim Baker* in pairs.

B. Write your name.

➤ Hold the Student's Book up and point to the first line. Say *First name.* Ask a student *What's your first name?* Repeat the person's first name as you point to the line. Write the name on the board. Repeat for the last name. Give several examples.

➤ Have students write their first and last names on the first form.

Option: Writing freehand will be a challenge for your students. To take small steps toward that task, print out and distribute Worksheet 0 to each student, with a model of their name at the top for them to copy many times.

Note: Students may have learned how to write their names before they learned the correct strokes. Don't let them carry on these incorrect writing habits. Model their names correctly before they write independently. Watch as they write to make sure they are trying to use the correct strokes.

Some students may also have learned to write their names in all capitals. Encourage them to practice writing the lowercase letters in their names.

➤ Have students complete the second form on their own. Note that students are now progressing from writing their name on the primer rule to writing it on a more authentic single line.

Additional Activities
Activity 1: Have students work with a partner to point to each letter in their name and spell it aloud.

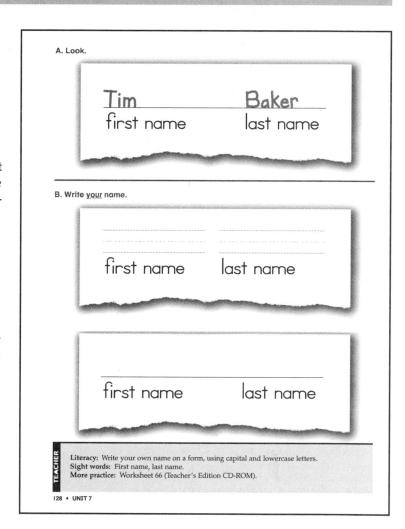

A. Look.

Tim   Baker
first name   last name

B. Write your name.

first name   last name

first name   last name

TEACHER
Literacy: Write your own name on a form, using capital and lowercase letters.
Sight words: First name, last name.
More practice: Worksheet 66 (Teacher's Edition CD-ROM).

128 • UNIT 7

Activity 2: Place lowercase Letter Cards a-z along the board rim in alphabetical order. One at a time, dictate the letters in your name or a student's name. Have individual students come up to the board and select each letter. Copy the letter on the board. Be sure to make the first letter a capital and point it out to the class. Then have the student return the card to its place in the alphabet. When the complete name is written on the board, point to it and say it clearly.

Worksheet Link: Worksheet 66
The worksheet changes the order of first and last names to prepare students for forms that require last name first. Be certain that students understand how to write their first and last name freehand before going on to the next literacy lesson.

TEACHER

Survival: Learn vocabulary for more relationships. Discuss national origin.
New language: Employer, co-worker, girlfriend, boyfriend / What's your [employer]'s name? /
Where is [he] from?

🎧 A. Look and Listen.

See "Look and listen" on page T17a.

🎧 B. Listen again and repeat.

See "Listen again and repeat" on page T17a.

> **Tapescript**
> 1. employer   2. co-worker   3. girlfriend
> 4. boyfriend

🎧 C. Listen and circle.

See "Listen and circle" on page T17a–b.

> **Tapescript**
> **Conversation 1**
> **A:** What's your employer's name?   **B:** Sam Lee.
>
> **Conversation 2**
> **A:** What's your girlfriend's name?   **B:** Alice Carter.

🎧 D. Look and listen.

See also "Look and listen" on page T9a.

➤ Say *My employer is [name of school director]. He / She is from [name of place].*

➤ Show the class a world map. Point to the countries *Brazil* and *Canada* as you say their names.

🎧 E. Listen again and repeat.

Additional Activities

Activity 1: Practicing contracting *Where* and *is*. Gesture to a male student and ask the class *Where is he from?* Hold up four fingers and repeat the question, touching a finger for each word. Then ask the contracted form *Where's he from?* Join the first two fingers together to represent the contraction of *Where* and *is*.

Repeat with a female student. You may want to point at different students and have the class form the contracted questions.

Activity 2: Have students bring in pictures of family, friends, and co-workers. Students work in small groups to ask and answer questions about the people, such as *What's her name? How do you spell that? Where's she from? How old is she?* (if a child).

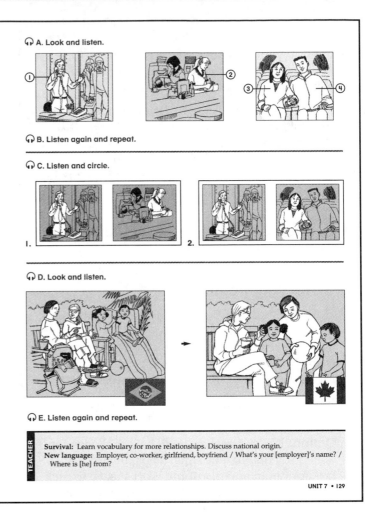

🎧 A. Look and listen.

🎧 B. Listen again and repeat.

🎧 C. Listen and circle.

1.   2.

🎧 D. Look and listen.

🎧 E. Listen again and repeat.

TEACHER

Survival: Learn vocabulary for more relationships. Discuss national origin.
New language: Employer, co-worker, girlfriend, boyfriend / What's your [employer]'s name? /
Where is [he] from?

UNIT 7 • 129

Activity 3 (Challenge): Copy and distribute Worksheet 0. Print the name of each student's country, and give each student his country name. Have each student say the name of the country and spell it for the class. The class writes it down freehand on the Worksheet (all capitals). Then identify each country on the map. Note: Most of your students will probably not be able to read or locate a country on a world map. This activity is simply to expose students to the concept of a world map.

> **Tapescript**
> **A:** What's your employer's name? **B:** Dan Casal.
> **A:** Where's he from? **B:** He's from Brazil.
>
> **B:** What's *your* employer's name? **A:** Lynette Jones.
> **B:** Where's she from? **A:** She's from Canada.

Authentic practice: Students listen to an authentic conversation about name, marital status, and national origin and then complete listening and speaking tasks, providing true information about themselves.

🎧 A. Listen and circle.

➤ Write the four names in this exercise on the board. Point to each name and spell it.

➤ Have students listen once first. Point to each letter of the names on the board as students listen.

➤ Play the cassette or read the tapescript aloud. Students circle the correct spelling of the name.

Tapescript

Conversation 1
A: Who's that? **B:** That's Hanna. She's my co-worker. **A:** Hanna. How do you spell that?
B: Hanna? H-A-N-N-A.

Conversation 2
A: There's my wife. **B:** What's her name?
A: Mei. **B:** M-A-Y? **A:** No. M-E-I.

🎧 B. Look and listen.

See also "Look and listen" on page T22a.

➤ Ask several students *What's your marital status? Are you single or married?* Asking these two questions together will clarify the meaning of the new, authentic question (What's your marital status?) and will prepare students for the Listen and respond activity.

➤ On a world map, identify the location of Haiti.

➤ Play the cassette or read the tapescript aloud as many times as necessary.

Additional Activity
Test comprehension. Hold the book up for the class to see. Point to the woman and ask *What's her name? Where is she from? Is she single or married?*

Tapescript

A: Could you please spell your name? **B:** My first name or my last name?

A: Your last name. **B:** Sure. It's M-A-R-T-I-N.

A: What's your marital status? **B:** I'm separated.

A: And where are you from? **B:** Haiti.

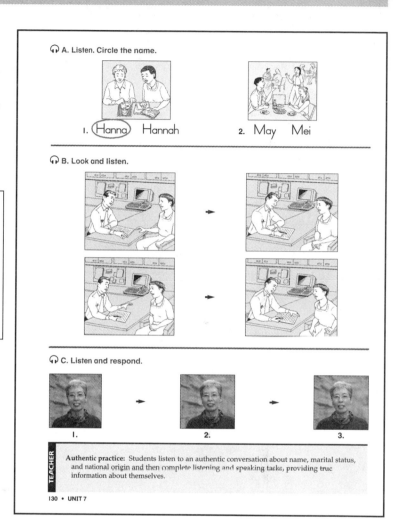

🎧 A. Listen. Circle the name.

1. (Hanna) Hannah   2. May Mei

🎧 B. Look and listen.

🎧 C. Listen and respond.

1.   2.   3.

Authentic practice: Students listen to an authentic conversation about name, marital status, and national origin and then complete listening and speaking tasks, providing true information about themselves.

130 • UNIT 7

🎧 C. Listen and respond.

See "Listen and respond" on page T22a.

Tapescript

Prompt 1: Could you spell your last name, please?
Prompt 2: What's your marital status? Are you single or married?
Prompt 3: Where are you from?

Listen and respond (possible student responses)

Prompt 1: [student spells last name]. **Prompt 2:** I'm single / married / divorced / separated / widowed. **Prompt 3:** I'm from [country name].

TEACHER

Literacy review: Review correspondence of capital and lowercase letters in alphabetical order.
More practice: Worksheet 67 (Teacher's Edition CD-ROM).
Literacy test: Teacher's Edition CD-ROM.

Circle.

See "Circle" on page T120.

Additional Activities

Activity 1: Write similar letter sequences on the board. Have students take turns coming up to the board and circling the matching letter. Make sure students always say the name of each letter as they do the exercise.

Activity 2: Concentration. Make multiple sets of any ten letter cards. Follow the instructions for Activity 2 on page T28.

Activity 3: Have students look around the classroom for three minutes to find printed letters. Have students take turns pointing to the letters they found and naming each one.

Activity 4: Test students' knowledge of the letter names. Show students Letter Cards in both lowercase and capital form. Correctly name the first card you show. After you speak, nod your head and say *Yes!* Then incorrectly name a letter. After you speak, shake your head and say *No!* Then invite students to say *Yes* or *No* as you call out correct and incorrect names of the letters.

Activity 5: Make multiple copies of any four lowercase Letter Cards. Line up several of the same lowercase Letter Cards on the board rim, but turn some of the cards on their sides or upside down. Invite students to come to the board to correct the orientation of the cards. For more challenge, combine different Letter Cards, both lowercase and capital, in the same line-up. Occasionally add in a letter from the previous lessons.

Activity 6: Play a memory game. Photocopy any eight lowercase Letter Cards. Give each student one set of each. Have students lay them out on their desks. Make sure the cards are all correctly oriented. Have students close their eyes. Call out four letters in a row. Have students recite the letters aloud and then open their eyes and find the letters in their card sets. Repeat calling out different letters. This game reviews letter names and develops students' visualization of letters.

Circle.   NAME _____

a	Ⓐ D	b	P B
c	C E	d	D B
e	O E	f	T F
g	G Q	h	N H
i	J I	j	J F
k	H K	l	I L
m	M W	n	U N
o	O D	p	D P
q	P Q	r	R B
s	Z S	t	J T
u	A U	v	Y V
w	V W	x	Z X
y	X Y	z	Z L

TEACHER

Literacy review: Review correspondence of capital and lowercase letters in alphabetical order.
More practice: Worksheet 67 (Teacher's Edition CD-ROM).
Literacy test: Teacher's Edition CD-ROM.

UNIT 7 • 131

Worksheet Link: Worksheet 67

Assign the worksheet for homework or in-class independent work. Follow the procedures for the above activity. Review students' work to make sure they can match the capital with the lowercase form of every letter in the alphabet.

Survival / civics review: Point and name things in the pictures. Make sentences about the pictures. Role-play conversations based on the pictures.
Tests: Teacher's Edition CD-ROM.

Talk about the pictures.

➤ Hold up the Student's Book and point between any two people in the picture. Have students name the probable relationship between the two people. *(mother, father, son, daughter, sister, brother, wife, husband, friend.)* Note: Students do not have the language to describe a relationship between the man and woman in the first picture.

➤ Have students point and name relationships and other things in the picture with a partner.

Possible student responses

mother / father / son / daughter / sister / brother / wife / husband / friend / co-worker / employer / girlfriend / boyfriend / (Unit 4:) shoes / socks / pants / shirts

---

Role-play conversations.

➤ Point to the father's speech balloon in the first picture and say *This is my son*. Then point to the teacher and gesture to elicit a student's response. *(What's his name?)* Model any of the other scenes.

➤ With a partner, students practice conversations.

➤ Ask pairs of students to present some of their conversations to the class.

Talk about the pictures. Role-play conversations.

Survival / civics review: Point and name things in the pictures. Make sentences about the pictures. Role-play conversations based on the pictures.
Tests: Teacher's Edition CD-ROM.

132 • UNIT 7

Role-play conversations (possible student responses)

(Father, son, and teacher)
A: (Unit 5:) Good morning. / Good afternoon. / (Unit 2:) Hello. (Unit 1:) I'm [first name, last name]. (Unit 7:) And this is my son. **B:** What's his name? **A:** [first name, last name]. **B:** How do you spell that? **A:** [all alphabet letters]. **B:** How old is he? **A:** He's [five] years old. **B:** (Unit 2:) What's your address and zip code? And your telephone number and area code? **A:** [address and zip code, telephone number and area code]. (Unit 5:) Oh, when is school? **B:** School is Monday to Friday, from [hour] to [hour]. **A:** (Unit 1:) Thank you. / Thanks. Bye. **B:** Bye. See you later, [son's name].

(Two women looking at photographs)
A: This is my daughter / son / husband. **B:** What's her / his name? **A:** [name]. **B:** (Unit 1:) That's a nice name. (Unit 7:) How do you spell that? **A:** [all alphabet letters]. **B:** Where's your husband from? **A:** [country name]. **B:** How old is your daughter / son? **A:** She's / He's [eight] years old.

(Bottom picture)
A: [Name], this is my friend / sister / wife / girlfriend / co-worker, [name]. [Name], this is my friend, [name]. **B:** (Unit 1:) Hi. Nice to meet you, [name]. **C:** Nice to meet you too, [name]. **B:** (Unit 7:) Where are you from? **C:** I'm from [place name]. (Unit 1:) And you? **B:** (Unit 7:) I'm from [place name]. (Unit 1:) What do you do? **C:** I'm a [occupation]. What about you? **B:** I'm a [cook] [too].

LESSON PLAN FOR STUDENT'S PAGE 133

TEACHER

Literacy: Recognize sound-symbol correspondence of D and Z as initial sound of known and unknown words. Trace D and Z.

This unit continues introducing students to the sounds of letters. In Unit 6, students learned the sounds of the letters M, B, P, F, V, H. In this unit, students will learn the sounds of D, Z, S, T, N, J.

🎧 A. Look and listen.

See "Look and listen" on page T98a.

🎧 B. Listen again and repeat.

See "Listen again and repeat" on page T98a.

Option: Make sure students understand the mechanics of forming the /d/ sound. Encourage them to look at your mouth as you say it. The tip of the tongue presses against the upper gum ridge and then releases a puff of air. Students can place their hands in front of their mouths as they say /d/ to feel a light puff of air. To help students identify the voiced quality of /d/, have them place their hands on their throats or cover their ears as they say it.

Tapescript
/d/, /d/, day

🎧 C. Look and listen.

See "Look and listen" on page T98a.

🎧 D. Listen again and repeat.

See "Listen again and repeat" on page T98a.

Option: Make sure students understand the mechanics of forming the /z/ sound. Encourage them to look at your mouth as you say it. Exaggerate baring and clenching your teeth. Have the class imitate you and produce a very long /z/ sound (as long as your breath). To help students identify the voiced quality of /z/, have them place their hands on their throats or cover their ears as they say it.

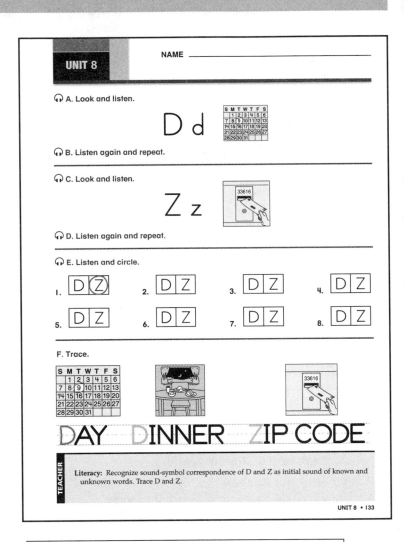

Literacy: Recognize sound-symbol correspondence of D and Z as initial sound of known and unknown words. Trace D and Z.

UNIT 8 • 133

Tapescript
/z/, /z/, zip code

🎧 E. Listen and circle.

See "Listen and circle M or B" on page T98b.

Additional Activity

Hand out a set of D and Z Letter Cards to each student. Read the words from the tapescript in a scrambled order and have students hold up the letter they hear.

Tapescript

1. zip 2. dip 3. zone 4. zebra 5. dab 6. dime 7. zoom 8. doom

---

F. Trace.

➤ Model the exercise. Place Vocabulary Cards 70, 107, 18, *(day, dinner, zip code)* on the board rim and write the words on the board. Point to a Vocabulary Card and its word on the board. Say the word and then trace its initial letter.

➤ Have students point to each picture, say its name, and then trace the letter. Pay attention to students' proper pronunciation of the letter sound and their correct strokes in writing the letter.

Note: The goal is for students to recognize the sound and trace the initial letter of each word. They should not be expected to sound out or read the remaining letters in the word.

Additional Activity

(Challenge): Review letter-sound correspondence. Show the class Letter Cards B, D, F, H, M, P, V, Z. Call on students to recite the letter name, a word that begins with the letter, and the sound it represents; for example, *D, day, /d/*. You may choose to pass out the Letter Cards to pairs or small groups of students and have them work together to think of a word for each letter.

NOTES

TEACHER

Literacy: Discriminate between D and Z as initial sound of known words.
  Listen and trace D and Z.
More practice: Worksheet 68 (Teacher's Edition CD-ROM).

A. Say the word. Circle D or Z.

See "Say the word. Circle M or B" on page T102.

Additional Activities

Activity 1: Review vocabulary words and their initial consonants. Hand out a set of D and Z Letter Cards to each student. Select Vocabulary Cards 18, 35, 39, 45, 70, 107, 129 (*zip code, discount store, drugstore, dress, day, dinner, divorced*). Hold up a Vocabulary Card and gesture to your ear to elicit students' naming the card. Then say *D? Z?* Have students hold up the letter they hear.

Activity 2 (Challenge): The sounds of D, P, and B are often confused. This activity helps students contrast the sounds and associate the letter sounds with words. Hand out a set of D, P, and B Letter Cards to each student. Select Vocabulary Cards 39, 78, 79, 89, 107, 119, 134 (*drugstore, bank, post office, pasta, dinner, daughter, boyfriend*). Hold up a Vocabulary Card and gesture to your ear to elicit students' naming the card. Then say *D? P? B?* Have students hold up the letter they hear.

🎧 B. Listen and trace.

➤ Model the writing of the letters D and Z. Count the strokes out loud as you write each letter on the board.

➤ Have students practice on the board and desktops.

➤ Model the exercise. Write the words DAY, ZIP CODE, and DRESS on the board. Point to and say each word, and then trace the initial letter.

Note: The goal for students is to recognize the sound and trace the initial letter of each word. They should not be expected to sound out or read the remaining letters in the word.

➤ As students listen to the words, have them trace the initial letter of each word.

Tapescript
1. day **2.** zip code **3.** dress

Worksheet Link: Worksheet 68

Assign the worksheet for in-class independent work. Follow the procedures for the above activities. Review students' work to make sure they understand the sound-symbol correspondence for D and Z before going on to the next literacy lesson.

TEACHER

Survival: Learn vocabulary for names of body parts.
New language: Head, neck, arm, wrist, hand, leg, ankle, foot.

🎧 A. Look and listen.

See also "Look and listen" on page T17a.

➤ Students listen with books closed. Play the cassette or read the tapescript aloud. Point to each body part on yourself as it is mentioned.

Additional Activity

Test comprehension. Say a vocabulary word and have students point to that body part in their books or on themselves.

🎧 B. Listen again and repeat.

See "Listen again and repeat" on page T17a.

Additional Activity

Point to a body part on yourself and have students say the word. Repeat the process with several words. Then have students do this activity in pairs. (Be sensitive to the fact that students from some cultures may not be comfortable with this activity. An alternative is to bring in pictures of people from magazines or newpapers.)

Tapescript

1. head 2. neck 3. arm 4. wrist 5. hand 6. leg
7. ankle 8. foot

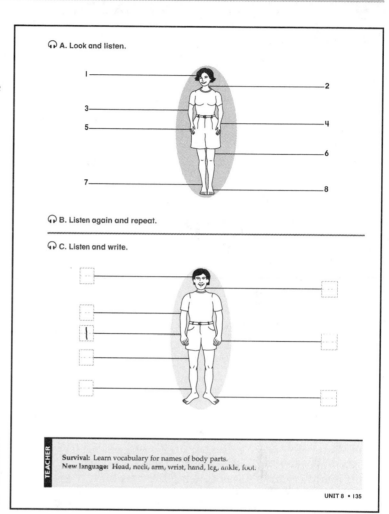

🎧 A. Look and listen.

🎧 B. Listen again and repeat.

🎧 C. Listen and write.

TEACHER

Survival: Learn vocabulary for names of body parts.
New language: Head, neck, arm, wrist, hand, leg, ankle, foot.

UNIT 8 • 135

🎧 C. Listen and write.

➤ Play the cassette or read the tapescript aloud as many times as necessary. Students write the numbers in the correct boxes.

Note: Students will move around the page to write the numbers. They will not follow top-to-bottom and left-to-right order on the page.

Additional Activities

Activity 1: Stand in a circle with the class. Have students take turns pointing to a body part on themselves as the class names it. (Bring in magazine pictures if students would prefer it.)

Activity 2: Play a memory game. Have students stand up. Call out four body parts in a row. Have students point to those four body parts in the same sequence. This activity reviews the names of body parts and develops students' sequencing recall.

Tapescript

1. wrist 2. hand 3. leg 4. foot 5. ankle 6. neck
7. arm 8. head

TEACHER

Survival: Report an injury, express concern, offer to get help, decline help.
Civics concept: You're expected to offer help to someone who is hurt or injured.
New language: What's wrong? / I hurt my [hand]. / Should I get help? / No, thanks. / I'm OK.

🎧 A. Look and listen.

See also "Look and listen" on page T9a.

➤ Set the scene. Hold the book up for the class to see. Point to the pictures and say *work*.

➤ Play the cassette or read the tapescript aloud as many times as necessary. Gesture to convey *I'm OK*. (Hold hand up briefly to dismiss concern.)

🎧 B. Listen again and repeat.

See "Listen again and repeat" on page T9a.

Additional Activities
Activity 1: Test comprehension. Hold the book up for the class to see. Point to the man and ask *What's wrong?* Note that the answer *He hurt his hand* uses the pronoun *he* and the possessive *his*. Both have been taught, but students have not previously put them together in this manner. This question may be too difficult for some students.

Activity 2: Practice new language. Put Vocabulary Cards 135–142 (body parts) on the rim of the board. Say *I hurt my hand* and point to the *hand* card or to your own hand. Repeat, but omit *hand* and point to a different Vocabulary Card or body part. Have students complete the sentence, using the new body part. Repeat this procedure until students can report an injury to several different body parts.

Tapescript

A: What's wrong?   **B:** I hurt my hand.

A: Oh, no! Should I get help?   **B:** No, thanks. I'm OK.

C. Pair work.

➤ Model the Pair work. Have students look at the cues in their book and name the five body parts (*hand, wrist, neck, ankle,* and *foot*). Invite a student to the front of the class. Ask the student *What's wrong?* If the student is confused, offer a possible response and repeat the question. Then ask *Should I get help?* Model again with another student. Clutch a body part as if in pain. Motion for the student to initiate the conversation.

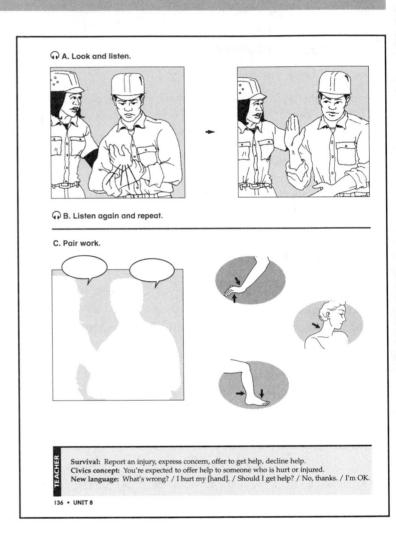

🎧 A. Look and listen.

🎧 B. Listen again and repeat.

C. Pair work.

TEACHER

Survival: Report an injury, express concern, offer to get help, decline help.
Civics concept: You're expected to offer help to someone who is hurt or injured.
New language: What's wrong? / I hurt my [hand]. / Should I get help? / No, thanks. / I'm OK.

136 • UNIT 8

➤ Divide the class into pairs. Students report an injury, express concern, offer to get help, and decline help.

➤ Have several volunteer pairs act out their conversations in front of the class.

Pair work (possible student responses)

A: What's wrong? **B:** I hurt my hand / wrist / neck / ankle / foot. **A:** Should I get help? **B:** No, thanks. I'm OK.

Your students can also say . . .

A: (Unit 1:) How are you? / (Unit 3:) What's the problem? / Do you need an ambulance? **B:** (Unit 1:) I'm fine. / (Unit 8:) I hurt my head / arm / leg.

TEACHER

Literacy: Recognize sound-symbol correspondence of S and T. Discriminate between S and T as initial sound of known and unknown words. Trace S and T.

🎧 A. Look and listen.

See "Look and listen" on page T98a.

🎧 B. Listen again and repeat.

See "Listen again and repeat" on page T98a.

Option: Exaggerate baring and clenching your teeth to produce the /s/ sound. Have the class imitate you and produce a very long /s/ sound (as long as your breath). To help students identify the voiceless quality of /s/, have them place their hands on their throats or cover their ears as they say it. Contrast this to the voiced sound of /z/. You may choose to hold up Vocabulary Cards 18, 50, 123 (*zip code, socks, sister*) and Number Card 7 and say the words. Have students repeat, focusing on their pronunciation of the initial sound.

Tapescript
/s/, /s/, sister

🎧 C. Look and listen.

See "Look and listen" on page T98a.

🎧 D. Listen again and repeat.

See "Listen again and repeat" on page T98a.

Option: To form the /t/ sound, the tip of the tongue presses against the upper gum ridge and then releases a strong puff of air. Place a thin strip of paper in front of your mouth to show how the paper reacts to the sound. Encourage students to practice with a piece of paper or even with their hands in front of their mouths so they can feel the burst of air. /t/ is unvoiced. Have students place their hands on their throats or cover their ears as they say /t/.

Tapescript
/t/, /t/, ten

🎧 E. Listen and circle.

See "Listen and circle M or B" on page T98b.

Additional Activities

Activity 1: Hand out a set of S and T Letter Cards to each student. Read the words from the tapescript in a scrambled order and have students hold up the letter they hear.

Activity 2: The significant difference between D and T is that the former is voiced and the latter is unvoiced. With students' hands to their throats, drill the pronunciation of the two sounds. Then hold up Vocabulary Cards 4, 32, 35, 119, 129 (*teacher, telephone, discount store, daughter, divorced*) and Number Card 10 and say the words. Have students repeat, focusing on the pronunciation of the initial sound.

Tapescript
1. tap 2. sap 3. tag 4. sag 5. ton 6. sun
7. send 8. tend

TEACHER

Literacy: Discriminate between S, T, D, and Z as initial sound of known words. Trace S and T.
More practice: Worksheet 69 (Teacher's Edition CD-ROM).

A. Say the word. Circle the letter.

See "Say the word. Circle M or B" on page T102.

Additional Activities
Activity 1: Hand out a set of B, D, F, H, M, P, S, T, V, and Z Letter Cards to each student. Select Vocabulary Cards 8, 18, 19, 22, 28, 31, 32, 70, 85, 89, 113, 114, 127 (*mechanic, zip code, bus, subway, fire, hospital, telephone, day, fish, pasta, soup, vegetables, married*). Hold up a Vocabulary Card and gesture to your ear to elicit the vocabulary word. Then have students hold up the letter they hear.

Activity 2: The sounds of B, D, and P are often confused. This activity helps students contrast the three sounds. Hand out a set of B, D, and P Letter Cards to each student. Select Vocabulary Cards 39, 78, 79, 89, 107, 119, 134 (*drugstore, bank, post office, pasta, dinner, daughter, boyfriend*). Hold up a Vocabulary Card and gesture to your ear to elicit the vocabulary word. Then say *B? D? P?* Have students hold up the letter they hear.

Activity 3: Concentration. Students can play in groups of three or four. For each group of students, photocopy the following two sets of cards:

Set 1: Vocabulary Cards 16, 41, 48, 91, 102, 103, 108, 114, 125 (*hotel, bakery, pants, milk, salad, drink, toast, vegetables, friend*).

Set 2: Letter Cards B, D, F, H, M, P, S, T, V.

Show each Vocabulary Card to the class to review the vocabulary before playing. Follow the instructions for Activity 1 on page T106.

Activity 4: Review letter-sound correspondences. Show the class Letter Cards B, D, F, H, M, P, S, T, V. Call on students to recite the letter name, a word that begins with the letter, and the sound it represents; for example, *T, ten, /t/*. You may choose to pass out the Letter Cards to pairs or small groups of students and have them work together to think of a word for each letter.

B. Listen and trace.

See "Listen and trace" on page T134.

Additional Activity
Lightly draw the letters M, B, P, F, V, H, D, Z, S, and T on the board. Invite individual students to the board to trace the letters with the correct stroke motions and sequences.

Tapescript
1. son **2.** six **3.** ten

Worksheet Link: Worksheet 69
Assign the worksheet for in-class independent work. Follow the procedures for the above activities. Make sure students understand the sound-symbol correspondence for S and T before going on to the next literacy lesson.

TEACHER

Survival: Learn names of places within buildings.
Civics concept: There are important standard signs in many places.
New language: Entrance, exit, restrooms, stairs, elevator, hall.
Sight words: ENTER, EXIT, PUSH, PULL, MEN, WOMEN, RESTROOMS, STAIRS, ELEVATOR.

🎧 A. Look and listen.

See also "Look and listen" on page T17a.

➤ Mime entering the room as you wave hello to the students. Point to the door and say *entrance*.

➤ Wave good-bye to the students and leave the room. Say *exit*. If there is such a sign in your class-room, point to it (or the door) and say *exit* again.

Option: Have students study the sight words embed-ded in the pictures. Point to the words in the pictures and say each word. Note: Sight words are words stu-dents recognize but don't necessarily read (sound out). There are many ways to acquaint students with sight words. Here we simply suggest you write the words on the board and say them.

Enter: Point to the word *enter* in Picture 1. Write it in large capital letters on the board. Point to the word and say it.

Pull: Write *pull* in large letters on the board. Point to the word and say it. Then mime pulling an imaginary object.

Exit: Write *exit* in large letters on the board. Point to the word on the board and say it.

Push: Write *push* in large letters on the board. Point to it and say it. Then mime pushing an imaginary object.

Women: Copy the symbol and the word *women* on the board. Point to the symbol and word and gesture to-ward some women in the class.

Restrooms: Write *restrooms* in large capital letters on the board. Point to the word and say it.

Men: Copy the symbol and the word *men* on the board. Point to the symbol and word and gesture to-ward some men in the class.

Stairs: Write *stairs* in large letters on the board. Point to the word and mime walking up a flight of stairs. Say *stairs*.

Elevator: Write *elevator* in large letters on the board. Point to the word and say it.

Option: Point to the sight words embedded in the pictures. Say the name of each word and then ask *How do you spell that?* Have students read the letters aloud.

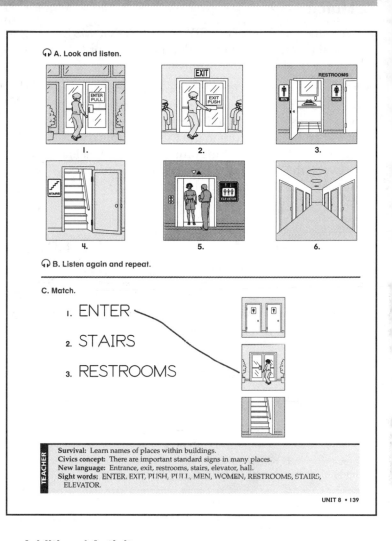

TEACHER

Survival: Learn names of places within buildings.
Civics concept: There are important standard signs in many places.
New language: Entrance, exit, restrooms, stairs, elevator, hall.
Sight words: ENTER, EXIT, PUSH, PULL, MEN, WOMEN, RESTROOMS, STAIRS, ELEVATOR.

UNIT 8 • 139

Additional Activity
Total Physical Response. Drill the concepts of *push* and *pull* with the class. Call out the word *push* and have students perform the appropriate motion to indicate they understood. Repeat with the word *pull*.

🎧 B. Listen again and repeat.

See "Listen again and repeat" on page T17a.

Additional Activity
With the class, walk through the school building. When you come to one of the six vocabulary items, point to it and to elicit the word. Repeat your walk though the building until students can correctly name the *entrance,* (emergency) *exit, restrooms, stairs, elevator* (if available), and *hall.*

(Continued on page T139b.) **T139a**

Tapescript

1. entrance 2. exit 3. restrooms 4. stairs
5. elevator 6. hall

C. Match.

➤ Write the words ENTER, STAIRS, RESTROOMS in capital letters on the board. Point to each word and say it. Have students repeat.

➤ Model the exercise. Tape Vocabulary Cards 143, 146, 145 *(entrance, stairs, restrooms)* on the board. Say *enter* as you point to its printed form on the board and then gesture to the three Vocabulary Cards. Invite a student to come up and draw a line between the word and the Vocabulary Card. Repeat with the other words.

➤ Have students point to each word, say the corresponding sight word, and draw a line connecting the word to its picture.

Additional Activity

Play a word hunt game. Give each student a printed form of a sight word they can find posted in the building. The most common words are *exit, stairs, restrooms, push,* and *pull.* Take a tour. Have students walk and look for the word in a sign. When students see an example of their word, stop walking and have the class compare the word and the sign. Then continue looking for other examples of the words in signs.

NOTES

_____

_____

_____

_____

_____

_____

_____

_____

_____

_____

_____

_____

_____

_____

_____

_____

_____

TEACHER

Survival: Learn vocabulary for directions within buildings. Ask for and give directions.
Civics concept: Signs help you find places.
New language: Down the hall / up [down] the stairs / on the right [left].

🎧 A. Look and listen.

See also "Look and listen" on page T17a.

➤ Review *left* and *right* with the class. With your back to the class, hold up your right arm and say *right*. Then hold up your left arm and say *left*. Have students mimic your movements as you say the words.

Additional Activity
Test comprehension. Say one of the phrases and have students identify the number of the picture.

🎧 B. Listen again and repeat.

See "Listen again and repeat" on page T17a.

Additional Activities
Activity 1: Practice new language. Point upward and say *Up the stairs.* Hold up three fingers and say the phrase again, touching a finger for each word. Repeat, but omit saying *up.* Point to the finger that represents the missing word. Have students supply *up.*

Point downward and say *Down the stairs.* Hold up three fingers and say the phrase again, touching a finger for each word. Repeat, but omit saying *down.* Point to the finger that represents the missing word. Have students supply *down.*

Repeat this procedure for the two phrases *on the right* and *on the left,* having students supply the words *right* and *left* as you gesture to the right and left walls of the classroom.

Activity 2: Total physical response. Call out the words *right* or *left* and have students raise the appropriate arm to indicate they understood. Repeat many times. Call out the words *up* or *down* and have students point upwards or downwards to indicate they understood.

Tapescript

1. down the hall 2. up the stairs 3. down the stairs 4. on the right 5. on the left
---

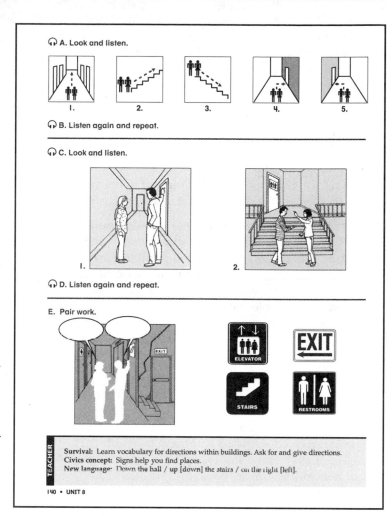

🎧 A. Look and listen.

1. 2. 3. 4. 5.

🎧 B. Listen again and repeat.

🎧 C. Look and listen.

1. 2.

🎧 D. Listen again and repeat.

E. Pair work.

ELEVATOR EXIT STAIRS RESTROOMS

TEACHER
Survival: Learn vocabulary for directions within buildings. Ask for and give directions.
Civics concept: Signs help you find places.
New language: Down the hall / up [down] the stairs / on the right [left].

140 • UNIT 8

🎧 C. Look and listen.

See also "Look and listen" on page T9a.

➤ Play the cassette or read the tapescript aloud as many times as necessary.

Option: To give students visual cues to the tapescript, place Vocabulary Cards 144, 145, and 146 *(exit, restroom, stairs)* on the board rim. Point to each card when it is mentioned in the conversation.

Option: Demonstrate the gestures associated with the following directions as students listen to the conversation: *down the hall, on the right* (point to the distance, as if pointing down a hall, then turn your hand to the

(Continued on page T140b.)

right); *up the stairs, on the left* (point as you move your hand upward, then turn your hand to the left).

Additional Activity

Total physical response. Go to the hallway outside your classroom. Give a volunteer student a simple set of directions to follow (for example, *down the hall, on the left*) and have the student follow the directions. Repeat with other students. With the class, go to a stairway landing and practice the phrases *up the stairs* and *down the stairs*.

⌒ D. Listen again and repeat.

See "Listen again and repeat" on page T9a.

Additional Activities

Activity 1: Test comprehension. Pointing to the appropriate picture, ask *Where's the exit? The restrooms?*

Activity 2: Practice new language. Place Vocabulary Cards 143, 144, and 147 (*entrance, exit, elevator*) on the board rim. Ask *Where's the exit?* and point to the *exit* card. Hold up three fingers and repeat the question, touching a finger for each word. Repeat, but omit the word *exit* and point to the *elevator* card. Have students supply the missing word. Repeat the substitutions until students can produce the three questions without errors.

Place Vocabulary Cards 145–146 (*restrooms, stairs*) on the board. Say *I'm looking for the restrooms* and point to the *restrooms* card. Hold up five fingers and repeat the sentence, touching a finger for each word. Repeat, but omit the word *restrooms* and point to Vocabulary Card 146 (*stairs*). Have students provide the missing word. Repeat the substitutions until students can produce the two statements without errors.

Note: Rather than introduce the more difficult skill of forming questions about plurals, students learn the sentence *I'm looking for the [restrooms]*.

Tapescript

Conversation 1
A: Excuse me. Where's the exit?
B: The exit? Down the hall, on the right.

Conversation 2
A: Excuse me. I'm looking for the restrooms.
B: The restrooms? Up the stairs, on the left.

E. Pair work.

➤ Hold up the Student's Book and point to the Pair work illustration. Model the Pair work. Ask the class *Where is the elevator?* When you receive a correct response, repeat the question and answer to reinforce the model. Then ask for directions to the other cues.

➤ Students ask for and give directions with a partner. They can use the Pair work picture or make up their own directions. Circulate around the classroom, offering help as needed.

Option: Have students stand up to practice these conversations. Encourage them to use gestures to explain their directions.

➤ Have several volunteer pairs act out their conversations in front of the class.

Additional Activity

Go into the hallway outside the classroom and ask students for directions to a place within the school building. Note: You may need to situate yourselves close to the locations (*exit, restrooms, stairs,* and *elevator*) to keep the directions simple.

Pair work (possible student responses)

A: Excuse me. I'm looking for the elevator / exit. Where are the stairs / restrooms? **B:** The [elevator]? Down the hall / on the right / on the left / up the stairs / down the stairs.

Your students can also say . . .

A: Where's the entrance? **B:** (Unit 2:) Right over there. / (Unit 4:) Across from the [elevator]. / Next to the [restrooms]. **A:** (Unit 1:) Thank you. / Thanks. **B:** You're welcome.

TEACHER

Literacy: Recognize sound-symbol correspondence of N and J. Discriminate between N and J as initial sound of known and unknown words. Trace N and J.

🎧 A. Look and listen.

See "Look and listen" on page T98a.

🎧 B. Listen again and repeat.

See "Listen again and repeat" on page T98a.

Option: Make sure students understand the mechanics of forming the /n/ sound. Encourage them to look at your mouth as you say it. It's a nasal sound; the air flows through the nose rather than the mouth. Have the class imitate you and produce a very long /n/ sound (as long as your breath). To help students identify the voiced quality of /n/, have them place their hands on their throats or cover their ears as they say it.

Tapescript
/n/, /n/, November

🎧 C. Look and listen.

See "Look and listen" on page T98a.

🎧 D. Listen again and repeat.

See "Listen again and repeat" on page T98a.

Option: Make sure students understand the mechanics of forming the /dʒ/ sound. Illustrate the brevity of the sound by opening your fist quickly. To help students identify the voiced quality of /dʒ/, have them place their hands on their throats or cover their ears as they say it.

Tapescript
/dʒ/, /dʒ/, June

🎧 E. Listen and circle.

See "Listen and circle M or B" on page T98b.

Additional Activities

Activity 1: Contrast /z/ and /dʒ/. The significant difference between /z/ and /dʒ/ is that the former is a long sound and the latter is a short sound. Have students focus on this difference. With their hands to their throats, drill the pronunciation of the two sounds.

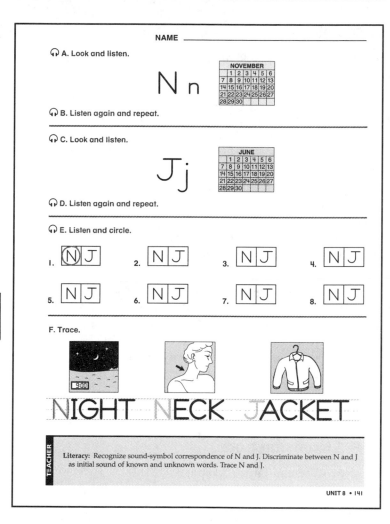

Activity 2: Give each student a set of F, H, J, N, V, and Z Letter Cards. Have students lay the cards out face up on their desks. Call out a letter sound (as opposed to the letter name). Have students select the letter from their sets, hold it up for you to see, and say its name.

Tapescript
1. net 2. jet 3. June 4. noon 5. nag 6. jag 7. job 8. nob

F. Trace.

See "Trace" on page T133b.

TEACHER

Literacy: Discriminate between N, J, D, T, S, and Z as initial sound of known words. Trace N and J.
More practice: Worksheet 70 (Teacher's Edition CD-ROM).

A. Say the word. Circle the letter.

See "Say the word. Circle M or B" on page T102.

Additional Activities
Activity 1: This activity contrasts the sounds of N and M and reviews the S and J sounds. Make multiple copies of Vocabulary Cards 42, 47, 50, 64, 91, 102, 110, 118, and 123 (*mall, jacket, socks, night, milk, salad, jam, mother, sister*) and Number Cards 6 and 9. Tape Letter Cards N, M, J, and S on the board. Pick up a Vocabulary Card. Point to it, say its name, and then place it under the appropriate letter. Have students do this activity in pairs. Review the students' word piles, picking up each Vocabulary Card and saying the word and its initial letter.

Activity 2: Review letter/sound correspondences. Show the class Letter Cards B, D, F, J, M, N, P, S, T, V, Z. Call on students to recite the letter name, a word that begins with the letter, and the sound it represents; for example, *T, ten, /t/*. You may choose to pass out Letter Cards to pairs or small groups of students and have them work together to think of a word for each letter.

⌒ B. Listen and trace.

See also "Listen and trace" on page T134.

➤ Model the writing of the letters N and J.

➤ Have students practice with their fingers on the board and desktops.

➤ Model the exercise. Write the words JUNE, NAME, and JULY on the board. Point to each word, say its name, and then trace its initial letter.

➤ Students trace J and N.

Tapescript
1. June **2.** name **3.** July

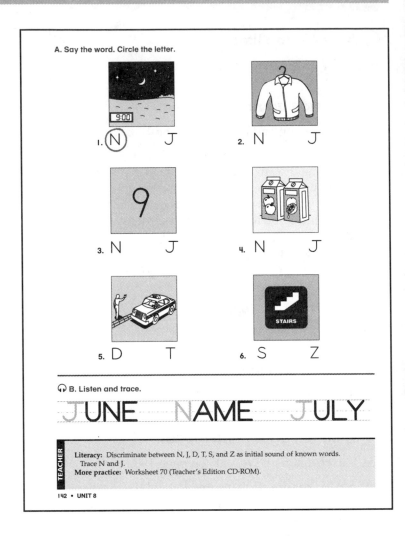

TEACHER

Literacy: Discriminate between N, J, D, T, S, and Z as initial sound of known words. Trace N and J.
More practice: Worksheet 70 (Teacher's Edition CD-ROM).

142 • UNIT 8

Worksheet Link: Worksheet 70
Assign the worksheet for in-class independent work. Follow the procedures for the above activities. Circulate around the classroom as students work to make sure they understand the sound-symbol correspondence for N and J before going on to the next literacy lesson.

TEACHER

Survival: Recognize and demonstrate understanding of common street signs.
Civics concept: Signs protect your safety and that of others. Obey them.
Sight words: STOP, WALK, DON'T WALK.

🎧 A. Look and Listen.

See also "Look and listen" on page T17a.

➤ Set the scene. Hold your book up for the class to see and say *street*.

➤ Play the cassette or read the tapescript aloud as many times as necessary.

➤ Introduce the new vocabulary:

Stop: Mime driving a car, say *stop*, and stop driving.

Walk: Mime walking and say *walk*.

Don't walk: Stand still in one spot and say *Don't walk*. Contrast *walk* and *don't walk* several times.

Option: Sight words are words students recognize but don't necessarily read (sound out). There are many ways to acquaint students with sight words. Here we simply suggest you write the words *stop, walk,* and *don't walk* on the board and say them.

Additional Activity
Total Physical Response. Drill the concepts of *walk* and *don't walk* with the class. Call out the word *walk* and have students walk to indicate that they understand. Then call out *don't walk* for students to stop. Repeat several times.

🎧 B. Listen again and repeat.

See "Listen again and repeat" on page T17a.

Additional Activity
Go to the nearest pedestrian crossing. Point to the walk sign and gesture for a student to tell the class what to do. Wait for the light to change. Again, have a student to read the sign aloud. Repeat two or three times. Look for a stop sign. Have students read the word.

Tapescript
1. stop 2. walk 3. don't walk

C. Match.

➤ Review the sight words. Write the words STOP, WALK, DON'T WALK in a column on the board, in the order they are written in the exercise. Point to each word and say it. Have students repeat.

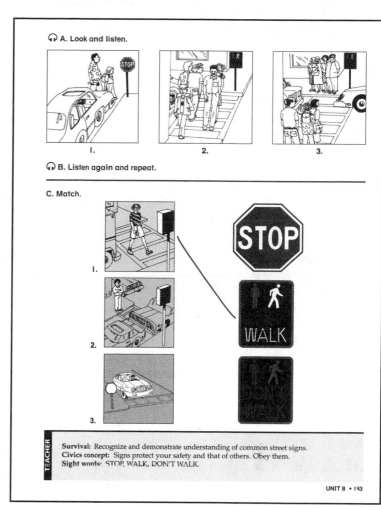

🎧 A. Look and listen.

1. 2. 3.

🎧 B. Listen again and repeat.

C. Match.

1.

2.

3.

STOP

WALK

DON'T WALK

TEACHER

Survival: Recognize and demonstrate understanding of common street signs.
Civics concept: Signs protect your safety and that of others. Obey them.
Sight words: STOP, WALK, DON'T WALK.

UNIT 8 • 143

➤ Model the exercise. Tape Vocabulary Cards 154–156 *(stop, walk, don't walk)* to the left of the words on the board, in the order they are placed in the exercise. Point to a Vocabulary Card and elicit the word. Invite a student to come up and draw a line between the Vocabulary Card and the word(s). Repeat with the two other cards.

➤ Have students complete the exercise.

Additional Activity
Make two large signs with the words *walk* and *don't walk*. Clear away the classroom furniture or go into the hallway. Stand far away from the students, lift up the *walk* sign, and have the students walk toward you. Lift up the *don't walk* sign and have the students stop. You may want to have only three or four students walk at a time and another student hold up the signs.

Survival: Warn someone about a danger. Recognize and understand signs that say
DANGER and CAUTION. Recognize and understand international "prohibited" symbol
(diagonal line through picture).
Civics concept: Signs can indicate danger. Recognize them and heed them.
New language: Uh-oh! / What's the matter? / Look at the sign. / Oh, thanks.
Sight words: NO SWIMMING, DANGER, POISON, NO SMOKING, CAUTION, FLAMMABLE.

🎧 A. Look and listen.

See also "Look and listen" on page T9a.

➤ Mime swimming. Point to the sign in the second picture, shake your head, and say *no swimming*.

🎧 B. Listen again and repeat.

See "Listen again and repeat" on page T9a.

Option: Introduce the high/low intonation pattern of *Uh-oh!* with a surprised or concerned look on your face.

Additional Activity
(Challenge): Illustrate the transference of the language to other situations. Before doing so, make sure that your students fully understand the context of the conversation on page 144. Then place Vocabulary Cards 159, 29, 30, *(no swimming sign, fire truck, ambulance)* on the board rim. Say *Look at the sign* and point to Vocabulary Card 159. Hold up four fingers and repeat the sentence, touching a finger for each word, but change the word *sign* to *ambulance*. Repeat this procedure until students can produce the sentences *Look at the ambulance* and *Look at the fire truck* error-free.

Tapescript
A: Uh-oh! B: What's the matter?
A: Look at the sign. B: Oh. Thanks.

🎧 C. Look and listen.

See also "Look and listen" on page T17a.

➤ Write the words DANGER and CAUTION on the board. Convey the meaning of each sign with gestures. For example, mime puffing on a cigarette, shake your head, and say *No smoking!* Mime putting out the cigarette.

Additional Activity
Bring to class magazine pictures of locations where one would find these danger signs (lakes, rivers, cleaning products, a gas station, a garage, a restaurant, an office building, etc.). Distribute the pictures, along with copies of Vocabulary Cards 157–160 (warning signs). Have students tape the signs onto the appropriate pictures (or group the pictures and signs together) and then show the class.

T144

🎧 A. Look and listen.

🎧 B. Listen again and repeat.

🎧 C. Look and listen.

 1.  2.

 3.  4.

🎧 D. Listen again and repeat.

Survival: Warn someone about a danger. Recognize and understand signs that say DANGER and CAUTION. Recognize and understand international "prohibited" symbol (diagonal line through picture).
Civics concept: Signs can indicate danger. Recognize them and heed them.
New language: Uh-oh! / What's the matter? / Look at the sign. / Oh, thanks.
Sight words: NO SWIMMING, DANGER, POISON, NO SMOKING, CAUTION, FLAMMABLE.

144 • UNIT 8

🎧 D. Listen again and repeat.

See "Listen again and repeat" on page T17a.

Tapescript
1. No swimming 2. No smoking
3. Danger—poison 4. Caution—flammable

If your students are ready . . .

Civics enrichment: Take a walk with your class through your building and point out all the danger signs. Use the context of each sign to explain the meaning.

Literacy: Review capital and lowercase correspondence. Trace initial consonant of known words in both capital and lowercase letters.
More practice: Worksheet 71 (Teacher's Edition CD-ROM).

A. Circle.

See "Circle" on page T120.

Additional Activities

Activity 1: Write a column of capital letters on the board and a second column of the same letters, in lowercase form and in a different order. Have students take turns coming up to the board and drawing a line between the matching letters. Make sure students always say the name and size of each letter as they do the exercise. (See the first paragraph on page T119a regarding *large* and *small*, *capital* and *lowercase*.)

Activity 2: For further practice, give each student a set of capital and lowercase Letter Cards B, D, M, N, P. Students work with a partner. Student A chooses a card and says the letter name and size without showing the card to Student B. B then finds the card in his own set. The two students check their cards to make sure they match. Students continue, taking turns, until all cards are matched.

B. Trace.

See also "Trace" on page T133b.

➤ Model the exercise. Place Vocabulary Card 91 (*milk*) on the board rim and write *milk* on the board twice—once in capitals and once in lowercase letters. Point to the Vocabulary Card and words on the board. Say *milk* as you point to each word and then trace the initial M and m.

➤ Students trace capital and lowercase letters in known words.

Additional Activities

Activity 1: Have students evaluate your handwriting. Write several examples of lowercase letter m on a primer-ruled line on the board. Include one or two examples of a malformed m (for example, in straight lines rather than curved). Have students take turns coming up to the board to cross out the incorrectly formed letters. Repeat this procedure with the lowercase letters b, d, f, h, j, m, n, p, s, t, v, z. You may also choose to have students erase the incorrect letters and write them correctly.

Activity 2: The lowercase form of the letters n, m, and h are difficult to distinguish visually. This activ-

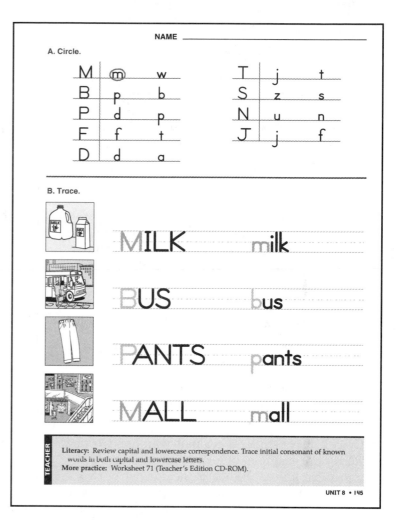

ity gets students to pay careful attention to each letter shape. Make multiple copies of the lowercase n, m, and h Letter Cards. Begin by lining up several of the same Letter Cards on the board rim, but turn some of the cards on their sides or upside down. Invite students to come to the board to correct the orientation of each card. For more challenge, combine different Letter Cards in the same line-up. Repeat the procedure again with the lowercase letters s and z, or the capitals of B, P, and D.

Worksheet Link: Worksheet 71

Assign the worksheet for homework or in-class independent work. Follow the procedures for the above activities.

TEACHER

Literacy: Trace initial consonant of known words in both capital and lowercase letters.
More practice: Worksheet 72 (Teacher's Edition CD-ROM).

Trace.

See also "Trace" on page T133b.

➤ Model the exercise. Place Vocabulary Card 28 (fire) on the board rim and write *FIRE* and *fire* on the board. Point to the Vocabulary Card and the words on the board. Say *fire* as you point to each word and then trace the initial capital and lowercase F.

➤ Students trace capital and lowercase letters F, D, T, S, N, J.

Additional Activities

Activity 1: Concentration. Students can play in groups of three or four. For each group of students, photocopy the following two sets of cards:

Set 1: Vocabulary Cards 45, 48, 84, 108, 110, 114, 126, 134, 136, 139, 142 (*dress, pants, meat, toast, jam, vegetables, single, boyfriend, neck, hand, foot*).

Set 2: Lowercase Letter Cards b, d, f, h, j, m, n, p, s, t, and v.

Show each Vocabulary Card to the class to review the vocabulary before playing. Follow the instructions for Activity 1 on page T106.

Activity 2: Have students evaluate your handwriting. Write several examples of lowercase letter m on a primer-ruled line on the board. Include one or two examples of a malformed m (for example, in straight lines rather than curved). Have students take turns coming up to the board to cross out the incorrectly formed letters. You may also choose to have students erase the malformed letters and write them correctly. Repeat this procedure with lowercase letters: b, d, f, h, j, n, p, s, t, v, and z.

Activity 3: Review vocabulary and initial consonants. Hand out a set of b, d, f, j, m, n, p, s, and t Letter Cards to each student. Hold for yourself a set of Vocabulary Cards 4, 19, 28, 42, 47, 48, 70, 91, 136, 154 (*teacher, bus, fire, mall, jacket, pants, day, milk, neck, stop*) Hold up a card and gesture to your ear to elicit the vocabulary word. Then have students hold up the letter they hear.

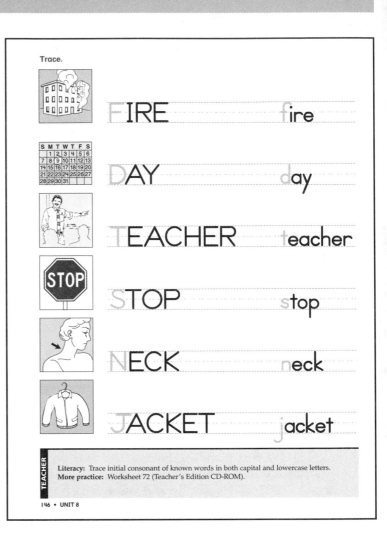

Trace.

FIRE   fire

DAY   day

TEACHER   teacher

STOP   stop

NECK   neck

JACKET   jacket

TEACHER **Literacy:** Trace initial consonant of known words in both capital and lowercase letters.
More practice: Worksheet 72 (Teacher's Edition CD-ROM).

146 • UNIT 8

Worksheet Link: Worksheet 72

Assign the worksheet for in-class independent work. Follow the procedures for the above activities. Circulate around the classroom to make sure students understand the sound-symbol correspondence for N and J.

Survival: Learn vocabulary for passenger restraints. Understand necessity of using passenger restraints in vehicles.
Civics concept: The law requires safety restraints. You must obey the law.
New language: Car, seat belt, car seat, booster seat, stroller, safety harness /
You have to use a [seat belt]. / Why? / It's the law.

🎧 A. Look and listen.

See "Look and listen" on page T17a.

Option: Help students understand the differences in these safety devices. Point to yourself and say *I? A seat belt*, and hold up the corresponding Vocabulary Card. Gesture to other students in the class and repeat the advice *You? A seat belt*. Show a picture of a school-age child (eight to ten years old) and say *He / She? A seat belt*.

Point to a picture of a baby or hold a pretend baby in your arms. Say *The baby? A car seat* and hold up the corresponding Vocabulary Card.

Point to a picture of a young child three to five years old, or gesture as if indicating a young child's height. Say *My daughter / son? A booster seat*, and hold up the corresponding Vocabulary Card.

Additional Activities
Activity 1: Test comprehension. Say a vocabulary word and have students identify the number of the picture.

Activity 2: Give each student a set of Vocabulary Cards 162–166 (*seat belt, car seat, booster seat, stroller, safety harness*). Have students lay the cards out face up on their desks. Call out a vocabulary word and have students select the card and hold it up for you to see.

🎧 B. Listen again and repeat.

See "Listen again and repeat" on page T17a.

Option: Demonstrate with hand motions the high/low pitch of two-word nouns (*seat belt, car seat, booster seat, safety harness*).

Option: To get students to fully associate letters with sounds, place the Letter Cards S, B, and H on the board rim. Say *seat, stroller, safety* and point to the letter S. Say *booster, belt* and point to the letter B. Say *harness* and point to the letter H. Have students repeat after you.

Additional Activity
Provide speaking practice. With students' books open, hold up a Vocabulary Card and have students say the

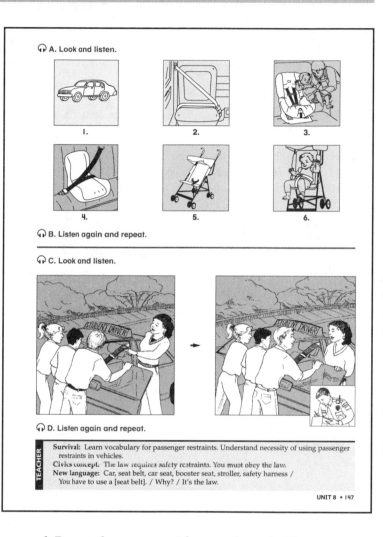

word. Repeat the process with several words. Then have students do this activity in pairs.

Tapescript
1. car 2. seat belt 3. car seat 4. booster seat
5. stroller 6. safety harness

🎧 C. Look and listen.

See also "Look and listen" on page T9a.

➤ Hold the book up for the class to see. Point to the following items in the picture and say their names: *car, students, teacher*.

(Continued on page T147b.)

➤ Play the cassette or read the tapescript aloud as many times as necessary.

Option: Give students visual cues to the dialogue. Mime putting on a seat belt to convey the meaning of *You have to use a seat belt.* Point to the inset picture of the police officer to convey the meaning of *the law.*

🎧 D. Listen again and repeat.

See "Listen again and repeat" on page T9a.

Additional Activities

Activity 1: Test comprehension. Say *You have to use a seat belt. Why?* (It's the law.)

Activity 2: Practice new language. Put Vocabulary Cards 162–164 *(seat belt, car seat, booster seat)* on the rim of the board. Say *You have to use a seat belt* and point to the *seat belt* card. Hold up seven fingers and repeat the sentence, touching a finger for each word. Repeat, but omit *seat belt.* Point to the two fingers that represent the missing phrase. Have students supply *seat belt.*

Say the sentence again, but this time change *seat belt* to *car seat.* Repeat this procedure until students can produce the sentence error-free, substituting *seat belt* with different words.

Tapescript

A: You have to use a seat belt.
B: Why?

A: It's the law.

If your students are ready . . .

Civics enrichment: The law in many places requires safety restraints. Show students pictures of people, young and old. Point to a picture and ask *Car seat? Booster seat? Seat belt?* Have students respond. Go through many examples of different ages so students understand who must wear each type of safety restraint.

Explain that seat belts are also required in the back seats of a car. Point to a picture of a car. Point to the front seats and say *You have to use a seat belt. It's the law.* Point to the back seats and repeat this phrase, gesturing to different students to show seat belts are required of everyone.

NOTES

_____

_____

_____

_____

_____

_____

_____

_____

_____

_____

_____

Authentic practice: Students listen to an authentic conversation at a medical reception desk and then complete listening and speaking tasks, providing true information about themselves.

🎧 A. Listen and circle.

➤ Prepare students for listening. Hold the book up for the class to see. Point to each picture to elicit the language it represents. For number 1 there are several possible phrases. If your students do not suggest *Turn right* and *Turn left*, remind them that this language from Unit 3 is also applicable.

➤ Students listen once without writing.

➤ Have students listen again and circle the picture that corresponds to each conversation.

Tapescript
Conversation 1 **A:** Where's the elevator? **B:** The elevator? Turn right at the end of the hall. **A:** Thanks. **Conversation 2** **A:** Buckle up! You have to use your seat belt. **B:** You're right. Thanks.

🎧 B. Look and listen.

See also "Look and listen" on page T22a.

➤ Set the scene. Have students look at the three pictures. Point to the pictures and say *hospital*.

Additional Activities

Activity 1: Test comprehension. Hold the book up for the class to see. Point to the woman and ask *What's the matter? What's her name?*

Activity 2: Teach new vocabulary. Have students study the pictures. Point to the following items and say their names: *form, pen.* Or bring in a blank form and a pen and use them as props as you read the tapescript or play the cassette.

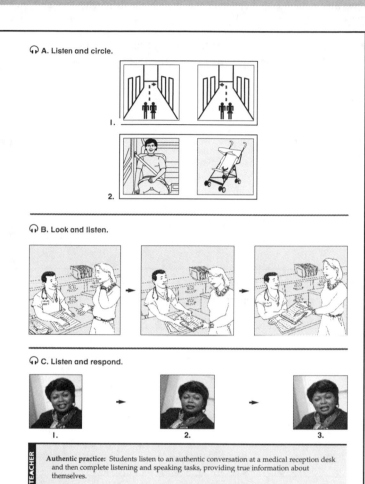

🎧 A. Listen and circle.

1.

2.

🎧 B. Look and listen.

🎧 C. Listen and respond.

1.   2.   3.

Authentic practice: Students listen to an authentic conversation at a medical reception desk and then complete listening and speaking tasks, providing true information about themselves.

148 • UNIT 8

Tapescript
A: Yes, ma'am. What's the problem? **B:** I hurt my neck. **A:** OK. Spell your name, please. **B:** Karen Kraft. K–A–R–E–N . . . last name K–R–A–F–T. **A:** Thank you, Ms. Kraft. Could you please fill out this form? Here's a pen. Please fill out both sides. **B:** Sure. No problem. **A:** Thank you. The doctor is ready. He's in Room 2, at the end of the hall. Feel better! **B:** Thank you very much.

(Continued on page T148b.)

🎧 C. Listen and respond.

See also "Listen and respond" on page T22a.

Note: The goal of this activity is to give students practice responding to authentic prompts, using the language they have learned so far, thus building confidence. Different students will say different things.

➤ Do this exercise several times to give students practice answering authentic questions.

➤ Have the class listen as you ask individual students the three question prompts.

Tapescript

Prompt 1: Spell your name, please.

Prompt 2: Thanks. Please fill out this form. Here's a pencil.

Prompt 3: Thank you. The doctor is in Room 3. It's down the hall across from the restrooms. Feel better!

Listen and respond
(possible student responses)

Prompt 1: [student spells name, any alphabet letters].

Prompt 2: (Unit 6:) Certainly. / (Unit 3:) OK. / (Unit 2:) Sure.

Prompt 3: (Unit 1:) Thank you. / Thanks.

NOTES

_____

_____

_____

_____

_____

_____

_____

_____

_____

_____

_____

_____

_____

_____

_____

_____

_____

_____

TEACHER

Literacy review: Review correspondence of capital and lowercase letters. Trace and write capital and lowercase letters as initial letters of known words.
More practice: Worksheets 73–74 (Teacher's Edition CD-ROM).
Literacy test: Teacher's Edition CD-ROM.

A. Circle.

See "Circle" on page T120.

Additional Activities

Activity 1: Copy and distribute capital and lowercase Letter Cards: B, D, F, J, M, N, P, S, and T. Have pairs of students work together to match the lowercase and capital cards.

Activity 2: Play a memory game. Photocopy lowercase Letter Cards b, d, f, h, j, m, n, p, s, t, v, and z and give each student one set. Have students close their eyes. Call out four letters in a row. Have students open their eyes and find the letters in their Letter Card sets. Repeat with different letters. This game reviews letter names as well as develops students' visualization of letters.

B. Trace.

See also "Trace" on page T133b.

➤ Model the exercise. Place Vocabulary Card 154 (stop) on the board rim and write STOP and stop on the board. Point to the Vocabulary Card and the capital and lowercase words on the board. Say stop as you point to each word and then trace the initial capital and lowercase S.

➤ Students trace capital and lowercase letters S, M, B, F, D.

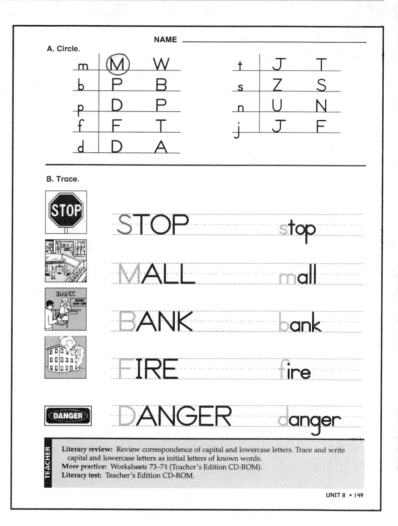

Additional Activities

Activity 1: Review vocabulary words and their initial consonants. Hand out a set of Letter Cards: B, D, F, H, J, M, N, P, S, and T to each student. Hold for yourself a set of Vocabulary Cards 8, 14, 16, 19, 23, 64, 70, 79, 81, 94 (mechanic, school, hotel, bus, taxi, night, day, post office, factory, juice).

Hold up a card and gesture to your ear to elicit the vocabulary word. Then have students hold up the letter for the sound they hear.

Activity 2: This activity integrates students' knowledge of vocabulary, initial consonant sounds, and their freehand writing skills. Place Letter Cards B, D, F, H, J, M, N, P, S and T along the board rim. Say one of the following known words: Mr., Ms., turn, March, June, July, September, November, December, nine, ten,

fifteen, please, number, Sunday, Monday, Tuesday, Friday, Saturday. Have a student come up the board and select the word's initial letter. Have the student copy the letter on the board and then return the letter to the board rim. Repeat the word and point to the letter on the board. (Note that these words are known but do not have corresponding Vocabulary Cards.)

Worksheet Link: Worksheets 73–74
Assign the worksheets for homework or in-class independent work. Follow the procedures for the above activities.

TEACHER

Survival / civics review: Point and name things in the picture. Make sentences about the picture. Role-play conversations based on the picture.
Tests: Teacher's Edition CD-ROM.

Talk about the picture.

➤ Name the following items and have students point to them in the pictures: *husband, wife, mother, son, stroller, hospital, restrooms, stairs, exit, entrance.*

➤ Hold up the book and point to the same items as above and have students say them. Point to the signs in the pictures. Have students say the sight or vocabulary words.

➤ Have students point to and name the things and places in the picture with a partner.

Possible student responses

stroller / hall / stairs / restrooms / exit / entrance / sign / hand / wrist / neck / ankle / foot / head / arm / leg / (Unit 7:) husband / wife / mother / son / (Unit 4:) shoes / pants / jacket / shirt / stockings / skirt

---

Role-play conversations.

➤ Hold the book up for the class to see. Point to the receptionist talking to the patient and say *What's the matter?* Then point to the patient to elicit a student's response (*I hurt my ankle*).

➤ Model any of the other conversations.

➤ Have students practice conversations appropriate to the contexts in the picture with a partner.

➤ Ask pairs of students to present some of their conversations to the class.

**Role-play conversations
(possible student responses)**

(Receptionist and patient)

A: (Unit 3:) What's the problem? / (Unit 8:)What's the matter? / What's wrong? **B:** I hurt my foot / ankle. **A:** (Unit 4:) Oh, I'm sorry. (Unit 1:) What's your name? **B:** [first name, last name]. **A:** (Unit 7:) How do you spell that? **B:** [any alphabet letters]. **A:** Are you single or married? **B:** I'm single / married / separated / divorced / widowed. **A:** (Unit 2:) What's your address and zip code? **B:** [address and zip code]. **A:** And what's your telephone

---

Talk about the picture. Role-play conversations.

TEACHER

Survival / civics review: Point and name things in the picture. Make sentences about the picture. Role-play conversations based on the picture.
Tests: Teacher's Edition CD-ROM.

150 • UNIT 8

---

number and area code? **B:** [telephone number and area code]. (Unit 5:) What time is it? **A:** It's 10:20. **B:** Oh, good, I'm early / on time. / Oh, no! I'm late!

(Woman with stroller and hospital employee)
A: Excuse me. I'm looking for / Where's the elevator / exit / entrance? / Where are the stairs / restrooms? **B:** The [restrooms]? Down the hall. / On the right. / On the left. / Up the stairs. / Down the stairs. / (Unit 2:) Right over there. / (Unit 4:) Across from the [elevator]. / Next to the [stairs]. **A:** (Unit 1:) Thank you. / Thanks. **B:** You're welcome.

(Elderly couple)
A: Uh-oh! **B:** What's the matter? / What's wrong? / (Unit 3:) What's the problem? **A:** (Unit 8:) Look at the sign! **B:** (Unit 1:) Thanks!

TEACHER

Literacy: Recognize and discriminate between C and G as initial sound of known and unknown words. Trace and write C and G.
More practice: Worksheet 75 (Teacher's Edition CD-ROM).

This unit continues to introduce students to the sounds of letters. In Unit 6, students learned the sounds of the letters M, B, P, F, V, H. In Unit 8, they learned the sounds of the letters D, Z, S, T, N, J. In this unit, they will learn the sounds of C, G, K. In Unit 10, they will learn the sounds of L, Y, R, W.

🎧 A. Look and listen.

See "Look and listen" on page T98a.

Option: You may want to show the class Vocabulary Card 160 (Caution: Flammable) as they listen to the word caution.

🎧 B. Listen again and repeat.

See "Listen again and repeat" on page T98a.

Option: Make sure students understand the mechanics of forming the /k/ sound. The mouth stays open and relaxed. Students can place their hands in front of their mouths as they say /k/ to feel the puff of air. To help students identify the voiceless quality of /k/, have them place their hands on their throats or cover their ears as they say it.

Tapescript
/k/, /k/, caution

🎧 C. Look and listen.

See "Look and listen" on page T98a.

🎧 D. Listen again and repeat.

See "Listen again and repeat" on page T98a.

Option: Make sure students understand the mechanics of forming the /g/ sound. /g/ is produced in the same manner as /k/, only it is voiced. To help students identify the voiced quality of /g/, have them place their hands on their throats or cover their ears as they say it.

UNIT 9 NAME _____

🎧 A. Look and listen.

C c CAUTION

🎧 B. Listen again and repeat.

🎧 C. Look and listen.

G g

🎧 D. Listen again and repeat.

🎧 E. Listen and circle.

1. ⓒ G 2. C G 3. C G 4. C G
5. C G 6. C G 7. C G 8. C G

F. Trace and write.

CAR car
GARAGE arage
COOK ook
GIRLFRIEND irlfriend

TEACHER
Literacy: Recognize and discriminate between C and G as initial sound of known and unknown words. Trace and write C and G.
More practice: Worksheet 75 (Teacher's Edition CD-ROM).

UNIT 9 • 151

Tapescript
/g/, /g/, garage

🎧 E. Listen and circle.

See "Listen and circle M or B" on page T98b.

(Continued on page T151b.)

Additional Activities

Activity 1: Hand out a set of C and G Letter Cards to each student. Read the words from the tapescript in a scrambled order and have students hold up the letter they hear.

Activity 2: Contrast the sounds of C and G. The significant difference between /k/ and /g/ is that /k/ is unvoiced and /g/ is voiced. Have students focus on this difference. With their hands to their throats, drill the pronunciation of the two sounds. Distribute the Letter Cards C and G and have students hold up the letter they hear as you model the two letter sounds. Then have students practice producing the sounds as others listen and identify the letters they hear.

Tapescript

1. could 2. good 3. cot 4. got
5. girl 6. curl 7. card 8. guard

F. Trace and write.

➤ Review the writing of the letters C and G. Count the strokes out loud as you write each letter in capital and lowercase form on the board.

   Option: Since students have learned the strokes, you may want to invite individual students to model the letters.

➤ Model the exercise. Write the first line of the exercise on the board. Show the class Vocabulary Card 20 (*car*). <u>Trace</u> the initial capital letter C of *CAR*. Then <u>write</u> the initial lowercase letter c of *car*.

➤ Have students identify the picture cues before they do the exercise.

➤ Have students work independently to trace and write the letters.

Additional Activity

Provide writing practice. Make a master copy of Worksheet 0 (blank primer rules) with the letters C and G in capitals and lowercase at the beginning of the lines. Make a copy for each student. Have students practice writing the letters. After each line of freehand practice, have them circle their best letters and mark a small x below any letters that need improvement.

Worksheet Link: Worksheet 75

Assign the worksheet for homework or in-class independent work. This worksheet gives students the opportunity to review their handwriting skills.

NOTES

_____

_____

_____

_____

_____

_____

_____

_____

_____

_____

_____

_____

Literacy: Reinforce sound-symbol correspondence of C, G, and K. Trace and write C, G, K.
More practice: Worksheet 76 (Teacher's Edition CD-ROM).

🎧 A. Look and listen.

See also "Look and listen" on page T98a.

➤ Students may be confused that two letters (C and K) represent the same sound. Show the class the Letter Cards C and K and make the /k/ sound to indicate that the two letters represent the same sound.

Note: Students have not yet learned the word *key*, but the illustration will provide the definition.

🎧 B. Listen again and repeat.

See "Listen again and repeat" on page T98a.

Tapescript
/k/, /k/, key

🎧 C. Listen and circle.

See "Listen and circle M or B" on page T98b.

Additional Activity
Hand out a set of K and G Letter Cards to each student. Read the words from the tapescript in a scrambled order and have students hold up the letter they hear.

Tapescript
1. kitchen **2.** garden **3.** good **4.** king

D. Trace and write.

See "Trace and write" on page T151b.

Additional Activities
Activity 1: Provide writing practice. Make a master copy of Worksheet 0 with the letters K and G in capitals and lowercase at the beginning of the lines. Make a copy for each student. Have students practice writing the letters. Have them evaluate their work after each line of freehand practice by circling their best letters and marking a small x below any letters that need improvement.

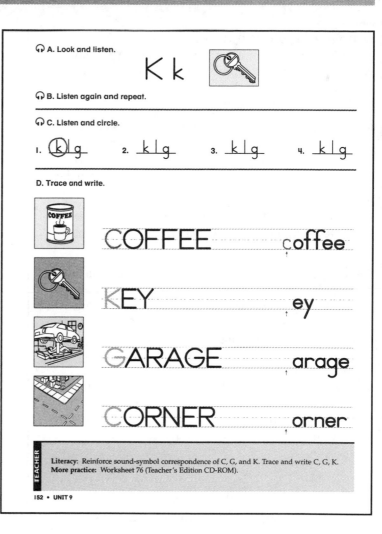

🎧 A. Look and listen.

K k

🎧 B. Listen again and repeat.

🎧 C. Listen and circle.

1. k l g   2. k l g   3. k l g   4. k l g

D. Trace and write.

COFFEE   coffee

KEY   ey

GARAGE   arage

CORNER   orner

Literacy: Reinforce sound-symbol correspondence of C, G, and K. Trace and write C, G, K.
More practice: Worksheet 76 (Teacher's Edition CD-ROM).

152 • UNIT 9

Activity 2: Have students evaluate your handwriting. Write several examples of a capital or lowercase letter K in a line on the board. Include one or two examples of a malformed K (for example, with diagonal lines pointing out at uneven lengths). Have students take turns coming up to the board to erase and re-write the incorrectly formed letters. Repeat this procedure with capital and lowercase G and C.

Activity 3: Copy and distribute Worksheet 0. Dictate letters (for example, *large G, small g*) and have students write the letters. Check students' work for good handwriting.

Worksheet Link: Worksheet 76
Assign the worksheet for homework or in-class independent work. Follow the procedures for the above activity.

TEACHER

Survival: Recognize U.S. bills and understand their monetary value. Ask for change.
Civics concept: It's OK to ask a stranger for change.
New language: A dollar, five, ten, twenty, fifty, a hundred dollars / Do you have change for [$10]? / Let me check. / Here you go. / Thanks so much.

Number Review Activities

Students learned numbers 1–50 in Unit 3. You may want to review these numbers with students before presenting the material on this page. The following are suggested review activities:

Review Activity 1: Round robin. Sit with the class in a circle. Start by saying *One* and then, with the gesture of two fingers up, prompt a student to say *two*. Continue around the circle, again and again, until the class has counted to 50.

Review Activity 2: Call out numbers in sequence. Every few numbers, clap instead of saying a number. Have students say the missing number.

Review Activity 3: The following hand-crossing activity helps students encode and memorize numbers by connecting kinesthetic activity (left/right) with words. Model the activity with a student volunteer. You and the student stand face-to-face, holding your hands out with palms up. Cross your right hand over to tap the student's opposing (right) hand and say *one*. Then cross your left hand over to tap the student's left hand and say *two*. Then invite the student to do the speaking and tapping *(three, four)*. Count up to 50 in this manner. Have students do this activity in pairs.

🎧 A. Look and listen.

See also "Look and listen" on page T17a.

➤ Show the class real $1, $5, $10, and $20 bills. Write the amount of each bill on the board with a dollar sign. Point to the bill and number on the board and say *[five] dollars*.

➤ Play the cassette or read the tapescript aloud as many times as necessary.

Additional Activity
Make copies of Vocabulary Cards 167–172 *($1, $5, $10, $20, $50, $100 bills)*. Give each student a set. Say a bill number and have students show you the Vocabulary Card.

🎧 B. Listen again and repeat.

See "Listen again and repeat" on page T17a.

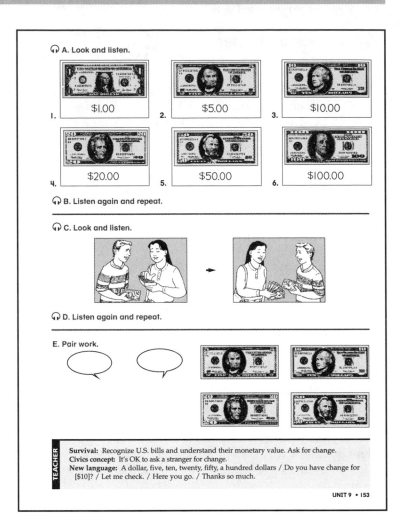

🎧 A. Look and listen.

1. $1.00   2. $5.00   3. $10.00
4. $20.00   5. $50.00   6. $100.00

🎧 B. Listen again and repeat.

🎧 C. Look and listen.

🎧 D. Listen again and repeat.

E. Pair work.

Survival: Recognize U.S. bills and understand their monetary value. Ask for change.
Civics concept: It's OK to ask a stranger for change.
New language: A dollar, five, ten, twenty, fifty, a hundred dollars / Do you have change for [$10]? / Let me check. / Here you go. / Thanks so much.

UNIT 9 • 153

Option: Have students tap out the syllables as they say each word. This will help them enunciate the often forgotten second syllable of numbers *twenty* and *fifty* and will prepare students to correctly say three-syllable numbers like *twenty-five*.

Option: To get students to fully associate letters with sounds in words they know, place the Letter Cards F, T, and H on the board rim. Say *five* and *fifty* and point to the letter F. Say *ten* and *twenty* and point to the letter T. Say *hundred* and point to the letter H. Have students repeat after you.

Additional Activity
Make many copies of Vocabulary Cards 167–172. Cut out the bills and distribute several bills to each student. Have students show each bill to the class and say the amount.

🎧 C. Look and listen.

See also "Look and listen" on page T9a.

➤ Show the class a ten-dollar bill. Say *Ten dollars. I need ONE dollar. I need change.*

Option: To give students visual cues to the dialogue, mime the conversation as the class listens to the cassette, or read the conversation aloud, acting out the parts. Use money (a $10 bill, a $5 bill, and five $1 bills) and a wallet as props. Hold out the $10 bill as the man asks *Do you have change for ten dollars?* Hand over the $5 bill and the five $1 bills as the woman says *Here you go.*

🎧 D. Listen again and repeat.

See "Listen again and repeat" on page T9a.

Option: Focus on intonation. If you have worked on the rising intonation pattern of *yes / no* questions in previous lessons, reinforce your instruction with the question *Do you have change for ten dollars?* Move your hand upward on the second syllable of *dollars.*

Option: If you focused on the /tʃ/ sound in previous units, reinforce your instruction with the words *change* and *check.* Illustrate that it is a plosive sound by placing a thin strip of paper in front of your mouth as you say the sound.

Tapescript

A: Do you have change for ten dollars?
B: Let me check.

B: Here you go.
A: Thanks so much.

Additional Activity

Practice new language. Place Vocabulary Card 169 ($10 bill) on the board rim. Ask *Do you have change for ten dollars?* Hold up seven fingers and ask the question again, touching a finger for each word. Repeat, but omit saying *ten.* Point to the Vocabulary Card that represents the missing word. Have students say the missing word. Repeat this procedure with Vocabulary Cards 167, 168, 170 ($1, $5, $20 bills).

E. Pair work.

➤ Model the exercise. Have students look at the cues in their book and name the four bills. Invite a student to the front of the class. Hand the student several copies of Vocabulary Cards 167 and 168 ($1 and $5 bills). If you have access to "play" money, as in a Monopoly game, that will work even better. Hold up Vocabulary Card 169 ($10) or a play $10 bill and ask *Do you have change for ten dollars?* Gesture for the student to find the change. Say *Thanks.* Then reverse roles.

➤ Students ask a partner for change. Circulate around the classroom, offering help as needed.

Option: Encourage students to stand while they speak, which will allow them to communicate more naturally with their bodies. Encourage them to say *Here you go* as they hand over the money.

➤ Have several volunteer pairs act out their conversations in front of the class.

Additional Activity

Distribute many copies of Vocabulary Cards 167–172 ($1 to $100 bills) or play money to students. Have students circulate around the room, asking each other for change. You will want to review the sentence *No, I'm sorry* before students practice these more open-ended conversations.

Pair work (possible student responses)

A: Do you have change for five / ten / twenty / fifty dollars? **B:** Let me check. Here you go.
A: Thanks so much.

Your students can also say . . .

A: (Unit 2:) Excuse me. (Unit 9:) Do you have change for a dollar / a hundred dollars? **B:** (Unit 2:) Sure. / (Unit 6:) Certainly. **A:** (Unit 1:) Thank you. / Thanks.

TEACHER

Survival: Recognize U.S. coins and understand their monetary value.
Civics concept: Money comes in the form of coins as well as bills.
New language: Penny, nickel, dime, quarter, half dollar.

🎧 A. Look and listen.

See also "Look and listen" on page T17a.

➤ Show the class the following real coins: *penny, nickel, dime,* and *quarter.* (Show a 50¢ piece and $1 coin if you have them.) Hold up each coin and say its name.

Additional Activity
Test comprehension. Give each student an array of coins. Say a coin name *(nickel)* or its value *(five cents)* and have students hold up the coin to show you.

🎧 B. Listen again and repeat.

See also "Listen again and repeat" on page T17a.

➤ After students understand that each coin has a name *(penny, nickel,* etc.) and represents an amount *(one cent, five cents,* etc.), begin to acquaint them with the meaning of the written amount. Write the amounts on the board. *($ .01, $ .05,* etc.) Hold up a coin, say its name, and then point to the amount on the board and say it.

Option: To show that the decimal point separates dollars and cents, draw a large decimal point on the board. Hold up three $1 bills, say *Three dollars,* and write a 3 to the left of the decimal point. Hold up a quarter, say *Twenty-five cents,* and write 25 to the right of the decimal point.

Additional Activities
Activity 1: Show the class a coin and have students call out the name of the coin and its value. Repeat the process with several coins. Then distribute coins to pairs of students for more practice.

Activity 2 (Challenge): Distribute coins to students. Make sure that the total value of each student's coins is less than a dollar. Have students show each coin to the class and say its name and value. Then have students count out the total value of their coins. Switch coins among students and repeat.

Tapescript
1. penny . . . one cent 2. nickel . . . five cents
3. dime . . . ten cents 4. quarter . . . twenty-five cents
5. half dollar . . . fifty cents 6. a dollar

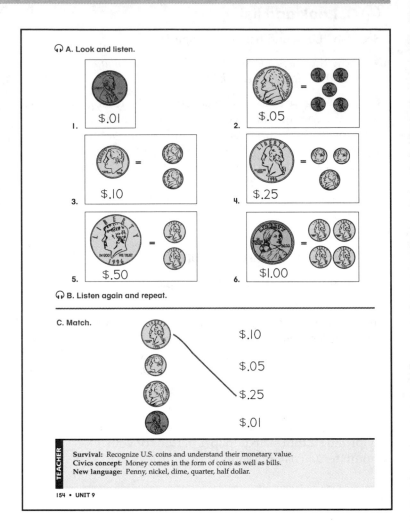

C. Match.

➤ Hold up the book for the class to see. Point to each picture and have students say its name and value.

➤ Students draw lines connecting each coin with its value.

Additional Activities
Activity 1: Place coins in a paper bag. Invite a student to reach in the bag and hold one coin. Ask the student *What is it? A penny? A nickel?* Have the student make a prediction and then pull the coin out of the bag. Have students do this activity in small groups.

Activity 2: Play a memory game. Give each student a set of coins and play bills. Have students close their eyes. Call out three coin and bill names in a row. Have students open their eyes and find the items in their sets.

TEACHER

Literacy: Read and say dollar and cent amounts in two ways. Trace dollar and cent amounts. Recognize the decimal point between dollars and cents.
More practice: Worksheets 77–78 (Teacher's Edition CD-ROM).

Introduce Numbers 51 to 99

Note: This page includes numbers 51–99. First introduce and practice the numbers before doing the exercises on the page.

➤ Review numbers 20–50. Write the numbers on the board in groups of ten. Point to each number and say its name. Have students repeat after you. Then do the same with 51–99. Point out that the numbers all follow the same pattern.

➤ Focus on pronunciation. Have students tap out the syllables as they say each number. This will help them enunciate the often forgotten second syllable of numbers 20 to 100 (for example, six-*ty*-three).

Additional Review Activities

Activity 1: Round robin. Sit with the class in a circle. Start by holding up one finger and saying *one*. Then, by holding up two fingers, prompt the student next to you to say *two.* Continue around the circle until the class has counted to 100. (You can also do this activity counting by tens.)

Activity 2: Count by tens from 10 to 100. Then repeat, but clap instead of saying a number (for example, *10, 20, CLAP*). Have students identify the missing number *(30)*.

Activity 3: Have students count to 100 with a partner. Follow the procedure for Review Activity 3 on page T153a.

🎧 A. Look and listen.

See also "Look and listen" on page T17a.

➤ Write $00.00 on the board. Point to the zeros preceding the decimal point and say *dollars*. Point to the zeros after the decimal and say *cents*.

➤ Play the cassette or read the tapescript aloud as many times as necessary.

Note: The cassette provides two ways to say the money amounts: the long form, which includes *dollars* and *cents*, and the short form, which omits the words *dollars* and *cents*. Make sure students wait to hear both ways.

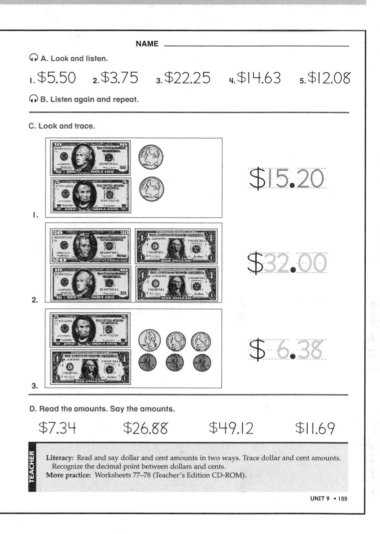

Additional Activity

Test comprehension. Say one of the money amounts and have students point to the amount in Exercise A. Circulate around the room to check students' responses.

🎧 B. Listen again and repeat.

See "Listen again and repeat" on page T17.

Note: Students listen and repeat each amount in the long form (with *dollars* and *cents*) and then listen and repeat each amount again, this time in the short form (omitting *dollars* and *cents*).

(Continued on page T155b.)

Additional Activities

Activity 1: Write dollar and cent amounts on the board. Point to each and say the amount in both the long and short form. Then point to amounts and have students call out the amounts.

Activity 2: Call out a dollar and cent amount in the long form and have an individual student repeat it to you in the short form. For example, Teacher: *Three dollars and eighty-two cents.* Student: *Three eight-two.*

Activity 3: Give each student a Number Card, 0–9. Give one student a card on which you have drawn a giant dot. Have the students stand up. Call out money amounts and have the students arrange themselves into the correct amount. Point to the numbers as you read them aloud.

Tapescript

1. five dollars and fifty cents
   five fifty
2. three dollars and seventy-five cents
   three seventy-five
3. twenty-two dollars and twenty-five cents
   twenty-two twenty-five
4. fourteen dollars and sixty-three cents
   fourteen sixty-three
5. twelve dollars and eight cents
   twelve-oh-eight

C. Look and trace.

Note: This exercise requires tracing of numbers. You may want to review number writing before beginning this exercise. You may want to assign Worksheet 28 for in-class tracing practice.

➤ Show the class several dollars and coins. Count out the total value and write it on the board.

➤ Students count the money in each picture, say the total, and trace the number amount.

Additional Activities

Activity 1: Copy and distribute Worksheet 78 (primer rules with dollar signs and decimal points). Copy and distribute Monopoly money or several copies of Vocabulary Cards 167–169 ($1, $5, $10 bills) and give each student a few coins. Have the students count their money and write the total amount on the worksheet. Review students' work, counting out each pile of money and checking to see if the written amount is correct.

Activity 2: Give individual students two sets of Number Cards 0–9 and a card on which you have drawn a dot. Call out a dollar amount. Have students arrange the amount with their cards. Circulate around the room to check their work. Repeat this procedure many times. If students are ready, have them take turns calling out dollar amounts.

D. Read the amounts. Say the amounts.

➤ Model the exercise. Write the four dollar amounts on the board. Point to the first amount and say *Seven dollars and thirty-four cents. Seven thirty-four.* Point to the second item and call on two students to say the amount, one in the short form and one in the long. Continue in the same manner.

➤ Students work with a partner to read and say the amounts. Or students say each amount individually, covering one ear to focus on their own speech.

Additional Activity

(Challenge): Distribute coins and "play" bills or Vocabulary Cards 167–169 to students. Call out an amount. Have students count out that amount with their sets of money. If students need change, encourage them to ask a neighboring classmate *Do you have change for [a dollar]?* Ask one or two students to count out their money to show you the amount. Students will use different combinations of coins and bills to reach the same amount, so their counting out loud will always be unique.

Worksheet Link: Worksheets 77–78

Assign Worksheet 77 for homework or in-class independent work. Follow the procedures for the above activities. Worksheet 78 is for in-class activities.

TEACHER

Literacy: Understand spoken monetary amounts. Listen and write dollar and cent amounts. Recognize the decimal point between dollars and cents.

🎧 A. Listen and circle.

See also "Listen and circle" on page T17a–b.

➤ Model the exercise. Write the dollar amounts for item 1 on the board. Say *sixteen seventy-seven* and trace the circle around the correct number.

➤ Play the cassette or read the tapescript aloud. Students circle the correct amount.

Option: You may want students to say each dollar amount before listening.

Additional Activities

Activity 1: With books open, call out one of the two dollar amounts in item 1. Have students point to the correct amount. Repeat this process with items 2–8. Then have students do this activity in pairs.

Activity 2: Create, copy, and distribute sets of dollar amount cards, using the same amounts that are on Student's Book page 156. Pairs of students sit facing each other. Student A chooses a card and says its amount without showing the card to Student B. B finds the card in his own set. The two students then check their cards to make sure they match.

Tapescript
1. sixteen seventy-seven
2. forty-three dollars and twenty-two cents
3. sixty-two oh-eight 4. three dollars and nine cents
5. one sixteen 6. one fifty-seven
7. two ninety-nine 8. eight forty-five

🎧 B. Listen and write.

➤ Model the exercise. Write $5.5__ on the board, with a small arrow, as in the Student's Book, to indicate the missing numer. Say *Five dollars and fifty cents* and fill in the missing 0.

➤ Play the cassette or read the tapescript aloud. Have students write the numbers to complete the amounts they hear.

Note: This is a challenging exercise. Students may need to listen to the same number several times. After each item, write the correct answer on the board for students to see.

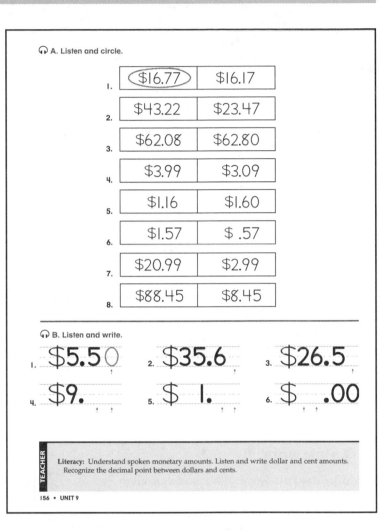

🎧 A. Listen and circle.

1.	($16.77)	$16.17
2.	$43.22	$23.47
3.	$62.08	$62.80
4.	$3.99	$3.09
5.	$1.16	$1.60
6.	$1.57	$ .57
7.	$20.99	$2.99
8.	$88.45	$8.45

🎧 B. Listen and write.

1. $5.50   2. $35.6   3. $26.5
4. $9.   5. $ 1.   6. $ .00

TEACHER **Literacy:** Understand spoken monetary amounts. Listen and write dollar and cent amounts. Recognize the decimal point between dollars and cents.

156 • UNIT 9

Additional Activity

(Challenge): Copy and distribute Worksheet 78. Have each student write down a dollar amount on the first line. Have students take turns dictating their amounts. The rest of the class listens and writes down the numbers on the remaining lines. After each item, write the numbers on the board for students to check.

Tapescript
1. five dollars and fifty cents
2. thirty-five sixty-one 3. twenty-six fifty-two
4. nine oh-one 5. one forty-four 6. ten dollars

TEACHER

Survival: Order and pay for food. Choose item and size from a menu.
Civics concept: Menus tell you the cost of food items.
New language: That's [$2.78].

🎧 A. Look and listen.

See also "Look and listen" on page T9a.

➤ Set the scene. Name several fast food restaurants in the neighborhood.

➤ Have students study the menu in the picture. Hold the book up for the class to see. Point to menu items and have students say the words.

➤ Play the cassette or read the tapescript aloud as many times as necessary.

🎧 B. Listen again and repeat.

See "Listen again and repeat" on page T9a.

Tapescript

A: A hamburger and small fries, please.
B: Something to drink?
A: No, thanks. That's all.

A: That's $2.78.
B: Here you go.

🎧 C. Pair work.

➤ Model the Pair work. Place some or all of Vocabulary Cards 91–95, 97–104 (*milk, coffee, tea, juice, water, sandwich, cheese sandwich, chicken sandwich, fish sandwich, hamburger, salad, drink, fries*) on the rim of the board. Write prices above each item. Invite a student to the front of the class. Ask *Can I help you?* Gesture toward the food cards to elicit a response. Listen to the student's response and then ask *Something to drink?* Tell the student the price and complete the transaction. Reverse roles and repeat the conversation.

➤ Divide the class into pairs. Students practice ordering and paying for food. Circulate around the classroom, offering help as needed.

➤ Have several volunteer pairs act out their conversations in front of the class.

Note: Students can use the menu in the picture and/or Vocabulary Cards 91–95, 97–104 (foods and drinks) to make their orders.

TEACHER
Survival: Order and pay for food. Choose item and size from a menu.
Civics concept: Menus tell you the cost of food items.
New language: That's [$2.78].
UNIT 9 • 157

Pair work (possible student responses)

A: A hamburger and small / medium / large fries, please. **B:** Something to drink? **A:** No, thanks. That's all. / Yes, please. A small / medium / large coffee / tea / milk / juice / water. **B:** That's [dollar amount]. **A:** Here you go.

TEACHER

Survival: Ask for prices of near and far singular items.
Civics concepts: It's OK to ask salespeople for a price. A sales tax is charged on many items.
New language: How much is this [that]? / plus tax.

🎧 A. Look and listen.

See also "Look and listen" on page T9a.

➤ Introduce *this* and *that*. Hold an object up and say *this*. Then point to an object far from you and say *that*. Repeat with various objects so students can see the different spatial relationships *this* and *that* establish.

➤ Set the scene. Point to the pictures and say *drugstore*.

Option: Introduce the expression *plus tax*. Write the price $4.95 on the board. Then say *$4.95 plus tax* and write the appropriate tax for your area below the price, add the numbers, and write the total. Point to the tax and say *plus tax*. You can also do this activity with receipts that show tax.

🎧 B. Listen again and repeat.

See "Listen again and repeat" on page T9a.

Additional Activity
Practice *this* and *that*. Gesture to something close to you and ask *How much is this*? Hold up four fingers and ask the question again. Touch a finger for each word. Repeat, but omit saying *this*. Instead, point to a near object. Have students supply the word *this*. Repeat the procedure, this time gesturing to an object far from you to elicit the word *that*.

Tapescript

A: How much is this? **B:** $4.95 plus tax.
A: And how much is that? **B:** $13.99.

If your students are ready . . .

Civics enrichment: Show students taxable and non-taxable objects from advertising fliers. Point to non-tax items and say *No tax*. Then point to tax items and say *Tax*.

C. Pair work.

➤ Model the Pair work. Place several objects (book, bottle of water, hairbrush, tissues) on the board rim. Write prices above each item. Invite a student to the front of the class. Hold up an object and ask *How much is this?* Gesture to the price to elicit a response.

🎧 A. Look and listen.

🎧 B. Listen again and repeat.

C. Pair work.

$1.99 + tax	$2.24 + tax
$6.89 + tax	$22.00 + tax
$2.99 + tax	$10.50 + tax

TEACHER
Survival: Ask for prices of near and far singular items.
Civics concepts: It's OK to ask salespeople for a price. A sales tax is charged on many items.
New language: How much is this [that]? / plus tax.

158 • UNIT 9

After the student responds, gesture to an item on the board rim and ask *How much is that?* Then gesture to reverse roles so the student asks the questions.

➤ Students practice asking a partner for prices of near and far singular items.

➤ Have several volunteer pairs act out their conversations in front of the class.

Pair work (possible student responses)

A: How much is this / that? **B:** [any dollar amount to $100] / plus tax.

Literacy: Recognize symbols as numbers, letters, words, or sentences.

A. Look and listen.

See also "Look and listen" on page T17a.

➤ Play the cassette or read the tapescript aloud as many times as necessary.

Note: The concept of a sentence will be the most difficult to grasp. Write several examples on the board. (For example, *Marco is a student.*) Highlight the beginning and ending features of sentences (capitals and periods). Point to the first letter and ask *Big letter? Small letter?* (See the note on page T119a regarding the terminology *big / small* and *capital / lowercase.*) Point to the period at the end and say *Stop.* Identify the capitals and periods in all the sentences.

You may also want to point out that words are separated by spaces. You can do this by reading the sentence aloud and placing your fingers between each word.

Additional Activity

Photocopy Letter Cards and Number Cards. Give each student several of each type of card all mixed together. Have students sort the cards into letters and numbers.

B. Listen again and repeat.

See "Listen again and repeat" on page T17a.

Additional Activities

Activity 1: Say single words, numbers, or letters. Have students listen and tell you whether each utterance is a *number, letter,* or *word.* This activity stimulates students' aural comprehension.

Activity 2: Play a word hunt game. Ask students *Where is a number?* Look around the class to identify a number on the wall or furniture. Invite students to show what numbers they found in the classroom. Repeat with *words* and *sentences.*

Tapescript
1. letter 2. word 3. sentence 4. number

C. Look at the picture. Circle the words.

➤ Model the exercise. Play the cassette or say *Look at the picture. Circle the words.* Hold the picture up for

the class to see and point to a word, say *word,* and circle it.

➤ Play the cassette or read the direction line aloud. Students circle all the *words* in the picture.

➤ Repeat the above procedure with *numbers* and *sentences* for Exercises D and E. Note that there is only one sentence in the picture.

Note: You may want to review all the words students circled before going on to the next step (circle the *numbers*). To check students' work, have them count the number of words they circled.

Additional Activity

Bring in advertising fliers. Have students circle the numbers, words, and sentences on them.

TEACHER

Literacy: Continue distinguishing letters, numbers, words, and sentences. Review sight words from Unit 8. Recognize beginning and end of sight words.
More practice: Worksheet 79 (Teacher's Edition CD-ROM).

A. Cross out.

➤ Model the exercise. Copy the first row on the board. Point to each item and name and classify it (for example, *6, number; 7, number; 3, number; exit, word.*) Then shake your head and cross out *exit*. You may need to repeat the modeling. This time just point to each item and classify it (for example, *number; number; number; word!*).

➤ Have students work individually to read across each line and cross out the item that does not belong.

Option: Go over the answers as a class by holding up the book for the class to see. Point to each item and elicit its classification *(number, letter, or word).* Identify the crossed out item in each line.

B. Circle the words.

Note: This is not a reading exercise. It is designed to introduce the concept that there should be spaces between words. This exercise may be quite difficult for some students and may require extensive demonstration.

➤ Review the sight words students have learned *(caution, danger, enter, exit, push, stop, no smoking, stairs).* Write each word on the board in capital letters. Point to each word and say it. Review all the words several times. Have students then say the words as you point to them. Leave the words on the board for students' reference.

➤ Model the exercise. Point to the words *CAUTION* and *DANGER* and read them aloud. Copy the first row of connected words on the board. Point to the single word *CAUTION* and then point to the connected words and ask *Where is the word caution?* Count and name the letters in the whole word *caution* and then identify the same letters in the connected words. Circle the word *CAUTION*.

➤ Have students work individually to circle the two sight words in each line.

Option: Identify the words in each line so students know what to look for.

A. Cross out.

6	7	3	E̶X̶I̶T̶
14	STOP	8	56
A	R	J	8
m	3	b	s
PUSH	PULL	ENTER	f

B. Circle the words.

1. (CAUTION)(DANGER)
2. ENTEREXIT
3. PUSHSTOP
4. NOSMOKING
5. EXITSTAIRS

TEACHER

Literacy: Continue distinguishing letters, numbers, words, and sentences. Review sight words from Unit 8. Recognize beginning and end of sight words.
More practice: Worksheet 79 (Teacher's Edition CD-ROM).

160 • UNIT 9

Option: Go over the answers as a class. Call out each word and ask *How do you spell that?* Write on the board the letters students dictate for each word.

Worksheet Link: Worksheet 79
Assign the worksheet for homework or in-class independent work. Follow the procedures for the above activities.

Survival: Learn vocabulary related to payment.
Civics concept: Money comes in a variety of forms other than cash.
New language: Cash, check, credit card, money order, receipt.

🎧 A. Look and listen.

See also "Look and listen" on page T17a.

➤ Introduce as much of the vocabulary as possible by showing these vocabulary items from your own wallet (for example, *cash, check, credit card, receipt*). (You may want to tape over your account information before you show the items to the class.)

➤ Play the cassette or read the tapescript aloud as many times as necessary.

Additional Activity

Test comprehension. Say a word and have students tell you the picture number in their books.

🎧 B. Listen again and repeat.

See "Listen again and repeat" on page T17a.

Additional Activities

Activity 1: Focus on stress patterns. Demonstrate with hand motions the high/low pitch of multisyllabic nouns (*credit card, money order, receipt*). Have students mirror the hand motions to reinforce the learning.

Activity 2: Provide speaking practice. Call out a picture number and have students say the word. Repeat several times. Then have students do this activity in pairs.

Tapescript

1. cash 2. check 3. credit card
4. money order 5. receipt

🎧 C. Listen and circle.

See also "Listen and circle" on page T17a–b.

➤ Model the exercise. Hold up Vocabulary Cards 179, 181–183 (*cash, credit card, money order, receipt*). Have students name the cards. Read the first conversation in the tapescript or play the first conversation on the cassette one time. When the conversation has finished, point to the two pictures in item 1. Have students listen again. Students circle the correct picture in their books.

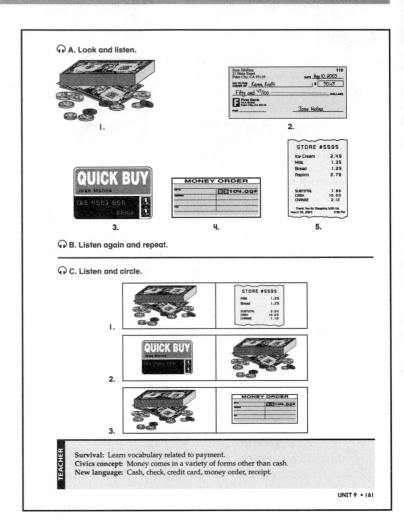

➤ Play the cassette or read the tapescript aloud. Students listen and circle the correct pictures.

Tapescript

Conversation 1
A: How will you be paying for that?
B: With cash.

Conversation 2
A: Cash or charge?
B: Charge.

Conversation 3
A: I need a money order.
B: OK. Just a minute.

TEACHER

Survival: Ask and answer questions about payment.
Civics concept: Payment can be made with a variety of devices other than cash.
   It's OK to ask for a receipt.
New language: Will that be cash or charge? / Cash. / Charge. / Can I have a receipt?

🎧 A. Look and listen.

See also "Look and listen" on page T9a.

➤ Set the scene. Hold the book up for the class to see. Point to the pictures and say *discount store*.

Option: To illustrate the meaning of *charge*, show the class a credit card and say *credit card—charge*. Repeat several times so students understand the two words have similar meanings.

Option: Give visual cues as students listen to the conversation. Place Vocabulary Cards 179, 181, 183 (*cash, credit card, receipt*) on the board rim. Point to the Vocabulary Cards (or hold up actual cash, credit card, and receipt) as they are mentioned in the conversation. Mime *Here you go.*

Additional Activity
Test comprehension. Point to each of the first two pictures and ask *Cash or charge?*

🎧 B. Listen again and repeat.

See "Listen again and repeat" on page T9a.

If your students are ready . . .
Civics enrichment: Teach the students which types of payment are typically accepted at known locations, for example—*Discount store: cash, credit card, check. Bank: cash, check, money order. Taxi: cash. Bus: cash.*

Tapescript
Conversation 1 **A:** That's $86.36. Will that be cash or charge? **B:** Cash. **Conversation 2** **A:** That's $42.11. Will that be cash or charge? **B:** Charge, please. **Conversation 3** **B:** Can I have a receipt? **A:** Sure. Here you go.

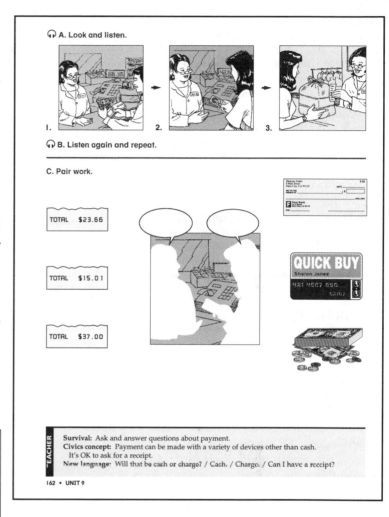

🎧 A. Look and listen.

1.   2.   3.

🎧 B. Listen again and repeat.

C. Pair work.

TOTAL $23.66

TOTAL $15.01

TOTAL $37.00

QUICK BUY
Sharon Jones
4821 4567 890
02/07

TEACHER

Survival: Ask and answer questions about payment.
Civics concept: Payment can be made with a variety of devices other than cash.
   It's OK to ask for a receipt.
New language: Will that be cash or charge? / Cash. / Charge. / Can I have a receipt?

162 • UNIT 9

C. Pair work.

➤ Hold the book up for the class to see. Point to each receipt and ask *How much?* Then point to each form of payment on the right and elicit the word.

➤ Model the Pair work with a student volunteer.

➤ Students ask and answer questions about payment with a partner.

➤ Have several volunteer pairs act out their conversations in front of the class.

Pair work (possible student responses)
A: That's [dollar amount]. Will that be cash or charge? **B:** Cash. / Charge. / Check, please. Can I have a receipt? **A:** Certainly. / Sure. Here you go.

Circle.

➤ Model the exercise. Have students study the pictures in the first row in their books. Hold your book up for the class to see. Point to the dollar amount to elicit the words from the students (*ten dollars*). Point to each picture in the first row and count out the money. Say the amount for each of the two pictures. ($6.00, $10.00.) Use your finger to trace the circle around the second picture.

Option: Before doing the exercise, have students practice saying both the long and short form of all the dollar and cent amounts (for example, *five eleven* and *five dollars and eleven cents*.)

➤ Have students complete the exercise individually. Circulate around the room to check students' work.

Option: Go over the answers as a class. Have students take turns reading the dollar amounts, counting the money, and indicating the correct picture to circle.

Additional Activities

Activity 1: Give individual students three sets of Number Cards 0–9 and a card on which you have drawn a dot. Call out a dollar amount. Have students arrange the amount with their cards. Circulate around the room to check their work. Repeat this procedure many times. If students are ready, have them take turns calling out dollar amounts.

Activity 2: Give each student one Number Card 0–9. Give one student a giant dot. Have the students stand up. Call out monetary amounts and have the students arrange themselves into the correct number. (Note: You will need to be conscious of how many of each number card there are in the classroom. If there is only one student with a 9, make sure the amounts you call out each contain only one 9.) Point to each number as you read the amount aloud.

Activity 3 (Challenge): Distribute coins and "play" money to students. Call out an amount. Have students count out that amount with their sets of money. If students need change, encourage them to ask a neighboring classmate *Do you have change for [a dollar]?* Ask one or two students to count out their money to show you the amount. Students will use

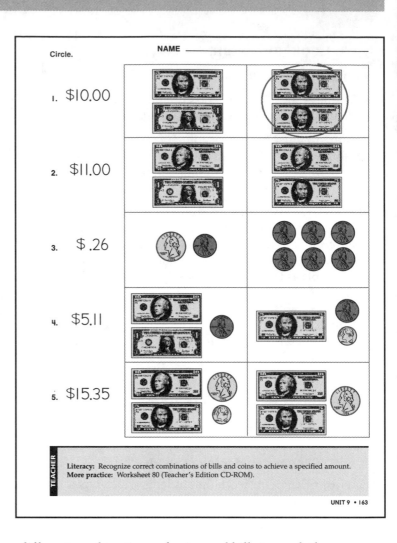

different combinations of coins and bills to reach the same amount, so their counting out loud will always be unique.

Worksheet Link: Worksheet 80
Assign the worksheet for homework or in-class independent work. Follow the procedures for the above activity.

Literacy: Understand, circle, and trace spoken monetary amounts.
More practice: Worksheet 81 (Teacher's Edition CD-ROM).

🎧 A. Look and Listen.

See "Look and listen" on page T9a.

🎧 B. Listen and circle.

➤ Point to each picture of money and have students count out the total amount.

➤ Play the cassette. Students listen to the conversations from Exercise A again. Have students circle the amounts they hear.

🎧 C. Listen and trace.

➤ Play the cassette or read the tapescript aloud. Have students listen to the conversations again and trace the amounts they hear.

Additional Activities

Activity 1: Return to Exercise B. Point to each picture and ask *How much?* Have students come to the board to write the number down.

Activity 2 (Challenge): Copy and distribute Worksheet 78. Have each student write down a dollar amount on the first line. Have students take turns dictating their amounts. The rest of the class listens and writes down the numbers on the remaining lines. After each item, write the amount on the board for students to check.

Literacy: Understand, circle, and trace spoken monetary amounts.
More practice: Worksheet 81 (Teacher's Edition CD-ROM).

164 • UNIT 9

Tapescript

Conversation 1
A: How much is this?
B: It's ten dollars.

Conversation 2
A: That'll be twenty dollars and twenty-five cents.
B: How much?
A: Twenty twenty-five.

Conversation 3
A: Do you have change for a twenty?
B: No. How much do you need?
A: I need a dollar fifty for the bus.
B: No problem. Here's the cash. You can pay me back tomorrow.

Worksheet Link: Worksheet 81

Assign the worksheet for in-class independent work. Model the exercise "Look and circle." Follow the procedures for "Look and trace" on page T155a.

TEACHER

Survival: Ask for prices of near and far plural items.
Civics concept: Salespeople expect you to ask them about the products they sell.
New language: How much are these [those]?

🎧 A. Look and listen.

See also "Look and listen" on page T9a.

➤ Introduce *these* and *those*. Hold several objects up to the class and say *these*. Then point to some same objects far from you and say *those*. Repeat with various objects so students can see the different spatial relationships the words *these* and *those* establish.

➤ Set the scene. Hold up the book for the class to see, point to the pictures, and say *department store*.

Option: Hold up a pair of shoes in your hand when *these* is mentioned, and point to a pair of shoes farther away when *those* is mentioned.

🎧 B. Listen again and repeat.

See "Listen again and repeat" on page T9a.

Additional Activities

Activity 1: Practice *these* and *those*. Gesture to some items close to you and ask *How much are these?* Hold up four fingers and ask the question again. Touch a finger for each word. Repeat, but omit saying *these.* Instead, point to some objects near you. Have students supply the word *these*. Repeat the procedure, this time gesturing at objects far from you to elicit the word *those*.

Activity 2: Contrast *this* with *these* and *that* with *those*. Place objects close to and far from you. Make sure some of the objects are individual (singular) and others are in a set (plural). Point to a set of objects close to you and ask *How much are these?* Then point to a singular item close to you and ask *How much is this?* Repeat a few times. Then do the same with *those* and *that*.

Tapescript

A: How much are these?   **B:** $45.99.   **A:** Thanks.
A: How much are those?   **B:** $30.

C. Pair work.

➤ Model the Pair work with a student volunteer and Vocabulary Cards 49–51, 54–58 (plural clothing items). Be sure to ask about prices of both near and far Vocabulary Cards.

🎧 A. Look and listen.

🎧 B. Listen again and repeat.

C. Pair work.

$10.00 $12.99

$47.99 $54.00

$2.50 $18.29

TEACHER
Survival: Ask for prices of near and far plural items.
Civics concept: Salespeople expect you to ask them about the products they sell.
New language: How much are these [those]?

UNIT 9 • 165

➤ Students ask a partner for the prices of near and far plural items.

Option: Distribute picture cut-outs from mail-order catalogs of plural clothing items. Give some to pairs of students and place some on the board rim so they have the appropriate near and far context to use the words *these* and *those*. You may also want to have students write prices on the clothing and use play money to expand the Pair work.

➤ Have several volunteer pairs act out their conversations in front of the class.

Pair work (possible student responses)

A: How much are these/those?   **B:** [any dollar amount to one hundred].   **A:** Thanks. / Thank you.

TEACHER

Authentic practice: Students listen to an authentic conversation about payment and then complete listening and speaking tasks, providing their own information.

🎧 A. Listen and circle.

➤ Hold the book up for the class to see. Point to each picture and say *check* or *credit card*.

➤ Give students visual cues to the dialogue as they listen the first time. Place Vocabulary Cards 179–181 (*cash, check, credit card*) on the board rim. Point to them when they are mentioned in the conversation.

➤ Play the cassette or read the tapescript aloud. Students listen and circle the correct form of payment.

Tapescript

Conversation 1
A: That comes to $53.28. Cash or charge?
B: Charge, please.

Conversation 2
A: How will you be paying for that?
B: Do you accept personal checks?
A: Yes. A check is OK.

🎧 B. Look and listen.

See also "Look and listen" on page T22a.

➤ Set the scene. Point to the pictures and say *grocery store*.

➤ Play the cassette or read the tapescript aloud as many times as necessary.

Option: Show the class Vocabulary Card 172 when the hundred dollar bill is mentioned.

Option: Illustrate the meaning of the question *How will you be paying for that?* Hold up Vocabulary Cards 179–181 (*cash, check, credit card*) or the actual items as you ask the question.

Tapescript

A: That'll be $29.48, including the tax. How will you be paying for that? **B:** Cash.

A: Oh. I can't make change for a hundred. Do you have anything smaller? **B:** Yes. Here you go.

A: Great. Thank you very much. Would you like a receipt? **B:** Yes, thanks.

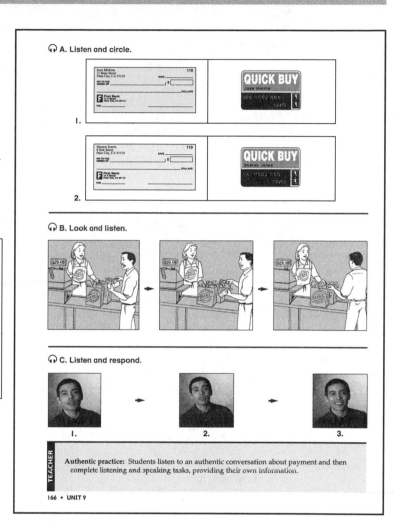

🎧 C. Listen and respond.

See "Listen and respond" on page T22a.

Tapescript

Prompt 1: How will you be paying for that?
Prompt 2: Would you like a receipt?
Prompt 3: Thank you very much.

Listen and respond
(possible student responses)

Prompt 1: Cash. / Charge. / Check. **Prompt 2:** Yes, please. / No, thanks. **Prompt 3:** You're welcome.

Literacy review: Write initial consonants in known words. Demonstrate recognition of sight words as groups of letters.
More practice: Worksheet 82 (Teacher's Edition CD-ROM).
Literacy test: Teacher's Edition CD-ROM.

⌒ A. Listen and circle.

See "Listen and circle M or B" on page T98b.

Additional Activities

Activity 1: Hand out a set of B, C, D, F, J, N, P, S, and T Letter Cards to each student. Have students hold up the letter they hear as you read each of the following words: *penny, nickel, dime, cash, fifty, ten, bank, stop, jacket.*

Activity 2: Play a memory game. Photocopy Letter Cards B, D, F, G, H, J, K, M, N, P, S, T, V, and Z and give each student one set. Have students close their eyes. Call out four letters in a row. Have students open their eyes and find the letters in their Letter Card sets. Repeat with different letters. This game reviews letter names and develops students' visualization of letters.

Activity 3: Use the same letter sets as in Activity 2. Have students lay the cards out face up on their desks. Call out a letter <u>sound</u>. Have students select the card from their own sets, raise it to show you, and say the letter <u>name</u>. Repeat with different sounds. Then have students take turns calling letter sounds as the class listens and identifies the letter.

Tapescript
1. milk **2.** fire **3.** hospital **4.** dollar
5. safety **6.** neck **7.** garage **8.** bakery

B. Write.

➤ Review the writing of the letters D, C, and S. Count the strokes out loud as you write each letter on the board.

> **Option:** Since students have learned the strokes, you may want to invite individual students to model the letters.

➤ Model the exercise. Write the first line of the exercise on the board. Show the class Vocabulary Card 157 (*danger*). Write the initial letter D.

➤ Have students identify the picture cues in the exercise and then work independently to write the first letters in the remaining two sight words.

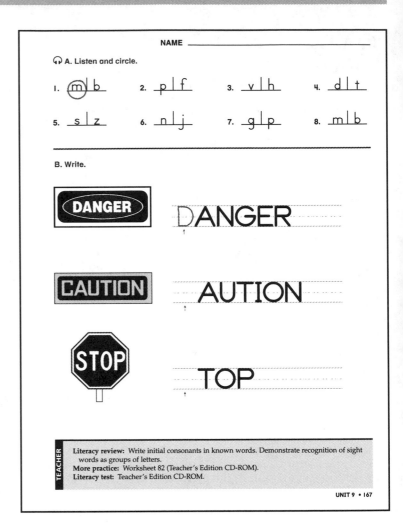

Additional Activity

Concentration. For each pair of students, photocopy the following two sets of cards:
Set 1: Vocabulary Cards 4, 117, 118, 119, 120, 121, 124, 132, 133 (*teacher, father, mother, daughter, son, husband, brother, co-worker, girlfriend*).
Set 2: Letter Cards B, C, D, F, G, H, M, S, and T.
Follow the instructions for Activity 1 on page T106.

Worksheet Link: Worksheet 82

Assign the worksheet for in-class independent work. Follow the procedures for the above activities. In the Write activity, make sure students identify whether the word is in lowercase or capitals before writing.

Survival / civics review: Point and name things in the pictures. Make statements about the pictures. Role-play conversations based on the pictures.
Tests: Teacher's Edition CD-ROM.

Talk about the pictures.

➤ Top picture: Say the following words and have students point to the items: *$2.00, $3.00, $5.00, twenty dollars, telephone, pants, shirts, jacket, booster seat, car seat, husband, wife.*

➤ Point to items with price tags in the picture. Ask *How much is this / that? How much are these / those?*

➤ Have students practice naming items and prices with a partner.

➤ Bottom picture: Say the following words and have students point to the items: *restaurant, mother, son, daughter, hamburger, small / medium / large fries, coffee, milk.*

➤ Have students name relationships, foods, and, sizes. Have students talk about the foods and relationships in the picture with a partner.

Possible student responses

(Top picture) change / twenty dollars / ten dollars / (Unit 8:) booster seat / car seat / (Unit 7:) husband / wife / (Unit 4:) shoes / pants / shirts / jacket / (Unit 3:) street / corner / telephone / (Unit 2:) house

(Bottom picture) cash / (Unit 7:) mother / son / daughter / brother / sister / (Unit 6:) hamburger / salad / fries / coffee / milk / sandwich / (Unit 2:) restaurant

---

Talk about the pictures. Role-play conversations.

Survival / civics review: Point and name things in the pictures. Make statements about the pictures. Role-play conversations based on the pictures.
Tests: Teacher's Edition CD-ROM.

168 • UNIT 9

Role-play conversations.

➤ Top picture: Point to the speech bubble of the man speaking to the woman about the coffee pot and say *Excuse me. How much is this?* Then point to the woman's speech bubble on the right to elicit a student's response.

➤ Have students practice conversations appropriate to the contexts in the picture with a partner.

➤ Ask pairs of students to present some of their conversations to the class.

➤ Bottom picture: Point to the cashier's speech bubble and say *That's $14.86.* Then point to the woman's speech bubble to elicit a student's response. *(Here you go.)*

➤ Proceed as with top picture.

Role-play conversations
(possible student responses)

(Yard sale)
A: Excuse me. How much is this / that? / How much are these / those? **B:** [any dollar amount up to $100]. **A:** Do you have change for twenty dollars? **B:** Let me check. Yes, here you go.

(Two women on the corner)
A: Excuse me. Do you have change for twenty dollars? **B:** Let me check. Yes, here you go. **A:** Thanks so much.

(Continued on page T168b.)

(Fast food restaurant)
A: (Unit 2:) Can I help you? **B:** Yes. (Unit 6:) Two hamburgers, a salad, and two fries. **A:** What size? **B:** Small and large, please. **A:** Something to drink? **B:** Yes, please. A coffee and two milks. **A:** Anything else? **B:** No, thanks. That's all. **A:** (Unit 9:) That's $14.86. Will that be cash or charge? **B:** Cash. Here you go. Can I have a receipt? **A:** (Unit 6:) Certainly. (Unit 1:) Thank you.

NOTES

_____

_____

_____

_____

_____

_____

_____

_____

_____

_____

_____

_____

_____

_____

_____

_____

_____

_____

_____

_____

_____

_____

LESSON PLAN FOR STUDENT'S PAGE 169

TEACHER

Literacy: Recognize sound-symbol correspondence of L and Y. Trace and write initial capital and lowercase L and Y for known words.

🎧 A. Look and listen.

See "Look and listen" on page T98a.

🎧 B. Listen again and repeat.

See "Listen again and repeat" on page T98a.

Option: Make sure students understand the mechanics in forming the /l/ sound. The tongue touches the gum ridge behind the front teeth. To help students identify the voiced quality of /l/, have them place their hands on their throats or cover their ears as they say it.

Tapescript
/l/, /l/, leg, lunch

🎧 C. Look and listen.

See "Look and listen" on page T98a.

🎧 D. LIsten again and repeat.

See "Listen again and repeat" on page T98a.

Option: Make sure students understand the mechanics in forming the /y/ sound. Exaggerate pulling back your lips. /y/ is voiced. To illustrate this, have students place their hands on their throats or cover their ears as they say it.

The significant difference between /y/ and /l/ is that the tongue doesn't touch the gum ridge in the former but it does in the latter.

Additional Activity
Provide listening practice. Hand out a set of L and Y Letter Cards to each student. Have students hold up the initial letter they hear when you say the following words: *you, yes, large, leg, your, late, lot, like, year, law, let.*

Tapescript
/y/, /y/, year

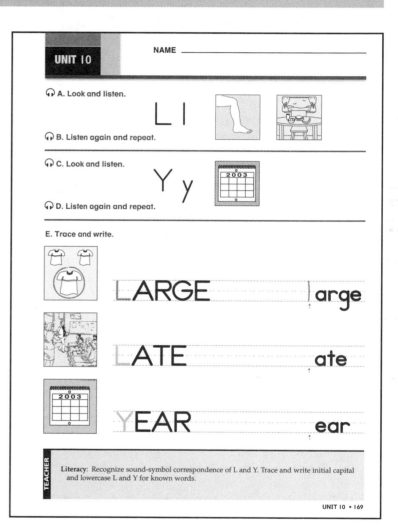

E. Trace and write.

See "Trace and write" on page T151b.

Additional Activity
Concentration. For each pair of students, photocopy the following two sets of cards:
Set 1: Vocabulary Cards 91, 108, 124, 165, 173, 174, 175 *(milk, toast, brother, stroller, penny, nickel, dime).*
Set 2: B, D, M, N, P, S, T Letter Cards.
Follow the instructions for Activity 1 on page T106.

Literacy: Recognize sound-symbol correspondence of R and W. Trace and write initial capital and lowercase R and W for known words.
More practice: Worksheet 83 (Teacher's Edition CD-ROM).

🎧 A. Look and listen.

See "Look and listen" on page T98a.

🎧 B. Listen again and repeat.

See "Listen again and repeat" on page T98a.

Option: Make sure students understand the mechanics in forming the /r/ sound. Exaggerate the tension in your lips. /r/ is voiced. To help illustrate this, have students place their hands on their throats or cover their ears as they say it.

Additional Activity
Contrast /r/ and /l/. The tongue doesn't touch the gum ridge when pronouncing /r/ but does when pronouncing /l/. Have students focus on this difference. Distribute the R and L Letter Cards and have students hold up the letter they hear as you model the two letter sounds. Then have students practice producing the sounds as others listen and identify the letters they hear.

Tapescript
/r/, /r/, receipt, restaurant

🎧 C. Look and listen.

See "Look and listen" on page T98a.

🎧 D. Listen again and repeat.

See "Listen again and repeat" on page T98a.

Option: Make sure students understand the mechanics in forming the /w/ sound. Exaggerate how you pucker your lips to form to sound. /w/ is voiced. To help illustrate this, have students place their hands on their throats or cover their ears as they say it.

Additional Activities
Activity 1: Contrast /r/ and /w/. There are two differences in the production of the sounds /r/ and /w/. When saying the /r/ sound, the tip of the tongue is high up. For the /w/ sound, it is low. The lips are also gathered tightly together to produce the /r/ sound. The lips protrude more when producing the /w/ sound. Have students focus on these differences. Distribute the R and W Letter Cards and have students hold up the letter they hear as you model the two letter sounds. Then have students practice producing the sounds as others listen and identify the letters they hear.

Activity 2: Hand out a set of L, R, W, and Y Letter Cards to each student. Have students hold up the initial letter they hear when you say the following words: *what, you, yes, where, rice, leg, your, late, restroom, like, year, water, let.*

Tapescript
/w/, /w/, week, widowed

E. Trace and write.

See "Trace and write" on page T151b.

Note: By this point, students have learned how to write all the letters of the alphabet in capitals and lowercase. They have also learned the sound-symbol correspondence for all consonants except Q and X.

Additional Activities

Activity 1: Provide writing practice. Make a master copy of Worksheet 0 with the letters R and W in capitals and lowercase. Make a copy for each student and have students practice writing the letters. Have them evaluate their work after each line of freehand practice. They should circle their best letters and mark a small x below any letters that need improvement.

Activity 2: Concentration. For each pair of students, photocopy the following two sets of cards:
Set 1: Vocabulary Cards 47, 82, 114, 125, 140, 145, 148, 155, 179 (*jacket, garage, vegetables, friend, leg, restroom, hall, walk, cash*).
Set 2: C, F, G, H, J, L, R, V, W Letter Cards. Follow the instructions for Activity 1 on page T106.

Activity 3: This activity integrates students' knowledge of vocabulary, initial consonant sounds, and their free-hand writing skills. Place the C, F, G, H, J, L, R, W, and Y Letter Cards along the board rim. Say one of the following words: *year, good, fifty, June, can, hi, receipt, where, like*. Have a student come up to the board, select the initial consonant, copy it on the board, and then return the letter to the board rim. Repeat the word and point to the letter on the board.

Worksheet Link: Worksheet 83

Assign the worksheet for homework or in-class independent work. Follow the procedures for the above activity.

NOTES

TEACHER

Survival: Learn verbs that represent work skills.
Civics concepts: Each work skill has a name. Speaking English is considered a work skill.
New language: Drive, clean, wash, paint, cook, sew, read, write, speak English.

🎧 A. Look and listen.

See "Look and listen" on page T17a.

Additional Activity
Play a memory game. Photocopy Vocabulary Cards 184–192 (workskill vocabulary) and give each student one set. Have students close their eyes. Call out two workskills in a row. Have students open their eyes and find the items in their Vocabulary Card sets. Repeat with different workskills.

🎧 B. Listen again and repeat.

See "Listen again and repeat" on page T17a.

Additional Activities
Activity 1: Call out a picture number and have students say the word. Repeat several times. Then have students do this activity in pairs.

Activity 2: Concentration. Photocopy Vocabulary Cards 184–192. Give two sets of the Vocabulary Cards to each pair of students. Follow the instructions for Activity 2 on page T28.

> **If your students are ready . . .**
>
> **Civics enrichment:** Say the name of an occupation and then the workskills used in that occupation. For example: *Teacher: read, write, speak English. Cook: cook. Housekeeper: clean, wash.*

> **Tapescript**
>
> **1.** drive **2.** clean **3.** wash **4.** paint **5.** cook **6.** sew **7.** read **8.** write **9.** speak English

🎧 C. Listen and match.

➤ Have students listen to the conversations twice. They should listen with pencils down the first time. On the second listening, students draw a line connecting each number to a picture.

Additional Activity
Make copies of Vocabulary Cards 184–192. Place the cards face down in a pile. Pick up one card and mime the action. Have students guess the action. Invite stu-

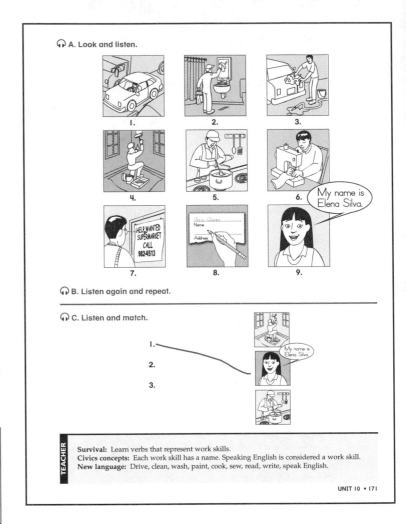

dents to pick up a card and mime the action as the class watches and names it.

> **Tapescript**
>
> **Conversation 1**
> A: Ms. Silva. Can you speak English?
> B: Yes, a little.
> A: Great. We have a good job for you!
>
> **Conversation 2**
> A: We're looking for a painter.
> B: Great! I can paint.
>
> **Conversation 3**
> A: Let's talk about your skills.
> B: Well, I can cook.
> A: That's excellent. There's a cook's job open at the Main Street Diner.

TEACHER

Survival: Describe one's workskills in an interview.
Civics concept: You get a job by applying for one.
New language: I need a job. / What are your skills? / I can [drive]. / Here's an application.
Sight word: JOBS.

🎧 A. Look and listen.

See also "Look and listen" on page T9a.

➤ Introduce the new vocabulary *job*. Say *I'm a teacher. My job? Teacher*. Give other examples of jobs your students have. *(Jose's job? cook.)*

➤ If possible, bring several examples of job applications to show the class.

Option: Introduce the word *skills*. Show the class Student's Book page 171. Point to the pictures of workskills. Say *Skills: drive, clean*, etc.

Additional Activity
Test comprehension. Hold up your book for the class to see. Point to the man in the picture and ask *What are his skills? Can he drive? Can he paint?*

🎧 B. Listen again and repeat.

See "Listen again and repeat" on page T9a.

Option: Have students tap out the syllables in the word *application*. Have students repeat after you until they have mastered the pronunciation. This is a key word in the conversation and in students' work lives.

Additional Activities
Activity 1: Practice new language. Place Vocabulary Cards 184–192 on the board rim. Point to Vocabulary Card 184 (*drive*). Say *I can drive*. Repeat, but substitute the word *drive* with another workskill. Repeat until students can easily substitute *drive* with various workskills.

Activity 2: Ask a student *Can you cook? Yes? No?* Encourage students to make their own statements about themselves. Then ask a student *What are your skills?* Show that the student can use his previous statements (*I can _____*) to answer.

C. Pair work.

➤ Model the Pair work with a student volunteer. Use Vocabulary Cards 184–192 as prompts.

➤ Students describe their workskills to a partner.

➤ Have several volunteer pairs act out their conversations in front of the class.

🎧 A. Look and listen.

🎧 B. Listen again and repeat.

C. Pair work.

TEACHER

Survival: Describe one's workskills in an interview.
Civics concept: You get a job by applying for one.
New language: I need a job. / What are your skills? / I can [drive]. / Here's an application.
Sight word: JOBS.

172 • UNIT 10

Tapescript

A: I need a job.
B: OK. What are your skills?

A: Well, I can drive and I can paint.
B: That's great. Here's an application.

Pair work (possible student responses)

A: I need a job. **B:** What are your skills? **A:** I can drive / wash / paint / cook / read / write.
B: That's great. Here's an application.

Your students can also say . . .

I can clean / sew / speak English.

TEACHER

Literacy: Recognize rhyming words and associate them with printed words.
More practice: Worksheet 84 (Teacher's Edition CD-ROM).

🎧 A. Look and listen.

➤ On this page, students begin to group words by similar sounds, in this case, rhyming endings.

➤ Have students close their books and listen as you recite the following rhymes: *cook, book, look*; *call, mall, hall, small*; and *dime, time*.

➤ Have students open their books to page 173. Play the cassette or read the tapescript out loud. Students point to each picture as you say the words or play the cassette.

🎧 B. Listen again and repeat.

➤ Play the cassette or read the tapescript aloud again. Have students point to the pictures as they repeat each word.

➤ You may want to have students say just the endings a few times to reinforce the relationship of the words and then listen and repeat again.

Additional Activities

Activity 1: Show the class Vocabulary Cards 1, 7, 33, 42, 59, 148, 175, 65 (*look, cook, call, mall, small, hall, dime, time*). Have students say each word.

Activity 2 (Challenge): Play a rhyming game. Say a word (*book*) and then show a Letter Card (C) for a student to form a rhyming word (*cook*). Review all the words on this page this way.

<table>
<tr><td colspan="2" align="center">Tapescript</td></tr>
<tr><td>1.</td><td>cook . . . book . . . look</td></tr>
<tr><td>2.</td><td>call . . . mall . . . hall . . . small</td></tr>
<tr><td>3.</td><td>dime . . . time</td></tr>
</table>

🎧 C. Look and listen.

➤ On the board, write each set of words in a column so that the endings (*–ook, –all, –ime*) all line up. Point to each column, say the end sound, and then say each word.

➤ Play the cassette or read the tapescript aloud as many times as necessary. Students point to each picture as they hear the word.

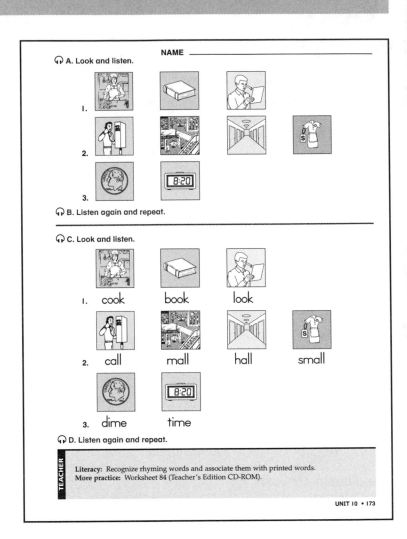

TEACHER

Literacy: Recognize rhyming words and associate them with printed words.
More practice: Worksheet 84 (Teacher's Edition CD-ROM).

UNIT 10 • 173

🎧 D. Listen again and repeat.

See "Listen again and repeat" above.

➤ Have students point to the words under the pictures as they listen and repeat.

➤ Demonstrate the following word chant several times and then have the class perform it with you:

Cook [CLAP] *book* [CLAP] *look!* [CLAP]
Call [CLAP] *mall* [CLAP] *hall* [CLAP] *small!* [CLAP]
Dime [CLAP] *time!* [CLAP]

Additional Activities

Activity 1: Have students sort the words according to their rhymes. Make multiple copies of Vocabulary Cards 1, 7, 33, 42, 59, 148, 175, 65 (*look, cook, call, mall, small, hall, dime, time*). Model the activity. Pick up a

Vocabulary Card. Point to it, say its name, and then place it on a desk. Pick up another card, say the word, and place on a different desk if it has a different sound. Repeat with the other Vocabulary cards, sorting the words into 3 piles, according to their end sounds. Have students do this activity in pairs.

Activity 2: Place the B, C, D, H, L, M, S, and T Letter Cards along the board rim. Say one of the words from the page. Have a student come up to the board, select the initial consonant of the word, copy it on the board, and then return the letter to the board rim. Repeat the word and point to the letter on the board.

Activity 3 (Challenge): On separate cards, write the words from Exercise C. Distribute the cards among the students. On the board, write three columns: *–ook, –all,* and *–ime.* Have students individually come up to the board and place their word cards in the correct column. Read each word to the class after it is placed.

Activity 4 (Challenge): On separate cards, write the words from Exercise C. Show each card to the class. Point to the end sound in each word (*–ook, –all, –ime*) and pronounce it. Then point to the initial consonant. Have students sound out the word (initial consonant + end sound).

Worksheet Link: Worksheet 84
Assign the worksheet for homework or in-class independent work. Follow the procedures for the Trace and write activity on T151b.

NOTES

TEACHER

Literacy: Recognize rhyming words and associate them with printed words.
More practice: Worksheet 85 (Teacher's Edition CD-ROM).

🎧 A. Look and listen.

See "Look and listen" on page T173a.

Additional Activity
Test comprehension. Say one of the words and have students point to the picture cue. Circulate around the room to check students' responses.

🎧 B. Listen again and repeat.

See also "Listen again and repeat" on page T173a.

➤ Isolate the /ð/ sound in *mother* and *brother*. Show the class how your tongue rests between your teeth as you blow. /ð/ is a voiced sound unlike the voiceless /θ/ of *three* or *thirteen*.

Additional Activity
Play a rhyming game. Say *mice* and then show a Letter Card (R) for a student to form a rhyming word *(rice)*. Review all the words on this page this way.

Tapescript
1. mother . . . brother
2. rice . . . mice
3. key . . . tea

🎧 C. Look and listen.

See also Exercise C on page T173a.

➤ On the board, write the first two sets of words in a column so that the endings line up. Point to each column, say the end sound, and then say the words (for example, *–other, mother, brother*).

🎧 D. Listen again and repeat.

See "Listen again and repeat" on page T173a.

Additional Activity
Have students practice rhyming words with a partner. Student A says one of the words on page 173 or 174. Student B says a word that rhymes with it. Students take turns.

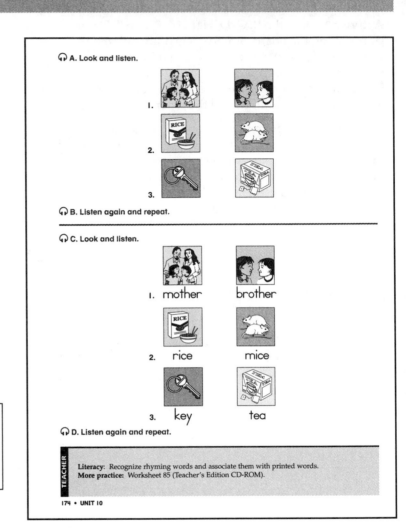

Worksheet Link: Worksheet 85
Assign the worksheet for homework or in-class independent work. Follow the procedures for the Trace and write activity on T151b.

> **Survival:** Learn vocabulary for occupations that don't require reading and writing
> or high-level proficiency in English.
> **Civics concept:** Adults of all ages, races, and both sexes can do many jobs.
> **New language:** Gardener, tailor, dishwasher, taxi driver, mover, packer, mason, companion, painter.

🎧 A. Look and listen.

See also "Look and listen" on page T17a.

➤ Gesture to yourself and say *I'm a teacher*. Gesture to a student and say the person's occupation. Give several more examples.

Additional Activity

Play a memory game. Photocopy Vocabulary Cards 4–9 and 193–197 (*teacher, student, housekeeper, cook, mechanic, babysitter, gardener, tailor, dishwasher, taxi driver, mover*) and give each student one set. Have students close their eyes. Call out three vocabulary items in a row. Have students open their eyes and find the items in their Vocabulary Card sets. Repeat with different vocabulary items. This game reviews vocabulary and develops memory recall in English.

🎧 B. Listen again and repeat.

See "Listen again and repeat" on page T17a.

Additional Activity

Provide speaking practice. Call out a picture number and have students say the word. Repeat several times. Then have students do this activity in pairs.

```
              Tapescript
1. gardener 2. tailor 3. dishwasher
4. taxi driver 5. mover
```

🎧 C. Look and listen.

See "Look and listen" on page T17a.

Additional Activity

Play a memory game. Photocopy Vocabulary Cards 193–201 (*gardener, tailor, dishwasher, taxi driver, mover, packer, mason, companion, painter*) and give each student one set. Have students close their eyes. Call out three or four vocabulary items in a row. Have students open their eyes and find the items in their Vocabulary Card sets. See the Activity in Exercise A above.

🎧 D. Listen again and repeat.

See "Listen again and repeat" on page T17a.

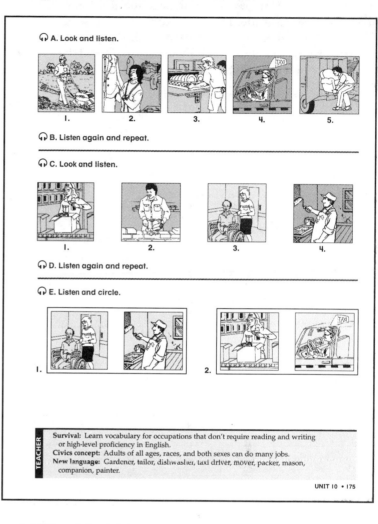

Additional Activities

Activity 1: Concentration. Photocopy Vocabulary Cards 193–201. Give two copies of the Vocabulary Cards to each pair of students. Follow the instructions for Activity 2 on page T28a.

Activity 2: To encourage students to continue associating workskills with jobs, place Vocabulary Cards 184–192 (workskills) on the board rim. One at a time, hold up Vocabulary Cards 193–201 (*gardener, tailor, dishwasher, taxi driver, mover, packer, mason, companion, painter*) and 4–9 (*teacher, student, housekeeper, cook, mechanic, babysitter*). Have students call out the workskills necessary for each job. Model by holding up the tailor card and saying *Tailor—sew*. You can also distribute both sets of job and workskills cards to pairs

(Continued on page T175b.)

of students for work with a partner. This activity reviews vocabulary from Unit 1 and reinforces the association between jobs and workskills.

Activity 3: This activity integrates students' knowledge of vocabulary, initial consonants, and free-hand writing skills. Place Letter Cards C, D, G, M, P, and T along the board rim. Say one of the occupations on page 175. Have a student come up to the board, select the correct initial consonant, copy it on the board, and then return the letter to the board rim. Repeat the word and point to the letter on the board.

Tapescript

1. packer 2. mason 3. companion 4. painter

🎧 E. Listen and circle.

See "Listen and circle" on T17a–b.

Additional Activity

Make copies of Vocabulary Cards 4, 6, 193–199, 201 (*teacher, housekeeper, gardener, tailor, dishwasher, taxi driver, mover, packer, mason, painter*). Place the cards

face down in a pile. Pick up one card and mime the occupation. Have students guess the occupation. Invite students to pick up a card and mime the action as the class watches and names the occupation. This activity reviews vocabulary from Unit 1 and helps students associate each occupation with its action and/or workskill.

Tapescript

Conversation 1
A: What do you do?
B: I'm a painter.
A: A painter? That's great.

Conversation 2
A: I need a new job.
B: What do you do?
A: Right now I'm a taxi driver.

NOTES

_____

_____

_____

_____

_____

_____

_____

_____

_____

_____

_____

_____

_____

TEACHER

Survival: Describe work experience in the U.S.
Civics concepts: Potential employers ask about prior work experience. It's important
   to give correct information.
New language: Do you have any experience in this country? / Yes, I do. / No, I don't. /
   right now / unemployed.

🎧 A. Look, listen, and read.

See also "Look and listen" on page T9a.

Note: This is the first time speech balloons contain
the text of spoken language. The purpose is for students to associate spoken speech with printed text. In
unit ten there are three opportunities for students to
observe and compare such language with what they
hear and say, and the experience is intended as an
orientation to reading, rather than a true reading activity. The paired utterances are almost the same,
with slight variations: *Yes, I can. / No, I cant. Yes, I do. /
No, I don't.* After students have listened to the cassette
and practiced repeating the conversation, you may
wish to ask students to point out the differences in
the two written variations. Or you may wish to read
the sentences in random order, asking students to
point to the language you have read.

➤ Review language previously learned in Unit 1.
   Approach a student and ask *What do you do?* Ask
   several other students in class.

➤ Introduce the word *experience.* Say *Experience is the
   time you work. I am a teacher. I have [five] years work
   experience.* Ask a student who works *What do you
   do?* After he answers, say *You are a [cook]. You have
   experience.* Ask *Are you a [cook] in this country?* If
   the student answers *Yes,* say *You have experience in
   this country.* Repeat with other students who work.

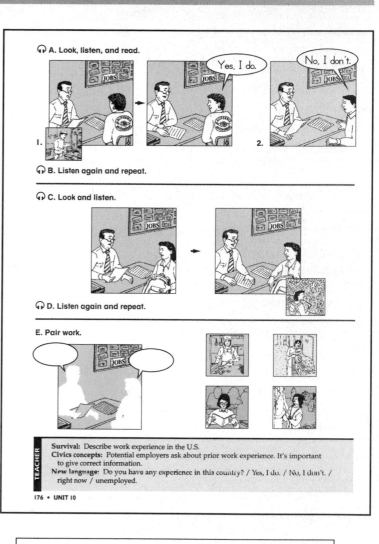

🎧 B. Listen again and repeat.

See "Listen again and repeat" on page T9a.

Option: Have students tap out the syllables in the
word *experience.* Have students repeat after you until
they have mastered the pronunciation. This is a key
word in the conversation and in students' work lives.

Additional Activity
Place Vocabulary Cards 7–9, 193–201 (*cook, mechanic,
babysitter, gardener, tailor, dishwasher, taxi driver, mover,
packer, mason, companion, painter*) on the board rim.
Ask each student *What do you do?* Gesture to the
Vocabulary Cards for a response. Then ask *Do you
have any experience in this country?* Give examples of
answers the first few times. Nod your head and say
Yes. I do. Shake your head and say *No I don't.* Have
students repeat the response.

Tapescript

Conversation 1
A: What do you do?
B: I'm a cook.

A: Do you have any experience in this country?
B: Yes, I do.

Conversation 2
A: Do you have any experience in this country?
B: No, I don't.

(Continued on page T176b.)

🎧 C. Look and listen.

See also "Look and listen" on page T9a.

➤ Introduce the word *unemployed*. Hold up the Student's Book. Point to the picture on the right and say *She needs a job. She is unemployed. Unemployed means no work, no job.* Repeat the sentence several times.

🎧 D. Listen again and repeat.

See "Listen again and repeat" on page T9a.

Option: Have students repeat after you until they have mastered the pronunciation of *unemployed*. To help students distinguish between the /n/ and /m/ sounds, say the word slowly and point to the N and M Letter Cards as you pronounce those sounds. This is a key word in the conversation and in students' work lives.

Tapescript

A: What do you do?
B: Actually, I'm a student right now.

A: Are you unemployed?
B: Yes.

E. Pair work.

➤ Model the Pair work with a student volunteer. Use Vocabulary Cards 7–9, 193–201 (*cook, mechanic, babysitter, gardener, tailor, dishwasher, taxi driver, mover, packer, mason, companion, painter*).

➤ Students work with a partner to describe their work experience in the United States.

➤ Have several volunteer pairs act out their conversations in front of the class.

Pair work (possible student responses)

A: What do you do? **B:** I'm a cook / housekeeper / student / tailor. **A:** Do you have any experience in this country? **B:** Yes, I do. / No, I don't. **A:** Are you unemployed? **B:** Yes. / No.

Your students can also say . . .

Actually, right now I'm a gardener / dishwasher / taxi driver / mover / packer / mason / companion / painter / (Unit 1:) teacher / babysitter / mechanic.

NOTES

_____

_____

_____

_____

_____

_____

_____

_____

_____

_____

_____

_____

_____

TEACHER

Literacy: Recognize that spaces go between words. Letters within words are not separated by spaces.
More practice: Worksheet 86 (Teacher's Edition CD-ROM).

A. Cross out.

➤ Write the sentence *Yes, I do* on the board. Make sure to leave a noticeable space between words. Read the sentence aloud and place your hand between each word. Then write the words all connected to each other. Demonstrate how your hand doesn't fit between the words. Point to the sentence with spaces and say *Yes!* Point to the connected words and say *No!* and cross it out.

➤ Have students work individually to cross out the words with no spacing in between.

Option: Review the page with the students. Hold the book up for students to see, and point to each item that is crossed out.

Option: Call out each word and ask *How do you spell that?* Write on the board the letters students dictate for each word. By naming the letters in each word, students pay attention to where each word ends.

Additional Activity
Write other known phrases on the board, some connected and some with spaces. Have students take turns coming up to the board and crossing out the phrases with no spaces between words.

B. Trace.

➤ Review the writing of lowercase letters. Draw primer rules on the board and lightly write the alphabet in lowercase. Have students take turns coming up to the board and tracing over several letters.

➤ Model the exercise. Draw a primer rule and four letter boxes on the board. Lightly write the first line of the exercise. Point to the word *rice* and say it. Invite a student to come up and trace the word.

➤ Point to each word in the book and say it before students do the exercise.

Option: Introduce students to *finger spacing.* Hold the Student's Book up for the class to see. Place your finger over each empty box in the phrases *first name, no smoking,* and *no swimming.* Have students do the same. In *Literacy Plus B,* as students learn to write whole words, they will find finger spacing is a useful method for separating words.

TEACHER

Literacy: Recognize that spaces go between words. Letters within words are not separated by spaces.
More practice: Worksheet 86 (Teacher's Edition CD-ROM).

UNIT 10 • 177

➤ Have students work independently to trace the letters.

Worksheet Link: Worksheet 86
Assign the worksheet for homework or in-class independent work. Follow the procedures for the above activities.

TEACHER

Literacy: Write name in boxes and on a line, as on a form. Do not skip boxes within each name. Leave a space between the two parts of a name.
More practice: Worksheet 87 (Teacher's Edition CD-ROM).

A. Look.

➤ Hold the book up for the class to see. Point to the first name, *Jen*, say it, and then place your finger over the blank box between the two names. Point to the last name, *Pratt*, and say it.

➤ Have students look at the names in the exercise. Say *Jen. How do you spell that? Pratt. How do you spell that?* By naming the letters in each word, students pay attention to the where each name ends.

B. Write your name.

Note: Capital letters are used in Exercise A. It is easier for students at this level to write capital letters over boxes. As you model Exercise B, use capital letters also.

➤ Model the exercise. Write your name in the boxes. Hold the book up for the class to see. Point to your first name, say it, and then place your finger over the blank box between the names. Point to your last name and say it.

➤ As students write their names, circulate around the classroom. Make sure students leave one empty box between their first and last names.

C. Look.

See "Look" above.

➤ Point to the first letter in each name and ask *Capital or lowercase?* (*Large or small?*) Point to the next letters and ask the question again.

D. Write your name.

Note: Initial capital and lowercase letters are used in Exercise C, and should be used in Exercises D and E, where students practice writing their names on a line.

➤ Model the exercise. Write your name on the line. Hold the book up for the class to see. Point and say your name.

➤ As students write their names, circulate around the classroom. Make sure students capitalize the first letter of each name.

A. Look.

J E N   P R A T T
NAME

B. Write your name.

NAME

C. Look.

Jen   Pratt
FIRST NAME   LAST NAME

D. Write your name.

FIRST NAME   LAST NAME

E. Write your name.

LAST NAME   FIRST NAME

TEACHER

Literacy: Write name in boxes and on a line, as on a form. Do not skip boxes within each name. Leave a space between the two parts of a name.
More practice: Worksheet 87 (Teacher's Edition CD-ROM).

178 • UNIT 10

E. Write your name.

➤ Model the exercise as before. Point to and say *Last name, first name.*

➤ As students write their names, circulate around the classroom. Make sure students write their last name first.

➤ Go back to Exercise D and make sure students recognize the difference in name order of the two lines. This recognition will be valuable for when they start filling out forms.

Worksheet Link: Worksheet 87
Assign the worksheet for homework or in-class independent work. Follow the procedures for the above activities.

T178

TEACHER

Survival: Learn singular and plural forms of machines, vehicles, and equipment.
New language: A truck, trucks / a car, cars / a copier, copiers / a lawn mower, lawn mowers / a cash register, cash registers / a bus, buses.

🎧 A. Look and listen.

See also "Look and listen" on page T17a.

➤ To make explicit the notion of plurals, point to the single truck in picture 1 and say *A truck. One truck.* Then point to the plural form and say *Trucks. Two trucks.* Repeat with one of the pictures containing more than two plural items to reinforce that the plural is not always *two.*

Additional Activity
Test comprehension. Say a word (singular or plural form) and have students point to the item in their books. Circulate around the room to check their answers.

🎧 B. Listen again and repeat.

See "Listen again and repeat" on page T17a.

Option: Have students tap out the syllables as they listen to each word. This will help underscore that the final plural sound for the first five items is a phoneme, not a syllable, and that that only the word *bus* adds a new syllable in its plural form (*buses*).

Additional Activity
Provide speaking practice. Call out a picture number and have students say the word in both singular and plural forms. Repeat several times. Then have students do this activity in pairs.

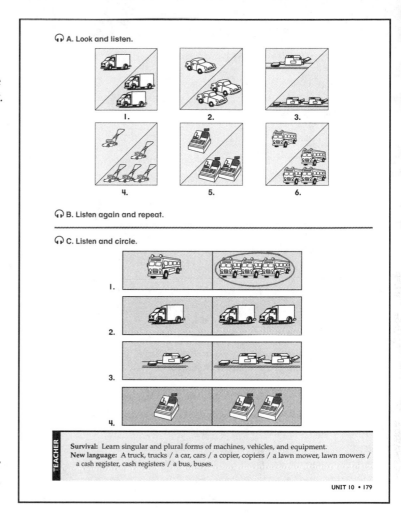

🎧 A. Look and listen.

1. 2. 3.

4. 5. 6.

🎧 B. Listen again and repeat.

🎧 C. Listen and circle.

1.

2.

3.

4.

TEACHER

Survival: Learn singular and plural forms of machines, vehicles, and equipment.
New language: A truck, trucks / a car, cars / a copier, copiers / a lawn mower, lawn mowers / a cash register, cash registers / a bus, buses.

UNIT 10 • 179

Tapescript
1. a truck/trucks
2. a car/cars
3. a copier/copiers
4. a lawn mower/lawn mowers
5. a cash register/cash registers
6. a bus/buses

🎧 C. Listen and circle.

See "Listen and circle" on page T17a–b.

Additional Activities

Activity 1: For more practice, students can work in pairs, saying a singular or plural form of one of the picture names as the partner points to it.

Activity 2: Concentration. Photocopy Vocabulary Cards 202–213. Follow the instructions for Activity 2 on page T28.

Tapescript
1. buses 2. trucks 3. a copier 4. a cash register

Survival: Answer interview questions about technology skills.
Civics concept: Employers ask about ability to use machines and equipment.
New language: Can you use a [cash register]? / Can you drive a [car]? / Yes, I can. /
No, I can't. / What skills do you have?

A. Look, listen, and read.

See also "Look, listen, and read" on page T176a.

➤ Introduce the word *computer*. Hold up the Student's Book for the class to see. Point to the computer and say the word.

➤ Play the cassette or read the tapescript aloud as many times as necessary.

Option: Give visual cues as students listen to the conversation. Place Vocabulary Cards 202, 204, 210, 214 (*truck, car, cash register, computer*) on the board rim. Point to the Vocabulary Cards as they are mentioned in the conversation.

Additional Activity

Test comprehension. Point to the interviewees in the pictures and ask *Can he use a cash register? Can he use a computer? Can she drive a car? Can she drive a truck?*

B. Listen again and repeat.

See "Listen again and repeat" on page T9a.

Option: Focus on pronunciation. *Can* and *can't* are difficult to distinguish. *Can't* is a slightly longer sound. You can illustrate this by drawing your fingers from your mouth to the air slowly when you pronounce *can't* and emphasizing the /t/ sound on the end of the word. Make a chopping motion to illustrate the brevity of *can*.

Additional Activities

Activity 1: Introduce the verbs used with each piece of machinery. Place Vocabulary Cards 19, 23, 202, 204, 206, 208, 214 (*bus, taxi, truck, car, copier, lawn mower, cash register*) on the board rim. Point to each and say the word and then say the verb that accompanies it; for example, Bus: *drive* a bus. Taxi: *drive* a taxi. Computer: *use* a computer. Copier: *use* a copier.

Activity 2: Practice *Yes, I can* and *No, I can't*. Say *Yes, I can*. Hold up three fingers and repeat the sentence, touching a finger for each word. Repeat, but omit saying *can*. Point to the finger that represents *can*. Have students say *can*. Repeat several times with the sentences *Yes, I can* and *No, I can't*.

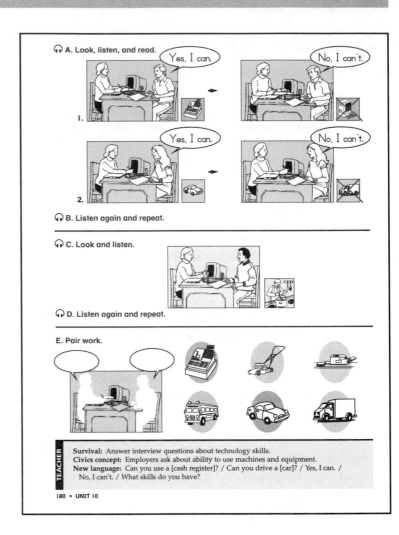

Activity 3: Practice answering questions. Hold up Vocabulary Card 210 (*cash register*) and ask a student *Can you use a cash register?* If the student answers with a simple *Yes* or *No*, encourage him to form the response *Yes, I can* or *No, I can't*. Ask another student more questions, using both verbs *use* and *drive*.

Tapescript

Conversation 1
A: Can you use a cash register? **B:** Yes, I can.
A: Can you use a computer? **B:** No, I can't.

Conversation 2
A: Can you drive a car? **B:** Yes, I can.
A: Can you drive a truck? **B:** No, I can't.

🎧 C. Look and listen.

See "Look and listen" on page T9a.

Option: Show that *What skills do you have?* is similar in meaning to *What are your skills?* Illustrate this by repeating both questions and making a gesture of equality with your hands.

Additional Activity

Test comprehension. Hold the book up for the class to see. Point to the man in the picture and ask *Can he cook?*

🎧 D. Listen again and repeat.

See "Listen again and repeat" on page T9a.

Additional Activity

Place Vocabulary Cards 184–192 (workskills) and 202–214 (vehicles and equipment from p. 179) on the board rim. Point to *drive* and say *I can drive a car.* Then ask a student *What skills do you have?* Point to the Vocabulary Cards to elicit a response. You may need to prompt the first few responses with the additional question *Can you [clean]?* Repeat with several students.

Tapescript

A: What skills do you have?
B: I can cook.

E. Pair work.

➤ Model the Pair work. Place Vocabulary Cards 184–192 (workskills) and 20, 23, 202, 206, 208, 210 (*car, taxi, truck, copier, lawn mower, cash register*) on the board rim. Point to each card and elicit the verb and the object if appropriate (for example, *drive a truck*).

Invite a student to the sit down at your desk. Sit down at the other side of the desk and say *What skills do you have?* Gesture to the Vocabulary Cards to elicit a response. After the student responds, ask *Can you [drive a truck]?* Ask a few more questions with *can*.

➤ Divide the class into pairs. Students ask and answer interview questions about technology skills. Circulate around the classroom, offering help as needed. Encourage students to use language from all three conversations on the page: *Can you [drive a car]? / What skills do you have?*

➤ Have several volunteer pairs act out their conversations in front of the class.

Pair work (possible student responses)

A: What are your skills? / What skills do you have? **B:** I can use a cash register / lawn mower / copier. **A:** Can you drive a bus / car / truck? **B:** Yes, I can. / No, I can't.

Your students can also say . . .

A: I can drive a taxi / wash / paint / cook / read / write / clean / sew / speak English. **B:** Do you have any experience in this country? **A:** Yes, I do. / No, I don't. **B:** Are you unemployed? **A:** Yes. / No. **B:** (Unit 1:) What do you do? **A:** (Unit 10:) Actually, right now I'm a gardener / dishwasher / taxi driver / mover / packer / mason / companion / painter / tailor / (Unit 1:) teacher / babysitter / mechanic / cook / housekeeper / student.

TEACHER

Literacy: Recognize letters and words written correctly on the line.

Circle.

➤ Draw a line on the board. Write your name on the line. Point to your name and say *Yes*. Then write your name incorrectly on the line (below, through, or above the line). Point to it and say *No*. Circle the correct form. Model your name several times, each time presenting other ways the word can be incorrectly placed.

➤ Model the exercise. Copy the first line on the board. Invite a student to come up and circle the correct form. Have students copy the circle in their book.

➤ Have students work independently to circle the correctly-written letters and words. Circulate around the room to check students' work.

Option: Go over the answers as a class. Hold the book up for the class to see as you point to the circled item on each line.

Additional Activity
Have students evaluate your handwriting. Write several examples of any letter on a line on the board. Include one or two examples of a misplaced letter (for example, not touching the bottom line). Have students take turns coming up to the board to erase and rewrite the incorrectly placed letters. Repeat this procedure with other letters of the alphabet and/or with words from previous "Trace and write" activities.

NAME _____

Circle.

1. (a)   a

2. r   r

3. S   S

4. | |

5. PUSH   PUSH

6. STOP   STOP

7. Karen Kraft   Karen Kraft

8. Yes, I can.   Yes, I can.

TEACHER

Literacy: Recognize letters and words written correctly on the line.

TEACHER

Literacy: Demonstrate ability to write capital and lowercase letters on lines.
More practice: Worksheet 88 (Teacher's Edition CD-ROM).

A. Write lowercase letters.

➤ Model the exercise. Hold the book for the class to see. Point to the first letter on the page and say *capital (large) A*. Point to the lowercase A and say *lowercase (small) A*. Point to the next letter, S, point to the blank space, and invite a student to come up to the board to write the lowercase s.

Option: Hold the page up for everyone to see and point to each letter to elicit its name and size before students do the exercise.

➤ Circulate around the room as students work independently to complete the exercise.

B. Write capital letters.

Follow the procedures for Exercise A.

Additional Activities

Activity 1: Give students the opportunity to correct you. Write any letter on the board correctly. As you write, nod your head and say *Yes!* Then write the letter incorrectly with an incorrect stroke sequence or motion. As you write, shake your head and say *No!* Then invite students to say *Yes!* or *No!* as you write other letters correctly and incorrectly. Repeat the activity several times, reviewing the writing of any of the letters.

Activity 2: Make copies of Worksheet 0 and distribute to students. Dictate letters (for example, large G, small g) and have students write the letters. Check students' work for good handwriting.

Worksheet Link: Worksheet 88

Assign the worksheet for homework or in-class independent work. Follow the procedures for Exercise A above.

A. Write lowercase letters.

A a   S ___   R ___   T ___

M ___   G ___   F ___   O ___

B. Write capital letters.

K k   ___ b   ___ d   ___ f

___ m   ___ v   ___ n   ___ o

___ a   ___ e   ___ r   ___ u

___ j   ___ y   ___ q   ___ g

TEACHER
Literacy: Demonstrate ability to write capital and lowercase letters on lines.
More practice: Worksheet 88 (Teacher's Edition CD-ROM).

182 • UNIT 10

TEACHER

Survival: Answer interview questions about present and prior experience and references.
Civics concept: It's important to bring references to a job interview.
New language: What did you do in your country? / I was a [mason]. /
Do you have references?

∩ A. Look, listen, and read.

See also "Look, listen, and read" on page T176a.

➤ Introduce *do* and *did*. Write the current year on the board. To the left of it, write a past year. Ask *What do you do?* and point to the current year. Then ask *What did you do?* Make a gesture for the past (waving you hand over your shoulder) and point to the other year on the board. Repeat the contrast several times.

Option: Give visual cues as students listen to the conversation. Place Vocabulary Card 199 *(mason)* on the board rim. Point to it when it is mentioned in the conversation. Make the present and past time gestures when appropriate.

∩ B. Listen again and repeat.

See "Listen again and repeat" on page T9a.

Additional Activity
Practice new language. Place Vocabulary Cards 6–9, 193–197 *(housekeeper, cook, mechanic, babysitter, gardener, tailor, dishwasher, taxi driver, mover)* on the board rim.

Ask the class *What did you do in your country?* Provide a possible answer: *I was a tailor.* Hold up four fingers and repeat the sentence, touching a finger for each word. Repeat, but omit *tailor*. Point to the finger that represents the missing word. Point to the Vocabulary Cards and have students supply a new occupation. Repeat several times with different occupations. Then ask individual students the question.

Tapescript

A: Do you have any experience in this country?
B: No, I don't.

A: What did you do in your country?
B: I was a mason.

∩ C. Look, listen, and read.

See also "Look, listen, and read" on page T176a.

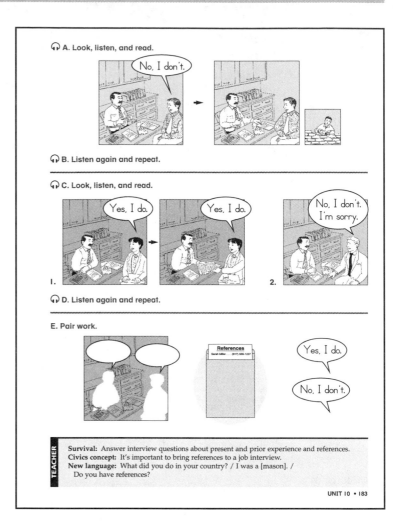

TEACHER

Survival: Answer interview questions about present and prior experience and references.
Civics concept: It's important to bring references to a job interview.
New language: What did you do in your country? / I was a [mason]. /
Do you have references?

UNIT 10 • 183

➤ After students listen, introduce the word *reference*. Write the current year and a previous year on the board. Point to yourself and to the previous year on the board. Say *I was a [gardener] in [year]. Now I need a job. My employer from [year] is my reference.* Point again to the references in the picture. Mime the actions of calling as you point to the current year on the board and say *My new employer can call my references.*

∩ D. Listen again and repeat.

See "Listen again and repeat" on page T9a.

Option: Have students tap out the three syllables in the word *reference*. Have students repeat after you until they have mastered the pronunciation. This is a key word in the conversation and in students' work lives.

Tapescript

Conversation 1
A: Do you have any experience in this country?
B: Yes, I do.

A: Do you have references?
B: Yes, I do.

Conversation 2
A: Do you have references?
B: No, I don't. I'm sorry.

E. Pair work.

➤ Model the Pair work. Invite a student to sit down at your desk. Sit down at the other side of the desk and ask *Do you have any experience in this country?* After the student responds, ask *What did you do in your country?* Then ask *Do you have references?* When you finish the conversation, reverse roles with the student and repeat the interview.

➤ Students answer a partner's questions about their prior work experience and references. Circulate around the classroom, offering help as needed.

➤ Have several volunteer pairs act out their conversations in front of the class.

Pair work (possible student responses)

A: What did you do in your country? **B:** I was a student / teacher / cook / babysitter / mechanic / housekeeper / gardener / tailor / dishwasher / taxi driver / mover / packer / mason / companion / painter. **A:** Do you have any experience in this country? **B:** Yes, I do. / No, I don't. **A:** Do you have references? **B:** Yes, I do. / No, I don't. I'm sorry.

Your students can also say . . .

A: What are your skills? / What skills do you have? **B:** I can use a cash register / lawn mower / copier. **A:** Can you drive a bus / car / truck / taxi? Can you wash / paint / cook / read / write / clean / sew / speak English? **B:** Yes, I can. / No, I can't. **A:** Are you unemployed? **B:** Yes. / No.

NOTES

_____

_____

_____

_____

_____

_____

_____

_____

_____

_____

TEACHER

Authentic practice: Students listen to an authentic job interview and then complete listening and speaking tasks, providing personal information.

🎧 A. Listen and write the last name.

➤ Hold the book up for the class to see. Point to and say the words *name* and *occupation*. Point to the name Luisa. Say *First name, Luisa. Last name?* and shrug.

➤ Play the cassette or read the tapescript aloud. Give visual cues to the conversation as students listen. Place Vocabulary Card 6 (*housekeeper*) on the board rim. Point to it when it is mentioned in the conversation. Write SOTO on the board when it is mentioned (and then erase it). Hold up the Student's Book and place your finger over the first empty box after *Luisa* to remind students to leave a blank box between first and last names.

➤ Have students listen again with pencil in hand. Point to the application when she begins to spell her last name. You may need to replay that part of the conversation several times.

Note: Make sure that students do not write in the space between the first and last names.

Tapescript

A: Good morning. Your name, please?
B: Luisa Soto.
A: Could you please spell Soto?
B: Sure. That's S–O–T–O.
A: What do you do?
B: I'm a housekeeper.

🎧 B. Look and listen.

See also "Look and listen" on page T22a.

➤ You may want to introduce the question *What machines or equipment can you operate?* Place Vocabulary Cards 202–214 on the board rim. Ask the question and answer it by pointing to a piece of machinery and saying *I can [use a lawn mower].* Repeat a few other examples of the question and response so that students begin to understand that the question can be answered similarly to *What are your skills?*

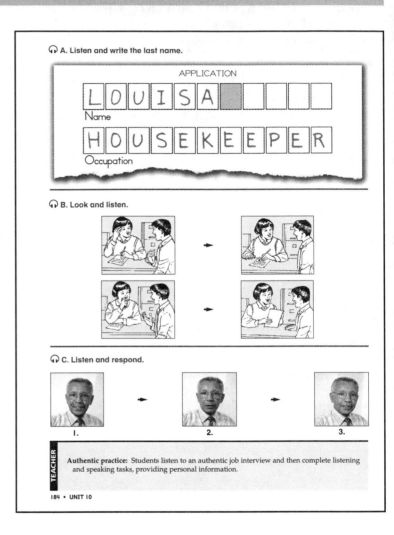

🎧 A. Listen and write the last name.

APPLICATION

L O U I S A ☐ ☐ ☐ ☐
Name

H O U S E K E E P E R
Occupation

🎧 B. Look and listen.

🎧 C. Listen and respond.

1.   2.   3.

TEACHER Authentic practice: Students listen to an authentic job interview and then complete listening and speaking tasks, providing personal information.

184 • UNIT 10

➤ Set the scene. Point to the man in Exercise B and say *He needs a job.*

Option: Provide visual cues. Point to Vocabulary Cards 188, 189, 184, 208 (*cook, sew, drive, lawn mower*) when they are mentioned in the conversation.

Additional Activity

Test comprehension. Hold the book up for the class to see. Point to the man in the pictures and ask *Is he unemployed? Does he have any experience in this country? What did he do in his country? What are his skills? Can he paint? Can he sew? Can he use a lawn mower? Can he use a copier?*

Tapescript
A: Your name, please.
B: James Kim.
A: What do you do, Mr. Kim?
B: Right now I'm unemployed.
A: Do you have any experience in this country?
B: Yes, I do. At the Downtown Restaurant.
A: What did you do in your country?
B: I was a cook.
A: What skills do you have?
B: I can cook. I can sew. I can drive.
A: What machines or equipment can you operate?
B: I can use a lawn mower.
A: Great. Here's an application. Please fill it out.

Tapescript
Prompt 1: What do you do?
Prompt 2: Do you have any experience in this country?
Prompt 3: What skills do you have?

Listen and respond (possible student responses)
Prompt 1: I'm a student / teacher / cook / babysitter / mechanic / housekeeper / gardener / tailor / dishwasher / taxi driver / mover / packer / mason / companion / painter.
Prompt 2: Yes, I do. / No, I don't.
Prompt 3: I can clean / wash / paint / cook / sew / read / write / speak English. / I can drive a car / taxi / truck / bus. / I can use a copier / lawn mower / cash register.

⌒ C. Listen and respond.

See "Listen and respond" on page T22a.

Note: The goal of this activity is to give students practice responding to authentic prompts, using the language they have learned so far, thus building confidence. Different students will say different things.

NOTES

_____

_____

_____

_____

_____

_____

_____

_____

_____

_____

_____

_____

_____

TEACHER

Literacy review: Write name, phone number, and area code on a form.
More practice: Worksheet 89 (Teacher's Edition CD-ROM).
Literacy test: Teacher's Edition CD-ROM.

A. Look.

➤ Hold the Student's Book up for the class to see. Say *name* and point to the word on the form. Point to the first name, *Jose,* say it, and then place your finger over the blank box between the first and last names. Point to the last name *Lopez,* and say it. Ask *What's his name?* Point to the letters and ask *Capital or lowercase?* (*Large or small?*)

➤ Point to the words *area code* and *phone number* and say them. Ask *What's his phone number?*

B. Write <u>your</u> name and phone number.

This exercise gives students the opportunity to practice writing their names in two different formats—in letter boxes and on lines. Focus on writing names with capital letters in the boxes and with initial capitals and lowercase letters on the lines.

➤ Model the exercise. Write your name in capital letters and your phone number in the boxes. Hold the book up for the class to see. Point to your first name, say it, and then place your finger over the blank box between your first and last names. Point to your last name and say it. Point to your phone number and say it.

➤ Point to your lettering and ask *Capital or lowercase?* (*Large or small?*)

➤ Model filling in the second form, using initial capitals and lowercase letters.

➤ As students write their names, circulate around the classroom. Make sure students leave an empty box between their first and last names.

Option: You may want to make numerous copies of this page and distribute to students so they can practice filling in their names and phone numbers until their work is error-free.

Optional Activity

Students evaluate your writing. Draw two lines on the board. Write the same name twice, one time correctly and one time poorly by misplacing the name, joining the first and last name, or using capital letters incorrectly. Invite a student up to the board to cross out the incorrectly written name. Repeat this proce-

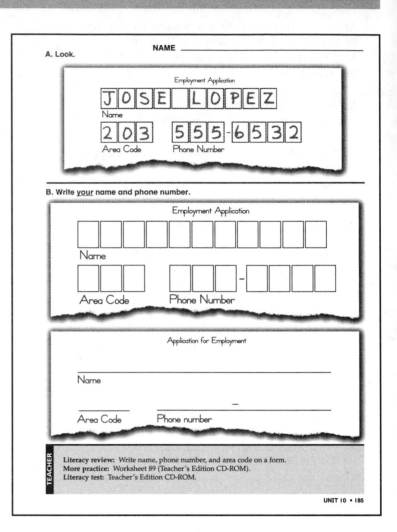

dure with other names, using either the boxed or line format on text page 185.

You can also do this activity with phone numbers, placing the numbers poorly on the line or grouping the numbers incorrectly so that the area code has only two digits and the exchange has four.

If your students are ready . . .

Civics enrichment: Make multiple copies of the top portion of a real job application and have students practice filling in their name, address and phone number.

Worksheet Link: Worksheet 89
Assign the worksheet for homework or in-class independent work.

TEACHER

Survival / civics review: Point and name things in the pictures. Make statements about the pictures. Role-play conversations based on the pictures.
Tests: Teacher's Edition CD-ROM.

Talk about the pictures.

➤ Hold up the Student's Book for the class to see and say the following as students point: *drive a bus, packer, computer, telephone, references.*

➤ Hold up the picture for the class to see and have students name what they see. Then ask *Can she drive a bus?*

➤ Have students talk with a partner about the people and objects in the pictures.

Possible student responses

packer / application / references / She can drive a bus / use a computer. She has references. (Unit 5:) office / (Unit 4:) shirts / pants / shoes / jacket / (Unit 3:) telephone / bus / street / corner

Role-play conversations.

➤ Point to the speech bubble of the man in the first interview scene and say *What skills do you have?* Then point to the woman's speech bubble to elicit a student's response (*I can drive a bus.*)

➤ In pairs, have students practice an interview appropriate to the cues in the picture.

➤ Ask pairs of students to present their interviews to the class. Repeat with the second interview scene.

Role-play conversations (Possible student responses)

A: (Unit 1:) What do you do? **B:** I'm a student / cook / babysitter / mechanic / teacher / housekeeper. / (Unit 10:) Actually, right now I'm a gardener / tailor / dishwasher / taxi driver / mover / packer / mason / companion / painter. **A:** Do you have any experience in this country? **B:** Yes, I do. / No, I don't. **A:** What did you do in your country? **B:** I was a [packer]. **A:** Are you unemployed? **B:** Yes. / No. **A:** What are your skills? / What skills do you have? **B:** I can clean / wash / paint / cook / sew / read / write / speak English / drive a car / taxi / truck / bus. **A:** Can you use a copier / lawn mower / cash register? **B:** Yes, I can. / No, I can't. **A:** Do you have references? **B:** Yes, I do. / No, I don't. I'm sorry. **A:** Here's an application.

Talk about the pictures. Role-play conversations.

TEACHER

Survival / civics review: Point and name things in the pictures. Make statements about the pictures.
Tests: Teacher's Edition CD-ROM.

186 • UNIT 10

T186

Alphabetical list of
Literacy Plus A vocabulary

The following is an alphabetical list of all vocabulary taught in *Literacy Plus A,* with corresponding unit, page number, and Vocabulary Card number (from the Flashcards packaged with this Teacher's Edition).

Vocabulary word	Unit	Page	Vocabulary card	Vocabulary word	Unit	Page	Vocabulary card
accident	3	49	27	a copier	10	179	206
afternoon	5	81	63	copiers	10	179	207
ambulance	3	49	30	corner	3	45	25
ankle	8	135	141	co-worker	7	129	132
apartment	2	28	11	credit card	9	161	181
arm	8	135	137	danger – no swimming	8	144	159
babysitter	1	17	9	danger – poison	8	144	157
bakery	4	63	41	daughter	7	117	119
bank	5	93	78	day	5	85	70
booster seat	8	147	164	dime (10 cents)	9	154	175
boyfriend	7	129	134	dinner	6	108	107
bread	6	99	87	discount store	4	63	35
breakfast	6	108	105	dishwasher	10	175	195
brother	7	117	124	divorced	7	125	129
bus	3	45	19	a dollar	9	153	167
	10	179	212			154	178
bus stop	2	28	12	don't walk	8	143	156
buses	10	179	213	down the hall	8	140	149
butter	6	108	109	down the stairs	8	140	151
cake	6	108	115	dress	4	67	45
call	3	49	33	dresses	4	68	56
car	3	45	20	drink	6	103	103
	8	147	161	drive	10	171	184
	10	179	204	drugstore	4	63	39
car seat	8	147	163	early	5	90	76
cars	10	179	205	eggs	6	108	111
cash	9	161	179	eight fifteen	5	81	66
a cash register	10	179	210	eight o'clock	5	81	65
cash registers	10	179	211	elevator	8	139	147
caution – flammable	8	144	160	employer	7	129	131
cereal	6	108	112	entrance	8	139	143
cheap	4	67	52	exit	8	139	144
check	9	161	180	expensive	4	67	53
cheese	6	99	86	factory	5	93	81
cheese sandwich	6	103	98	father	7	117	117
chicken	6	99	83	fifty dollars	9	153	171
chicken sandwich	6	103	99	fire	3	49	28
clean	10	171	185	fire truck	3	49	29
coffee	6	99	92	fish	6	99	85
companion	10	175	200	fish sandwich	6	103	100
computer	10	180	214	five dollars	9	153	168
cook	1	17	7	foot	8	135	142
	10	171	188	friend	7	117	125

T187

Vocabulary word	Unit	Page	Vocabulary card	Vocabulary word	Unit	Page	Vocabulary card
fries	6	107	104	night	5	81	64
fruit	6	99	90	no smoking	8	144	158
garage	5	93	82	office	5	93	80
gardener	10	175	193	oil	6	99	96
girlfriend	7	129	133	on the left	8	140	153
grocery store	4	63	38	on the right	8	140	152
half dollar (50 cents)	9	154	177	packer	10	175	198
hall	8	139	148	paint	10	171	187
hamburger	6	103	101	painter	10	175	201
hand	8	135	139	pants	4	67	48
hardware store	4	63	40	parking lot	2	28	17
head	8	135	135	pasta	6	99	89
highway	3	45	26	penny (one cent)	9	154	173
hospital	3	49	31	post office	5	93	79
hotel	2	28	16	press	3	49	34
house	2	28	10				
housekeeper	1	17	6	quarter (25 cents)	9	154	176
a hundred dollars	9	153	172				
husband	7	117	121	read	10	171	190
				receipt	9	161	183
ice cream	6	108	116	restaurant	2	28	15
					4	63	36
jacket	4	67	47	restroom	8	139	145
jackets	4	68	58	rice	6	99	88
jam	6	108	110				
juice	6	99	94	safety harness	8	147	166
				salad	6	103	102
large	4	72	61	sandwich	6	103	97
late	5	90	77	school	2	28	14
a lawn mower	10	179	208		5	86	73
			209	seat belt	8	147	162
leg	8	135	140	separated	7	125	128
listen	1	2	2	sew	10	171	189
look	1	2	1	shirt	4	67	43
lunch	6	108	106	shirts	4	68	54
				shoes	4	67	49
mall	4	63	42	single	7	125	126
married	7	125	127	sister	7	117	123
mason	10	175	199	skirt	4	67	44
meat	6	99	84	skirts	4	68	55
mechanic	1	17	8	small	4	72	59
medium	4	72	60	socks	4	67	50
milk	6	99	91	son	7	117	120
money order	9	161	182	soup	6	108	113
month	5	89	74	speak English	10	171	192
morning	5	81	62	stairs	8	139	146
mother	7	117	118	stockings	4	67	51
mover	10	175	197	stop	8	143	154
				street	3	45	24
neck	8	135	136	stroller	8	147	165
nickel (5 cents)	9	154	174	student	1	17	5

Vocabulary word	Unit	Page	Vocabulary card	Vocabulary word	Unit	Page	Vocabulary card
subway	3	45	22	vegetables	6	108	114
supermarket	2	28	13				
	4	63	37	walk	8	143	155
				wash	10	171	186
tailor	10	175	194	water	6	99	95
taxi	3	45	23	week	5	85	71
taxi driver	10	175	196	widowed	7	125	130
tea	6	99	93	wife	7	117	122
teacher	1	17	4	work	5	86	72
telephone	3	49	32	wrist	8	135	138
ten dollars	9	153	169	write	1	2	3
three twenty	5	81	69		10	171	191
toast	6	108	108				
train	3	45	21	year	5	89	75
a truck	10	179	202				
trucks	10	179	203	zip code	2	39	18
twelve forty-five	5	81	68				
twelve thirty	5	81	67				
twenty dollars	9	153	170				
uniform	4	67	46				
uniforms	4	68	57				
up the stairs	8	140	150				

Placement Test

INSTRUCTIONS FOR USING THIS TEST

This test is designed to place preliterate students in *Literacy Plus A* or *B*. *Literacy Plus A* is designed for beginning students who are not literate in any language. *Literacy Plus B* is for beginning students who are literate in their own language but not in English.

A student who begins in *Literacy Plus A* should continue his or her studies in *Literacy Plus B*. A student who completes *Literacy Plus B* may continue his or her studies in an ESL textbook for literate students.

The student answer sheets

The two student answer sheets are photocopiable, and each contains a name and date line.
• **Test 1** determines whether a student is literate in English.
• **Test 2** determines whether a student is literate in his or her native language.

Testing sequence

Greet the student in English or in the student's native language. Write the student's name and the test date at the top of the answer sheet in the spaces provided. Give the student the answer sheet and a pen or a pencil. Be sure the answer sheet is turned so that **Test 1** is face up, but oriented AWAY from the student, to determine if the student is familiar with print. Watch to see if the student orients the answer sheet in the right position when the test begins. The instructions for the test may be given in the student's native language if necessary.

Test I: Literacy in English

Point to item 1. Say *What's your name?* If student responds, say *Please write your name on the line.*

Point to item 2. Say *What's your address?* If student responds, say *Please write your address on the line.*

Point to item 3. Say *Please write this number on the line. Thirty-three.*

Point to item 4. Say *Look at the letters.* Say each letter in order as you point to it. Pause at the blank where the C would go. Say *Write the letter.* Pause to give the student time to write the letter in the box. Continue with the rest of the letters, indicating the blank each time and asking the student to write the letter. Pause long enough each time for the student to write.

Point to item 5. Say *Look at the numbers.* Say each number in order as you point to it. Pause at the blank where the 15 would go. Say *Write the number.* Pause to give the student time to write the number in the box. Continue with the rest of the numbers, indicating the blank each time and asking the student to write the number. Pause long enough each time for the student to write.

Point to item 6 (the form). Say *Now please fill out this form.*

Point to item 7. Say *Please read number 7 and write your answer here.*

Scoring and placement

➤ If the student has been able to orally answer the questions in items 1, 2, and 3, and write the answers to five or more items legibly and on the lines, consider placing the student in an ESL textbook for literate students.

➤ If the student has been unable to write the answers to five or more items legibly and on the lines, administer **Test 2**.

Test 2: Literacy in the native language

Test 2 should be administered in the student's native language.

Give the student the answer sheet for **Test 2**. Make sure the answer sheet is face up. Ask the student if he or she can write in [student's language]. Ask the student to write a description of daily life at home. If the student is unsure what is expected, it is OK to explain further. For example, tell the student to write what he or she does in the morning, the afternoon, at night; what he or she eats for breakfast, lunch, and dinner; what time meals are eaten; what kind of work he or she does, etc. Explain that there is no "right" answer, that this is just a sample of the student's writing. If the student has questions about the task, answer them freely.

Scoring and placement

➤ If the student is able to comfortably write two or more sentences that are legible, on the lines, and with appropriate spacing between words, place the student in *Literacy Plus B*.

➤ If the student is unable to write even one sentence, writes something, but with difficulty, or does not write anything, place the student in *Literacy Plus A*.

The student answer sheets for both tests follow.

Student's name _____

Date of test _____

Test I: Literacy in English

1. _____

2. _____

3. _____

4. A B ☐   D E ☐   G H ☐   J K ☐

5. 12 13 14 ☐   16 17 18 ☐   20 ☐ ☐

6.

name _____

address _____

_____

date of birth _____

7. Write the name of your country. _____

Student's name _____

Date of test _____

Test 2: Literacy in the native language

_____

_____

_____

_____

_____

_____

_____

_____

_____